THE PAPACY SINCE 1500

These original essays offer thought-provoking perspectives on the complex evolution of the papacy in the last 500 years, from the pope as an Italian Renaissance prince to the pope as a universal pastor concerned with the well-being and salvation of human beings everywhere on earth. Structured by detailed studies of some of the most significant popes in this evolution, this volume explores how papal policies and actions were received as the popes sought to respond to the political, cultural, and social circumstances of their time. Included are essays examining pontificates from that of Julius II, warrior as well as patron of the arts, to the era of the French Revolution and Napoleon, as well as Paul VI's pleas for peace during the Cold War and John Paul II's itinerant, prophetic, and hierarchical model of a pastoral papacy in the age of television and the internet.

JAMES CORKERY is Associate Professor of Systematic Theology, Milltown Institute of Theology and Philosophy, Dublin. He is the author of *Joseph Ratzinger's Theological Ideas: Wise Cautions and Legitimate Hopes* (2009).

THOMAS WORCESTER is Professor of History, College of the Holy Cross, Worcester, MA. He is the editor of *The Cambridge Companion to the Jesuits* (Cambridge, 2008) and the co-editor (with Gauvin Bailey, Pamela M. Jones, and Franco Mormando) of *Hope and Healing: Painting in Italy in a Time of Plague, 1500–1800* (2005).

THE PAPACY SINCE 1500

From Italian Prince to Universal Pastor

EDITED BY

JAMES CORKERY AND THOMAS WORCESTER

CAMBRIDGE
UNIVERSITY PRESS

CAMBRIDGE UNIVERSITY PRESS
Cambridge, New York, Melbourne, Madrid, Cape Town, Singapore,
São Paulo, Delhi, Dubai, Tokyo, Mexico City

Cambridge University Press
The Edinburgh Building, Cambridge CB2 8RU, UK

Published in the United States of America by Cambridge University Press, New York

www.cambridge.org
Information on this title: www.cambridge.org/9780521729772

First published 2010
Reprinted 2010

Printed in the United Kingdom at the University Press, Cambridge

A catalogue record for this publication is available from the British Library

Library of Congress Cataloguing in Publication data
The papacy since 1500 : from Italian prince to universal pastor / [edited by] James Corkery,
Thomas Worcester.
p.   cm.
Includes bibliographical references and index.
ISBN 978-0-521-50987-9 – ISBN 978-0-521-72977-2 (pbk.)
1. Papacy–History.   I. Corkery, James.   II. Worcester, Thomas.   III. Title.
BX955.3.P35 2010
262′.130903–dc22   2010016804

ISBN 978-0-521-50987-9 Hardback
ISBN 978-0-521-72977-2 Paperback

Contents

Illustrations

Notes on contributors

JAMES CORKERY, SJ, is Associate Professor of Systematic Theology at the Milltown Institute of Theology and Philosophy in Dublin. In 2006 he was a visiting international Jesuit scholar at the College of the Holy Cross, Massachusetts. He is an editorial correspondent of *The Way* and a member of the Steering Committee and the Council of the Irish School of Ecumenics Trust. His publications include articles on theological anthropology, spirituality, and culture, and on the writings of Joseph Ratzinger. He is the author of *Joseph Ratzinger's Theological Ideas: Wise Cautions and Legitimate Hopes.*

THOMAS WORCESTER, SJ, is Professor of History at the College of the Holy Cross, Massachusetts, and he has also held the Wade Chair at Marquette University. He is the author of *Seventeenth-Century Cultural Discourse: France and the Preaching of Bishop Camus*, and co-editor (with Pamela M. Jones) of *From Rome to Eternity: Catholicism and the Arts in Italy, ca. 1550–1650*. Editor of *The Cambridge Companion to the Jesuits*, Worcester has served on the editorial board of *Studies in the Spirituality of Jesuits* and is a member of the advisory board of *Theological Studies.*

SHEILA BARKER is a fellow at the Medici Archive Project, Florence; she has taught at the American University of Rome. Her works include "Art, Architecture, and the Plague of 1656," in *La peste a Roma 1656–1657*, edited by Irene Fosi.

FREDERIC J. BAUMGARTNER is Professor of History at Virginia Polytechnic Institute and State University. He is the author of several books including *Louis XII, France in the Sixteenth Century*, and *Behind Locked Doors: A History of the Papal Elections.*

CHARLES R. GALLAGHER, SJ, was a visiting fellow at the Geneva School of Diplomacy and International Relations; he has taught at the

College of the Holy Cross. His publications include *Vatican Secret Diplomacy: Joseph P. Hurley and Pope Pius XII.*

KENNETH GOUWENS teaches history at the University of Connecticut; he has been a fellow of Villa I Tati and of the American Academy in Rome. Among his works is *Remembering the Renaissance: Humanist Narratives of the Sack of Rome.*

LINDA HOGAN is Professor of Ecumenics and head of the Irish School of Ecumenics, Trinity College Dublin; she has also taught at the University of Leeds. Her publications include *Confronting the Truth: Conscience in the Catholic Tradition.*

PAMELA M. JONES is Professor of Art History at the University of Massachusetts Boston. She is the author of *Federico Borromeo and the Ambrosiana: Art Patronage and Reform in Seventeenth-Century Milan* and *Altarpieces and their Viewers in the Churches of Rome from Caravaggio to Guido Reni.*

THOMAS MASSARO, SJ, is Professor of Moral Theology at the Boston College School of Theology and Ministry. His books include *Living Justice: Catholic Social Teaching in Action* and *United States Welfare Policy: A Catholic Response.*

CIARÁN O'CARROLL is a priest of the Archdiocese of Dublin and a specialist in the religious history of nineteenth-century Ireland. He has taught at the Milltown Institute and at St. Patrick's College Maynooth; he is the author of *Paul Cardinal Cullen: Portrait of a Practical Nationalist.*

JOHN F. POLLARD is a fellow of Trinity Hall, Cambridge, and Emeritus Professor in Modern European History at Anglia Ruskin University. His books on the papacy include *Money and the Rise of the Modern Papacy: Financing the Vatican, 1850–1950* and *The Unknown Pope: Benedict XV (1914–1922) and the Pursuit of Peace.*

GEMMA SIMMONDS, CJ, lectures on ecclesiology and spirituality at Heythrop College, London. She has published a translation of Henri de Lubac's *Corpus mysticum*; she is the author of "Women Jesuits?," in *The Cambridge Companion to the Jesuits.*

Acknowledgements

We owe a debt of gratitude to those who have made this book possible. Thomas Worcester thanks the College of the Holy Cross for a summer faculty fellowship that facilitated his research on Pius VII. Worcester also thanks Marquette University, where he held the Wade Chair for 2008–09, an appointment that provided generous funding and time for scholarly endeavors. Julie Tatlock, Worcester's research assistant at Marquette, merits special praise for her work. James Corkery thanks the Irish province of the Society of Jesus for financial support of this project, and the Jesuit community at the College of the Holy Cross for its generous welcome during the editing of this book. Worcester and Corkery thank the Jesuit community at Dooradoyle, Ireland, for a warm welcome; they thank Pamela M. Jones for providing several photographs of Rome; they thank Simon Smith, SJ, for assistance with proofreading; and they acknowledge the gracious technical assistance of Mary Morrisard-Larkin in preparing the manuscript for submission to Cambridge University Press.

Introduction

James Corkery and Thomas Worcester

Many images could have been selected for the cover of this book; we chose Corot's *View of Rome*, painted in 1826–27. It offers a particular angle of perspective on the dome of St. Peter's, the Castel Sant'Angelo, and the Ponte Sant'Angelo across the Tiber river. The St. Peter's Basilica that exists today, and is seen in Corot's image, was begun shortly after 1500, and over these last five centuries it has become a central place for the pope to function as pastor, celebrating sacraments and preaching and teaching. The basilica has also served as the venue for the two most recent ecumenical councils, councils called by the pope. The Castel Sant'Angelo (begun in 135 CE) was originally the tomb of the Emperor Hadrian, and popes for centuries used it as a fortress for protection against enemies and/or as a prison. This tomb, fortress, and prison thus evokes the history of the pope as a princely head of state, and successor to the caesars.

This book places special emphasis on how two roles of the pope – prince and pastor – have evolved over the past 500 years. Attention is also paid to the role of patron, a role closely associated with that of prince. Though the pope has become principally if not exclusively a pastor, a kind of universal pastor, the chapters that follow explore some of the complexities of how he has become that. It will become clear that it has not been through a simple, linear evolution, and still less solely through free choices made by popes. If the pope as prince was frequently challenged, so too has been his role as universal pastor, as a pastor claiming a kind of universal jurisdiction and doctrinal authority throughout the world. What popes have done is less the focus of this book than is the question of how performance of certain functions or roles has been perceived, promoted, and/or critiqued. How the roles of prince and patron have been largely replaced by that of pastor alone will be examined, as well as how that transition has been elicited from the papacy by a wide variety of factors and forces at times beyond papal control.

What this book is *not* should perhaps be underlined. It is not another general history of the papacy; there are already many excellent works of that genre, Eamon Duffy's among them.[1] Nor is it a comprehensive, chronological, or alphabetical account of one pope after the next, such as many fine dictionaries and encyclopedias offer. Rather, this book examines a number of especially significant popes since about 1500, significant for the ways in which their pontificates reveal tensions about, reactions to, developments in, and changes in the role or roles of the pope as prince and/or pastor.

Renaissance Rome is where this book begins. John W. O'Malley, in his work on preaching before the papal court in the late fifteenth and early sixteenth centuries, has studied the kind of preaching that was done in that time and place. The preachers were usually members of religious orders; the pope himself did not preach, though much of the preaching was done in his presence.[2] That the pope rarely if ever preached may come as a surprise to those familiar with the papacy of John Paul II or of other recent popes. Preaching has come to be a major part of the pastoral role of the pope, and the pastoral role has come to take precedence over any other roles. Much has changed in the last 500 years.

To be more specific in chronology, by the papacy "since 1500" we mean the papacy since the pontificate of Julius II (1503–13), Giuliano della Rovere. Julius was the epitome of what is sometimes referred to as a Renaissance pope. He lived as an Italian prince of that time, and thus he spent much of his efforts on war, seeking to defend and, better yet, extend his territory on the Italian peninsula. He was even called the warrior pope, and, wearing armor, he led troops into battle.[3] The beneficiary of nepotism – his uncle was Sixtus IV, who made the young Giuliano a cardinal – Julius II bribed his way to election as pontiff, replacing Pius III, who died less than a month after his election. Though Julius did not have as many mistresses and illegitimate children as some bishops of Renaissance Rome, his daughter Felice played a prominent role in early sixteenth-century Rome, as a recent biography of her makes clear.[4] Pope Julius was one of the great Renaissance patrons of the arts, choosing the very best artists of the

[1] Eamon Duffy, *Saints & Sinners: A History of the Popes* (New Haven: Yale University Press, 1997).

[2] John W. O'Malley, *Praise and Blame in Renaissance Rome: Rhetoric, Doctrine, and Reform in the Sacred Orators of the Papal Court, c. 1450–1521* (Durham, NC: Duke University Press, 1979). O'Malley has recently published an overview of papal history: *A History of the Popes: From Peter to the Present* (Lanham, MD: Sheed & Ward, 2010).

[3] See Christine Shaw, *Julius II, the Warrior Pope* (Oxford: Blackwell, 1993).

[4] See Caroline Murphy, *The Pope's Daughter: The Extraordinary Life of Felice della Rovere* (Oxford: Oxford University Press, 2006).

day, Michelangelo among them. The pope as patron of the arts emerged as equal to the pope as pastor or as warrior prince. Julius laid the foundation stone of the new St. Peter's Basilica, the basilica we see today. One of the ways in which he financed his bellicose and cultural enterprises was through the sale of indulgences, and Martin Luther's critique of such practices is usually considered the beginning of the Protestant Reformation.[5]

Frederic J. Baumgartner's chapter in this volume highlights how Julius, who may have chosen this name in imitation not of an earlier pope but of Julius Caesar, was perceived as above all a prince and warrior devoted to expansion and defense of his territories, the Papal States, and to driving French troops out of Italy. Julius was seen as impetuous, prone to fits of rage, and ready to put all sorts of things up for sale, indulgences included, in order to fill the papal treasury. The role of Julius as patron of artists such as Michelangelo, Bramante, and Raphael was seen at the time as an integral part of his role as prince, but also as part of his role as supreme pastor of the Catholic Church. Baumgartner points out that many of the negative assessments of Julius came from outside the Papal States and indeed outside Italy.

Many of the popes in the sixteenth century came from the most powerful families in Italy. Julius II's family, the della Rovere, was actually of relatively modest standing compared with the Medici, the family of Julius's successor, Leo X (1513–21). Though the Protestant Reformation was well underway by the end of his pontificate, Leo seems to have had other priorities, including patronage of the arts and fascination with a pet elephant given to him by the King of Portugal.[6] Leo was not the only Medici pope; his cousin Giulio, whom he had made Archbishop of Florence and a cardinal, reigned as Clement VII (1523–34). Kenneth Gouwens's chapter in this volume examines Clement's eventful pontificate, including the 1527 sack of Rome by troops of Emperor Charles V. For an extreme case of a negative response to, or reception of, a pope's actions, it would be hard to find a better example than this. Clement and the entire city of Rome paid dearly for papal support of the French in the on-going wars between France and the Holy Roman Empire. Gouwens shows how Clement was more successful in promoting Medici power in Florence than he was in pursuing his many goals as Bishop of Rome. Still, Gouwens makes clear that, as patron of the arts, Clement was viewed favorably, for he extended

---

[5] For Luther on the papacy, see Scott Hendrix, *Luther and the Papacy: Stages in a Reformation Conflict* (Philadelphia: Fortress Press, 1981).
[6] See Silvio Bedini, *The Pope's Elephant* (Nashville: Sanders, 1998).

papal support not only to the visual arts but to music and literature. Gouwens also considers both hostile assessments of Clement – especially as prince – made in the 1520s and 1530s, and how recent historiography has been more balanced in its accounts of Clement's reign.

Paul III succeeded in convoking a council at Trent. One of the most interesting things about the Council of Trent, meeting between 1545 and 1563, is its reform decrees calling on bishops and parish priests to get their act together, reside in their dioceses and parishes, and make pastoral ministry their priority. Such changes surely were an innovation for many clerics in that era. The silences of Trent are also interesting. These stand out: there is nothing at Trent on the church expanding outside Europe, in the Americas and elsewhere, even though by the time the council met such expansion was very considerable. And there is no decree at Trent on papal authority, despite repudiation of the papacy by Luther, Calvin, and other Protestant reformers. It is true that in the closing session of Trent, in 1563, the council fathers voted to seek papal confirmation of the council's canons and decrees, confirmation that was obtained from Pope Pius IV. In the following years implementation of Trent was promoted by popes such as Pius V. For example, the council had asked the pope to oversee publication of a revised Roman missal, and Pius V did that.[7]

In her chapter, Pamela M. Jones considers what led to Pius V (1566–72) being canonized as a saint a century and a half after his death. In other words, she examines post-mortem reception of Pius V, especially by his successors as pope. Jones highlights tensions in the image of Pius V that emerged beginning with the pontificate of Sixtus V (1585–90), who initiated the process for beatification and eventual canonization of Pius V. Pius was remembered both as a warrior, most especially as one of the leaders of a coalition that led to a naval victory over the Turks at Lepanto in 1571, and as a man of intense prayer before the crucifix and of deep devotion to Our Lady of the Rosary.

In the decades after Trent, as the papacy took more seriously its pastoral role, popes also strove to keep up, as it were, with other heads of state. Post-Tridentine popes worked hard as princes and as pastors.[8] And

---

[7] For an excellent summary of what Pius V did as pope, see A. D. Wright, *The Early Modern Papacy: From the Council of Trent to the French Revolution, 1564–1789* (New York: Longman, 2000), 272–80.

[8] See Paolo Prodi, *The Papal Prince: One Body and Two Souls: The Papal Monarchy in Early Modern Europe*, trans. Susan Haskins (Cambridge: Cambridge University Press, 1987). See also Prodi's revised version, *Il sovrano pontefice: un corpo e due anime: la monarchia papale nella prima età moderna* (Bologna: Il Mulino, 2006).

they were very image-conscious, as we might say. The rebuilding of Rome, architecturally and spiritually, was a primary concern;[9] the completion of the new St. Peter's, intended to be the largest church in Christendom, was a major focus for popes through the mid-seventeenth century. Papal rituals also helped to promote the dignity, the authority, the mystique of the papacy. Peter Burke has argued that the sixteenth and seventeenth centuries were a kind of high-water mark for elaborate rituals that were designed to display the pre-eminence of the pope in both temporal and spiritual realms. Julius II had founded the Swiss Guards, and there were other mercenary troops employed by popes, but the lack of an army comparable to that of most princes or kings had to be compensated for in some way, and in part, at least, by ritual: its magnificence, its complexity, its ability to display hierarchical order. For example, most visitors to the pope had to genuflect at two points as they crossed a room to meet the Holy Father; then they knelt to kiss his foot. For some occasions, trumpets were sounded when the pope made his entrance, carried in procession on a throne and surrounded by large fans of ostrich or white peacock feathers. When a new pope took possession of his cathedral – St. John Lateran – triumphal arches were erected for the procession to the basilica, and fountains flowed with wine. When the pope gave his *urbi et orbi* blessing from the loggia of St. Peter's, not only were bells rung but cannons were fired.[10]

The *urbi et orbi* blessing was for the city of Rome and for the world. Post-Tridentine popes focused not only on Rome, but on the entire world, a world in which the Catholic Church was increasingly present, through the efforts of missionaries sent to the corners of the earth. When Pope Gregory XV created the Congregation for the Propagation of the Faith, in 1622, he acted as a kind of universal pastor, seeking to ensure a greater measure of papal supervision of evangelization beyond the limits of Catholic Europe. Gregory's efforts sought also to limit the power of Catholic monarchs over the church in their realms, but in the following centuries it was the monarchs of Spain, Portugal, and France that limited papal authority the most severely.

[9] See Frederick McGinness, *Right Thinking and Sacred Oratory in Counter-Reformation Rome* (Princeton: Princeton University Press, 1995).
[10] Peter Burke, "Sacred Rulers, Sacred Priests: Rituals of the Early Modern Popes," in *The Historical Anthropology of Early Modern Italy: Essays on Perception and Communication* (Cambridge: Cambridge University Press, 1987), 168–82. On the rituals for taking possession of St. John Lateran, see also Irene Fosi, "Court and City in the Ceremony of the *possesso* in the Sixteenth Century," in Gianvittorio Signorotto and Maria Antonietta Visceglia, eds., *Court and Politics in Papal Rome, 1492–1700* (Cambridge: Cambridge University Press, 2002), 31–52.

Of seventeenth-century popes, none stands out more for his patronage of the arts, and for his efforts to function as a significant prince on the international stage, than Urban VIII (1623–44). Well known for his patronage of the sculptor and architect Gianlorenzo Bernini, whom he considered a "Michelangelo of his own,"[11] Urban also supported the other arts, including music.[12] Urban's pontificate fell within the period of what we now call the Thirty Years' War (1618–48). His efforts to play a significant role in that major war and in its resolution were largely frustrated by a variety of factors. The pope was seen by many as an ineffectual prince. In her chapter in this volume, Sheila Barker examines criticism of Urban disseminated by pasquinades: brief, anonymous satirical writings, usually written in verse, both during and after Urban's reign. Though later generations would deplore the condemnation of Galileo's heliocentrism, a condemnation made under Urban VIII's authority, Barker shows how in Italy, at least, in Urban's own time, a range of other alleged papal faults were considered far more significant.

From the 1640s on, Jansenists, taking their initial inspiration from Cornelius Jansen's work on St. Augustine, emphasized the sinfulness of humanity and the authority of Augustine, an authority they placed above that of the pope. Gemma Simmonds's chapter offers a sympathetic account of Jansenist non-reception of papal teaching authority in the second half of the seventeenth century. She shows how Jansenists juxtaposed what they identified as ancient traditions of Augustinian theology and of conciliarist ecclesiology with more recent and "novel" papal efforts to exercise absolute doctrinal authority and to turn aside Augustinian tradition. Simmonds also points out that the Jansenist spokesman Blaise Pascal, in his *Provincial Letters* of 1656–57, mentioned the papal condemnation of Galileo as an example of papal fallibility.

The eighteenth century was a time of enormous challenges to the popes, and not solely from a resilient Jansenism. One of the biggest changes in the exercise of the papal office over the last 500 years has been in the role of heads of state in church matters such as appointment of bishops. Whereas cathedral chapters had often chosen bishops in the Middle Ages, in the early modern era (1500–1800) Catholic monarchs enjoyed that prerogative, in Portugal, Spain, and France. National churches, under royal patronage, existed in no small tension with a papacy of increasingly international

[11] Howard Hibbard, *Bernini* (New York: Penguin, 1990), 68.
[12] See Frederick Hammond, *Music and Spectacle in Baroque Rome: Barberini Patronage under Urban VIII* (New Haven: Yale University Press, 1994).

pretensions. The Catholic monarchs of Europe were pleased to control episcopal nominations in their kingdoms, but they wanted more than that. By the 1700s, kings pushed hard against papal interference in their territories; separation of church and state was not the monarchs' goal, but rather the thorough subjection of national churches to kings. Pope Benedict XIV (1740–58) was the first pope to utilize the encyclical as a way of making the papal magisterium function in a universal way, but he did so in an age when his role as universal pastor was contested by many voices, not least those of the Catholic heads of state.[13]

Worse was to come for the papacy. The French Revolution and Napoleon seemed for a time to have nearly destroyed it. The Papal States were occupied repeatedly by French troops; Pope Pius VI (1775–99) died in France, a prisoner of Napoleon. His successor, Pius VII (1800–23), was elected in a conclave held in Venice. As Cardinal and Bishop Chiaramonte, the future Pius VII was considered a moderate, or at least as somewhat open to some of the Revolution's ideals. But agreement between Pius VII and Napoleon on a concordat governing church and state in France did not prevent Napoleon's troops from suppressing the Papal States and taking Pius VII prisoner. But this pope outlived Napoleon's empire and returned to Rome a hero in 1814. Thomas Worcester's chapter explores reception of Pius VII, and finds that being seen as persecuted by and as a survivor of Napoleon's imperialism served Pius and the papacy very well.

In an age of restoration of monarchical authority, not only did Ultramontanists seek to restore the pope's authority to what it had been before what they saw as the horrors of the eighteenth and early nineteenth centuries, but they wanted the pope to play a greater and more direct role as head of the church than had ever been the case. Pius IX (1846–78) was happy to oblige. Ciarán O'Carroll's chapter examines how Pius IX fought a losing battle to retain the Papal States, and yet won, at the same time, a greater role as pastor of the universal church, especially as teacher of doctrine. The pope may no longer have been a prince as well as a pastor, but as pastor he was stronger than before. Conciliarism was rejected not only by a pope but by a council when Vatican I affirmed the possibility for the pope to speak infallibly, if certain conditions were fulfilled, on matters of faith or morals. O'Carroll also shows how under Pius IX centralization of the Catholic Church progressed rapidly, and how Ireland in particular helped to lead the way in enthusiastic reception and implementation of an Ultramontanist vision of the church.

---

[13] On Benedict XIV, see Duffy, *Saints & Sinners*, 191–93.

Though it would be hard to overstate the role of reaction against the French Revolution in nineteenth-century European Catholicism, by the end of the century, Pope Leo XIII (1878–1903) pointed in some other directions. He encouraged French Catholics to accept and work within the political structures of the Republic. In his 1891 encyclical, *Rerum novarum* (literally, "Of New Things"), Leo applied a Thomistic understanding of natural rights to the question of capital and labor in the industrial age. He insisted that the state has a duty to intervene in the economy to protect the dignity of workers. Laissez-faire capitalism Leo presented as a threat to human rights no less menacing than a socialism that would confiscate all private property. Some papal encyclicals never get much attention and are quickly forgotten, perhaps deservedly; Thomas Massaro's chapter shows how *Rerum novarum* is most certainly not in that category. In many places, Catholic politicians and labor leaders were inspired by Leo's teaching and put it into practice. Popes after Leo XIII saw fit to recall and update the themes of his *Rerum novarum*: for example, Pius XI's *Quadragesimo anno* (1931), John Paul II's *Centesimus annus* (1991), and Benedict XVI's *Caritas in veritate* (2009).

From the reign of Pope Leo XIII on, the publication of encyclicals and other papal documents, on doctrinal and spiritual matters as well as on questions of social justice, became a very major part of what popes did. The pope as a spokesman for human rights and human dignity eventually became a part of what people expected of a pope – and not just what Catholics expected, but others as well. A defense of human rights that was grounded in a theory of natural rights could be directed to a worldwide audience, not solely to a Christian one that recognized biblical imperatives. While Leo's Thomism no doubt had elements of a very conservative looking-back to what was imagined as a golden age of thirteenth-century philosophy and theology, it also helped to point ahead to a prophetic style of papal discourse which popes such as Paul VI and John Paul II frequently employed.

But, as may be repeated many times, the development of the papacy has rarely been in a straight line. It has been a matter of two steps forward and one back, and perhaps one sideways. Leo XIII's successor, Pius X (1903–14), had none of the zeal for Catholic intellectual life that animated his predecessor, and he pursued a relentless campaign against historical critical scholarship, perceived as a threat to Catholic doctrine. Yet Pius X also is remembered for encouraging frequent reception of communion and for allowing a younger age for first communion than had previously been the common practice. He was eventually beatified and canonized.

Pius X died just as World War I began. When the Papal States existed, popes had often hired troops to fight wars for them, and entered into political and military alliances just like any other state. Since 1870, there had been no papal state. Charles R. Gallagher's chapter considers both how and why Benedict XV adopted an "impartial" stance in time of war, and the generally negative reception of this stance. During World War I, the impartiality of Benedict XV (1914–22) irritated governments on both sides, which suspected him of really favoring their enemies.[14] Gallagher gives special attention to British reception (or non-reception) of Benedict's policies during that war. It was also during World War I that Benedict published the Code of Canon Law. This publication surely reinforced the role of the pope as universal lawmaker in the church. But Benedict's efforts to broker a peace deal in World War I failed, and when the Armistice of 1918 came, he was refused the right to send a representative to the peace conference at Versailles.

Pius XI (1922–39) resolved the "Roman Question" through the 1929 Lateran Accords, signed by the Holy See and by the Kingdom of Italy. The pope was once again a head of state (Vatican City). John F. Pollard's chapter considers how from Pius XI's creation of Vatican Radio in the early 1930s, the pope has become a kind of electronic pastor, with technological advances allowing his message to reach the ends of the earth. The "impartial" stance of Pius XII (1939–58) during World War II, and especially his alleged silence in the face of the extermination of millions of Jews, remains controversial. Critics continue to contend that Pius XII should have played a more public and prophetic role, in particular by exposing and denouncing the Holocaust. Pollard considers especially the significance of Vatican Radio broadcasts in helping to sort out such heated questions. For the post-World War II era, Pollard examines the pope on television and in film, up to John XXIII (1958–63). "Reception" of the pope henceforth included viewing him on one's own television screen; the pope could be seen and heard live, in one's own home, everywhere. The Ultramontanist bishops of the First Vatican Council could not have dreamt of such a vast opportunity to promote a pope-centered church.

October 1962 saw the first sessions of the Second Vatican Council (1962–65), a council called by Pope John, but one that did most of its work in the pontificate of Paul VI (1963–78). John O'Malley, in his recent book *What Happened at Vatican II*, argues that the council adopted a new

---

[14] See John F. Pollard, *The Unknown Pope: Benedict XV (1914–1922) and the Pursuit of Peace* (London: Geoffrey Chapman, 1999).

style of discourse. Unlike earlier councils that had delineated what was Catholic and what was not by issuing condemnations and drawing firm boundaries, Vatican II put in place "a model largely based on persuasion and invitation." This new style relied heavily on concepts such as dialogue, cooperation, partnership; "Vatican II so radically modified the legislative and judicial model that had prevailed since the first council, Nicaea, in 325, that it virtually abandoned it."[15]

If O'Malley is right, a key question for the papacy since that of Paul VI is whether or not the pope has adopted such a new style. Linda Hogan's chapter looks at reception of both Paul VI and John Paul II (1978–2005) in their teachings on sex and on war. Paul VI's 1968 encyclical, *Humanae vitae*, stands out as a case of controversial papal teaching. Some might call the encyclical prophetic. Its reception was often negative, especially in Europe and North America. But Paul's teachings on war and peace also met with mixed reception. As Vatican II met, Paul VI traveled to places where no pope had been before. Modern technology had made possible a different style of the papacy, as itinerant as it was Roman. Paul VI's 1965 address to the United Nations helped to establish a new model of the papacy: one that was prophetic, on pilgrimage, and concerned to promote the good of all human beings in this world, not solely their salvation in the next. In the very year in which the United States dramatically increased its war effort in Vietnam, Paul VI pleaded for there to be no more war. The prophetic voice, however, is actually quite a different one from what O'Malley attributes to Vatican II.[16] The prophet proclaims uncomfortable or unpopular truths and is rarely conciliatory or collaborative.

It is easy to pass over the brief pontificate of John Paul I, some thirty-three days in August–September 1978. He turned out to be the last Italian pope in a tradition of Italians-only popes that had lasted since 1523. But even in his brief pontificate, John Paul I managed to make a significant change that his two successors have followed: he abandoned the ritual of coronation with the tiara. This was no small innovation, especially for turning the page on some of the more imperial trappings of the papacy.

Pope John Paul II developed Paul VI's itinerant model of the papacy further, with much more travel, all around the world. He also published many encyclicals and other writings in defense of human life and human dignity. Indeed, the prophetic style characterized much of John Paul's

[15] John O'Malley, *What Happened at Vatican II* (Cambridge, MA: Harvard University Press, 2008), 11.

[16] O'Malley discusses prophetic culture as one of four cultures in his *Four Cultures of the West* (Cambridge, MA: Harvard University Press, 2004), 37–75.

papacy, inspiring many, but also alienating others.[17] James Corkery's chapter considers how John Paul sought to function as a universal pastor, for the entire Catholic Church and perhaps the entire world, in an age of jet travel, as well as faxes, email, internet. Corkery shows how John Paul was present, often in person, and certainly electronically, throughout the world. Reception of such a presence was often enthusiastic, but was the enthusiasm matched by acceptance and implementation of his teachings?

[17] For assessment of Paul VI and John Paul II by a prominent progressive among US bishops, see Rembert G. Weakland, *A Pilgrim in a Pilgrim Church: Memoirs of a Catholic Archbishop* (Grand Rapids, MI: Eerdmans, 2009), esp. 210–20, 401–08.

CHAPTER I

Julius II: prince, patron, pastor

Frederic J. Baumgartner

Dozens of popes have been honored as saints, and several known as "the Great," but only one – Julius II – is called *terribile*. The sense of the word as used in Julius's era was that of a man who possessed an iron will, vehement determination, and the capacity to awe in deed and word. It did not embody an evil connotation but meant someone who had those qualities far beyond those of an ordinary person, who could take his actions to excess, often with bad consequences for himself and others.[1] The early sixteenth century saw other rulers who made a powerful mark on their times – Charles V; Francis I; Suleiman the Magnificent; Henry VIII; Ivan IV, the other *terribile* of history – but all of them had decades to achieve their place; Julius earned his in less than ten years as pope. It was as politician, head of the Catholic Church, and patron of arts that Julius made his mark on history as *Papa Terribile*.

Julius II is the epitome of the Renaissance pope in nearly every respect except nepotism, lagging behind Sixtus IV, his uncle, and as a father, having only a daughter, Felice, and thus fewer children than several popes of the era.[2] When on November 1, 1503 Giuliano della Rovere was elected pope, he announced that he would be Julius II. It is unlikely that he meant to honor the previous Julius, an obscure fourth-century pope, but whether he intended simply to keep his own name or to emulate Julius Caesar is uncertain. When Genoa congratulated him as a native of Liguria, Genoa's region, on his election, it declared that he had "the soul of a Caesar."[3] Undoubtedly he came to think of his office, if not himself, as imperial. One of many examples to make the point was the

---

[1] Julius was called *terribile* during his lifetime, usually by the Venetians. See M. Sanuto, *I diarii*, ed. F. Stefani, 58 vols. (Venice, 1879–1903), IX–XI; and L. von Pastor, *The History of the Popes from the Close of the Middle Ages*, trans. F. Antrobus, 40 vols. (St. Louis: Herder, 1969), VI, 214n.

[2] Julius may have had two more daughters, but evidence is weak. See I. Cloulas, *Jules II: le pape terrible* (Paris: Fayard, 1990), 127.

[3] Pastor, *History*, VI, 212n. Some popes kept their baptismal names, as Adrian VI and Marcellus II did after Julius.

medal cast to celebrate his victory at Bologna, which was inscribed *Iulius Caesar Pont. II.*[4]

Named a cardinal in 1471 by Sixtus IV at about the age of twenty-eight, della Rovere served his uncle as Grand Penitentiary, as papal legate to France, and as commander of the papal armies. These offices gave him experience and a taste for power and, with the revenues from several abbeys and eight sees that he held as a pluralist prelate, a huge income. He demonstrated many of the characteristics that would mark him as pope, such as zeal for war and a keen eye for building. He gained a reputation as a generous and discriminating patron of artists and architects: building or rebuilding three palaces in Rome; assembling an excellent collection of antique sculpture; and commissioning a bronze tomb for his uncle after Sixtus died in 1484, which is described as the most opulent monument of the fifteenth century.[5] He was never reticent about putting his family's symbol – an oak tree – on his projects.

At the conclave to elect Sixtus's successor, della Rovere was too young to be *papabile*, but he acted as pope maker, assembling the coalition of cardinals who elected Innocent VIII. It was obvious from the first that della Rovere was his right-hand man. Innocent was among the least aggressive popes of the era, and what warlike activity took place during his reign is attributed to della Rovere's influence.[6] His abrasive personality began to rub on Innocent, and his clout with the pope was reduced late in the reign. Nonetheless, shortly before Innocent died, he refused to hold a consistory until della Rovere recovered from gout, "because he needed him."[7]

At Innocent's death in July 1492, della Rovere, now about age fifty, was regarded as *papabile*. The French king Charles VIII sent his cardinals with gold to support him, since he had come to admire the cardinal when he was legate in France. When the conclave deadlocked, Roderigo Borgia emerged as a compromise, becoming Alexander VI. Although Borgia and della Rovere had been cordial rivals for two decades, they had a bitter falling-out soon after the election. In early 1493 della Rovere

[4] R. Weiss, "The Medals of Julius II (1503–1513)," *Journal of the Warburg and Courtauld Institutes* 28 (1965), 163–83. See also C. Stinger, "Roma Triumphans: Triumphs in the Thought and Ceremonies of Renaissance Rome," *Medievalia et Humanistica* 10 (1981), 189–201; Loren Partridge and Randolph Starn, *A Renaissance Likeness: Art and Culture in Raphael's Julius* (Berkeley: University of California Press, 1980), 47–59.
[5] L. Ettlinger, "Pollaiuolo's Tomb of Pope Sixtus IV," *Journal of the Warburg and Courtauld Institutes* 16 (1953), 239–74.
[6] C. Shaw, *Julius II: The Warrior Pope* (Oxford: Blackwell, 1993), 62–70.
[7] Quoted in ibid., 79.

was banished to Ostia. The first recorded episode of his notorious temper occurred there, when he received word that Alexander had named as a cardinal his son Cesare, who later resigned the office in order to carve a principality out of the Papal States. Della Rovere was so enraged at the news that he was heard "bellowing and shouting" in his chamber.[8] Late in 1493 he fled to France, where he helped persuade Charles VIII to invade Italy in 1494. Louis XII's succession to the French throne in 1498 gave him a powerful friend who told him that in making his plans for Italy he would follow his advice. Louis's plans included winning Milan, which he claimed as an inheritance. Aware of this, Ludovico Sforza of Milan wrote to his agent in France to deal with della Rovere, since he was "the one who can do the most, because of his authority and wealth, and he is the one on whom all lean."[9]

After France seized Milan in 1500, della Rovere returned to Italy and was at his hometown in August 1503 when he heard of Alexander VI's death. He wrote to the cardinals in Rome demanding that they not enter conclave until he arrived. They solved the problem of facing a deadline for starting the conclave by delaying Alexander's funeral, creating an embarrassing situation with the corpse in the heat. Louis expected della Rovere to support the candidacy of his right-hand man, Cardinal d'Amboise, for whose election Louis had prepared since becoming king. Della Rovere was never anyone's tool, and he complained that the French had reneged on a promise to make him pope. He was there, he said, to look after his own interests and nobody else's. If he were not elected, he would work for the election of a good Italian, not a "barbarian," as Italians of that era called any non-Italian.[10]

With della Rovere and d'Amboise at odds, the conclave turned to Cardinal Piccolomini, who was in such poor health that he missed the ballot that elected him. He was chosen because he was not expected to live long; he exceeded expectations by dying twenty-six days after his coronation. The opportunity for which della Rovere had waited for thirty years was at hand. He used the time after Pius III's election well, winning d'Amboise's support by convincing him that the cardinals would not elect a Frenchman and gaining Cesare Borgia's cardinals by promising him that he would keep command of the papal army. Della Rovere was so certain of his election that he had his pontifical ring engraved before the conclave. And elected he was, in the shortest conclave since the system still used

---

[8] Ibid., 91.   [9] Ibid., 108.
[10] A. Giustinian, *Dispacci*, ed. P. Villari, 3 vols. (Florence, 1876), II, 181.

today was created in the 1200s – on the first ballot ten hours after the cardinals assembled.

Julius II's election was regarded as having involved extensive simony, which occurred in most elections of the era but probably never so blatantly as in 1503.[11] The Spanish cardinals reputedly received 150,000 ducats.[12] Julius nonetheless issued a bull banning simony. His bull, written in January 1505 but first published in 1510, declared all simoniacal elections at any level void and meriting excommunication. In respect to papal conclaves, if cardinal electors not guilty of simony believed that it had occurred, they could appeal to a general council and the Catholic rulers to overturn the election.[13] Although Julius's bull did not make simony disappear from conclaves, it was far less common by 1600.

The news of the new pope's election was well received across Catholic Europe, although there was surprise expressed that someone with so many enemies and so formidable a temper had been chosen. Louis XII sent an envoy to express his pleasure that a good friend had become pope. As usual, the ambassadors of the Italian states at the papal court wrote about the policies he was expected to pursue. The agent from Ferrara wrote that the Romans believed Julius's reign would be "glorious, peaceful, genial, and free-handed … We have a pope who will be both loved and feared."[14] The Venetian ambassador reported that Julius lacked the patience to listen to what others were saying and that his mind was always racing ahead of what he was being told. He rarely consulted anyone, and the few whom he did consult had little influence on him. Once he made a decision, he expected it to be carried out immediately: "Whatever was in his mind had to be carried out, even if he should perish in the attempt." Yet he preferred to do everything himself. The Venetian noted that despite his age of about sixty years, he looked and acted much younger. Except for gout, he showed no signs of infirmity, which remained true for most of his reign. When gout did lay him low, he was furious with his body for betraying him.[15] In short, he was impetuous, calm, cunning, candid, stubborn, vigorous, violent, warmhearted, generous, tightfisted – all summed up in the word *terribile*.

---

[11] A Venetian wrote that the papacy "falls to the highest bidder." Ibid., 255. Pastor, *History*, VI, 209n., states categorically that simony occurred.

[12] F. Gregorovius, *History of the City of Rome*, trans. A. Hamilton, 8 vols. (New York: AMS Press, 1967), VIII, 16n.

[13] Ibid., 440; Sanuto, *Diarii*, XI, 530.

[14] Quoted in Pastor, *History*, VI, 211.

[15] Sanuto, *Diarii*, XI, 722–843; a Venetian reported that Julius also suffered from the French disease (syphilis). Here and elsewhere in this chapter translations are mine unless otherwise stated.

As pope in that era, Julius II had three major roles to fill – those of ruler of the Papal States and a major power of Italy, supreme pastor of the Catholic Church, and patron of art and letters. Since the papacy's permanent return to Rome in 1420, the popes had been deeply involved in Italian politics. The ambassadors at Rome were not certain what policies Julius would enact as pope; they knew that he had made many promises to get the votes of cardinals, especially to Cesare Borgia, which would be difficult to fulfill. Julius's solution was to act as if he had not made most of them, although many promised ecclesiastical promotions were completed.

The promise to Borgia to maintain him in power in the Papal States was one that Julius had no intention of keeping. Shortly after his election he told Niccolò Machiavelli, then Florentine agent in Rome, that he was determined to have the Papal States under his control and was ready to use force if necessary.[16] His handling of Borgia was so well crafted that it was a major factor in his reputation as a consummate politician. Julius made it seem as if he was content to allow Venice, bitterly hostile to Borgia, to seize several cities in the Romagna, part of the Papal States, which Borgia controlled. Once Venice had sufficiently worn down his forces, Julius ordered him to be arrested and taken to Rome. After extensive negotiations, he was allowed to go to Spanish-controlled Naples in exchange for those fortresses that his forces still occupied. The viceroy of Naples put him on a ship for Spain, and he passed out of Julius's life. With Borgia gone, Julius turned to recovering the papal cities. Before he could do it, he needed to fill his treasury, revitalize the papal army, and assert papal authority in the rest of the Papal States. Insisting on pocketing every ducat owed to the papacy and spending as little as possible, which gained him a reputation of being both avaricious and miserly, he achieved the first two goals and, thereby, the third. In the course of recovering the papal cities Julius won the title of "the Warrior Pope."

Bologna had been independent of papal authority for decades. In 1506 Julius ordered Giovanni Bentivoglio, its tyrant, to give up his power, threatening that otherwise he would come in person to force him out. When the ultimatum was rejected, Julius assembled a force and marched on Bologna with most of the cardinals and curia in tow. The pope hoped to win the cooperation of France and Venice against Bologna, but when they dithered in committing their forces, he marched anyway. Machiavelli, who accompanied him, admired the way he dealt with their procrastination: "When

<hr />

[16] Machiavelli, quoted in Weiss, "The Medals of Julius II," n. 26.

he saw that he was getting nothing from them ... he decided to make them both to come to his judgment by giving them no time to deliberate."[17] By acting without them, Julius gave them a distasteful choice of seeing the papacy defeated or going to his aid. Louis XII agreed to send troops for the papal army, while Venice pledged neutrality.

Marching north to Bologna, the papal party crossed the rugged Apennines.[18] Julius several times had to dismount and go on foot for a mile or more because of the narrow path. He was described as bearing the trip's burdens as if he were still young. After arriving at Bologna, he excommunicated Bentivoglio and placed an interdict on the city. Those spiritual weapons, along with the papal and French forces, persuaded Bentivoglio to flee and the city authorities to open the gates to the pope. Julius made a triumphal entry into Bologna on November 11, 1506; it was one of the most spectacular events of his reign. Julius never stinted on spending money for enhancing papal prestige. Newly minted coins with the inscription "Bologna freed by Julius from the tyrant" were tossed to the people. He ordered the construction of a fortress, for which he laid the first stone before returning to Rome. Since Venice still held several papal cities, Julius skillfully created the League of Cambrai in 1508, combining France, Spain, and the Holy Roman Empire against Venice. France, providing most of the League's forces, routed Venice in May 1509 and forced it to concede the cities.

Having achieved that goal, Julius now turned his attention to driving the "barbarians" out of Italy – *fuori i barbari* – beginning with the French as the most visible of the non-Italians. He succeeded in keeping it from Louis that he was subverting the league into an anti-French alliance until he was ready to spring it on him in 1510, when he excommunicated Duke Alfonso d'Este of Ferrara, France's closest ally in Italy, charging d'Este with plotting to depose him. Louis responded with spiritual and temporal weapons, calling a synod of the French church to assess its ties with Rome and sending an army to defend Ferrara.

When the French crossed the Po river in late 1510, Julius took it as a signal for war. Hoping to seize Ferrara before the French could intervene, he sent the papal army with Swiss and Spanish allies against Mirandola, which was regarded as the key to Ferrara. When the attack stalled, Julius took command of his forces in January 1511. Cardinals had often

---

[17] Machiavelli, *Discourses on Livy*, trans. H. Mansfield (Chicago: University of Chicago Press, 1996), 304.

[18] Sources for the next paragraphs: Giustinian, *Dispacci*, III; Sanuto, *Diarii*, X; Pastor, *History*, VI, 247ff; Shaw, *Julius II*, 146ff.

commanded armies, as Julius did for Sixtus, but it was unheard of for a
pope. Furthermore, the weather was atrocious, and Julius had been seriously ill the previous months. He took up residence in a building so close
to the walls that shots from defenders killed two aides. He kept a ball and
presented it to the shrine of the Virgin of Loreto, to whom he attributed
his protection from harm.

No episode of Julius's life so defined him as did this event. The Venetian
ambassador quoted him as saying as he left for Mirandola: "Let's see if I
have bigger balls than the King of France."[19] When he arrived there, he
made everyone tremble by cursing them, using words that the ambassador refused to put on paper. He did not stop with words but pushed and
shoved those who angered him. Even his nephew, a captain, steered clear
of Julius to avoid his rage. The pope spent most of the three days while
his men bombarded the walls under a flimsy shelter unbothered by the
blowing snow and flying cannon balls. When the city surrendered after a
breach was opened, Julius refused to wait until barricades were removed
from a gate; a ladder was placed on the rubble, and he entered through the
breach. His aides persuaded him not to slaughter the garrison and sack the
city, as he had wanted; the episode's final scene had the pope traversing the
streets demanding that his soldiers return to camp or be hanged.

"The Warrior Pope at the siege of Mirandola" remains the indelible
image of Julius, in part because of Francesco Guicciardini's statement:

It is certainly a strange event, and not seen before, that the king of France, a
secular prince of an age not yet past its vigor and in good health, trained from
his youth in handling arms, should be taking his repose … and on the other
side, to see the highest priest, vicar of Christ, old and infirm, involved in person
in waging a war stirred up by him against Christians, as a leader of soldiers; he
exposed himself to hardships and perils, retaining nothing of the pontiff but the
robes and the name.[20]

Whether he wore armor at the siege is uncertain. It is commonly said that
Erasmus presents him in *Julius Excluded* as being armored at the gates of
heaven, but the text in fact refers to his papal robe "shining all over with
gold and silver," although underneath it he "clattered with horrendous
arms."[21] Jean Lemaire de Belges, however, describes Julius as wearing "the
armor of war, which he never takes off."[22]

[19] Sanuto, *Diarii*, XI, 721.
[20] Francesco Guicciardini, *The History of Italy*, trans. Sidney Alexander (Princeton: Princeton
     University Press, 1984), 149.
[21] K. Sowards, ed., *The Julius exclusus of Erasmus* (Bloomington: Indiana University Press, 1968),
     46–48. Pastor, *History*, VI, 343n., states that Julius's armor was preserved in the Vatican.
[22] J. Lemaire de Belges, *Traité de la différence des schismes et des conciles* (Lyons, 1511).

Two months later Julius made another entry into Bologna, during which he rode a spirited horse, not his usual mule. An observer reported that the horse bolted at a noise and that Julius, bringing it under control, looked more like a captain putting his horse through its paces than an aged pope with the burdens of the world on him.[23] Julius's bravado was shaken in April 1512, when the French won the Battle of Ravenna against papal and allied armies. Expecting the French to march on Rome and depose him, Julius prepared to flee, but when word came of their horrendous losses, he recovered his nerve. He drew up a bull deposing Louis XII and giving the throne to Henry VIII of England, promising that he would go to Paris and place the French crown on Henry's head if he seized the city. The pope's renewed optimism drew largely from the success that he had in bringing the Swiss into an alliance. He had long courted them and in 1506 gave them the honor of providing men for his bodyguard, thus creating the Swiss Guard. In May 1512 the Swiss committed themselves to providing 18,000 men to the papacy. By June the French were retreating from Italy, and the papal allies had invaded France.

A victorious Julius was hardly magnanimous. Bologna, which had welcomed the French six months earlier, was treated harshly; Louis was excommunicated and an interdict placed on France; and the campaign against the Duke of Ferrara continued unabated. Ferdinand of Aragon was eager for peace with the duke, who held Spanish prisoners. Ferdinand's ambassador at Rome found dealing with Julius very exasperating. He told a cardinal that in the madhouse at Valencia a hundred people were chained up who were less mad than the pope.[24]

The image of Julius II in history draws heavily on his activities as the ruler of the Papal States and a major power in Italy; but he was first of all the supreme pastor of the Catholic Church, and he made his mark in that role nearly as boldly as he did in politics. His acts in that sphere were less controversial. One right the pope had was that of the appointment of cardinals, although he was expected to convoke a consistory of the existing cardinals and get their opinions on his proposed choices. Within a month after his election Julius gave red hats to two of his nephews along with a nephew of d'Amboise to repay him for his support in the conclave. Despite the early appearance that Julius would act in the same way as his predecessors in respect to nepotism, he named only two more relatives as cardinals, never having more than two at a time in the College of Cardinals. Also unlike his predecessors, he named mostly Italians to the college.

---

[23] Shaw, *Julius II*, 273–74, citing the papal master of ceremonies.
[24] Ibid., 304–05.

Convinced that Louis XII would stop at nothing to win d'Amboise's election as pope, Julius named few French cardinals; this reticence was one of the issues that raised tensions between king and pope. Julius was hardly more generous to his erstwhile allies; he was convinced that the papacy was an Italian institution and that Italians ought to control it.

Julius's second nomination of cardinals in 1505 occasioned a row with the existing cardinals; they wanted attrition in the college, because Alexander VI's increase in their number above the traditional number of twenty-four had reduced their incomes. The cardinals at the consistory were treated to one of *Papa Terribile*'s public tantrums; for several it was the first time they had seen him truly angry. The Venetian ambassador reported that Julius's shouting was heard well away from the consistory hall. Only after an eight-hour session did the cardinals and pope emerge with a consensus on nine new red hats. While none of the total of twenty cardinals whom Julius appointed during his reign would become pope and none would have major roles in church history, only one is regarded as an unworthy choice.

Julius was accused of appointing as cardinals those who held valuable church offices that they had to return to the pontiff, who could sell them to others. There is enough evidence of such a pattern to suggest that it did motivate him in giving out red hats. Julius's need for money to conduct his aggressive politics led him to increase the practice of venality, already established by 1503. Its most profitable form was the creation of new offices, which Julius did in large number, creating over 200 in the course of his reign.[25] In England it was common opinion that the request to canonize Henry VI failed because "Julius II was too dear, and the king would not come to his rates."[26] The sense that everything was for sale at Julius's court became greater with the use of indulgences as a fiscal device. Sixtus IV had issued a bull in 1476 that extended the applying of indulgences to the dead in Purgatory while emphasizing the power of the pope alone to issue them. One means of obtaining an indulgence was donating money to the church for a crusade or charity, but the papacy quickly found that the practice provided vast sums for any purpose. Julius took full advantage of the practice, creating numerous indulgences, especially the infamous St. Peter's Indulgence in 1507. Erasmus's critiques of indulgences are well known, and Martin Luther's even better known; but attacks also

---

[25] P. Partner, *The Pope's Men: The Papal Civil Service in the Renaissance* (Oxford: Clarendon Press, 1990).
[26] J. Foxe, *Acts and Monuments*, 8 vols. (reprinted New York: AMS, 1965), III, 758.

appeared from others. Jacques Almain, a theologian at the University of Paris, denounced the granting of indulgences for the dead in Purgatory as a misuse of indulgences which showed that the pope was capable of falling into doctrinal error.[27]

Almain's criticism appeared as part of a vast French campaign against Julius after he turned the League of Cambrai against France. The major weapon that Louis XII wielded against this "wolf in sheep's clothing"[28] was calling a council for the purpose of deposing Julius as an antipope. In April 1511 Louis convoked a national synod, which agreed that Julius was guilty of simony at his election and other sins, and that the French king had the authority to assemble a council to depose him if he refused to step down. Louis then called on the prelates of Catholic Europe to meet at Pisa in September 1511. Only four cardinals, sixteen bishops, and a few other clerics were present at Pisa; they declared Julius an antipope and named an Italian cardinal as papal administrator until an election was held. Julius responded by excommunicating the attendees, placing an interdict on Pisa, and convoking his own council for the Lateran in Rome. Besides denouncing the "schismatics" at Pisa, this council was instructed to reform the church and organize a crusade against the Turks. The Fifth Lateran Council opened in April 1512 with some one hundred prelates present, mostly Italians. It accepted Julius's bull excommunicating those at Pisa, declared that only the pope could call a council, and proclaimed its intention of reforming the church.

Thus began the "war of the councils."[29] Julius chose Giles of Viterbo, whom he had helped become general of the Augustinian Hermits, to give the opening sermon for his council. Giles was Julius's favorite preacher for good reason: in 1507 he proclaimed that Pope Julius had vastly surpassed Julius Caesar in lands that he controlled because of the conquests made by Portugal and Spain.[30] At the council Giles strongly defended the right of the papacy to call a council and excommunicate and depose schismatic kings and cardinals. He also defended Julius's use of arms to secure control of the Papal States and attributed the recovery of Bologna to divine providence, although he denounced war among Christians in general. Giles proclaimed that Julius had only the purest motives in

[27] J. Almain, *Libellus de auctoritatae ecclesiae et conciliorum generalium* (Paris, 1512).
[28] P. Gringore depicts him thus in *Le jeu du prince des sotz* (1512); in *Recueil générale des sotties*, ed. E. Picot, 3 vols. (Paris, 1909–12), II, 132–73.
[29] Cloulas's term in his *Jules II*.
[30] Quoted in N. Temple, "Julius II as Second Caesar," in M. Wyke, ed., *Julius Caesar in Western Culture* (Oxford: Blackwell, 2006), 127n.

convoking his council and enumerated his great accomplishments on behalf of the church: this great pope would now reform the church and defeat the Turks.[31]

At the council's fifth session in February 1513, the last that the gravely ill Julius attended, Cristoforo Marcello, a Venetian, gave an address that could have served as an epitaph that the pope might have written himself: Julius had fought a just war against the enemies of the church and Italy, generously funding an army with his own money and undergoing the awful rigors of war without flinching. Having driven the enemy out of Italy, he had given his fatherland joy and peace and earned for himself an immortal name. Even greater glory would be his, now that he could turn his attention to purifying the church as its physician and husbandman; the children of God "now raise their eyes full of joy and hope to the bridegroom who has come to deliver her; almost as if God were again on Earth."[32]

The theologian Thomas Cajetan also gave a sermon to the council defending papal supremacy and denouncing the schismatic council at Pisa, which was quickly published. A copy reached Louis XII, who ordered the Sorbonne to refute it. The task was given to Almain. He argued that papal power was not absolute; if the pope sinned or erred, the Christian princes had the authority to oversee the church until he repented or was replaced. Almain then demonstrated how grievously Julius had sinned and erred. Simony, avarice, pride, lust, and drunkenness were among his vices, but his worst sin was leading armed men against other Christians. Did not Jesus tell Peter, "Put up the sword!"? In regard to erring princes the pope can use only fatherly admonition, not excommunications, interdicts, and arms. Because Julius used such forms of coercion against the French king, he was an antipope; the council must depose him and elect another.[33]

Louis XII sponsored a propaganda campaign against Julius to keep popular support in face of the papal interdict and the heavy taxes needed for the French army in Italy. For it he drew on the writers of farcical plays called *sotties*. As can be imagined, Julius's many vices, real or supposed, and pretensions to power were wildly lampooned. One vice attributed to him was drunkenness. There is no question that Julius liked wine.[34] Jean Beaufils, an author of a life of Julius, declared that he was "a great drinker and devourer

---

[31] Sanuto, *Diarii*, XIV, 203ff.   [32] Quoted in Pastor, *History of the Popes*, VI, 429.

[33] Almain, *De auctoritate ecclesiae*, 46.

[34] Pastor, *History*, VI, 223n., notes that papal disbursements for wine first appeared in Julius's accounts but states that only his enemies called him a drunkard. Erasmus often does so in *Julius Excluded*.

of wine, the stronger the better."[35] The *sotties* panned him as a falling-down drunk, to great humorous effect among audiences. What is considered the best of them, Pierre Gringore's *Jeu du prince des sotz*, presented the pope as the Obstinate Man with his companions, Simony and Hypocrisy, who seek to stir up discord between France and Italy. Gringore accused him of being allied with murderers and thieves.[36] Another French author, Jean Bouchet, wrote a fictional letter to Henry VIII from Henry VII to persuade him not to join the pope in war on France. What faith, he asked, can anyone have in this Julius who does not hesitate to put on armor instead of cope and mingle with rude soldiers?[37] With few exceptions the Catholic princes rejected the council at Pisa, as did most Italians. Its welcome in Pisa was so unfriendly that it soon moved to Milan; when the French were forced out of Milan, the council collapsed. On his deathbed Julius barred the schismatic cardinals from participating in the coming conclave.

Julius was convinced that what he was doing was essential for the independence and authority of the papacy and the Catholic Church. While hardly a saintly man he was devout in his own way, celebrating or attending Mass regularly. He had a deep devotion to Our Lady of Loreto and often made pilgrimages to her shrine. He also was an advocate of the doctrine of transubstantiation and chose Raphael to paint the *Mass of Bolsena* in the Vatican, which commemorated a thirteenth-century miracle supporting the doctrine. Raphael depicted him deep in meditation at the consecration of the Host.

Most artistic and architectural works produced for Julius were commissioned to glorify the papacy. Already noted for his largesse and keen eye as a cardinal, once he became pope he had access to great wealth and the best artists and architects. It is usually said that he was fortunate to have Raphael, Bramante, and Michelangelo active during his reign to produce great works for him, but it is equally true that they were lucky to have him as a patron with his sense of grandeur, iron will, and access to vast resources to impel them to create many of the Renaissance's masterpieces. It can be argued that without Julius's patronage, they would not have achieved much of the great work that established their reputations.[38]

---

[35] J. Britnell and C. Shaw, "A French Life of Pope Julius II: Jean Beaufils and his Translation of Platina," *Bibliothèque d'humanisme et renaissance* 72 (2000), 114.
[36] Gringore, *Jeu du prince.*
[37] N. Hochner, *Louis XII: les dérèglements de l'image royale* (Paris: Champ Vallon, 2007), 165–66. Hochner gives further examples from French authors accusing Julius of wearing armor.
[38] But apparently Leonardo da Vinci and Julius never met. G. Vasari, *The Lives of the Artists*, trans. J. Bondanella (Oxford: Clarendon Press, 1991), says that Leonardo first went to Rome at Leo X's election.

Julius's relationship with Michelangelo was highly tempestuous. The artist had a temper and ego equal to the pope's, and the word *terribile* was also applied to him, appropriately by Julius himself.[39] The story of the association between the two is well known, but one episode reveals much about the character of both men. In 1505 Julius commissioned Michelangelo to sculpt a colossal tomb for him, but soon after the artist had begun, the pope turned his attention to building the new St. Peter's. Fiercely angry that he had not been paid and his work interrupted, Michelangelo fled to Florence and refused to return to Rome despite appeals from Julius and Florence, which Pope Julius was pressing to return him to Rome. A Florentine told Michelangelo that he was behaving toward the pope in a way "the king of France would not have dared."[40] In 1506, after Bologna had submitted, Julius decided that he wanted a statue of himself placed in front of the cathedral to remind its people that he was their sovereign. He ordered Michelangelo to sculpt it, and the artist agreed, although he said that he was going with a rope around his neck. At his audience with Julius, Michelangelo told him that he had left Rome because he felt the pope's men had mistreated him. When a nearby prelate tried to calm the agitated pope by saying that artists do not know how to behave because all they know is their art, Julius turned in fury to him: "You are the ignoramus and the wretch. Get out of my sight and go to the devil!"[41] The statue that Michelangelo created in two months was made of 14,000 pounds of bronze. When Julius came to see it before returning to Rome, the artist asked him whether he should place book or sword in the pope's hand. Julius replied: "Put a sword there. I know nothing of literature."[42] After the Bentivogli regained control of the city in 1511, the statue was wrecked and the bronze used for a huge cannon derisively called La Giulia.

Julius's relationship with Raphael was far less troubled; his art reflected his personality – calm and graceful. He arrived in Rome in late 1508, and Julius put him to work with other painters in the new apartments in the Vatican Palace. He was so impressed with Raphael's painting that he commissioned him to do frescos for the new papal library, which included one of his great works, *The School of Athens*. Perhaps Raphael's best-known artwork is his portrait of Julius II himself. Begun in late 1511, it was

[39] Pastor, *History*, VI, 215.
[40] A. Condivi, *The Life of Michelangelo*, trans. A. Wohl (University Park: Pennsylvania State University Press, 1999), 37.
[41] Ibid., 38.
[42] Vasari, *Lives*, 438. Michelangelo put neither in Julius's hand but had it lifted in a blessing or, some said, a curse on the city.

presumably finished before the pope shaved off his famous beard in early 1512. Julius grew the beard, the focal point of the painting, while he was at Bologna in 1510 and seriously ill. Whether he grew it because he was too ill to be shaved or had made a vow not to shave until the French were driven from Italy, it elicited a great deal of comment.[43] Some suggested that he was imitating Caesar, who swore that he would not shave until he had avenged a defeat inflicted by the Gauls. All popes since 1370, and most clerics, had been clean-shaven, but, probably because of Raphael's portrait, all but two popes for the next two centuries had beards.[44] Julius shaved his in April 1512, expressing his optimism that the French would be forced from Italy.[45]

In his own era Julius was best known as the pontiff who ordered Constantine's basilica of St. Peter to be demolished and replaced by the "new" St. Peter's. That the old St. Peter's was decrepit was obvious, but Julius apparently intended only to have a chapel added to house the tomb that he had asked Michelangelo to do, and he commissioned Bramante to draw up plans. He produced such a stunning design for a largely new building that the pope put him to work on it. He wanted, however, to turn the building so that the obelisk on Vatican Hill, which Caligula had placed there, would be directly in front. Julius refused, because it required moving Peter's tomb, and "the sacred must be kept unchanged."[46] (The obelisk was moved to its location in St. Peter's Square in 1586.) After the first stone was laid in 1506, Bramante set to work demolishing sections of the old basilica and soon persuaded Julius that the whole structure had to come down, since leaving parts in place would be unsafe. There was strong opposition to demolishing the ancient basilica; many cardinals, for example, objected. The basilica took a century to complete, and when it was completed, with contributions from Michelangelo, Bernini, and others, it was reduced by a third in size from Bramante's plan.

Julius II died on February 21, 1513, after what all agreed was an exemplary deathbed scene, begging forgiveness of those he had wronged and commending his soul to God while refusing to make a cardinal of a

---

[43] Cloulas, *Jules II*, 201, citing a Bolognese chronicler on Julius's vow. See M. Zucker, "Raphael and the Beard of Julius II," *The Art Bulletin* 59 (1977), 524–33, for canon law on clerical beards and comments on Julius's beard.

[44] Julius's two successors were not bearded; after them the next clean-shaven pope was elected in 1700.

[45] Sanuto, *Diarii*, XIV, 86.

[46] J. O'Malley, *Giles of Viterbo on Church and Reform* (Leiden: Brill, 1970), 125.

grand-nephew he believed was unworthy, despite his relatives' pleas. He
surely must have been pleased with himself in how he had trumped the
king of the barbarians, restored papal authority in the Papal States, and set
underway several of Europe's greatest art projects. A pope's funeral was set
by tradition, so he had no say in his; but there was an outpouring of grief
among the Romans, who came in huge numbers to pay their last respects.
Julius's master of ceremonies wrote that in his forty years in Rome he had
never seen such a throng at a pope's funeral. "Weeping, they prayed for his
soul, calling him a true pope and Vicar of Christ, a pillar of the Apostolic
Church, an enemy of tyrants ... declaring that this pope had delivered
Italy from the barbarians."[47] The tomb in which Julius wanted to be buried
in the new St. Peter's was finished only in 1545 and placed in San Pietro in
Vincoli, his titular church as a cardinal.

As soon as Julius die, there were comments on his place in history.
Machiavelli, who knew him well, extolled him for being successful in all
that he attempted: "He merits the greater praise because he did everything to increase the power of the Church and not of any private person."[48]
He commented about the failure of Giovanipagolo Baglioni, the tyrant
of Perugia, to seize or even kill Julius when the pope entered that city in
1505 without his forces and unarmed. Machiavelli found it striking that
Baglioni,

who did not mind being publicly (called) incestuous and a parricide ... did not
dare to make an enterprise where everyone would have admired his courage and
which would have left an eternal memory of himself, being the first who would
have shown the Prelates how little esteemed are they who live and reign as they
do, and would have done an act, the greatness of which would have overcome
every infamy and every danger that could have resulted from it.[49]

Guicciardini equally lauded Julius the politician:

A Prince of inestimable spirit and resolution, but impetuous and given to boundless schemes ... worthy undoubtedly of the highest glory had he been a secular
prince, or if the same care and purpose which he had used to exalt the Church to
temporal greatness by the arts of war had been employed to exalt it in spiritual
matters by the arts of peace.[50]

[47] Quoted in ibid., 437.
[48] Niccolò Machiavelli, *The Prince and the* Discourses, ed. M. Lerner (New York: Random House,
1950), 43. It is never certain in *The Prince*, however, when Machiavelli intended irony.
[49] Machiavelli, *Discourses on Livy*, trans. H. Mansfield (Chicago: University of Chicago Press, 1996),
book I, chap. 28.
[50] Guicciardini, *History of Italy*, 273.

The Venetians, of course, despised him. Their ambassador wrote: "This pope was the ruin of Italy. If only he had died five years ago for the good of Christianity, this republic, and all Italy."[51]

Many northern humanists were equally negative. François Rabelais in *Pantagruel* has a character go to the nether world and see there the great figures of history in their eternal occupations; for example, Alexander the Great patches breeches, and Julius Caesar tars boat bottoms. The four popes among the many famous names include Alexander VI, selling rats, and Julius II, who sells tarts, "but they trimmed off his huge, ugly beard." His tarts are stolen, and the pastry shop owner badly beats him. Meanwhile, Lemaire de Belges apes Julius, "so all those poor worldly kings and popes had to kiss his feet – and how he swaggered as he gave them his blessing, saying 'Buy your pardons, you rascals, buy them. They're a good bargain.'"[52]

Erasmus was in Bologna at the time of Julius's 1506 triumph, and the pope appalled him. Besides certainly being the author of *Julius Excluded* with its cleverly satirical attack, he filled his letters and works with biting comments about him: "Warring, conquering, triumphing, acting the very Julius."[53] He wrote a poem that hints at approving tyrannicide in respect to Julius.

> Your name fits you perfectly,
> For you are certainly another Caesar.
> He too was once *pontifex maximus*,
> He too arrived at tyranny by a path of crime,
> Pleasing to him, no less than to you.
> Was faith broken for the sake of power.
> He scorned the gods, in this too you are Julius.
> The whole world he churned with blood,
> Battle and gore; here too you are another Julius.
> …
> That you be Julius wholly one thing alone
> Is lacking, that another Brutus should befall you.[54]

The Protestants were even more hostile, if that be possible. Luther, whose trip to Rome in 1510 made it likely that he had seen Julius, rendered

---

[51] Sanuto, *Diarii*, XV, 561.

[52] François Rabelais, *Gargantua and Pantagruel*, trans. B. Raffel (New York: Norton, 1990), 224–27.

[53] Desiderius Erasmus, *Correspondence*, trans. R. Mynors, 5 vols. (Toronto: University of Toronto Press, 1974), I, 420–21.

[54] The full poem is in Sowards's introduction to *Julius exclusus*, 19. I have given the text as abridged in J. Tracey, *The Politics of Erasmus* (Toronto: University of Toronto Press, 1978), 27.

disparaging remarks about him, as in his *Table Talk*, where he called Julius "a monster in power above all others, an ungodly, warlike and fierce man."[55] John Calvin wrote: "It is well known what sort of vicars of Christ we shall find: Julius, Leo, Clement, Paul, who never grasped anything of Christ except what they learned in Lucian's school," likely a reference to Lucian's satirical attacks on Greek religion.[56] John Foxe declared that Julius was more dedicated to war than to Christ. On his way to battle, Foxe alleges. Julius threw the keys of St. Peter into the Tiber, saying that since the keys did not serve his purpose, he would now take up St. Peter's sword.[57] Foxe further claimed that over 200,000 people were slain in the seven years of Julius's wars.

In the decades to come, Julius II became a symbol of what Protestants condemned about Rome, but for many Catholics as well, he epitomized everything that needed reforming in the papacy. It has proved most difficult to find any affirmative comments about him even in Catholic literature. Only in the twentieth century have there appeared more positive assessments of *Il Papa Terribile.*[58]

[55] Martin Luther, *Luther's Works*, ed. H. Lehman, 55 vols. (Philadelphia: Fortress Press, 1967), LIIII, 347.
[56] John Calvin, *Institutes of the Christian Religion*, ed. J. McNeill (Philadelphia: Westminster Press, 1960), 1146.
[57] Foxe, *Acts and Monuments*, IV, 16–117.
[58] Pastor and Shaw both give final assessments for Julius that are on balance favorable. For a positive interpretation of his role in the Fifth Lateran Council, see Nelson Minnich's works.

CHAPTER 2

Clement VII: prince at war

Kenneth Gouwens

The elevation of Cardinal Giulio de' Medici as Pope Clement VII in November 1523 occasioned rejoicing. The pontificate of Adrian VI (1522–23, family name Dedel) had been marked by fiscal retrenchment and cultural austerity, but now many expected a return to the golden days of Leo X (1513–21, family name Medici), Giulio's cousin. Nor was this hope baseless: as a cardinal, Giulio de' Medici had been the patron of artists, architects, and literati, including Raphael, Michelangelo, and Machiavelli. Late in Leo's pontificate, he had negotiated a critical alliance between the papacy and Charles V, King of Spain (1516–56) and Holy Roman Emperor (1519–56), so as to counterbalance the growth of French power on the Italian peninsula. In addition, he had participated in drafting the bull that threatened Martin Luther with excommunication. In short, he came to the See of Peter with a reputation for generosity in cultural patronage, prudence in political judgment, and commitment to the needs of the church. Thus when Pietro Bembo predicted in 1523 that "Clement will be the greatest and wisest, as well as the most respected pope whom the Church has seen for centuries," he had substantial grounds for optimism.[1] Nor was he alone: the historian Francesco Guicciardini later observed of Clement that "it was universally believed that he would be a greater pope and accomplish greater deeds than any of those who till that day had been seated in that chair."[2]

Such predictions could scarcely have been more wrong. In just over a decade, the papacy suffered spectacular political disasters that necessitated in turn a draconian curtailment of expenditure on the arts. In his effort to keep a balance of power between Charles V and Francis I, both of whom

---

[1] Ludwig von Pastor, *The History of the Popes from the Close of the Middle Ages: Drawn from the Secret Archives of the Vatican and Other Original Sources*, ed. F. I. Antrobus et al., 40 vols., 3rd edn. (London: Kegan Paul, 1901–33), IX, 247.

[2] Francesco Guicciardini, *The History of Italy*, trans. Sidney Alexander (Princeton: Princeton University Press, 1969), 363.

were fielding large armies on the Italian peninsula, the pope forged alliances that included alternately one or the other of them. That policy –
above all the anti-Imperial League of Cognac formed in 1526 – led to Rome
being sacked by Charles V's troops in May of 1527. Subsequently, the pope
himself was held hostage for half a year and was forced to pay exorbitant
fines. Upon his release he again found himself struggling to steer a middle course between the French and Spanish–Imperial sides. Ultimately,
he allied firmly with the emperor, not least because he required Charles's
assistance to regain control of Florence, which had expelled the Medici
in 1527. But any hope for Italian autonomy from foreign intervention had
been lost.

Ecclesiastically, Pope Clement fared little better: beyond the spread of
the Lutheran heresy in the north and the loss of Henry VIII's England
from the Catholic fold, Turkish incursions into Eastern Europe threatened even greater disruptions of Christendom.[3] Rhetoric about the
need to launch a crusade against the Turks, a staple since the fall of
Constantinople in 1453, intensified during Clement's pontificate, but
his efforts to unite Christian princes toward that end were no more successful than others' had been. Finally, while Clement was a committed
patron of the arts, economic constraints prevented him from supporting them on a lavish scale. The Sack of Rome caused a flight of literati
and artists from Rome so great that Ludwig von Pastor, the historian of
the popes, identified that event as marking "the end of the Renaissance,
the end of the Rome of Julius II and Leo X."[4] Both in textbooks and in
course syllabi, the years of Clement's pontificate have remained a conveni-
ent endpoint for the "High Renaissance" in Rome and, not infrequently,
for the Renaissance as a whole conceived as a distinct historical period.[5]
Upon his death, Clement bequeathed to his successor Paul III (1534–49,
family name Farnese) an Italian peninsula largely under Spanish control, a treasury that was severely depleted, a Rome from which artists and
intellectuals had dispersed, and a church riven by multiple schisms.

Contemporaries marveled at how spectacularly things had gone wrong.
Thus the Florentine diplomat Francesco Vettori, best known today as a
friend and correspondent of Machiavelli, quipped that Clement "endured
a great labor to become, from a great and respected cardinal, a small and
little-esteemed pope"; but Vettori did not plumb far into the reasons

---

[3] The bull excommunicating Henry VIII was issued at last on July 11, 1533.
[4] Pastor, *History*, X, 443.
[5] See, e.g., Denys Hay and John Law, *Italy in the Age of the Renaissance 1380–1530* (London: Longman,
      1989).

for this dissonance.[6] Guicciardini, in retrospect, explained the apparent anomaly less as a change than as a kind of unveiling: in effect, once Giulio had emerged from Leo's ample shadow, his own fundamental flaws of character – including miserliness, timidity, vacillation, and indecision – became manifest and had far-reaching consequences. Thus a fatal weakness of character subverted the pontiff's own goals.

Guicciardini's searing assessment, which appeared in his masterly *History of Italy*, has proved highly influential upon subsequent interpretations of Clement VII, who until recently has had virtually no advocates. The present chapter, by contrast, draws upon recent revisionist accounts that require us to reconsider the longstanding consensus.[7] Clement's failures must be viewed above all in the context of major changes in the dynamics of European politics. As warfare on the Italian peninsula intensified in the mid-1520s, the imperative of autonomy required enormous financial outlays to field standing armies. Political survival perforce eclipsed ecclesiastical reform as a short-term goal, and the costs of war necessitated the curtailment of expenditures on culture. Within the constraints of the limited options available to him, Clement pursued policies largely consistent with those of his illustrious predecessors Julius II and Leo X; but in the 1520s, those policies could but fail. Even as fiscal shortfall forced him to reduce his patronage, he continued to support a few exceptional artists including Sebastiano del Piombo and Michelangelo. But reform of the Church, to which his successors would turn, required resources and concerted secular support that the second Medici pope was unable to muster.

INAUSPICIOUS BEGINNINGS AND POLITICAL APPRENTICESHIP

Giulio de' Medici's life was marked from its outset by tragedy: on April 26, 1478, exactly a month before his birth, his father, Giuliano (brother of Lorenzo "the Magnificent"), was murdered in the cathedral of Florence by political enemies of their family. Born illegitimately to

[6] Francesco Vettori, *Sommario della storia d'Italia*: "... durò una gran fatica per diventare, di grande e riputato cardinale, piccolo e poco stimato papa." Quoted and trans. in T. C. Price Zimmermann, *Paolo Giovio: The Historian and the Crisis of Sixteenth-Century Italy* (Princeton: Princeton University Press, 1995), 60.

[7] Judith Hook, *The Sack of Rome, 1527* (London: Macmillan, 1972); Maurizio Gattoni, *Clemente VII e la geo-politica dello Stato Pontificio* (Vatican City: Archivio Segreto Vaticano, 2002); and Kenneth Gouwens and Sheryl E. Reiss, eds., *The Pontificate of Clement VII: History, Politics, Culture* (Aldershot: Ashgate, 2005).

a mother whose identity remains uncertain, he may have spent his first seven years in the care of the architect Antonio da Sangallo the Elder. Thereafter, Lorenzo raised him alongside his own sons Giovanni and Giuliano in the Palazzo Medici in Florence. When Giovanni, aged sixteen, assumed his duties as a cardinal in March of 1492, Giulio joined his retinue. But Lorenzo died only weeks later, and his son Piero, who assumed leadership of the family, proved unable to maintain the family's unofficial control of Florence. In 1494, as a French army menaced the city, the Medici were expelled from it. Thereafter, Giulio contributed to efforts to re-establish his family in Florence, for example by helping to arrange the marriage in 1509 of Piero's daughter Clarice to the prestigious banker Filippo Strozzi. Only in 1512, however, with the assistance of Spanish troops dispatched by Ferdinand of Aragon, did the Medici regain control of Florence.

The following year, Cardinal Giovanni's elevation as Pope Leo X dramatically enhanced the family's sway. Leo named Giulio Archbishop of Florence and soon created him cardinal, and in 1517 made him Vice-Chancellor of the Church. When in 1519 Leo's nephew Lorenzo di Piero de' Medici was seriously wounded while prosecuting the pope's war on Urbino, Cardinal Giulio took over both command of the army and, briefly, unofficial rule of Florence, serving with distinction in both capacities. Meanwhile, assisted by benefices bestowed upon him by Leo, Giulio had emerged as a generous and discriminating patron of the arts, and as a cardinal he commissioned two enduring masterpieces of painting: Sebastiano del Piombo's *Raising of Lazarus* and Raphael's *Transfiguration*. If political and cultural concerns overshadowed Cardinal Giulio's religious leadership, there was at least some evidence of the latter: for example, in 1517 he presided over a Florentine synod which promoted moral reform of the clergy and decreed punishments for simony as well as for carnal sins.[8]

Upon Leo X's death on December 2, 1521, Giulio de' Medici emerged as a leading candidate for the papacy. When his own advancement was blocked, he nominated the elderly Adrian of Utrecht as a compromise candidate who could be counted upon to be staunchly loyal to Charles V.[9] Following Adrian's death in 1523 Cardinal Giulio was exceptionally well prepared and ideally positioned for his elevation as Clement VII.

---

[8] W. David Myers, "Humanism and Confession in Northern Europe," in Gouwens and Reiss, eds., *Pontificate*, 381.

[9] Pastor, *History*, X, 22–23.

THE ROAD TO POLITICAL DISASTER

Imperial support, both political and financial, had been essential to Pope Clement's election, and Charles V had good reason to expect the new pope's loyalty. The Duke of Sessa, one of the emperor's agents in Rome, wrote to him at the end of the conclave that "The Pope is entirely your Majesty's creature."[10] But Clement soon showed himself to be committed more strongly to the *libertà d'Italia* – that is, the freedom of the peninsula from foreign domination – which would be necessary for him to maintain political autonomy. To the disappointment of Sessa, he refused to join an offensive alliance against France, instead trying to arrange a general armistice that he claimed might prepare the way for concerted action against the Turks, and he maintained impartiality regarding the conflict between Francis I and Charles V.[11] But as those sovereigns increased their forces in Italy, pressure to ally with one or the other became irresistible. After the French captured Milan from the Imperialists in October 1524, the pope's renewed proposals of an armistice were rejected by both sides. Believing that Francis I had gained a decisive military advantage, in December Clement formed an alliance with France and Venice.

This decision issued in disaster: on February 24, 1525, at Pavia, an Imperial army soundly defeated the French and took Francis I prisoner. In one stroke the balance of power had shifted, and Charles V now posed an immediate threat. The pope entered into negotiations with the Imperial Viceroy of Naples, Charles de Lannoy, and on April 1 they concluded a treaty that guaranteed Imperial protection both for the Papal States and for Medicean control of Florence. But the emperor refused to cede the strategically situated towns of Reggio and Rubiera to the papacy, as the treaty had stipulated, and he seemed intent on incorporating the Duchy of Milan into the Spanish Monarchy; meanwhile the pope, wary of Spain's growing dominance, explored strategies for countering it.[12] The freeing of Francis I in March 1526 renewed hope for effective resistance to Spanish hegemony on the peninsula, and so on May 22, Clement joined with France, Venice, and Francesco Sforza of Milan in the League of Cognac against Charles V.

Disillusionment soon followed. Over the summer months, as the league failed in efforts to wrest Milan and Siena from Imperial control,

[10] Ibid., IX, 253.
[11] Letters of Clement to Francis I (April 10, 1524) and to Charles V (April 14, 1524), summarized in Pastor, *History*, IX, 259.
[12] Ibid., IX, 278–99.

the tensions among its constituent members became painfully apparent. In part, its leaders could not agree on how to proceed. While the commander of the papal forces in the league's armies, Francesco Guicciardini, pushed for a rapid attack on the citadel of Milan, the commander of the Venetian troops, Francesco Maria della Rovere (1490–1538), the Duke of Urbino, who outranked Guicciardini, insisted upon waiting for Swiss and French support. More fundamentally, the signatories to the league had joined it for different reasons: while the Venetians sought to secure their own interests in northern Italy, the French cared only about conquering the Regno di Napoli.[13] Meanwhile, the emperor's forces grew stronger: in autumn 1526 the German knight Georg von Frundsberg led over 12,000 *Landsknechte* (pikemen) into northern Italy, where, in February 1527, they joined the Imperial army under the command of Charles de Bourbon.

In accordance with the papacy's shifting military fortunes and expectations, Pope Clement alternately sought terms of peace and forestalled their conclusion. By March of 1527, the virtually unopposed advance of Bourbon's army toward Rome made the situation desperate enough that Clement at last concluded an armistice with Charles de Lannoy. But the truce proved ineffective: Bourbon and his men refused to accept its terms and pressed onward, laying siege to Rome on May 6. Although Bourbon was killed in the initial assault, by sunset nearly the entire city was under Imperial control, and Clement could only watch from atop the papal fortress, the Castel Sant' Angelo, as the victors sacked the city below. A month later, by which time it had become clear that his allies were not coming to his rescue, he capitulated. Only in December, with the assistance of Cardinal Pompeo Colonna (1479–1532), a staunch Imperial partisan, did the pope manage to escape Rome.

Once freed, Clement directed his energies to regaining territories that the papacy had lost and to restoring the Medici to power in Florence, from which a popular revolt had driven them just days after Rome was sacked. Initially, he explored the possibility of renewing alliances with northern Italian powers and with France, but the failure of French attempts to conquer Naples made clear that Clement needed once again to seek an alliance with Charles V. In May of 1529, the pope and emperor reached terms of peace, and on February 24, 1530 – the emperor's birthday and the fifth anniversary of the Imperial victory at Pavia – Clement officially crowned

[13] Maurizio Gattoni, *Clemente VII e la geo-politica dello Stato Pontificio* (Vatican City: Archivio Segreto Vaticano, 2002).

Charles as Holy Roman Emperor.[14] Henceforth, the two remained allies. The struggle for the *libertà d'Italia*, so central to earlier papal policy, was over.

The catastrophes resulting from Clement VII's policies have tended to obscure an important fact: his policies were, in large part, of a piece with those that earlier Renaissance popes had pursued with positive results. Both Julius II and Leo X had shifted alliances as suited their purposes. Thus in 1508 Julius had formed the League of Cambrai with France, the Holy Roman Empire, and Spain, with the goal of despoiling Venice of various territories, but by 1511 he was allied in a "Holy League" with Venice, England, and the empire against France. Leo X initially joined the Emperor Maximilian, Ferdinand of Aragon, and Henry VIII of England in the League of Mechlin (1513) against Louis XII of France, but in 1516 he agreed to the Concordat of Bologna with Louis's successor, Francis I. Upon Maximilian's death in 1519, Leo initially supported Francis I to succeed him, partly because Leo feared that if Charles of Spain should become emperor he would be too powerful. But when Leo could not prevent Charles's election, he jettisoned France to ally with the winner.

The key difference for Clement was that large foreign armies were now continuously present on Italian soil, immediately threatening the territorial states. As the case of Milan poignantly demonstrated, an Italian polity could change hands repeatedly between the greater powers, and to its own detriment. Concern for self-preservation often trumped any willingness to dispatch troops far from one's own boundaries. In short, foreign intervention transformed Italian politics, its pressures contributing to the unreliability of the pope's allies.

DYNASTIC POLITICS AND THE RENAISSANCE PAPACY

Despite Clement's reputation for indecision and waffling, he was remarkably consistent and indeed successful in his efforts to ensure his family's control over Florence and to provide for the future of the Medici *nipoti*, Ippolito (1510–35), Alessandro (1510–37), and Catherine (1519–89).[15] When Clement was gravely ill in early 1529, he elevated Ippolito to the cardinalate. The conquest of Florence in 1529–30 by Charles V's troops led to its

---

[14] Before the coronation, Charles was technically "emperor-designate" rather than "emperor." The present chapter follows convention in calling him "emperor" from the time of his election in 1519.

[15] Barbara McClung Hallman, "The 'Disastrous' Pontificate of Clement VII: Disastrous for Giulio de' Medici?," in Gouwens and Reiss, eds., *Pontificate*, 29–40.

being given over to Medicean control, and at Charles's behest Alessandro became its duke in 1532. Thus the city came under overt, hereditary Medicean rule. Clement also orchestrated the betrothal of Alessandro to the emperor's natural daughter, Margaret. On the other hand, to the emperor's consternation, the pope arranged for Catherine to marry Duke Henri of Orléans (1519–59), and himself presided over the ceremony in Marseilles in 1533. At the time of his death Clement VII left the Medici with a foothold in the government of the church, dynastic control over Florence, and connections by marriage with the two most powerful royal houses in Europe.

In aiming to create a hereditary territorial state for his family, Clement followed papal precedents: Alexander VI had hoped to establish a state in central Italy for his son, Cesare Borgia (1475–1507); Julius II had set up his kinsman Francesco Maria della Rovere as Duke of Urbino; and Leo X, with his cousin Giulio's full support, dug deep into the papal and Florentine treasuries to bankroll the wars of Urbino, ultimately expelling della Rovere so as to replace him with Lorenzo de' Medici. Clement's dynastic strategy for Florence was distinct from the others not in its aspirations but in its long-term success: the Florentine state remained under Medici rule for the next two centuries.

This success is all the more remarkable in that rival Italian families could and did draw upon the Emperor Charles V's support against the pope, which enabled them to challenge the pope more effectively than had previously been possible. Take for example Pompeo Colonna, scion of one of the most powerful noble families of Rome. In 1511, at a time when Julius II was seriously ill, Colonna had rallied the Roman people in an attack on papal overlordship of the city. The coup failed, and as a result Colonna was deprived of his ecclesiastical dignities; but his power and influence remained such that Leo X rehabilitated him and thought it wise in 1517 to elevate him to the cardinalate. In the short run, the strategy of co-optation worked, and in the conclave of 1523 Colonna's support ultimately made Clement's election possible. But he offered that support grudgingly, not least because it appeared that Cardinal Orsini, a Francophile, might otherwise prove victorious. Although Clement named Pompeo Vice-Chancellor of the Church, the cardinal remained ambitious for the papacy.

Tensions between the two became explosive in 1526 after Clement aligned the papacy with the French in the League of Cognac against Charles V. In September 1526, with cognizance of the emperor's representative Hugo de Moncada, Pompeo led an attack on the Vatican in an attempt to wrest political control from Pope Clement and possibly even to kill him.[16] The pope narrowly escaped, and Moncada mediated a truce highly unfavorable to the pope. Soon Clement retaliated: like Julius II, he deprived Colonna of his ecclesiastical dignities and benefices. This time, however, the consequences were dire. Although the evidence remains sketchy, it appears that Pompeo Colonna himself intended to join the Imperial forces in the attack on Rome in May 1527.[17] Following the sack, Colonna was able to act as an intermediary between the occupying troops and their Roman captives, and in December he helped engineer the pope's escape; but this assistance came at the price of significant political and territorial concessions. Charles V, for his part, rewarded Pompeo's loyalty by naming him Imperial Viceroy of Naples.

The rivalry between Pope Clement and Francesco Maria della Rovere also had its roots in earlier pontificates.[18] Francesco Maria had become Duke of Urbino in 1508, an advancement made possible by special dispensations from Julius II.[19] But in 1516 Leo X, with full support of Cardinal Giulio de' Medici, deposed della Rovere on dubious grounds so that Urbino could be conferred upon Lorenzo (the Younger) de' Medici. Following Lorenzo's death in 1519, della Rovere retook the duchy by force of arms, and in 1523 Adrian VI reinstated him in his ducal title. But Clement, still hoping to establish the Medici in Urbino, refused to invest the duke.

Clement's treatment of della Rovere was certainly no worse than Leo's, but it had more serious consequences. Dispossessed and unemployed, Francesco Maria accepted a post as mercenary leader of the Venetian contingent of troops in the League of Cognac's army. Notoriously, in this capacity he did not engage Bourbon's army or attempt to block its advance on Rome nor, once the city had been taken, did he come to the pope's rescue. To be sure, the Venetians had not been eager to commit their troops to a southern strategy; but contemporaries blamed della Rovere for his stalling, and his partial responsibility for the Sack of Rome cannot easily be dismissed.[20]

[16] Hook, *Sack*, 93–115.
[17] Judith Hook, "Clement VII, the Colonna and Charles V: A Study of the Political Instability of Italy in the Second and Third Decades of the Sixteenth Century," *European Studies Review* 2 (1972), 281–99.
[18] Cecil H. Clough, "Clement VII and Francesco Maria Della Rovere, Duke of Urbino," in Gouwens and Reiss, eds., *Pontificate*, 75–108. On p. 75, Clough notes that Francesco Guicciardini, Gian Matteo Giberti, and Luigi Guicciardini all blamed della Rovere for allowing Bourbon's army to gain access to Rome.
[19] Particularly problematic was his murder of Cardinal Alidosi in 1511, for which Julius II absolved him. Ibid., 79.
[20] Ibid., 77–78.

Like Colonna, della Rovere ultimately triumphed. In December 1529, as a condition for joining in a league with both the pope and the emperor, the Venetians insisted upon the investment of their lieutenant-general with his duchy and titles. Probably under pressure from Charles V, Clement acceded. Then in February, in his capacity as Prefect of Rome – an office that Leo X had stripped from him but to which he was now restored – della Rovere stood in a place of honor in Charles V's coronation ceremony. Finally, in 1533, the emperor restored to della Rovere several fiefs of which he had been deprived by Charles in 1516 at the urging of Leo X.[21] The contrast in Charles's behavior, with respect both to della Rovere and to the pope, neatly encapsulates how much his influence within Italy had grown in the intervening years.

Clement VII would not be the last pontiff to promote his own family's interests or to confront armed resistance from other powerful families, as Paul III's blatant nepotism and his wars against Ascanio Colonna, Pompeo's kinsman, would make clear. But Clement's pontificate marks a critical moment when foreign intervention came to have a decisive impact upon the family politics of the Renaissance papacy. Ultimately he recognized this fact and managed to work effectively within its strictures. In sum, in the limited context of his pursuit of family objectives, Pope Clement appears surprisingly decisive and at least modestly successful.

PATRONAGE OF CULTURE

Following Clement's election, artists, musicians, and literati shared in the expectation of a return to the lavish patronage of Leo X. The contrast with his predecessor was stark: a Bolognese envoy wrote that Clement "granted more favors on the first day of his reign than Adrian did in his whole lifetime"; later, the biographer of artists Giorgio Vasari would credit the new pontiff with having revived the arts in a single day.[22] Leading artists, sculptors, and architects, including Giovanni da Udine, Baccio Bandinelli, and Baldassare Peruzzi, participated in the design of ephemera for his coronation, which expressed splendor without displaying the excesses and frivolities (e.g., jesters) that Leo's had featured.[23] Soon thereafter, Clement persuaded the outstanding Latinist Jacopo Sadoleto to return to

---

[21] Ibid., 106–07.
[22] Quoted, respectively, in Pastor, *History*, IX, 244, and Sheryl E. Reiss, "Clement VII," in *Hochrenaissance im Vatikan: Kunst und Kultur im Rom der Päpste I 1503–1534*, exhibition catalogue (Bonn: Kunst- und Ausstellungshalle, 1999), 57.
[23] Reiss, "Clement VII," 55; Pastor, *History*, IX, 248.

papal service as domestic secretary. In December the pope appointed a sixty-man commission to manage the construction of the new St. Peter's Basilica (a project begun by Julius II). Work proceeded under the direction of Antonio Sangallo the Younger and, initially, also of Peruzzi.

Noted as a patron of the so-called *arti minori*, including tapestry, metalwork, maiolica, and woodwork, Clement was also a connoisseur of illuminated manuscripts. He collected gems and was a patron of goldsmiths, including the flamboyant autobiographer Benvenuto Cellini. The painters and sculptors he sponsored included many erstwhile members of the workshop of Raphael (d. 1520) such as Giulio Romano and Gianfrancesco Penni, who completed the frescos in the Sala di Costantino in the Vatican *stanze* in 1524. Probably that same year, Polidoro da Caravaggio and Giovanni da Udine decorated the hot bath (*stufetta*) in Clement's apartments in the Castel Sant' Angelo. Around this time, too, Giovanni da Udine and Sangallo the Younger worked on fountains for the pope's Villa Madama on the Monte Mario. New talent arrived in the Eternal City, notably the painters Rosso Fiorentino and Parmigianino. The abundance of artistic innovation in mid-1520s Rome has led some scholars to identify a particular "Clementine style": an eclectic, mixed style (*stile mescolato*) expressive of the confidence and creativity of the early pontificate that would subsequently influence courts throughout Europe.[24] In short, there appeared to be every reason to expect that Clement would be a great patron – every reason, that is, except for the precarious state of papal finances.

Under any circumstances, Clement might have had difficulty maintaining the ambitious patronage of the early pontificate. Upon his death in 1521 Leo had left the treasury empty – a fact that helps to explain and even vindicate the supposed stinginess of his two immediate successors.[25] From 1525 onward papal commissions were few, and skyrocketing war expenses accelerated the decline. The Sack of Rome was an unmitigated disaster for the artists, many of whom sought gainful and safer employment elsewhere: Polidoro went to Naples, Rosso to King Francis I's Château de Fontainebleau, Parmigianino initially to Bologna, then to Parma, and Cellini to Florence and then Mantua. Those closest to the pope may have

[24] André Chastel, *The Sack of Rome, 1527*, trans. Beth Archer (Princeton: Princeton University Press, 1983), esp. 149–78. For reappraisals of Chastel's thesis, see Gouwens and Reiss, eds., *Pontificate*, esp. Linda Wolk-Simon, "Competition, Collaboration, and Specialization in the Roman Art World, 1520–27," 253–76. Wolk-Simon emphasizes how few of the key commissions in Rome prior to the sack emanated from the pope.
[25] Clough, "Clement VII and Francesco Maria Della Rovere," 93.

felt the impact of the sack the most: thus Sebastiano Luciani, known as "del Piombo" after he became the Keeper of the Papal Seal in 1531, wrote that year to his friend Michelangelo: "I still don't seem to myself to be that Sebastiano that I was before the sack; I can't return anymore to that state of mind."[26]

Nor, indeed, could the papal coffers soon recover. Yet there was modest cultural revival from 1529 onward. Clement recalled Cellini to Rome, making him *maestro delle stampe* at the papal mint, and commissioning him to make a jewel-encrusted golden morse (button or clasp) for the pontiff's embroidered cope. Designed to be worn on ceremonial occasions both with the tiara, symbol of the pope's secular *Imperium*, and with the jeweled miter, which represented his role as supreme pontiff, this morse was Cellini's first masterpiece.[27] As part of an effort to rehabilitate and dignify his image, the pope also commissioned Sebastiano del Piombo to paint several portraits of him.[28] By far his most famous commission, however, was one dating from late 1533 or early 1534 and completed long after his death: Michelangelo's *Last Judgment*.

Michelangelo represents a special case in Clement's patronage. The two had been acquainted since youth, when both were lodged in the Palazzo Medici in Florence. Upon hearing of Clement's election in November 1523, Michelangelo wrote to his quarry superintendent in Carrara: "You will have heard that Medici is made pope, which I think will gladden everyone. For this reason, with respect to art, many things will be accomplished here."[29] The following month, the artist and the pope met in Rome, and Clement confirmed his financial support for two architectural projects in the church of San Lorenzo in Florence: the new sacristy and the library. At least initially, financing was not an issue: Clement wrote that Michelangelo should spend "whatever monies he wanted," telling him "to

---

[26] Sebastiano to Michelangelo, February 24, 1531: "Ancora non mi par esser quel Bastiano che io era inanti el sacco; non posso tornar in cervello ancora." Gaetano Milanesi, ed., *Les correspondants de Michelange*, I: *Sebastiano del Piombo*, with French trans. by A. Le Pileur (Paris: Librairie de l'Art, 1890), 38. Here and elsewhere in this chapter translations are mine unless otherwise stated.

[27] Denise Allen, "Designed by the Dictates of Ceremony: Cellini's Cope-Morse for Clement VII," in Renate L. Colella et al., eds., *Sonderdruck aus Pratum Romanum: Richard Krautheimer zum 100. Geburtstag* (Wiesbaden: Reichert Verlag, 1997), 13–25.

[28] Two outstanding portraits, painted about 1531, are now in the Getty Museum in Santa Monica, CA, and in the Kunsthistorisches Museum, Vienna. See Pierluigi Leone de Castris, "Kultur und Mäzenatentum am Hof der d'Avalos in Ischia," in Sylvia Ferino-Pagden, ed., *Vittoria Colonna: Dichterin und Muse Michelangelos* (Vienna: Kunsthistorisches Museum, 1997), 66–107, with full-page color plates of the two portraits on 100–01.

[29] Paola Barocchi and Renzo Ristori, eds., *Il carteggio di Michelangelo*, 5 vols. (Florence: SPES, 1965–83), III, 1: "Arete inteso chome Medici è facto papa, di che mi pare si sia rallegrato tucto el mondo; ond'io stimo che qua, circha l'arte, si farà molte chose." Letter dated November 25, 1523.

spare no expense" and "not to worry about the cost."[30] The pope also tendered specific recommendations: for example, with respect to the library's construction, he indicated where Michelangelo should get the best travertine to make lime, the quality of the lime to be used in making stucco, and how many coats were to be applied.[31] The working relationship between the two was so close that one leading scholar has described Clement as "both patron and collaborator" to Michelangelo.[32] While the pope trusted him to do everything in the way he wanted to ("a vostro modo"), the work in San Lorenzo shows evidence of the pope's personal preferences, including "a tendency to favor novel solutions, and to push for the unorthodox and the *recherché*."[33] It would be tempting, on the basis of this admittedly unique example, to speculate about what Clement's patronage of art might have looked like had he enjoyed the resources of Julius II or Leo X. In any case, it does demonstrate convincingly that Clement VII lacked neither aesthetic sensitivity nor the will to support the arts: what he lacked, increasingly, was the means to do so.

As a patron of music, Pope Clement was similarly engaged and attentive to detail. Known not only to enjoy listening but to have a good singing voice, he may have been the most musically competent pope in the entire sixteenth century.[34] He had his own chamber ensemble, and he also sponsored outstanding performers including the lutenist Francesco da Milano, who accompanied him when he went to Bologna in 1533 to meet Charles V.[35] Clement also took pains to maintain the Sistine Chapel choir at twenty-four members, balanced among the vocal parts and comprising only competent singers – matters about which Leo had been unconcerned. After the sack depleted the choir's ranks, Clement dispatched the singer and composer Jean Conseil to France and Flanders to recruit new singers, and soon it had returned to full strength. Its lasting reputation was such that in the 1560s Clement's pontificate would be recalled as a golden age for the papal choir.[36]

[30] William E. Wallace, "Clement VII and Michelangelo: An Anatomy of Patronage," in Gouwens and Reiss, eds., *Pontificate*, 189–98, at 190. See also William E. Wallace, *Michelangelo at San Lorenzo: The Genius as Entrepreneur* (Cambridge: Cambridge University Press, 1994).

[31] Wallace, "Clement VII and Michelangelo," 192.

[32] Ibid., 192–93.

[33] Caroline Elam, "Michelangelo and the Clementine Architectural Style," in Gouwens and Reiss, eds., *Pontificate*, 199.

[34] This is the judgment of Richard Sherr, "Clement VII and the Golden Age of the Papal Choir," in Gouwens and Reiss, eds., *Pontificate*, 230. One contemporary went so far as to call Clement "one of the best musicians alive now in Italy" (ibid., n. 16).

[35] Victor Anand Coelho, "Papal Tastes and Musical Genres: Francesco da Milano 'Il Divino' (1497–1543) and the Clementine Aesthetic," in Gouwens and Reiss, eds., *Pontificate*, 278.

[36] Ibid., 229.

Clement also drew to Rome many literati. Some, such as Sadoleto, he lured to appointments as secretaries. Others such as Pietro Alcionio, who had relied upon Giulio de' Medici for support in Florence, hastened to Rome without any certain prospects. Two humanists in particular, Angelo Colocci and Johann Goritz, sponsored informal gatherings at which those with curial day-jobs feasted, engaged in poetry competitions, and in general participated in a renewal of Roman culture through the imitation of classical and early Christian models.[37] But by 1525, as opportunities for employment were severely constrained, the infighting among the humanists grew ugly.[38] By April of 1527 Sadoleto, who was privy to political intelligence, knew enough to leave Rome.[39] Many, including Erasmus's correspondent Paolo Bombace, died in the sack itself.[40] Cristoforo Marcello, who had given at least two sermons in the presence of the pope, was unable to raise the ransom demanded of him by the Spanish troops and was tortured to death.[41] Goritz managed to escape Rome after being reduced to poverty, but he died soon thereafter.[42] Agazio Guidacerio (1477?–1540), probably a professor of Hebrew at the University of Rome in 1524, had dedicated a commentary on the Song of Songs to Clement VII, but after he lost his library in the sack he sought opportunities elsewhere.[43] And Alcionio, who was wounded while fleeing into the papal fortress when Rome was attacked, subsequently sought patronage from the pope's nemesis, Pompeo Colonna.[44]

As Clement worked to rebuild the papal bureaucracy in the latter half of his pontificate, he again employed humanists in administrative capacities: for example, the poet Giovanni Battista Sanga (1496–1532), who in 1526 had been a papal envoy to the French and English courts, served as a protonotary from 1528 to 1531.[45] Colocci, who himself was twice captured

---

[37] On Colocci, see Ingrid D. Rowland, *The Culture of the High Renaissance: Ancients and Moderns in Sixteenth-Century Rome* (Cambridge: Cambridge University Press, 1998); on Goritz, see Julia Haig Gaisser, "The Rise and Fall of Goritz's Feasts," *Renaissance Quarterly* 48 (1995), 41–57.

[38] On the increasingly agonistic culture of Roman humanism in the years 1525–27, see Gaisser, "Rise and Fall," 55; and Anne Reynolds, *Renaissance Humanism at the Court of Clement VII: Francesco Berni's* Dialogue against Poets *in Context* (New York: Garland Publishing, 1997).

[39] Kenneth Gouwens, *Remembering the Renaissance: Humanist Narratives of the Sack of Rome* (Leiden: Brill, 1999), 107–08.

[40] Julia Haig Gaisser, *Pierio Valeriano on the Ill Fortune of Learned Men: A Renaissance Humanist and his World* (Ann Arbor: University of Michigan Press, 1999), 114, 271.

[41] Ibid., 43–44, 92, 304.

[42] Ibid., 220, 294–95.

[43] Paul F. Grendler, "Italian Biblical Humanism and the Papacy, 1515–1535," in Erika Rummel, ed., *Biblical Humanism and Scholasticism in the Age of Erasmus* (Leiden: Brill, 2008), 247–49. In 1530 Francis I appointed Guidacerio royal lecturer of Hebrew in the Collège de France in Paris.

[44] Gouwens, *Remembering the Renaissance*, 31–72.

[45] Reynolds, *Renaissance Humanism*, 87–102.

and ransomed before managing to escape Rome, subsequently returned. Some evidence suggests that in 1532 Clement had plans to sponsor a program of biblical translation in Rome.[46] But there could be no return to the literary patronage that distinguished the initial years of the pontificate. One reason for this may be that Clement's appreciation of literature was not on a par with his delight and engagement with art: evidently he valued humanists more for their clerical services than for their literary compositions.[47] But even in art, only smaller-scale projects moved forward.

EFFORTS AT REFORM AND PASTORAL CARE

Initial predictions that Clement would be the "angelic pastor" who would usher in a new golden age in church and society soon foundered. Attempts to stanch the spread of Luther's movement were hampered from the outset by faulty intelligence from sources at the Imperial court. Thus in 1525 misinformation prompted Clement to write letters to several German princes congratulating them on their supposed victory over the Lutherans, and as late as 1531 sources in the Imperial court actually wrote to Rome that Luther's chief defender, Frederick, the Elector of Saxony, had become reconciled with the church and had begun to restore Catholicism in his territories.[48] While Clement was surely too quick to latch onto such hopes, others did so as well. The chief impediment to resolving the Lutheran schism, however, was politics, initially within the German states and subsequently on a Europe-wide scale. In early 1524 Clement dispatched Cardinal Campeggio to Germany, but the legate was unable to heal the schism within those territories whose princes or civil authorities supported it, and the problems worsened.[49] Subsequently, the conflict between Charles V and Clement perforce reduced attention to Luther. Following the reconciliation of emperor and pope in late 1529, Charles got Clement to agree to a general council of the Church, but negotiations stalled over the particulars of where it would be held, who would be invited, and how it could be orchestrated in such a way that it did not provide opportunity for either France or England to use it to political advantage.

---

[46] Grendler, "Italian Biblical Humanism," 274. We do not know whether this hope was realized.
[47] Julia Haig Gaisser, "Seeking Patronage under the Medici Popes: A Tale of Two Humanists," in Gouwens and Reiss, eds., *Pontificate*, 308–09, advances this argument, noting that the pope was "apparently so indifferent to classical poetry that [Pierio] Valeriano had to argue for the importance of studying the text of Virgil."
[48] Pastor, *History*, X, 119–20, 129, 165.   [49] Ibid., X, 113–23.

Francis I, who proved unwilling to help restore order in Germany, would not agree to a council unless it were on his own terms. Henry VIII, meanwhile, was lobbying for the annulment of his marriage to Catherine of Aragon. As was his wont, Clement temporized when confronted with a lose–lose situation: if he acquiesced to Henry VIII's request, he would enrage Charles V, who was the nephew of Queen Catherine; but if he did not, he risked schism in England. Clement forbade the king to marry so long as the matter of the annulment was unresolved in Rome, where the Rota, a judicial panel within the curia, was considering it. Henry's marriage to Anne Boleyn in January 1533 forced the issue. A few months later Clement officially rejected the king's request for the annulment and then excommunicated him.

Strife within Europe impeded the pope's efforts to launch a crusade against the Turks: so long as Christian princes were at war with one another they could not unite to address the threat from without. Clement's urgent appeals to them to aid Hungary in 1526 came to nothing, even after the decisive Turkish victory at Mohács (August 29), following which King Louis II of Hungary was killed. Although the Imperial army and navy won important victories in 1532, the dissensions among Francis I, Henry VIII, and Charles V prevented the concerted effort that circumstances required.

Given the precariousness of papal politics and finances combined with the Lutheran schism and the Turkish threat, it is perhaps not surprising that Clement VII gave only limited attention to the need for internal reform of the church, but he does appear to have desired it. While a cardinal, he had founded the Confraternity of Charity, which fostered lay piety and outreach to the needy, and as pope he endowed it with the church of San Girolamo in Rome.[50] In early 1524 he appointed a special commission of cardinals to address the issue of reform, and in consistories that autumn a range of proposals were implemented to improve the competence and morals of Roman clergy. Also in 1524 Clement enacted legislation concerning reform of the secular and regular clergy in other major urban centers including Naples, Venice, and Milan, and he ordered a general reform of the Carmelites. But as political exigencies became all-consuming, little came of these initiatives. The scale of change required was beyond what he could accomplish without broad-based support, and churchmen increasingly agreed that a general council was needed.

[50] Ibid., X, 394.

Although Clement paid lip service to convening a council, he found ways to avoid doing so. In part, he was anxious that a council might use his illegitimacy as grounds for deposing him. But there were also structural reasons for postponement: if necessary reforms were implemented, as many subsequently would be in the Council of Trent (1545–63), the papal bureaucracy would lose revenue from sinecures and from the sales of offices and privileges at a time when fiscal pressures were already great. Clement resisted creating cardinals for income until 1527, when the need for revenue became desperate, and his sole nepotistic creation was Ippolito de' Medici. But the system of spoils in the church was so deeply ingrained that it would require more commitment to reform, and indeed a greater ability to implement it, than Clement VII ever demonstrated.

CONCLUSION

Military crises and to a lesser extent efforts at family advancement overshadowed and blocked Clement VII's evidently sincere desire to be a good pastor. The political and economic disasters of his pontificate resulted less from novelty or incompetence, however, than from a drastically changed field of politics in which approaches that had worked for his predecessors were no longer effective. He was surely naive in the hopes that he placed in Christian princes, who found the need for the defense of Christendom from the Turks less compelling than the desire for political advantage over one another and eagerness for territorial aggrandizement within Europe.

While Clement's accomplishments as prince, patron, and especially pastor fell far short of his aspirations and of the expectations of others, his intentions and his abilities do not bear out Guicciardini's bleak assessment.[51] His "strong reluctance to spend" was not a fundamental part of his character, as his initial expenditures make clear, but instead became absolutely essential to the solvency of the papacy. It is not enough to marvel, as Guicciardini does, at Clement's indecision, which did not have significant consequences until the escalation of the Italian wars after the Battle of Pavia in 1525. The historian may be correct in characterizing the pontiff as seemingly "directed rather than counseled" by his advisors and, in preferring the advice of one and then another, steering an uneven course that satisfied no one. But it is worth remembering that Guicciardini himself was one of those counselors – indeed, one of those who advised Clement to enter into the ill-fated League of Cognac. The fact is that no one had

---

[51] See esp. Guicciardini, *History*, 363, the source of the following brief quotations.

a clear vision at the time of where the political decisions of the mid-1520s would lead. More generally, in the first decades of the sixteenth century, observers of the political scene including Machiavelli, Vettori, and not least Guicciardini commented repeatedly upon the limited ability of individuals to shape, let alone predict, the course of history.[52] How successful, one wonders, might either Julius II or Leo X have been in the tumultuous 1520s? Guicciardini's unflattering portrait of Pope Clement remained intact for centuries largely because it was in nobody's interest to challenge it. But the historian's dictum that "the magistracy shows forth the man" must be qualified by realistic expectations of what any supreme pontiff could have accomplished in Clement VII's stead.

---

[52] John M. Najemy, *Between Friends: Discourses of Power and Desire in the Machiavelli–Vettori Letters of 1513–1515* (Princeton: Princeton University Press, 1993); Felix Gilbert, *Machiavelli and Guicciardini: Politics and History in Sixteenth-Century Florence* (Princeton: Princeton University Press, 1965), 236–301.

CHAPTER 3

The pope as saint: Pius V in the eyes of
Sixtus V and Clement XI

Pamela M. Jones

Michele Ghislieri, a Dominican father and former Inquisitor-General, reigned as Pope Pius V from 1566 until 1572.[1] Not only is Pius V the only early modern pontiff to have been canonized, but he was the first pope raised to sainthood since Celestine V in 1313 and the last to be so honored until Pius X was canonized in 1954.[2] This chapter focuses on the reception of Pius V during the reigns of two popes who considered him worthy of sainthood: Sixtus V (1585–90, family name Peretti), who started Pius's beatification process, and Clement XI (1700–21, family name Albani), who canonized him on May 22, 1712. Through close analysis of visual and written sources, I will explore continuity and change in these popes' formation of Pius V's image, which culminated in the creation of his official persona as a canonized saint. I will also examine Clement XI's use of the new saint's image to create a leadership position for himself within European politics and to assert traditional powers and prerogatives for the papacy during one of the most turbulent periods in its history.

When Pius V's papal successors looked back on his pontificate, they would have recognized that although brief, it had been momentous. Pius V had been a pope of decisive deeds: he oversaw the implementation of the decrees of the Council of Trent (1545–63), had the Roman catechism, breviary, and missal published, fought against the Huguenots in France, excommunicated the Protestant Elizabeth I of England, formed the Holy League that defeated the Ottoman Turks at Lepanto, and in the victory's aftermath established the feast of the Rosary, a devotion instituted by his order. But Pius's successors likewise knew that his reputation also rested

---

[1] Scholarship on Pius is vast. Recent studies include Virginio Giacomo Bono, *San Pio V Ghislieri: quinto centenario della nascità di S. Pio V* (Garbagnate Milanese: Anthelios, 2004); and Maurilio Guasco and Angelo Torre, eds., *Pio V nella società e nella politica del suo tempo* (Bologna: Il Mulino, 2005). For a brief biography, see J. N. D. Kelly, "Pius V, St.," in *The Oxford Dictionary of Popes* (Oxford: Oxford University Press, 1986), 268–69.
[2] Kelly, *Oxford Dictionary*, throughout.

on his personal qualities; humble, ascetic, and prayerful, he was a reformer who practiced what he preached. In essence, Pius V's deeds and personal qualities made him a consummate post-Tridentine pontiff.

Pius may also be seen as embodying the five universal qualities that Donald Weinstein and Rudolph Bell have identified as characterizing perceptions of Roman Catholic holiness from 1000 to 1700: supernatural grace, asceticism, good works, evangelical activity, and the exercise of power in defense of the church.[3] Although it is well known that more than any other event of his reign the victory over the "infidels" at Lepanto helped to shape Pius's posthumous reputation, Pope Saint Pius V's official persona was not exclusively martial, but also pastoral and prayerful.

PIUS V AND SIXTUS V

Prior to ascending the papal throne as Pius V, Michele Ghislieri was acquainted with Felice Peretti, later to be elected Pope Sixtus V.[4] Both men served Pope Pius IV as inquisitors, and both were members of mendicant orders; Ghislieri was a Dominican, Peretti a Franciscan. As Pius V, Ghislieri became Peretti's mentor, raising him to the episcopate and then to the cardinalate, thus setting the stage for his spectacular ecclesiastical career. Pius died in 1572, and Peretti's prominence in curial affairs waned during the subsequent reign of Gregory XIII (1572–85, family name Buoncompagni). But Cardinal Peretti's star soon rose again, for he was elected pope following Gregory's death in 1585, taking the pontifical name Sixtus V (reigned 1585–90). As pope, he proved to be an able statesman who strengthened the Holy See by reorganizing papal finances. Like his mentor Pius V, Sixtus was a reformer and defender of the faith who enhanced the spiritual tenor of Rome, but unlike Pius, Sixtus also enhanced the Eternal City's physical appearance through artistic patronage.

Sixtus V played a key role in creating a posthumous image of Pius V as a holy man. Expressed visually and in writing, this image was inextricably linked to Sixtus's initiation of the beatification process for Pius by starting to compile the requisite documentation.[5] Beatification, a necessary step

---

[3] Donald Weinstein and Rudolph M. Bell, *Saints and Society: The Two Worlds of Western Christendom, 1000–1700* (Chicago and London: University of Chicago Press, 1982), 159.

[4] See Kelly, "Sixtus V," in *Oxford Dictionary*, 271–73; and Steven F. Ostrow, *Art and Spirituality in Counter-Reformation Rome: The Sistine and Pauline Chapels in S. Maria Maggiore* (Cambridge: Cambridge University Press, 1996), 5–117.

[5] Paolo Alessandro Maffei, *Vita di S. Pio Quinto sommo pontefice, dell'ordine de' Predicatori* (Rome: Giacomo Tommasini, 1712), 436. The Roman Church's three official levels of sanctity – venerable, blessed, and saint – were standardized by Urban VIII in decrees of 1625 and 1634, but

on the way to canonization, was a lengthy process that involved research, reports, and trials concerning the candidate's piety, deeds, and miracles. These findings required verification and approval by a committee of cardinals and other ecclesiastics known as the Congregation of Rites. After receiving the pontiff's imprimatur, the congregation would hold a series of meetings before the papal decree of beatification could be issued. Surely Sixtus, who was already sixty-three years old when he was elected pope, assumed that he would not live long enough to beatify Pius; his aim was to ensure that the process got off to a good start. Despite this, Sixtus's conceptualization of Pius's holiness elicited resistance from the start.

SIXTUS V'S IMAGE OF PIUS V

Pius V's image had a prominent place in one of Sixtus's most important artistic commissions, the decoration of the Sistine Chapel in the right transept of Santa Maria Maggiore in Rome. The chapel was built by Domenico Fontana between 1585 and 1589 and decorated by a team of sculptors and painters. The left arm of the chapel is dominated by the polychrome marble tomb monument to Pope Pius V (Figure 3.1), designed by Fontana with sculptures attributed to several little-known artists.[6] A white marble portrait of Pius V is given pride of place at the lower center. Enthroned and wearing the papal tiara, Pius blesses the viewer. Below, a Latin inscription reads, "Pope Sixtus V, a Franciscan, placed this expression of gratitude to Pope Pius V, a Dominican."[7] Green marble columns separate the pope's portrait from two flanking white marble reliefs. The one on the left shows Pope Pius consigning the standard of command to Marcantonio Colonna, and its inscription reads:

Pius V, on forging an alliance with Philip II, King of Spain, and with the Republic of Venice, [defeated] Selim, Tyrant of the Turks, who had become insolent after

---

causes for beatification and canonization already involved long processes in the late sixteenth century. See Peter Burke, "How to Be a Counter-Reformation Saint," in *The Historical Anthropology of Early Modern Italy: Essays on Perception and Communication* (Cambridge: Cambridge University Press, 1987), 48–62.

[6] Alexandra Herz, "The Sixtine and Pauline Tombs: Documents of the Counter-Reformation," *Storia dell'arte* 43 (1981), 241–62. Silli and Spantigati provide brief discussions, but without explicit reference to the papal reception of Pius: Antonino Silli, *San Pio V: note agiographiche ed iconographiche* (Rome: Biblioteca B. Angelico, 1979), 23–25; among Spantigati's numerous studies, see Carla Enrica Spantigati, "Il culto di San Pio V nella diffusione delle immagini," in Fulvio Cervini and Carla Enrica Spantigati, eds., *Il tempo di Pio V, Pio V nel tempo: atti del Convegno Internazionale di Studi, Bosco Marengo, Alessandria, 11–13 marzo 2004* (Alessandria: Edizioni dell'Orso, 2006), 318–19.

[7] Here and elsewhere in this chapter, translations are mine unless otherwise stated.

3.1 Monument to Pope Pius V, Santa Maria Maggiore, Rome. Photo by Alinari/Art Resource, NY.

many victories. He conquered Cyprus with an enormous fleet and was threatening Christendom with extinction. Pius made Marcantonio Colonna Admiral of the Papal Fleet, and defeated the enemy at Lepanto with prayer and arms: 30,000 killed, 10,000 taken captive, 158 ships captured, 90 sunk, 15,000 Christians freed from slavery.

The relief at the lower right represents Pius V consigning the captain's baton to the Count of Santa Fiora against the Huguenots; it likewise bears an inscription:

When Charles [IX] was king, France was troubled by treasons and by the nefarious arms of heretics. So troubled was he concerning the kingdom and religion that Pius V thought it best to take action by putting Count Sforza of Santa Fiora in command of the papal troops of cavalry, infantry, and auxiliaries. Santa Fiora saved France from danger and after the enemy had been defeated, he announced a victory. [Through him Pius] restored both the kingdom and religion to the king. Pius hung trophies captured from the enemy in the Lateran Basilica.

The smaller reliefs on the upper register amplify the scenes below them. The relief above the pope's portrait represents the coronation of Pius V. On the left is the Battle of Lepanto, and on the right the triumph over the Huguenots in France. Pius's papal coat of arms is displayed in the pediment at the apex of the monument. Thus the tomb monument proclaims Sixtus's image of Pius V as a successful champion of the Roman Catholic faith, the vanquisher of both heretics and infidels, and the defender of papal primacy and universality. In overall effect, this monument representing Pius V as a papal prince is quite bellicose.

The decorative program of the Sistine Chapel as a whole, as examined in detail by Steven F. Ostrow, is highly complex, and not all of its themes concern us.[8] However, building on Ostrow's work, further consideration may be given to the resonance of Pius's tomb within the chapel. Dedicated to the Most Blessed Sacrament, the Sistine Chapel is also the locus for devotion to the relic of the *Presepio* (crib) located under the altar; fashioned as an oratory, it reputedly contains stones from the cave of the Nativity in Bethlehem and pieces of hay from Jesus' manger.[9] Thus the tomb of Pius V, conqueror of the Turks, was situated in a chapel containing highly venerated relics from the Holy Land, the Lord's birthplace, which had yet to be wrested from Muslim control. This strengthened the spirit of crusade proclaimed by Pius's tomb monument. In addition, the Sistine Chapel's prominently placed Tabernacle of the Blessed Sacrament proclaimed a distinctly Roman Catholic theology in contradistinction to that of Protestant

[8] On the chapel as a Franciscan shrine, see Ostrow, *Art and Spirituality*, 5–117; on Pius's tomb, see ibid., 52–57. Although Pius wanted to be buried in his native town of Bosco near Alessandria, where he had had his tomb built according to a different iconography, Sixtus had his body (which still resided provisionally in St. Peter's) transferred to the Sistine Chapel in Santa Maria Maggiore in 1588. On these matters, see also studies cited in n. 6 above.

[9] Ostrow, *Art and Spirituality*, 23–35, 293 n. 81. The *Presepio* had been in the basilica since the seventh century; Sixtus had it moved to his chapel.

heretics, who did not believe in transubstantiation.[10] These elements of the
chapel's decoration linked Pius's crusades against Muslims and Protestants
to his life of prayer and devotion to Christ. Nevertheless, the tomb's martial imagery made it clear that more than prayer was needed to overcome
infidels and heretics in order to unite the world under the Vicar of Christ.

As papal patron of the arts at Santa Maria Maggiore, Sixtus V had complete freedom in projecting his image of Pius V. And by positioning his
own tomb opposite that of his mentor, Sixtus – shown kneeling in prayer
surrounded by depictions of his own deeds – proclaimed himself Pius's
legitimate temporal and spiritual successor.[11] However, Sixtus's coeval
sponsorship of a written hagiography of Pius, meant to hasten his beatification, did not go unchallenged. The biography in question was Girolamo
Catena's *Vita del gloriosissimo papa Pio Quinto* (*Life of the Most Glorious
Pope Pius V*), published in Rome in 1586 with a dedication to Sixtus V,
who had sponsored and paid for it. When the Spanish Inquisition immediately censured Catena's *Vita* as "defective and prejudicial," Sixtus was
enraged.[12] As Miguel Gotor noted, Catena's biography makes it clear that
Pius V intended not simply to uphold the papacy's pre-existing rights, but
to "change relationships between secular and ecclesiastical authorities by
force, in favor of the latter."[13] It might be added that from a Spanish perspective Catena's discussion was also unacceptable for what it implied
about Sixtus's own objectives as pope. When in 1587 a revised edition of
Catena's book was issued in order to satisfy Spain, Sixtus must have realized how difficult it would be to advance Pius's cause for beatification.

Catena's *Vita* illuminates Sixtus's view of Pius in other ways that deserve
analysis. The revised edition, published in Rome in 1587, is 367 pages long,
and only twenty-one pages are devoted to Michele Ghislieri's life before
his election as pope. The synopsis of Ghislieri's early life highlights his
poverty, humility, chastity, asceticism and prayer, and enumerates the
positions he held, starting with his entrance into the Dominican order at
age fourteen, and continuing with his inquisitorial work, his appointments
to the episcopate and cardinalate, and his reforming zeal. As to Catena's
treatment of Pius's pontificate, much emphasis is given to his defense of
papal prerogatives and powers, and not merely in Spain, for the scope is

[10] See ibid., 46–51, for the tabernacle's role in the chapel as a new Bethlehem.
[11] On Sixtus's gesture, see ibid., 52–57; on the tomb's iconography, see Herz, "The Sixtine and Pauline Tombs," esp. 256–57, 261.
[12] Catena's book is discussed by Miguel Gotor, "Le vite di San Pio V dal 1572 al 1712 tra censura, agiografia e storia," in Guasco and Torre, eds., *Pio V*, 207–49, esp. 222–29.
[13] Ibid., 229.

pan-European; thus discussion extends to Pius's relationships with a wide variety of secular rulers; his diplomacy and battles against Protestant heretics, particularly in France, but also in England and Germany; his efforts to create a Holy League to fight the Muslim Turks; and various battles against the infidels.

Catena gives a great deal of attention to the Battle of Lepanto, providing details about military strategy, and listing the names of the Christian and Turkish captains – and even of their ships. He also mentions that while the battle was underway, Pius, who was in Rome, had a vision of the victory; although this vision later became a central theme in the iconography of Pope Saint Pius V, it was the battle itself – not the vision – that was central to Sixtus's image of his mentor, as likewise demonstrated by the tomb monument in Santa Maria Maggiore. Of the 346 pages that Catena devoted to Pius's reign, only about sixty focus on the pontiff's character, reforms, pastoral work, and religious devotions in contexts that are not directly related to his crusades against heretics and infidels.

An examination of the anonymous engraved frontispiece to Catena's *Vita* (Figure 3.2) will conclude our discussion of the persona that Sixtus shaped for Pius.[14] As in the tomb monument, so too in the engraving, Pius's portrait is the largest pictorial element. The engraved portrait shows Pius in profile, hands clasped in prayer before a crucifix. A Latin inscription identifies the pope: "Pius V, Pontifex Maximus, who came from Bosco, [member] of the order of Preachers." Around the oval compartment in which the portrait is confined, another Latin inscription reads, "But God forbid that I should glory, save in the Cross of Our Lord Jesus Christ." This indicates that Pius's victories were accomplished not through military might alone, but through divine intervention, which the pope sought through prayer. In a pediment resembling the one at the summit of the tomb monument is found the pontiff's coat of arms.

The tomb monument and engraving are also structured similarly in that the imagery treating the fight against infidels is placed on the left, the fight against heresy on the right. Flanking Pius's engraved portrait on the left side are three figures standing united in a fraternal embrace. They signify the Holy League that Pius formed to fight the Turks. Pius is depicted as the central figure wearing the papal tiara. On the left, the Kingdom of Spain is represented by King Philip II's half-brother, Don Juan of Austria, commander of the papal fleet, who wears a plumed helmet; on the right, the Republic of Venice is represented by the doge, who

---

[14] Illustrated here is the frontispiece of the 1586 edition, which was re-used for the 1587 edition.

3.2 Frontispiece to Girolamo Catena's *Vita del gloriosissimo papa Pio Quinto*, 1586.
Biblioteca Casanatense, Rome.

wears a Phrygian-style headdress. The Latin word above the niche is partly obscured, but the inscription below it reads: "A league having been struck versus the Turks, victory [was achieved]." Vanquished Turks in chains are displayed with their weapons in the scene below, while the Battle of Lepanto is depicted at the bottom center.

To the right of Pius's engraved portrait are two female figures, between whose heads the dove of the Holy Spirit hovers. Above them is the word "Gratitude," and below them is the inscription "The destruction of heretics." In one hand, the woman on the left displays a paten, the dish that holds the Eucharistic bread during the Mass, and in the other a tabernacle, in which the consecrated Hosts are reserved; the engraved tabernacle resembles that in the Sistine Chapel where Pius's tomb monument stands. The second engraved female figure holds the crown that Pius was able to restore to Charles IX of France; at her feet the Huguenots' heretical books are engulfed in flames. The final scene, below these figures, represents the Count of Santa Fiora's defeat of the French Protestants.

In sum, Sixtus V employed visual and written imagery to proclaim his mentor a pontiff worthy of beatification because of his defense of papal primacy and universality and his fight against infidels and heretics. Sixtus did not ignore the role that divine intervention in answer to Pius's prayers played in his victories; yet his presentation of Pius V as inquisitorial and warlike downplayed his personal piety and pastoral spirit, thus heightening the controversy surrounding his deeds. Sixtus's Pius, the papal prince, was simply too polemical to promote successfully.

PIUS V AND THE PAPACY'S CHANGING FORTUNES IN THE SEVENTEENTH AND EARLY EIGHTEENTH CENTURIES

On May 1, 1672, one hundred years after Pius's death and eighty-seven years after Sixtus V ascended the papal throne, Pius V was beatified by Clement X (family name Altieri). Only a brief analysis of Pius's official image as a Blessed can be provided in this short study. Instead, emphasis will be placed on the official image of Pope Saint Pius V that was decreed at his canonization on May 22, 1712 by Clement XI. In order to understand Clement XI's conceptualization of Pius V's holiness, however, a sketch of the papacy's changing fortunes in the seventeenth and early eighteenth centuries is warranted.

Pius V's policies and spiritual aspirations, which were formulated in light of the decrees of the Council of Trent, inspired Sixtus V at the end of the sixteenth century, as we have seen. But Trent's influence was still strong well after Sixtus's death. All of the popes who ruled between 1621 and 1655 devoted some of their energies toward the implementation of the council's decrees, and this was even true of the late seventeenth-century pontiff Innocent XI (1676–89, family name Odescalchi).[15] Among popes who drew inspiration from the Council of Trent, even those who found Pius V's lifestyle and reforms overly severe would have appreciated his desire to put Trent's decrees into practice.

The ever-weakening position of the papacy in European politics also had an impact on perceptions of Pius V's exemplarity. Bernard Dompnier's characterization of the mid-seventeenth century as a watershed period for the papacy deserves attention in this context.[16] According to Dompnier, three factors contributed to the papacy's declining power. First, in 1648 the Peace of Westphalia, which was ratified by secular leaders in opposition to the Holy See, decreed religious division in Europe. Not only had the papacy lost its clout, but the treaty brought a definitive end to the papacy's long-held goal of achieving unity among Christian princes. Second, papal universality and primacy were increasingly challenged by secular rulers, whose political theory and practice tended toward absolutism, and resulted in the creation of national churches over which the papacy was to be given no control. And third, the popes were simultaneously experiencing difficulties in ruling the Papal States because of depleted finances.

Despite these disastrous conditions, pontiffs of this era continued to try to influence secular rulers in the same ways as Pius V had done, viewing with nostalgia the halcyon days of his reign when the office of pope still carried both spiritual and temporal weight. Clement XI, who looked at the reign of his post-Tridentine predecessor in precisely this way, sought to harness Pius V's symbolic power by canonizing him.

CLEMENT XI AND THE CANONIZATION OF PIUS V

On November 23, 1700 Giovanni Francesco Albani, an erudite nobleman and former secretary of papal briefs, was elected Pope Clement XI (reigned 1700–21). Christopher M. S. Johns has characterized the scholarly Clement as both "combative and indecisive," traits that hardly boded well for the Holy See during its then perilous position, which even a more

---

[15] Bernard Dompnier, "Continuità della riforma cattolica," in Marc Venard, ed., *Storia del cristianesimo: religione–politica–cultura*, IX: *L'età della ragione (1620/30–1750)*, ed. Paola Vismara (Rome: Borla, 2003), 195–318, esp. 195–98.

[16] Ibid., 195–98, on which my analysis is based.

politically gifted pontiff would have found daunting.[17] What was needed
was a radical rethinking of papal goals and ways to achieve them in a
changed world, something that was well beyond Clement XI's conceptual
range, for as Johns notes, "Clement still held a Counter-Reformation view
of European politics unrealistic at the dawn of the modern era, and his
diplomacy was directed accordingly."[18]

Given Clement's Counter-Reformation attitude and the fact that he
faced the same kinds of problems that had earlier beset Pius V, albeit
under changed circumstances, it was inevitable that he looked to Pius as a
role model.[19] Like Pius, Clement aspired to defend papal privileges as well
as to raise a crusade against the Turks. Although Clement's appreciation
of Pius V has long been recognized, the timing of his decision to canonize
his pontifical predecessor demands fuller analysis than it has previously
received.

In 1696 Pope Innocent XII (reigned 1691–1700, family name Pignatelli),
Clement XI's immediate predecessor, signed a commission allowing
the Congregation of Rites to consider additional miracles performed by
Blessed Pius V.[20] About five years later, on May 16, 1705, the congregation approved two of the five miracles and presented them to Clement for
his consideration.[21] That it took Clement another five years to approve the
miracles of a pope he so deeply respected requires explanation.

During these years Clement was embroiled in one of the most complex political problems the papacy had ever experienced: the War of the
Spanish Succession.[22] On November 1, 1700, a few weeks before Clement
XI ascended the pontifical throne, King Charles II of Spain died without a direct heir, having bequeathed his kingdom to Philip, Duke of

---

[17] Christopher M. S. Johns, *Papal Art and Cultural Politics: Rome in the Age of Clement XI*
(Cambridge: Cambridge University Press, 1993), 2.

[18] Ibid., 1.

[19] In this short study I cannot do justice to Clement's artistic patronage, in which Pius figured both
before and after his canonization, on which see Johns, *Papal Art*, 8–10, 118–19; Steven F. Ostrow
and Christopher M. S. Johns, "Illuminations of S. Maria Maggiore in the Early Settecento,"
Burlington Magazine 132:1049 (1990), 528–34.

[20] Maffei, *Vita*, 461. The Roman edition of 1712 was published by Francesco Gonzaga.

[21] Luca Antonio Chracas, *Distinto raccolto di quanto si è operato nella canonizatione de' quattro santi.
S. Pio V. Pontefice, dell' ordine de' Predicatori, S. Andrea Avellino, de' chierici regolari Teatini, S.
Felice da Cantalice, laico professo dell' ordine de' Minori di S. Francesco Cappuccino. S. Catarina da
Bologna, dell' ordine di S. Chiara* ... (Rome: Giovanfrancesco Chracas, 1712), 3.

[22] On the Spanish Succession from the papacy's viewpoint, see Stefano Andretta, "Clemente XI,"
in Massimo Bray, ed., *Enciclopedia dei papi*, 3 vols. (Rome: Istituto della Enciclopedia Italiana,
2000), III, 405–20, esp. 407–10; Johns, *Papal Art*, 19–20; C. B. O'Keefe, "Clement XI," in *The
New Catholic Encyclopedia*, 2nd edn. (Detroit: Thomson Gale, in association with the Catholic
University of America, Washington, DC, 2003), III, 788–89.

Anjou, Louis XIV's grandson. Threatened by an increase in France's power, England, the Netherlands, Prussia, and Austria put forward their own claimant: Archduke Charles of Austria. Clement XI recognized the French claimant, thereby angering Emperor Leopold I of Austria. In 1705 – the very year in which Clement received Pius V's miracles for approval – Emperor Leopold died and was succeeded by his son Joseph I, who invaded the Papal States, taking Parma and Piacenza and besieging Ferrara. At first, Clement XI fought against the emperor and his allies, but the pope's own allies soon abandoned him. When Prince Hesse-Cassel's Protestant army reached Bologna, Clement feared that Rome would be sacked, as it had been in 1527 to disastrous effect. Therefore Clement backed down, and on January 15, 1709 recognized Archduke Charles as the legitimate heir.

Clement XI's humiliation of January 1709 was devastating, both personally and for the papacy as an institution: it highlighted his own tendency to vacillate, while underscoring the inability of the papacy to defend its own temporal lands or to exert an influence on secular rulers. At precisely this moment, Clement returned to the question of Pius V's miracles. After beseeching God's help in making the decision, Clement approved the miracles on March 16, 1710, ten months after his humiliation. On July 8 the Congregation of Rites ruled in favor of Pius's canonization.[23]

Clement chose to issue the decree of canonization on August 4, the feast of St. Dominic, founder of Pius's religious order.[24] In his *Vita di S. Pio Quinto sommo pontefice* (*Life of Saint Pius V Supreme Pontiff*) of 1712, written for Clement XI, Paolo Alessandro Maffei tactfully omitted references to the papacy's weaknesses and Clement XI's personal failings. But Maffei's following comment is best understood in the context of the political situation just synopsized:

By means of this decree published on such a noteworthy day, Clement XI intended not only to add new and very clear splendor to the said order of St. Dominic, such a worthy personage of the Catholic Church, but to promote the greater glory and honor of the Apostolic See, by imploring – in such calamitous times – the special, suitable, and necessary protection of a pope saint, in whom were always marvelously conspicuous a perpetual study to propagate religion, an indefatigable effort to restore the old observance of ecclesiastical discipline, a continual vigilance in extirpating errors, and an invincible and constant vigor in sustaining the laws of the Roman Church.[25]

[23] Maffei, *Vita,* 462.   [24] Ibid., 462; Chracas, *Distinto raccolto,* 3.
[25] Maffei, *Vita,* 462.

In short, because Pius V had been everything he himself wanted to be, Clement XI hoped to employ Pope Saint Pius V as a powerful figurehead.

Clearly, Clement needed to bolster his own position in 1710, hence his decision to approve Pius's miracles so that he could be canonized; but there was more to the timing than that. One result of Clement XI's political embarrassment in 1709 was that the majority of European powers were promised what they wanted: the installation of an Austrian Habsburg on the Spanish throne in order to limit France's power, which was already unusually strong under Louis XIV. Of course, with the treaties of Utrecht (1713) and Rastatt (1714) all this would change, resulting in Philip of Anjou being crowned the first Bourbon king of Spain.[26] But in 1710 Clement could not have foreseen that.

In 1710, therefore, Clement XI had every reason to believe that having just sided with the empire against France, he might have a chance to unite Christian rulers (other than Louis XIV) under the inspiration of Pope Saint Pius V in order to fight the Turks, thus regaining a commanding position in European politics, while also following in the saint's footsteps in defeating the infidel. This is suggested not merely by the way political events unfolded, as just discussed, but also by the ways in which Clement XI's image of Pius V departed from that of Sixtus V. First, Clement's vision of Pius the holy warrior was directed more at Turkish infidels than at European heretics; the most crucial difference, however, was that Clement's Pius V was not merely warlike, but also prayerful and pastoral.

CLEMENT XI'S IMAGE OF POPE SAINT PIUS V

Although different from Sixtus V's image, Clement XI's image of Pius V as both warlike and prayerful was not entirely new; in essence, it had already been codified at the time of Pius's beatification in 1672. Certainly this vision of Blessed Pius V was expressed in the pictorial decoration of St. Peter's on the occasion of his beatification ceremony, but detailed descriptions are lacking.[27] Let it suffice, therefore, to synopsize the pictorial decoration of Santa Maria sopra Minerva in Rome, where the Dominicans held their own beatification celebration a week later.[28] The Minerva's imagery was created in conformance with Pius's official iconography as a Blessed.

---

[26] See n. 22 above.
[27] See Maffei, *Vita*, 435–45, on the beatification ceremony in St. Peter's.
[28] Ibid., 445–52.

On the church's façade, Pius's fight against both infidels and heretics was emphasized by depictions of Don Juan of Austria charged with command of the papal forces, Pius's vision of the Battle of Lepanto in the presence of the Madonna of the Rosary, and the Count of Santa Fiora's victory over the Huguenots.

Inside the church, Pius's role as conqueror of the Turks was seen in Lazzaro Baldi's *Pius's Vision of the Battle of Lepanto*, prominently displayed in the tribune; Baldi's painting had served as the Blessed's standard during the beatification ceremony in St. Peter's the week before, and had subsequently been given to the Dominicans for their church.[29] Among the paintings on the walls, one represented Marcantonio Colonna being placed in command of the Holy League's fleet, while a whole series of paintings of Blessed Pius's miracles, including the miracle of the crucifix, completed the decorative program.

Clement XI, who was obviously intimately familiar with Blessed Pius's official image, could see how, with minor revisions, it could be used symbolically for the benefit of the Holy See, and even to help polish his own tarnished persona. As Antonio Silli and Carla Enrica Spantigati have each noted, the vision of the Battle of Lepanto and the miracle of the crucifix became the most popular themes in the iconography of Pope Saint Pius V.[30] What requires explanation is why Clement XI chose to revise Blessed Pius's image by giving greater emphasis to those particular themes in the iconography of Pope Saint Pius V. This question will be addressed in connection with the visual imagery designed for Pius's canonization ceremony in St. Peter's, Maffei's official hagiography of Pius, and an anonymous engraving made to commemorate Pius's elevation to sainthood.

Pius V was one of four holy persons whom Clement XI canonized on May 22, 1712; the others were Andrea Avellino, a Theatine priest; Felice da Cantalice, a lay Capuchin; and Catherine of Bologna, a Poor Clare. The imagery displayed at the canonization ceremony in St. Peter's centered on all four saints. But Pius V, as a former pontiff, was given precedence among the four by the Congregation of Rites when establishing the order in which they were presented during the ceremony.[31] Thus, for example, the coat of arms of Pius's Dominican order was carried into the church at the head of the procession.

---

[29] Ibid., 446; Maffei mentions Baldi by name. Canonization standards were normally given to churches of the same religious order or national affiliation as the new saint, a point made by Spantigati, "Il culto di San Pio," 314, in connection with Baldi's painting.

[30] Silli, *San Pio V*, 46; Spantigati, "Il culto di San Pio," 317.

[31] Chracas, *Distinto raccolto*, 8–9.

The façade of St. Peter's was decorated with a painting, *The Triumph of the Four Glorious Saints*.[32] The whole interior of the basilica was draped in red damask trimmed in gold and was lit by elaborate candelabra and torches. The four saints' coats of arms were displayed under the cornice, while over-life-size stucco sculptures of them stood in the four niches of the crossing.

Canonizations, like beatifications, depended on the verification of post-humous miracles, some of which presumably figured in the decorations of St. Peter's.[33] However, records of the decorative program are incomplete,[34] and the only miracles documented as having been depicted are ones said to have occurred during the saints' lifetimes; these paintings, four per saint, were displayed along the nave. The saintly pope's first miracle to be represented was that of the holy dust: the Polish ambassador asked Pius to give him a relic of Rome, so the pontiff bent down with a handkerchief and collected some dust from the ground in St. Peter's Square; when the ambassador unfolded the handkerchief both it and the dust were soaked with the blood of Rome's early Christian martyrs. The second miracle centered on Pius's exorcism of a possessed woman by making the sign of the cross. The third concerned a fire at the Duke of Sessa's palace; miraculously, two portraits of Pius were its only contents to survive unharmed. And the fourth was Pius's vision of the victory of Lepanto, which occurred in Rome at the very time when the battle took place. Also depicted in the nave were virtues, two per saint, presumably represented as female personifications; Pope Saint Pius V was represented by Justice and Religion.

Although our knowledge of the ceremony's decoration is rather schematic,[35] a few basic conclusions may be drawn. First, the pope as saint was proclaimed to be the most important of the four. This is the way the Congregation of Rites decreed it, and the way Clement XI surely saw it. Second, Pius was associated specifically with justice and religion.

Pius's four miracles recorded as having been displayed in the nave of St. Peter's should be considered particularly telling. The miracle of the dust emphasized Pius's and Clement's shared view of Rome as the temporal and spiritual center of Christianity. That Pius's portraits had survived a conflagration underscored the power and efficacy of images, as decreed at the

[32] Ibid., 9.
[33] Of the roughly one hundred miracles treated selectively, and at times vaguely, by Mattei (*Vita*, 399–420), about fifty-eight were posthumous.
[34] Chracas, *Distinto raccolto*, 8–10.
[35] It is possible to reconstruct neither the iconography of the apparatus – a temporary theater-like structure placed in the presbytery – nor the inclusion or placement of the saints' posthumous miracles, some of which must have been depicted.

Council of Trent, while simultaneously serving as proof of the pontiff's
inviolable holiness.

It is noteworthy that the other two miracles drew attention to Pius as
pastor, for as Simon Ditchfield has noted in a different context, Pius's identification with Christ as "the supreme priest" was central to his Eucharistic
devotion, and also to his conception of his role as Vicar of Christ.[36] Several
exorcisms were attributed to Pius, both in St. Peter's and in Santa Maria in
Aracoeli, so it is impossible to know whether a specific one was intended
or the painting was meant to evoke all of them.[37] However that might
be, Christ himself had cast out demons, and had given the apostles and
disciples the power to do so. Not only had exorcism long been considered
a pastoral duty, but it was believed that certain kinds of demons could be
cast out only by means of prayer and fasting, two practices especially associated with Pius.

The final miracle in question was Pius's vision of the Battle of Lepanto,
one of the scenes most important to his saintly iconography. Instead of the
battle per se this theme emphasized Pius's prayerfulness and his devotion
to the Madonna of the Rosary. Because this image is no longer extant, the
theme will be discussed below in relation to a surviving engraving. Let it
suffice to stress here that the vision of Pope Saint Pius V that Clement XI
proclaimed at his canonization ceremony was intended to burnish the papacy's image in terms of the sanctity of the Holy See's territory; the devotion to martyrs, relics, and images; the successful fight against infidels,
accomplished through a Holy League but also through prayer and divine
intervention; and the papal pastor's Christlike ability to care for souls.

Like the ceremony in St. Peter's, Maffei's biography of Pope Pius V
expresses the Albani pope's view of his new saint. At 470 pages, Maffei's
biography is about a hundred pages longer than that of Catena, from which
it drew inspiration, as is well known.[38] Maffei's treatment of Ghislieri's life
before his election – in fifty-three pages – resembles that of Catena.

Yet it has not been recognized that Maffei's treatment of Pius's reign
in Books II–V differs in important ways from that of Catena. Maffei's
Book II gives roughly even treatment to three themes: pastoral initiatives,
the fight against heretics, and the fight against infidels. In Book III, pastoral themes receive as much attention as the fight against heretics and the

---

[36] Simon Ditchfield, "Il papa come pastore? Pio V e la liturgia," in Guasco and Torre, eds., *Pio V*,
159–78, esp. 171.

[37] My synopsis is based on E. J. Gratsch, "Exorcism," in *The New Catholic Encyclopedia*, V, 551–53.

[38] On Maffei (1653–1716), see Johns, *Papal Art*, 24; Ditchfield, "Il papa come pastore?," 168. Maffei,
Vita, viii, noted his reliance on Catena and others.

coronation of Grand Duke Cosimo I de' Medici, with the fight against infidels scarcely mentioned. The years 1570–71 are covered in Book IV, which is entirely devoted to the crusade against the Muslims and the victory at Lepanto; this includes prayer and divine intervention. Finally, in Book V, which treats the last year of Pius's life, most attention is given to pastoral matters (twenty-seven pages), while the pope's fight against the infidel (seventeen pages) and his death and funeral (seventeen pages) receive equal emphasis.

Because the pastoral component of Pius's official image as a canonized saint has been largely overlooked,[39] it is worth noting that Maffei records Pius as having exhorted bishops to reside in their dioceses, so as to preach and save souls; urged the clergy to cure residents of the East and West Indies of superstitions; promoted the foundation of seminaries; reformed the breviary and missal and given indulgences to persons who recited the Office of the Virgin; consoled persecuted English Catholics during Elizabeth I's reign; instituted the feast of the Rosary to thank the Virgin for the victory at Lepanto; been on the Seven Churches pilgrimage in Rome; and led a life devoted to prayer.

This written image of Pope Saint Pius V found visual expression in an engraving placed before the title page to Maffei's book: *The Miracle of the Crucifix* (Figure 3.3), whose inscription reads, "Painted by Domenico Muratori, engraved by Girolamo Rossi."[40] That Muratori also helped design the decorations for Pius's canonization ceremony in St. Peter's points to the consistency of Pius's persona as created by Clement XI.[41] The engraving shows Pius V genuflecting in prayer before a crucifix, while two angels on the right hold his papal tiara; this miracle is also described in Maffei's text:

St. Pius customarily prayed before an image of the crucifix [carved] in relief. It happened one evening that when he tried to kiss its feet according to his usual custom, the holy figure [the sculpture] withdrew them from him more than once. The pontiff was surprised by this miraculous event, and reasonably doubted that the purpose of the Lord's great miracle was to save him from an evil person's plot. [But] Pius ordered that the holy feet [of the crucifix] be wiped with a hot piece of bread, which, when fed to a dog, was so poisonous that it killed the animal immediately.[42]

[39] Pius's pastoral role is analyzed with an emphasis on the liturgy by Ditchfield, "Il papa come pastore?"

[40] This illustration, here reproduced from the Venetian edition, was also used in the Roman edition of the same year.

[41] Spantigati, "Il culto di San Pio," 315.   [42] Maffei, *Vita*, 399–400.

3.3 Girolamo Rossi after Domenico Muratori, *The Miracle of the Crucifix*. From Alessandro Maffei's *Vita di S. Pio Quinto sommo pontefice*, Venice, 1712. With permission of the Ministero per i Beni e le Attività Culturali, Rome.

To return to the engraving in Maffei's tract, under the crucifix there is a book, which is inscribed with a passage that also appeared in the anonymous engraving to Catena's tract: "But God forbid that I should glory, save in the Cross ..." This passage, taken from St. Paul's letter to the Galatians, 6:14, continues, "of the Lord Jesus Christ, by whom the world is crucified unto me, and I unto the world." In the engraving to Catena's book (Figure 3.2), the small portrait of Pius in prayer is flanked by imagery and inscriptions referring to his fight against infidels and heretics. By contrast, the engraving to Maffei's book depicts only Pius's life of prayer, specifically his devotion to Christ's Passion; the inscription makes it clear that Christ's grace accounts for any praiseworthy deeds or virtues that may be associated with the pontiff. As an ideal pastor, Pius, like St. Paul in his pastoral letter to the Galatians, emulates Christ by being crucified metaphorically in the service of his flock. Placed as it is at the very beginning of Maffei's long tract, this engraving sets a distinctive tone for the text that follows it.

Pope Saint Pius V's official image may be summed up by examining an anonymous engraving made to commemorate his canonization (Figure 3.4).[43] Like other images commemorating beatifications and canonizations, this one consists of a large depiction of the holy person in the center surrounded by small scenes of miracles around the perimeter, each with its own explanatory caption; a long inscription at the bottom center provides biographical information about the new saint.

Before examining in detail the significance of the engraving's central scene, brief note should be made of Pius's sixteen miracles represented around it. Twelve of them were posthumous miracles in which people's physical ailments were healed by contact with a relic or piece of clothing worn by Pius, or by praying to him. Four miracles that occurred during the pontiff's life were represented in St. Peter's for the canonization ceremony, and of them only the miracle of the dust does not appear in the engraving; instead, two separate scenes of exorcism are portrayed. Given that the engraving commemorates Pius's canonization, it is likely that its posthumous miracles were also represented in St. Peter's on that occasion.

The engraving's main scene is *Pius V's Vision of the Battle of Lepanto*; in it Pius kneels in prayer before a crucifix on an altar. An angel extends his arms toward the crucifix and the lilies beside it, thereby underscoring the intercessory roles of Christ and the Madonna of the Rosary; behind Pius, through a window, the Battle of Lepanto is seen. As mentioned, a painting

---

[43] The undated engraving can be connected with the canonization because it contains a miracle approved by Clement only in 1710.

3.4 *Pope Pius V's Vision of the Battle of Lepanto with Scenes of his Miracles*, 1712.
© Biblioteca Apostolica Vaticana, Vatican City.

by Lazzaro Baldi on the same theme had served as the standard during Pius's beatification ceremony in 1672, and the same miracle also figured in the decoration of St. Peter's for the canonization ceremony.[44]

The meaning that the miraculous vision had in Clement XI's eyes is clarified by Maffei's treatment in the *Vita*. Maffei begins his discussion of the Battle of Lepanto by highlighting Pius's ministry to the soldiers, noting that he conceded a plenary indulgence to them and sent priests from ship to ship to give them the opportunity for confession and provide them with moral support. Maffei continues:

[44] The engraving is not based on Baldi's various paintings, on which see Silli, *San Pio V*, 43; Spantigati, "Il culto di San Pio," 317.

I am not going to describe at length the circumstances of the action that have already been recorded by historians, but will stop [to discuss] only a few things that pertain directly to the story of Saint Pius and his glory. One finds written that during that day and the entire night preceding it, [Pius] redoubled his prayers, and had them carried out in all the convents and monasteries of Rome, that he showed himself to be more concerned than usual with the enterprise [of achieving victory over the Turks], toward which end he had shed so many tears, and had sent to heaven so many sighs and very fervent prayers, with which he merited being heard, moving the mercy of God in favor of the Christians. And for himself he merited the consolation of receiving the early revelation of the very full victory to be obtained. Because while Pius was in his rooms in the Vatican Palace meeting with some ministers, and ... the general treasurer, he suddenly broke off from them and opened a window and raised his eyes to heaven, where he looked fixedly for a long time; afterwards, closing it, and showing himself to be full of great things, he turned graciously to the treasurer and said to him, "This is not the time to transact business. Go thank God because our armada has fought with that of the Turks and at this very hour [ours] has won." Upon leaving, he saw the Holy Pontiff throw himself down, genuflecting, with his hands joined [in prayer] to thank God for the grace obtained.[45]

Catena makes the same points in his biography of 1586, yet his overall trajectory differs from Maffei's.[46] After discussing Pius's vision and the subsequent report that the victory really had taken place, both Catena and Maffei relate salient events of the battle. Then their accounts diverge. Catena next compares the fight at Lepanto to various conflicts in antiquity; continues with a discussion of the number of galleys taken at Lepanto; and devotes the subsequent chapter to the celebration in Rome of Colonna's victory. By contrast, Maffei's account places more emphasis on the pontiff as pastor by omitting those themes and devoting a chapter to Pius's institution of the feast of Santa Maria della Vittoria (St. Mary of Victory).

As Maffei explains,[47] Pius attributed the victory to the Madonna of the Rosary, whose intervention had been beseeched by brothers of the Confraternity of the Holy Rosary; this lay brotherhood was dedicated to the recitation of the Rosary, a devotion founded by Pius's own Dominican order.[48] In thanks to the Madonna, therefore, the pontiff instituted October 7 as the feast of Santa Maria della Vittoria. Pius's successor, Gregory XIII, changed the feast's name to that of the Madonna

---

[45] Maffei, *Vita*, 223–24.
[46] This comparison centers on Catena, *Vita* (212–29) versus Maffei, *Vita* (223–43).
[47] Maffei, *Vita*, 240–43.
[48] The importance of the Dominican order to Pius figures in all the studies cited herein; also see Michele Miele, "Pio V e la presenza dei Domenicani nel corso della sua vita," in Guasco and Torre, eds., *Pio V*, 27–48.

of the Holy Rosary and ordered that it be celebrated on the first Sunday
of October. In Baldi's painting, as in the canonization engraving's main
scene, the Madonna of the Rosary is present while Pius receives the revelation of the Holy League's victory over the Turks. This theme had appeared
in art and literature ever since 1571, but whereas the battle itself had been
central to Sixtus V's image of his mentor as papal prince, the themes of
the devout pontiff's vision of the victory and the miracle of the crucifix
were central to the official iconography of Pope Saint Pius V, as officially
decreed by Clement XI.

In conclusion, Clement XI's pope as saint was both a defender of the
faith and a pastor, a pontiff who unified Christian princes against the infidel and cared for the souls of his flock. Yet Clement's aim of employing
Pope Saint Pius V to help him recoup for the papacy its former temporal
and spiritual ascendancy was unrealistic in the changed circumstances of
the early eighteenth century. As the product of an essentially *retardataire*
vision, Pope Saint Pius V could have been no more powerful in the eyes
of Clement's opponents than the reigning pontiff himself. Recently, in
2000, John Paul II beatified two popes, Pius IX and John XXIII; some
would argue that Pius IX – like his namesake Pius V – represents the past,
whereas John XXIII represents the future. When or whether either will be
canonized remains to be seen.

CHAPTER 4

Pasquinades and propaganda: the reception of Urban VIII

Sheila Barker

A FLORENTINE HERITAGE

At first it might not seem relevant that Maffeo Barberini, the future Urban VIII, began his life in Medicean Florence, having been born there on April 5, 1568, and baptized that same day at the Florence Baptistery.[1] He left almost no trace on the city that he left at a young age, with the exception of a showy plaque on the façade of the Carmelite monastery of Santa Maria Maddalena de' Pazzi, where two of his nieces lived until 1639.[2] Yet, in certain ways, the city left its trace on him. The signal aspects of his personality and papacy – humanistic learning oriented to the Greek letters, the use of art to further a political agenda, a tactical alternation of French and Habsburg alliances, a prophetic inclination, an ambition to establish a dynastic rule, and a fascination with astrology – all could be seen as a Florentine cultural legacy.

His education began under the Jesuits of Florence. Beginning in 1584, he studied briefly at the Jesuit College in Rome, and by 1586 he had obtained degrees in canon and civil law at the University of Pisa. He returned to Rome to enter the curia in 1588, taking a post that his uncle had purchased for him. From this same uncle, Maffeo Barberini soon afterwards received a large inheritance that enabled him to serve as

---

[1] All documents from the Archivio di Stato di Firenze, Florence (henceforth ASF), Fondo Mediceo del Principato (henceforth MdP), were located thanks to the Medici Archive Project's Documentary Sources Database, for which the author is grateful. The baptismal record is in the Archivio dell'Opera di S. Maria del Fiore di Firenze, Florence, Registri battesimali, Maschi, reg. 14, fol. 102. For published and archival sources on Maffeo Barberini, see Georg Lutz, "Urbano VIII," in Massimo Bray, ed., *Enciclopedia dei papi*, 3 vols. (Rome: Istituto della Enciclopedia Italiana, 2000), III, 317–21.

[2] Peter Rietbergen, *Power and Religion in Baroque Rome: Barberini Cultural Policies* (Leiden: Brill, 2006), 179. See Giacinto Gigli, *Diario di Roma*, ed. Manlio Barberito, 2 vols. (Rome: Editore Columbo, 1994), I, 325, for the transfer of Innocenzia and Maria Grazia Barberini to a Roman Carmelite monastery.

nuncio extraordinary to the court of Henry IV Bourbon and Maria de'
Medici in 1601. His success in this role led to his elevation to the cardinalate under Paul V in 1606. In 1622 Gregory XV made Maffeo Barberini
cardinal protector of the Greek College, and named him to the newly
created Congregation for the Propagation of the Faith.[3] Shortly thereafter, on August 6, 1623, he was elected to the papal throne. Summing
up his papacy of nearly twenty-two years, a contemporary chronicler,
Giacinto Gigli, wrote:

In that course of time, it was as if there had been two pontificates. This is because
while Urban was healthy, for fourteen or fifteen years, he governed with great
prudence, and, had he died the first time he fell sick, he would have been praised
by everyone and held in high esteem and considered among the best popes on
record. But when he lost his health, governing by means of his nephews, his pontificate changed its nature, and with the excessive taxation that aggrieved the
public, and the unsuccessful war, which was a source of tears for many, he managed to earn everyone's hatred ...[4]

DEATH AND *DAMNATIO MEMORIAE*

When, on July 29, 1644, the Roman public learned that Urban VIII had
died the previous day, they at first rejoiced. Exhilaration then gave way
to fury. Gathering in mobs under the fanatic lead of Mgr. Ferdinando
Cesarini (1604–46), formerly the patron of Galileo's student Benedetto
Castelli, they surged toward the Palazzo dei Conservatori – these "cus-
todians" were Rome's leading civic magistrates – on the Capitoline Hill.[5]
Here they intended to exact revenge against the "Barbarian tyrants" – that
is, the Barberini family – by reviving the custom of destroying the statues
of hated popes upon their death.[6] Their target was a marble statue of the
pope displayed here since 1640; in happier times, it had been carved by
Gian Lorenzo Bernini at the commission of the Roman Senate to honor
Urban as a savior of the Roman people.[7]

   When the mob reached the Palazzo dei Conservatori, they found it bar-
ricaded and occupied by soldiers armed with pikes, muskets, and heavy
artillery. The soldiers had been stationed here by Cardinal Girolamo

[3] For Urban VIII's early life and career, see Lutz, "Urbano VIII," 298–302.
[4] Gigli, *Diario*, I, 425. Here and elsewhere in this chapter translations are mine unless otherwise stated.
[5] Ibid., I, 426. Galileo dedicated the 1623 *assayer* to Cesarini's brother Virginio (1596–1624).
[6] Stanislao Fraschetti, *Il Bernini: la sua vita, la sua opera, il suo tempo* (Milan: Hoepli, 1900), 153, 154 n. 1.
[7] Ibid., 151–53. For the commission see Gigli, *Diario*, I, 331–34.

Colonna, Grand Constable of the Kingdom of Naples, in anticipation of the rioters' iconoclastic designs upon Urban's majestic image. With the angry populace halted in Michelangelo's Piazza del Campidoglio, Cesarini took advantage of the charged moment to lambaste two of the former pope's favorites: Marco Antonio Malagigi, a musician, and Bernini himself (who was rumored to be inside the Campidoglio protecting his statue). The mob then moved on to a secondary target, a life-size plaster effigy of the pope in the courtyard of the Jesuit College in Rome, which also had been made by Bernini. This time, no one stopped them from pulverizing the pope's likeness.[8]

The aggression of this ritual attack upon Urban's effigy pales in comparison to the ruthlessness of the character assassinations committed after his death. Many of these took the form of pasquinades, anonymous lampoons, usually of a political nature, that were written most often in verse, in either Latin or the vernacular; their name derived from the custom of publicly displaying these writings beside the so-called "talking statue" near the Piazza Navona nicknamed Pasquino. Among the reams of anonymous pasquinades and satires written against the pope were some that Giacinto Gigli attributed to Ferdinando Cesarini himself, including the wickedly successful "Papa Gabella" ("The Taxation Pope"):[9]

> O Taxation Pope
> You astound me even in death
> And I'm left without a breath
> To sustain my rebel hopes
> O Taxation Pope ...
> By Urban and his brother's sons
> More damage has been done
> Than by Vandal, Goth, or Hun
> To my beloved Rome
> O Taxation Pope.[10]

While interregnums in early modern Rome naturally gave occasion for uncensored critiques of the previous papacy, there was no recent precedent for the flood of scabrous writings during the Barberini vacant

[8] Fraschetti, *Il Bernini*, 154. On the statue, see Gigli, *Diario*, I, 332.
[9] Gigli, *Diario*, II, 429, names a second author of these pasquinades: Monsignor Stefano Vaio.
[10] "O Papa Gabella / Pur morto ti miro / E più non sospiro / La mia sorte rubella / O Papa Gabella ... / Han fatto più danno / Urbano e nepoti / Che vandali e Gothi / A Roma mia bella / O Papa Gabella." Gigli, *Diario*, I, 427. Pasquinade found in ASF, MdP 6425, fol. 456 (second copy at fol. 493).

see.[11] Even a cynical statesman like Gigli found many of them to be "overly vicious and unbecoming of Christians in their defamation of a pope, even making false accusations, as if [Urban VIII] had died a godless and evil tyrant."[12]

In general, these satirical writings are uniform in their themes: the greed of the Barberini family, their self-serving war against Duke Odoardo Farnese, the spoliation of ancient Rome for their own building projects, the pope's impious indifference to Gustavus II Adolphus's invasion of Catholic territories, the pope's excessive taxation of the Romans, and his unabashed bias toward France.[13] With these attacks the anonymous pasquinade writers defamed Urban's performance in each of the three major categories of papal activity – as prince, patron, and pastor.

In light of these scathing posthumous pasquinades, penned (presumably) by the inhabitants of Rome, it might at first seem that Urban's reign was an unmitigated disaster for the image of the papacy. Yet the historian Georg Lutz recently insisted that Urban's pontificate not be hastily dismissed as a failure.[14] Surely, then, a wider consideration of Urban's reception, in both geographic and temporal terms, is in order. To this end, this chapter will examine Urban's reign, particularly those characteristics that were common fodder for the pasquinades, in the context of the changing historical reception of his papacy, and in light of Urban VIII's own keen concern with the public perception of his papacy.

FRANCOPHILE, AS THE OCCASION REQUIRED

After Urban's death, pasquinades as well as political tracts accused him of deep-rooted Francophilism accompanied by a secret desire for the demise of the Habsburgs.[15] This charge has cast a long shadow over Barberini historiography. Granted, recent research has corroborated the anti-Medicean status of some of Urban's ancestors (as well as those of Pope Clement VIII Aldobrandini, who fostered Maffeo Barberini's curial career), and indeed,

---

[11] These writings have been found in Rome, Berlin, Ancona, London, and Frankfurt; see Ludwig von Pastor, *Storia dei papi dalla fine del Medio Evo*, trans. Pio Cenci, 15 vols. (Rome: Desclee, 1961), XIII, 898 n. 2. Cf. Laurie Nussdorfer, *Civic Politics in the Rome of Urban VIII* (Princeton: Princeton University Press, 1992), 245–48.

[12] Gigli, *Diario*, II, 429.

[13] E.g. The pasquinade in ASF, MdP 6425, fol. 458: "Epitaffio ad uso di Sonetto. Qui giace Papa Urbano Maffeo tiranno / Collega di Gustavo e di Luigi …"

[14] Lutz, "Urbano VIII," 316.

[15] See e.g. "Discorso politico sopra gl'interessi, e fini dei principi dell'Europa; fatto in occasione del conclave di Papa Urbano VIII nel quale fù assunto al pontificato il Cardinale Panfilio nominato Innocenzio X l'anno 1644," ASF, MdP 6426, fols. 238v–240r.

many anti-Medici exiles enjoyed French asylum or entered Francophile communities.[16] This distant family history does not, however, appear to implicate Maffeo. His parents were firmly settled in grand ducal Florence, calling into question any claims for their overt anti-Medicean identity. Their probable pro-Medici stance is further indicated by the fact that Maffeo's brother Carlo married a woman from a staunchly Medicean background: Costanza Magalotti, daughter of Vincenzo Magalotti, a Florentine senator, and Clarice Capponi. Casting further doubt on his supposed Francophilism are testimonies of Maffeo Barberini's early orientation toward Spain. In 1606 a Medici agent in Paris wrote to inform the Florentine court that Cardinal Maffeo Barberini was pro-Spanish, and that this was the cause of Henry IV's endeavors to upset Maffeo's loyalty.[17] Similar evidence comes from a detractor who, despite denouncing the Francophilism of Urban's papacy, nonetheless acknowledged that while a cardinal, Maffeo Barberini had obsequiously cultivated a Spanish clientele: "Gushing over every poor and wretched Spaniard, he would not suffer that any one of them should go away without having received some favor given [the cardinal's] position in the Prefecture of Justice ...."[18]

The anonymous author of the previous statement dismissed these instances as hypocritical dissimulation meant to mask Maffeo's true sympathy for France while he courted Spanish support for his election to the papacy. While it might be debated whether Maffeo's Hispanophile bias was genuine or feigned, it is entirely appropriate to contextualize such displays of favor in light of the cardinal's ambitions. Because he was an aspirant to the papacy, it behooved him to avoid being excluded from candidacy by either the Spanish king or the French king, both of whom held the power of the *jus exclusivae* veto.[19] Given the tensions between the two courts, it would have been easier to ride two horses with one saddle than always to appear equally amenable to the rival Catholic sovereigns, yet Maffeo did eventually endeavor to be perceived as neutral. This is even evident in his poetic activity, for between 1619 and 1620 he penned the "Ode to St. Laurence" to appeal to Spain, and, almost as a pendant, the "Ode to St. Louis IX" to appeal to France.[20]

[16] Irene Fosi, *All'ombra dei Barberini: fedeltà e servizio nella Roma barocca* (Rome: Bulzoni, 1997), 46; see also Lutz, "Urbano VIII," 298.

[17] Letter of Cosimo Baroncelli to Belisario Vinto, October 13, 1606, in ASF, MdP 8844, fol. 521.

[18] "Discorso politico," fol. 238r.

[19] Maria Antonietta Visceglia, "Factions in the Sacred College in the Sixteenth and Seventeenth Centuries," in Gianvittorio Signorotto and Maria Antonietta Visceglia, eds., *Court and Politics in Papal Rome, 1492–1700* (Cambridge: Cambridge University Press, 2002), 107–08.

[20] Rietbergen, *Power and Religion*, 110.

If manifesting political neutrality was an expedient for attaining the papacy, it was not always an ideal posture during Urban VIII's pontificate, despite the predominant view of modern historiography that, during the Thirty Years' War between the Habsburgs and France, papal neutrality served as a strategy for protecting the territorial integrity of the Papal States, carried forth under the old slogan of *libertà d'Italia*.[21] The drawbacks of a façade of neutrality were made evident when he attempted to negotiate a peace between France and Spain during the War of Valtellina. Apparently the pope thought he could protect the Holy See's interests by proffering papal nuncios as neutral mediators. This strategy first began to collapse when the pope lost his credibility as an impartial "common father" to the two crowns; evidence of this failure is found in a letter written in 1625 by the nuncio to Madrid, Giulio Sacchetti, in which he complained to the other nuncio, Francesco Barberini, that Spain and France "will neither trust nor follow the counsel and directives of His Holiness, who is endeavoring as a good father and mediator."[22] Then, in 1626, the French and Spanish ministers secretly determined that Roman mediation was unnecessary to their diplomatic efforts, and they struck the Peace of Monzón without consulting the nuncios.[23] The utter disregard of these Catholic nations of the Holy See's interests in a dispute that centered on Italian lands was experienced by Urban as both a political humiliation and a derailment of his pastoral mission as peace-maker.[24]

In the next phase of his papacy, Urban seems to have ceased striving to appear neutral or impartial in international affairs. Therewith he adopted a "Realpolitik" approach that insured the relevance of papal interests to other European courts.[25] It remained both effective and tenable insofar as Urban continuously shifted his favor between France and Habsburg Spain. This alternation is demonstrated not only by the well-known Spanish dissatisfaction with the supposed Francophilism of the Barberini pontificate (a view promulgated by the pasquinades), but also by the many instances of tension between Rome and Paris.[26] By vacillating between two rival

[21] On Urban's neutrality, William Nassau Weech, *Urban VIII: Being the Lothian Prize Essay for 1903* (London: Archibald Constable, 1905), and Fosi, *All'ombra*, 70.

[22] Quoted in Fosi, *All'ombra*, 85. See also ibid., 89.

[23] Lutz, "Urbano VIII," 304–05.

[24] Cf. Fosi, *All'ombra*, 91; and Lutz, "Urbano VIII," 305.

[25] Such an approach was advocated by Gabriel Naudé; see Alberto Merola, "Richelieu, Mazzarino, e le *Considérations politiques* di Naudé," in Alberto Merola, Giovanni Muto, Elena Valeri, and Maria Antonietta Visceglia, eds. *Storia sociale e politica: omaggio a Rosario Villari* (Milan: Franco Angeli, 2007), 302–22.

[26] French criticisms are voiced in Leonor d'Estampes de Valençay, *Remonstrance de l'Eglise gallicane a nostre très-sainct père le papa Urbain VIII* (Paris: [s.n.], 1625); and *Libre discours contre la grandeur*

Catholic powers, Urban VIII kept those courts guessing, doubting, and unable to predict his next political move.

NEPOTISM AS GOOD GOVERNMENT

Nepotism was a key tactic in this strategy of alternating favor, yet it was the aspect of the Barberini papacy that early critics identified as its greatest fault. Upon Urban's death, Giacinto Gigli, in the passage quoted earlier, blamed the decline of the Barberini pontificate upon the prominence of the pope's nephews.[27] A similar judgment had been formed by the Venetian correspondent Giambattista Nani already in 1640. According to Ludwig von Pastor, Nani believed that were it not for Urban VIII's "weakness for his relatives, he would have been one of the greatest rulers of his age as a consequence of his irreproachable conduct, his learning, and his political acumen."[28] During the following papacy of Innocent X (1644–55, family name Pamphili), public outcry against the Barberini family led to the formal investigation, beginning in the summer of 1645, of their handling of papal finances during the War of Castro. In this inimical climate, Antonio Barberini *iunior* felt compelled to seek asylum in Mazarin's France. Following the curia's sequestration of Barberini assets in December of 1645, Antonio's brothers, Francesco and Taddeo, also fled to France.[29] Yet there was soon evidence of a changed attitude toward the Barberini: within three years, Francesco Barberini was back in Rome.[30] Then, in July of 1653, Antonio, too, was welcomed back to Rome following the family's exoneration of all charges and the sealing of their alliance with the Pamphili through the marriage of the grand-nephew of Urban to the grand-niece of Innocent X.[31]

When Maffeo Barberini was elected pope, nepotism was a long-established papal practice. Though the 1567 constitution *Admonet nos* had

---

et puissance temporelle du pape: pour la deffence de nostre roy très chrestien, & des libertez de l'Eglise gallicane (Paris?: s.n., 1626?). Tensions culminated in 1642, when Richelieu was blamed for instigating the Farnese rebellion, and the French ambassador left Rome in protest over Portuguese matters; see Gigli, *Diario*, I, 372–73. On the strained relations between the Barberini and France after Urban's death, see Gigli, *Diario*, II, 434; and Olivier Poncet, "The Cardinal-Protectors of the Crowns in the Roman Curia during the First Half of the Seventeenth Century: The Case of France," in Signorotto and Visceglia, eds., *Court and Politics in Papal Rome*, 165–66.

[27] Gigli, *Diario*, I, 425.
[28] Pastor, *Storia dei papi*, XIII, 899.
[29] Ibid., XIV, 41–43.
[30] Ibid., XIV, 50–51. Taddeo died in exile.
[31] Gigli, *Diario*, II, 681–85. Maffeo di Taddeo Barberini (1631–85) married Olimpia Giustiniani (1641–1729) in 1653.

curtailed the abusive aspects of so-called *grande nepotismo*, the cardinal-nephew position had continued under *piccolo nepotismo* to gain importance, becoming in effect an "official alter-ego" of the pope under the reign of Paul V (1605–21).[32] *Piccolo nepotismo* would not have been tolerated for as long as it was (its repression began only in 1679 under Innocent XI) had it not presented at least some pragmatic benefits to contrast with its extraordinary drain on finances.[33] Antonio Menniti Ippolito has described two such benefits: first, the direction of largesse toward a pope's own family upheld the dignity of his throne, and second, the nomination of papal nephews to high ranks within the curia enabled a pope to trust those who helped him govern.[34] For a large portion of Urban's pontificate, the Roman public considered the papal nephews to have governed local affairs successfully, especially during the period when plague and war threatened the city (1629–34).[35] The fact that contemporaries later seized upon Urban's *piccolo nepotismo* as a cause of his downfall suggests that there was something discernibly different about Urban's nepotism in comparison to that which prevailed in previous papacies.

One notable characteristic of Barberini nepotism involved cardinal protectorships; in particular, Urban VIII seems to have appreciated how the nomination of a cardinal nephew to these positions could (under certain circumstances) insulate the papal throne from the factionalism of European politics and, at the same time, enhance the general power of his family.[36] Also contributing to these aims was Urban's parallel tactic of bestowing as many of the curial offices as possible upon his two nephews, Francesco Barberini (1597–1679) and Antonio Barberini (1607–71).[37] Several of those offices were partisan in nature, as were the cardinal protectorships; thus, with these delicate roles concentrated in the hands of those whom he trusted, Urban was in a position to reclaim the papacy's status as an institution *super partes*. There were drawbacks to this nepotistic arrangement. For instance, it was expected that Urban's nephews would incur enmity as a result of the partisan roles they were taking on. Indeed,

---

[32] Poncet, "The Cardinal-Protectors," 160. See also Antonio Menniti Ippolito, *Il tramonto della curia nepotista: papi, nipoti e burocrazia curiale tra XVI e XVII secolo* (Rome: Viella, 1999), 16, 46, 72–73.

[33] On the abolition of *piccolo nepotismo* in 1692, see Menniti Ippolito, *Il tramonto*, 16. The costs of Urban VIII's nepotism were calculated in 1638 and 1642 at 100,000 scudi annually, plus an additional 595,000 scudi over seventeen years for the purchase of titles and territories. Ibid., 75–79.

[34] Menniti Ippolito, *Il tramonto*, 15–17, 77, 82.

[35] See Gigli, *Diario*, I, 248. See also Fosi, *All'ombra*, 104.

[36] Rough precedents – albeit limited and (therefore) not entirely successful – could be found under the Aldobrandini and Borghese pontificates. Poncet, "The Cardinal-Protectors," 170–71.

[37] See Gigli, *Diario*, I, 225, 236, 309. See also Menniti Ippolito, *Il tramonto*, 44.

this point was later invoked to justify the wealth they had acquired from the papal coffers, with the argument that they deserved an indemnity against the opponents they had acquired in the course of service to the papal throne.[38]

Following the failure of Barberini diplomacy with the Peace of Monzón, Francesco Barberini assumed the burden of multiple partisan roles, acting from 1626 as cardinal protector of Sicily, Aragon, and Portugal (three of the six total Spanish protectorships) as well as cardinal protector of the Catholics of England, Scotland, and Switzerland.[39] Beginning in 1628, Francesco was also serving as superintendent of the Holy See, with duties and powers that later pontiffs would largely consign to the pontifical secretary of state.[40] Thus Francesco had inherited the conundrum that formerly was Urban's: unable to operate with strict impartiality yet unwilling to alienate either France or the Habsburgs, he distributed his favor episodically to achieve a semblance of balance.[41] This balance became more imperative when the pope undertook to groom Francesco for papal candidacy in the eventuality of his own death, an ambition which required Francesco to appear as unbiased as possible so as to avoid being blocked by a *jus exclusivae* veto in the next conclave.[42]

A way out of this bind presented itself when the *brevet* of co-protector of France was offered to Antonio Barberini *iunior* in September of 1633. An *avviso* from Rome dated June 23, 1634, recounts the ceremonies surrounding his eventual acceptance of the role, as well as the gift from Louis XIII of a diamond cross in a jeweled case decorated with a miniature painted portrait of the king and a seven-and-a-half-carat diamond. An accompanying letter explained that Antonio's acceptance of these gifts was an acknowledgement of the protection that he and his family had from the French king, who would send armed troops to protect them if necessary. When the gifts and the letter were presented to Antonio, however, he first obtained the permission of his uncle the pope before accepting them, thus

---

[38] See Menniti Ippolito, *Il tramonto*, 78.   [39] Poncet, "The Cardinal-Protectors," 172.

[40] See Menniti Ippolito, *Il tramonto*, 47; and Lutz, "Urbano VIII," 304. Until 1628 the secretary of state Lorenzo Magalotti, Urban VIII's brother-in-law, handled affairs.

[41] Alberto Merola, "Barberini, Francesco," in *Dizionario biografico degli italiani*, 71 vols. (Rome: Istituto della Enciclopedia Italiana, 1960–64), VI, 173–74. Francesco had to convince the French ambassador that his protectorship would not affect papal neutrality; see Poncet, "The Cardinal-Protectors," 172.

[42] Cf. Poncet, "The Cardinal-Protectors," 170, on the case of Cardinal Bentivoglio. For the hope that Francesco would succeed Urban VIII, see Sheila Barker, "Art in a Time of Danger: Urban VIII's Rome and the Plague of 1629–1634," unpublished PhD thesis, Columbia University (2002), 375.

demonstrating Urban's control over his nephews' political alliances.[43] As shown by Olivier Poncet, Francesco was obliged by his brother's impending polarization either to compensate with a strongly Spanish stance (which would have blemished his candidacy in the next conclave) or to renounce the partisan role of crown protector altogether. Two months before the diamond cross was sent to Antonio, Francesco opted for the latter.[44]

Although his nephews held many posts and offices, it was the crown protectorships which enabled Urban to pursue his interests in the arena of European politics without leaving the confines of trust that existed within his own family. After being instructed by the pope privately, Urban's nephews in turn conducted their business with representatives of other courts, who could never be certain of the degree to which the nephew was acting either independently and on the basis of his own considerable authority, or as Urban's transparent alter ego. In these circumstances, foreign agents and ambassadors encountered more difficulty than ever in perceiving the esoteric interests of the Roman court and in pursuing their own.[45] A seventeenth-century visitor described the climate created by Urban's nepotism:

Many ministers get lost in this court because they know where they are but not those whom they are with: when they believe themselves to be dealing with a republic they find it is a monarchy, and like bouncing balls they find themselves tossed from republic to monarchy, and then from monarchy to republic, that is, a republic without a head and a monarchy without counselors.[46]

In consideration of this use of nepotism to mask papal interests and obfuscate the Roman court's power structure, it is possible to understand why Georg Lutz has suggested that the "deficiencies and exaggerations" of the Barberini pontificate ultimately reinforced papal government.[47] Nevertheless, the criticism and enmity it focused on the papal nephews led to drastic changes. After Antonio's *brevet* of protectorship was withdrawn by Mazarin in 1644, papal nephews were never again nominated to protectorships, and, as a collateral consequence of the discontinuation of

---

[43] *Avviso* of June 23, 1634, ASF 4027a, fol. 407.

[44] Poncet, "The Cardinal-Protectors," 174–76, sees Francesco unwittingly forced into this renunciation; here it is recast as a strategy to improve Francesco's *papabilità*. Having renounced the post, Francesco demonstrated his neutrality by his mediations, on which see Rietbergen, *Power and Religion*, 27, 43.

[45] Marzio Bernasconi, *Il cuore irrequieto dei papi: percezione e valutazione ideologica del nepotismo sulla base dei dibattiti curiali del XVII secolo* (Berne: Peter Lang, 2004), 47–56.

[46] Quoted in ibid., 55.

[47] Lutz, "Urbano VIII," 316.

this practice, the role of the pontifical secretary of state was expanded to fill the vacuum left in its wake.[48]

RELUCTANT WARRIOR

Urban famously reproached his nephews for mismanaging the War of Castro, but detractors laid the blame for the instigation of this conflict at the feet of the pope himself, whom they represented as a greedy warmonger.[49] As seen already with regard to Urban's nepotism, the charge of bellicosity was painted with the broadest of brushes in the pasquinades, and likewise a nuanced analysis is needed to determine the degree to which it reflects a more general reception of Urban's performance.

To begin with, it should not be forgotten that the Roman populace had several times over celebrated the Barberini papacy's militant posture with lasting testimonies. The earliest example, commissioned from Bernini by the Roman Senate in 1630, is the monumental marble memorial in the church of Santa Maria in Aracoeli, whose lengthy inscription and sculpted allegories of the terrestrial church militant and (as suggested here) the celestial church militant commemorate the achievements of the pope's deceased brother Carlo Barberini, General of the Church. In a second instance, the Roman Conservatori commissioned from Alessandro Algardi and Bernini a portrait statue (based on an ancient torso) of Carlo Barberini in Julius Caesar's armor, displayed in their palace since 1630. Also in this category is Bernini's marble statue of Urban VIII (Figure 4.1), which, as mentioned at the opening of this chapter, was targeted during the Barberini vacant see; commissioned by the Conservatori, it bears their inscription thanking the pope for "having preserved Rome from pestilence and war, having added the Duchy of Urbino to the Papal States, and having maintained the security of the state in time of greatest need and peril."[50] The early historiography may have been overly influenced by the slogans of the pasquinades, for here we find that Urban's tutelage of the church's temporal interests and his expansion of its territories (as with Urbino, Ferrara, and Medola) is denigrated as overweening personal ambition, and likened to the truculence

---

[48] Poncet, "The Cardinal-Protectors," 175; Menniti Ippolito, *Il tramonto*, 50.

[49] Gigli, *Diario*, I, 364. See such pasquinades as "Urbanus Octavus Pontifex Maximus non Optimus," ASF, MdP 6425, fol. 256: "… tormenta bellica conflavit: armamenta, et Arces extruxit, et artificioso studio bella in Republica Christiana componit …"

[50] On these works, see Rudolph Wittkower, *Bernini: The Sculptor of the Roman Baroque* (Oxford: Phaidon, 1981), 249–50, 258.

4.1 Gian Lorenzo Bernini and workshop, *Pope Urban VIII*, 1635–40.
Palazzo dei Conservatori, Rome.

of Julius II.[51] Beginning with Giacinto DeMaria in 1898, however, modern historians have acknowledged Urban's military preparedness as a prudent means of discouraging Spanish incursions into the church state, and they have framed his territorial conquests within the analogous state-building of other monarchs and republics of his time.[52]

Already during Gregory XV's pontificate, Maffeo Barberini had articulated his conviction that a strong army was key to protecting the papacy's prestige and securing its neutrality, a principle that William Weech associated with "Si vis pacem, para bellum."[53] Apart from his well-known build-up of the church's defenses, beginning with the massive armory underneath the Vatican library, new foundries for making cannons, a new fortress, arsenals at Tivoli and Orvieto, and the fortified ports at Santa Marinella and Civitavecchia, Urban VIII also occasionally adopted a stance that was more minatory than prudent.[54] In 1627, for instance, he had soldiers far flung in Lombardy without any apparent cause, as reported by a traveling Florentine correspondent.[55]

Despite all his shrewd military maneuvering, the success of Urban's early temporal government is overshadowed by the overwhelmingly negative assessment, in both historical times as well as modern, of the War of Castro (1641–44). Seventeenth-century critics charged that it lacked moral justification, and that its true motive was the greed of the Barberini family. More pragmatic, the modern critics decry the incompetent leadership that led to an immense waste of resources without any apparent benefit, pointing out that this war emptied the Vatican of several million scudi, and yet when the Peace of Ferrara was concluded shortly before the pope's death in March of 1644, no net gains had been attained.[56] It will not be possible here to analyze the war that Urban mounted against Duke Odoardo Farnese, who, with French backing, had disrupted the Roman economy by reneging on his debts to the city's largely Hispanophile nobility (ironically, Farnese had employed this money in his campaigns against the

[51] Ferdinando Gregorovius, *Urbano VIII e la sua opposizione alla Spagna e al imperatore* (Rome: Fratelli Bocca, 1879), 5, 128.
[52] Giacinto DeMaria, "La guerra di Castro e la spedizione de' presidii (1639–1649)," *Miscellanea di storia italiana* 35:4 (1898), 191–256, esp. 191–95.
[53] Lutz, "Urbano VIII," 304; Weech, *Urban VIII*, 85.
[54] See Pastor, *Storia dei papi*, XIV, 865–89; and Weech, *Urban VIII*, 134.
[55] Letter of Domenico di Santi Pandolfini, February 10, 1627, ASF, MdP 6108, fol. 1075.
[56] Rietbergen, *Power and Religion*, 10. On the war's cost, see Ulrich Köchli, "Die Krise nach dem Papsttod: Die Barberini zwischen Rom und Frankreich 1644–1654," in Daniel Büchel and Volker Reinhardt, eds., *Modell Rom? Der Kirchenstaat und Italien in der frühen Neuzeit* (Cologne: Böhlau, 2003), 64.

Spanish in Lombardy).[57] It will, however, be suggested that both brands of critic have underestimated the Scylla-and-Charybdis situation through which Urban was forced to navigate.[58]

Pressured to undertake the war by the bilked Roman investors, Urban seemed poised for a swift success in October of 1641, when papal troops took Castro.[59] But in early 1643 it was clear that the victory would be a Pyrrhic one, because Farnese had forged a potent chain of allies (France, Tuscany, and Venice) who supported his vindictive strike against Rome.[60] Such a strike under the French ensign would have obliged the pope to call upon the King of Spain for help, whatever the cost.[61] A victory over Farnese thus promised disaster for Rome. It is little wonder that Urban opted to protract the state of war with minimal means and without making any advances that would have aggravated international tensions, while hoping for diplomatic resolution.[62]

Unaware of the impasse confronting Urban, the Romans grew anxious at the pope's reluctance to pursue his course. Among them was the chronicler Giacinto Gigli, who remarked in September of 1642 on the apparent folly of their leader:

… the Pope, having taken Castro and other places belonging to that state, and the [Farnese] palace and garden in Rome, did not take any further action, and with everyone expecting that he would naturally take the city of Parma, which for many months had been his primary goal, all were now awestruck, and the duke, who in the meantime had struck alliances with the Venetians and the Duke of Modena and others, now grew bold, and began making raids in the papal territories, backed up by 3,000 cavalry and 400 foot soldiers.[63]

By the time the pope realized that he could not outspend his opponent in the maintenance of a ready army, he had already lost the support of the Romans, who resented the new taxes on foodstuffs and the forced collection of silver. Though it was an utter capitulation, the 1644 Peace of Ferrara was seized upon as an opportunity to neutralize mounting international

---

[57] Gigli, *Diario*, I, 365–69. Cf. DeMaria, "La guerra di Castro," 197. Farnese's French support is noted in Gigli, *Diario*, I, 373.

[58] Cf. Rietbergen, *Power and Religion*, 26.

[59] On the shared economic interests of the Barberini and the Roman nobility, see Lutz, "Urbano VIII," 316.

[60] Gigli, *Diario*, I, 391. Cf. DeMaria, "La guerra di Castro," 213; and Rietbergen, *Power and Religion*, 57.

[61] DeMaria, "La guerra di Castro," 205, laid the foundation for this explanation of Urban VIII's dilemma by pointing to the Italian "system of equilibrium" between France and Spain, which caused the pope "continual anxiety."

[62] Cf. Rietbergen, *Power and Religion*, 57.

[63] Gigli, *Diario*, I, 369.

tensions and regain a modicum of public confidence in the last sickly months of the pope's life.[64]

Through hearsay circulating in late 1642, the pope is known to have criticized his nephew Taddeo for bungling his military strategy and misusing funds allotted for conscripting 30,000 soldiers, instead mustering "only" 10,000 of them; Urban also apparently blamed Francesco for hesitating to inform him about Taddeo's failings.[65] But if the hypothesis put forth here is correct, the pope may have been exploiting court gossip to put into circulation the idea that his best intentions had been snared by his wayward nephews – sufficiently piquant gossip to distract his enemies from recognizing that the stalling of his campaign was deliberate, and that Rome could not risk a victory. This explanation that the nephews were the primary reason for the failure of the war was so widely accepted that Urban's successor, Innocent X (1644–55), presumed that an aggressive military campaign was still a viable option for the Holy See in this system of delicate equilibrium between Spanish and French footholds in Italy, and he launched a second War of Castro in 1649.[66] From this circumstance, it can at least be concluded that Urban VIII's botched Italian war had not noticeably tarnished the perception of the military strength of the church state.

PIETY WITHOUT HUMILITY

A number of the pasquinades that appeared after Urban's death charged him with impiety for refusing to direct Vatican funds to the distant war waged by the Holy Roman Emperor, Ferdinand II, against the Protestant armies of the Swedish king, Gustavus II Adolphus.[67] It was left to a German, Ferdinand Gregorovius, to repudiate the charge by reframing the history of that war in a strictly political way, although Lutz has recently raised the question again, claiming that Urban obstructed the goals of the "pure Catholicism" of the Habsburgs.[68] It seems improbable, however,

---

[64] Ibid., I, 392, 398, 417–22.

[65] Ibid., I, 364.

[66] It is noteworthy that, while Innocent X did raze the city of Castro, almost at the same moment French troops swarmed into Campania to aid Masaniello's Neapolitan rebellion, and then made their presence felt in Rome, where rioting and assassination attempts left the papal family in a state of terror.

[67] The charge was surely made by Hispanophile authors, since it echoes the defiant accusation made toward Urban VIII by the Spanish cardinal Gaspar de Borja y Velasco (1584–1645) in March of 1632, on which see Pastor, *Storia dei papi*, XIV, 444–45, 1026–28.

[68] Lutz, "Urbano VIII," 306.

that Urban's contemporaries would have taken seriously the claim that he acted impiously during the Swedish king's campaigns. Urban had fervently and publicly applied his sacerdotal offices to the Catholic cause during that phase of the Thirty Years' War, making three special processions with the Madonna of Santa Maria dell'Anima (the church of the German Empire) and proclaiming in December of 1631 a major jubilee at three basilicas plus Santa Maria dell'Anima "so that people would pray to God for Emperor Ferdinand, besieged by the war against the heretics and the King of Sweden."[69]

Moreover, the pope met the challenge posed by Protestant religious propaganda in the form of German broadsheets portraying Gustavus Adolphus as a providential savior.[70] When Gustavus Adolphus was killed in November of 1632 during the Battle of Lützen, the pope wrote a letter to the emperor in which he represented the recent events in eschatological terms, terms which formerly he had confined to his private correspondence with Tommaso Campanella.[71] His letter began with a recognition of their common victory – "We turn to the Lord God of divine justice, because He has exacted vengeance against the arrogant and has liberated the Catholics from their most inexorable enemy" – but then it directed at the emperor himself a warning that a "terrible God destroys the puffs of ire of the kings of this earth."[72] Urban then began to circulate more widely his eschatological interpretation of events – whereby God was now providentially directing worldly affairs in order to destroy sin and exalt His church – by means of a silver medal minted in 1634 by Ottaviano Raggi.[73] It carried Urban's portrait on the recto, and on the verso was the motto *Vincit Deus* above the image of the Archangel Michael, the warrior angel of Revelation (12:7–9) who conquers Satan in the Armageddon of the final millennium.

Pietro da Cortona began his fresco *Allegory of Divine Providence* (1633–39) at Palazzo Barberini in these very years (Figure 4.2). Here, among emblematic portraits of his relatives, Urban is represented by papal insignia unified with imperial laurels, while through esoteric symbolism the return of the Golden Age is heralded, and Urban VIII

[69] Gigli, *Diario*, I, 212; see also Barker, "Art in a Time," 237.
[70] See John Roger Paas, "The Changing Image of Gustavus Adolphus on German Broadsheets, 1630–3," *Journal of the Warburg and Courtauld Institutes* 59 (1996), 205–44.
[71] See, e.g., letter of Campanella to Urban of April 6, 1628 in Tommaso Campanella, *Lettere*, ed. Vincenzo Spampanato (Bari: G. Laterza e Figli, 1927), 227, no. 57.
[72] Quoted in Pastor, *Storia dei papi*, XIV, 467.
[73] *Avviso* from Rome of February 2, 1634, ASF, MdP 4027a, fol. 315.

4.2 Pietro da Cortona, *Allegory of Divine Providence*, 1633–39. Palazzo Barberini, Rome.

is identified with both the angelic pope and the last world emperor.[74]
The image projects the Barberini pope as the divinely designated
apocalyptic renovator of the world – the great leader who Campanella
predicted would reign at the time of the eclipse of 1630, or just afterward.[75] By means of Girolamo Teti's elaborately illustrated book about
the palace and its decorations, *Aedes Barberinae ad Quirinalem descrip-
tae* (*A Description of the Palazzo Barberini on the Quirinale*, 1642),
Urban's eschatological vision was carried to elite audiences across the
continent.

Despite the success of Cortona's fresco, there is little evidence that any
but the court poets took interest in Urban's apocalyptic tenor.[76] After his
death it was mocked in the pasquinades:

> Finally Urban VIII has died,
> Who deemed his own papacy eternal;
> Chasing this depraved dream while alive
> He's gained a throne infernal.[77]

Urban's successor, Innocent X, refrained from eschatological discourse,
either out of modesty or out of deference to the Spanish crown. However,
the next pope, Alexander VII (1655–67, family name Chigi), would gently
reawaken the expectations of an angelic pope that Urban VIII had raised
against Protestants' Lion of Judah, Gustavus Adolphus; the occasion presented itself with the dramatic conversion and abdication of Gustavus
Adolphus's daughter and heir, Christina of Sweden.[78]

A ROMAN PARNASSUS AND ITS EXILE

The pasquinade about the ravages of Barberini patronage upon the Pan-
theon's bronze beams, "Quod non fecerunt barbari, fecerunt Barberini,"
has been repeated *ad nauseam* ever since.[79] But its derision of the family's

[74] Barker, "Art in a Time," 393–411. Cf. Roberto Rusconi, *Profezia e profeti alla fine del Medioevo* (Rome, Viella: 1999).

[75] Tommaso Campanella, *Articuli prophetales*, ed. Germana Ernst (Florence: La Nuova Italia, 1977), 76–8.

[76] E.g. Gugliemo Dondini, SI, *Orationes duae altera de Christi domini cruciatibus in sacello pontifi- cum vaticano* (Rome: ex typographia haeredum Francisci Corbelletti, 1641).

[77] Undated sonnet, "È pur morto alla fine Urbano ottavo," ASF, MdP 6425, fol. 458.

[78] On the revival of millenarian prophecies during the papacy of Alexander VII, see Peter Burke, "*Donec auferatur luna*: The Façade of S. Maria della Pace," *Journal of the Courtauld and Warburg Institutes* 44 (1981), 238–39.

[79] See Gaetano Bossi, *La pasquinata "Quod non fecerunt barbari fecerunt Barberini"* (Rome: Filiziani, 1898). Bossi attributes it to Carlo Castelli of Modena.

rapacious appropriation of Rome's public treasures and their lack of appreciation of Roman antiquities is more humorous than substantive. Urban
and his nephews systematically patronized poetry, music, science, art,
architecture, *and* archeological preservation, in testimony of their claim
that the Golden Age had returned and that it was centered in Rome.[80]
No longer dressed in the lugubrious and austere costume of the Counter-
Reformation, Rome appeared *briosa*, vibrant, learned, and elegant in the
ornaments fashioned by Bernini and Pietro da Cortona, and by such for-
eign-born artists as Simon Vouet, Valentin de Boulogne, Claude Lorrain,
Nicolas Poussin, and François du Quesnoy.[81] Even if the papacy's universal
character had begun to dissipate in the seventeenth century, Urban VIII's
artistic patronage assured Rome the cultural prestige befitting a world
capital.

The Barberini family's cultural and artistic patronage complemented
the pope's pastoral mission by rendering Rome praiseworthy and fascinating to European élites of almost any confession. Herein was the
motivating force behind the Barberini family's support of a vast network
of international scholarly correspondence and exchange, whose clearing house was, in all effects, the multi-faceted intellect of Cassiano dal
Pozzo, as celebrated in Gabriel Naudé's 1641 *Epigrammata in virorum lit-
eratorum imagines, quas illustrissimus eques Cassianus a Puteo sua in bib-
liotheca dedicavit* (*Epigrams on the Portraits of Men of Letters, which the
Illustrious Cavalier Cassiano dal Pozzo Solemnly Installed in his Library*).
Amplifying the range of this program of cultural outreach were a number
of books consisting of an ekphrastic celebration of Rome's artistic and
literary ferment; by means of these, the virtual image of the city was carried throughout the continent. Some examples include Leone Allacci's
luxurious volume, *Apes Urbanae: sive de viris illustribus, qui ab anno
MDCXXX per totum MDCXXXII* (*Urbane Bees: or, Illustrious Men, from
the Year MDCXXX through MDCXXXII*, 1633), which touts Barberini
Rome's flourishing literary culture. Rome's renovated appearance was
first brought to the attention of Europe's bibliophiles by Pompilio Totti's
1638 publication *Ritratto di Roma moderna* (*Portraits of Modern Rome*).
This was followed in 1644 by Fioravanti Martinelli's *Roma ricercata nel*

---

[80] On Barberini's library, see Rietbergen, *Power and Religion*, 140; On libraries' social importance, Irene Fosi, "La presenza fiorentina a Roma tra Cinque e Seicento," in Büchel and Reinhardt, eds., *Modell Rom?*, 62.

[81] Pastor, *Storia dei papi*, XIII, 911–1000.

suo sito e nella scuola di tutti gli antiquarii (*Rome Examined on Site and in the School of All Antiquarians*).

Such glowing cultural portraits of the papal city were meant to reach Europe's intellectual élites, entice their curiosity, and ultimately bring them into the fold of the Roman bishop, thus complementing the grassroots missionary work carried out in distant lands. The conversion of Lucas Holstenius (1596–1661), who later became librarian to Cardinal Francesco Barberini, was the paradigm for this "high-end proselytism." Even the warm welcome that Cardinal Francesco Barberini offered in 1639 to a traveling Calvinist poet from England, John Milton, can be inserted within this pattern of cultural patronage for religious ends.

Natural philosophy and science had at least a foothold in this program of cultural patronage, as can be seen in Maffeo Barberini's early support of Galileo Galilei, Tommaso Campanella, and the Academy of Linceans. Nevertheless, in recent centuries Urban VIII has generally come to be seen as an opponent rather than a protector of science because of the Holy Office's condemnation of Galileo in 1632, in the midst of his pontificate. Suggestions by various historians over the years that Urban somehow mitigated the consequences of the judgment against the astronomer have done little to soften what has now become the most prevalent criticism of Urban's pontificate.[82]

By contrast, however, the same seventeenth-century pasquinade writers who scoured Urban VIII's pontificate to discover even marginally disputable aspects that could be recast in diabolical terms would pass over the Galileo affair with a surprising silence. They failed to seize upon, for instance, the utter irony by which the early years of Galileo's house-arrest were carried out in a Medici villa whose property adjoined a villa once owned by Maffeo Barberini.[83] Today it is perhaps difficult to comprehend why Urban VIII's contemporaries denounced so resoundingly his supposed lack of piety – a charge they based on his refusal to engage in a pan-

---

[82] The scholarly reassessment of Urban's relationship with Galileo began with Sante Pieralisi, *Urbano 8. e Galileo Galilei; memorie storiche* (Rome: Poliglotta, 1875). It was renewed with Paolo Redondi, *Galileo eretico* (Turin: Einaudi, 1983), and was recently underlined by Ernan McMullin, ed., *The Church and Galileo* (Notre Dame, IN: University of Notre Dame Press, 2005). Also relevant are the essays of Enrica Schettini Piazza, "I Barberini e i Lincei: dalla *mirabile congiuntura* alla fine della prima Accademia (1623–1630)," in Lorenza Mochi Onori, Sebastian Schütze, and Francesco Solinas, eds., *I Barberini e la cultura europea del Seicento* (Rome: De Luca Editori d'Arte, 2007), 117–26; and John Beldon Scott, "Galileo and Urban VIII: Science and Allegory at Palazzo Barberini," in Onori, Schütze, and Solinas, eds., *I Barberini*, 127–36.
[83] Documenting this residence, see the letter of Maffeo Barberini of September 1, 1617, ASF, MdP 6077, fol. 435.

European war – and yet they found no cause for criticism in the fact that Galileo had been condemned under his pontificate. If for no other reason than this surprising circumstance, his reception serves as a benchmark of the alteration that has henceforth taken place in the criteria by which papal performance is judged.

CHAPTER 5

Jansenism versus papal absolutism

Gemma Simmonds

Eight hundred years after the foundation of the monastery of Port-Royal des Champs, from which it emerged, Jansenism continues to be the subject of repeated misrepresentation. Like the word "Puritan," "Jansenist" has become detached from its historical moorings to serve as a catch-all phrase for rigidity, sanctimoniousness, and oppressive religious austerity. Jansenism's admirers depict it as a religiously inspired social and political movement whose espousal of such varied causes as the rights of the lower clergy, the emancipation of slaves, and the restoration of civil status to Jews and Protestants places it in the forefront of social, political, and philosophical radicalism.[1] In terms of ecclesiology, the fostering of stronger roles for the laity and especially women in the church, and the emphasis on the need for a return to original sources in the theological and liturgical field, including the use of the Scriptures and missal in the vernacular, have brought about comparisons with the movements that resulted in the Second Vatican Council.[2] In the seventeenth century both the French crown and the papacy saw Jansenism as a major threat to their increasingly absolutist claims to power. Insofar as Jansenists placed the conscience of the individual and the Augustinian tradition above both hierarchies, they had a point.

Jansenism's claims to represent the pure Augustinian and patristic tradition within the church inevitably led to a crisis in church governance and authority, since the Jansenists and the Port-Royal circle in general cited the biblical and patristic traditions, in which they excelled, over the modern "innovation" of a dominant papal authority. They never called

---

[1] Alexander Sedgwick, *Jansenism in Seventeenth-Century France: Voices from the Wilderness* (Charlottesville: University Press of Virginia, 1977), 201–02.
[2] F. Ellen Weaver, "Liturgy for the Laity: The Jansenist Case for Popular Participation in Worship in the Seventeenth and Eighteenth Centuries," *Studia liturgica* 19 (1989), 47–59. The first recorded case of a celebration of the Mass in French in Jansenist circles was at Versailles in 1794. See also Linda Timmermans, *L'accès des femmes à la culture (1598–1715): un débat d'idées, de Saint François de Sales à la marquise de Lambert* (Paris: Champion, 1993), 14–16, 692–94.

themselves "Jansenists," preferring the name "disciples of St. Augustine." Their crisis of conscience lay in their claim that, in condemning them, the church was condemning St. Augustine and therefore itself. Profound and long-lasting theological dilemmas lay within the controversy, which led to a major and enduring crisis over the changing face of the papacy and papal authority. The prospect of internal dissidence not controlled by the clerical machine raised fears of a hidden enemy within that caused a panic in Rome equal to its hostility to Geneva.[3] The crushing of Port-Royal and the Jansenist movement was the inevitable outcome of an alliance between the French monarchy and the authorities in Rome, both of which saw within this movement the seeds of their own destruction.

The religious quarrels of the Catholic and Protestant reformations found their expression in increasingly divergent interpretations of the doctrines of St. Augustine. Jansenism has undoubtedly come to encapsulate problems of liberty and virtue, in both the theological and secular senses. The relationship between theology and history is vital to any study of the movement and provokes wider questions about themes and theological pressure points that continue to be provocative. Questions of liberty revolve around the primacy of the individual conscience and its relation to authority, whether in terms of belief, governance, or sacramental practice. Questions of virtue ask whether Christianity can exist within a profane secular framework and subject itself to the possibility of a reduction to religious formalism, or if the only viable option for membership of the church in all its Gospel vigor is withdrawal to a sacralized retreat. Such questions are as relevant to the twenty-first century as they were to the seventeenth, as would appear from the rise of religious fundamentalisms across the world in the face of post-modern uncertainties.

One of the most important contributions of Port-Royal to the church of seventeenth-century France lies in the painstaking scholarship that gave ordinary Catholics access to the Scriptures and the Fathers as a source of doctrinal and devotional reflection.[4] Port-Royal spearheaded reforms in biblical and patristic scholarship and in the liturgy which led to widespread criticism that by democratizing theology Jansenism was giving women and ignorant lay people ideas above their station.[5] Jansenism

---

[3] See Jean-Louis Quantin, "Le rêve de la communauté pure: sur le rigorisme comme phénomène européen," in Bernard Cottret, Monique Cottret, and Marie-José Michel, eds., *Jansénisme et puritanisme* (Paris: Nolin, 2002), 169.

[4] Jean-Louis Quantin, *Le catholicisme classique et les Pères de l'église: un retour aux sources (1669–1713)* (Paris: Institut d'Études Augustiniennes, 1999).

[5] Timmermans, *L'accès des femmes à la culture*, 14–16, 674–98, 788–89.

landed on a faultline in the theology of the time concerning grace and nature, which involved theologians in a feud over the relationship between grace and free will that no one could win. The attempt by the pope and his curia, most of them jurists rather than theologians, to resolve the matter by the imposition of silence only raised a further controversy over papal authority, questioning the role of the pope to pronounce on expert matters of theology on which he was no expert. Questions about the sacraments and Christian sources became questions about authority and governance.

A search of the contents of Denzinger's *Enchiridion symbolorum* (*Handbook of Creeds*) reveals that throughout the history of the church there has been a persistent link between legislation on Augustine's teaching and its interpretation and legislation on papal authority in doctrinal matters.[6] Some modern commentators have presented Jansenism as an idea before its time, emphasizing its positive aspects of "an ecclesiology that understood the church in terms of the body of Christ and gave equal value to all the members, a biblical-liturgical spirituality, and a great love of the early church accompanied by serious patristic scholarship."[7]

This discussion of Jansenism will concentrate on the first generation of Jansenists, from when the Abbé de Saint-Cyran, friend of Cornelius Jansen, became spiritual director of Port-Royal in 1633 until the publication of the anti-Jansenist bull *Unigenitus* in 1713. Later Jansenism became such a different movement and involved such a different group of adherents that it cannot be considered in the same framework. Early Jansenism was a movement at the heart of the Catholic Reformation. Jansenism after *Unigenitus*, and the increasingly restrictive legal measures required to enforce it, drove large numbers of otherwise faithful Catholics into positions of opposition to pope and crown which later developed into political and ideological stances that would not have been recognized by Port-Royal's first generation. The nuns and the *Messieurs* who lived in retirement at Port-Royal des Champs called themselves "friends of the truth."[8] The word "truth" and persecution in its cause are a constant theme in the letters of Mère Angélique Arnauld, reforming Abbess of Port-Royal.[9] Attacks on Jansen constituted, for her, an attack on Augustine, on God, and on the church.[10] Jacqueline Pascal, sister of Blaise and a nun of Port-Royal, saw matters in

---

[6] Heinrich Denzinger, *The Sources of Catholic Dogma*, trans. Roy Defferari, 30th edn. (St. Louis: Herder, 1957), 339–40.

[7] F. Ellen Weaver, "Scripture and Liturgy for the Laity: The Jansenist Case for Translation," *Worship* 59 (1985), 510–21, at 510.

[8] Angélique Arnauld, *Lettres*, 4 vols. (Utrecht: Aux Dépens de la Compagnie, 1742), I, 363.

[9] Ibid., I, 292, 483.   [10] Ibid., I, 292.

even starker terms, with the women of Port-Royal taking the place of bishops as guardians of the truth since the bishops had abandoned their vocation: "since our bishops have no more courage than women, women must learn to have the courage of bishops. But if it is not up to us to defend the truth, it is certainly up to us to die for it."[11]

The 1516 concordat, signed by Pope Leo X and François I, made the king effective head of the church in France, placing the nomination of sees and benefices in his right. The assertion of Gallican privileges over Roman authority and the struggle to establish Gallicanism as the predominant model for the French church in opposition to growing post-Tridentine Ultramontanism lies at the heart of many of the undercurrents in the story of Jansenism and its feud against the Society of Jesus.[12] It coincides historically with the emergence of France's national identity. It became common in some church and court circles to perceive the Society of Jesus as a threat to the autonomy of the Gallican Church through its espousal of the papacy as the ultimate authority within the church, whatever the country.

If Jansenism appeared to threaten growing royal absolutism, it was also perceived as a threat to the rising power of the papacy. Antoine Arnauld was the chief theological voice of Port-Royal. The preface to his *On Frequent Communion*, published in 1643, refers to SS. Peter and Paul as "the two heads of the church who make but one whole."[13] Given that the Holy Office had formally issued the decree *De duplici capite ecclesiae* in 1647 condemning such a theory, it needed only this for those hostile to Jansenism to detect a threat to papal authority by declaring Paul and Peter to have equal primacy and advocating a French patriarchate in succession to Paul and in rivalry with Rome.[14]

The Pragmatic Sanction of Bourges, drawn up between the French crown and the papacy in 1438, proclaimed the supremacy of a general council over the pope, restricting his rights and making them effectively subject to the royal will. The decree *Sacrosancta* of the Council of Basel established the "liberties" of the Gallican Church, but with the council's dissolution in 1449 this attempt to make conciliarism the norm in church governance came to grief. The Pragmatic Sanction was replaced by the

[11] See Jacqueline Pascal's letter of June 1661 to Angélique de Saint-Jean on the signing of the formulary in Victor Cousin, *Études sur les femmes illustres et la société du XVIIe siècle: Jacqueline Pascal*, 6th edn. (Paris: Didier, 1877), 325–26. Here and elsewhere in this chapter translations are mine unless otherwise stated.

[12] Nigel Abercrombie, *The Origins of Jansenism* (Oxford: Clarendon Press, 1936), 207.

[13] Antoine Arnauld, *De la fréquente communion* (Paris: Vitré, 1644), preface, 27.

[14] See Abercrombie, *Origins*, 202, and Bruno Neveu, *L'erreur et son juge: remarques sur les censures doctrinales à l'époque moderne* (Naples: Bibliopolis, 1993), 616.

Concordat of Bologna in 1516. The Gallican Church retained a strong independence from Rome and from papal influence in appointments to ecclesiastical office. The Council of Trent succeeded in establishing papal authority firmly over that of the council. This triumph over the conciliarist view of church governance was to have long-lasting repercussions in the Jansenist controversy of the following century.

The quarrel between Jansenists and Jesuits embraced not only the traditional French resistance to excessive papal authority but an ecclesiology which valued the direct relationship between Christ and the individual conscience over any structures of power.[15] Another movement with which Jansenism has been linked is Richerism.[16] This tendency was named after Edmond Richer, a conciliarist who argued against papal supremacy in favor of a church and church property under the unique power of the king. More dangerously, he postulated that the power of the keys rests in the church and not the pope, and that apostolic succession resides as much in the lower clergy as in the bishops. This culminated in a theory of apostolic succession of the clergy, as descendants of the seventy-two disciples sent out into the world by Jesus, in opposition to control by the higher clergy, and lay beneath the Jansenist clergy's acceptance of the revolutionary Civil Constitution in 1790.[17] This theory struck at the heart of episcopal Gallicanism, undermining the *curés'* obedience to pope and prelates and making them autonomous sources of power within their own parishes. The memory of the Wars of Religion made the connection between religious controversy and political subversion a very real fear in the minds of Europe's rulers in the seventeenth century. This identification of Jansenism with heresy and the political and social upheavals it brought in its wake was to cost the Port-Royal circle dearly.

Cornelius Jansen's monumental work *Augustinus* was the main source of reference for Port-Royal's espousal of Augustine as the ultimate source of theological authority. In 1650 the Sorbonne appealed for judgment on five propositions from it that were considered heretical. These were that some of God's precepts are impossible even for just human beings, who

[15] Jacques-M. Grès-Gayer, "Le gallicanisme d'Antoine Arnauld: éléments d'une enquête," *Chroniques de Port-Royal* 44 (1995), 31–51.
[16] See Émile Jacques, *Philippe Cospeau: un ami-ennemi de Richelieu 1571–1646* (Paris: Beauchesne, 1989), 189–94.
[17] See Edmond Préclin, "Edmond Richer (1559–1631): sa vie, son œuvre, le richérisme," *Revue d'histoire moderne* (1930), 241–69, 321–36, but also Viguerie's discussion of opposing theories regarding the Jansenist provenance of the constitution in Jean de Viguerie, *Christianisme et révolution: cinq leçons d'histoire de la Révolution française* (Paris: Nouvelles Éditions Latines, 1986), 73.

lack the grace to make them possible; that fallen human nature cannot resist interior grace; that fallen human nature chooses to do good or evil following interior necessity, but a proper moral choice is made only if free from external constraint; that the Semi-Pelagians argued the necessity of interior grace for all acts including the initial assent of faith, but committed heresy in asserting that the human will has the choice to follow or resist this grace; and that it is Semi-Pelagianism to believe that Christ died for all, thus implying that he died only for the elect and denying the universality of grace. The matter was referred to the General Assembly of the Clergy and sent on again to Rome by eighty-five bishops. The examination lasted two years, and its ten final sessions were presided over by the pope himself, a show of power not lost on the French clergy or court. The pro-Jansenists listed three possible interpretations of the chosen propositions: it might be possible to consider them as tainted with traces of Calvinism, Pelagianism, or a variety of Semi-Pelagianism. If this were true, they were to be rejected. But they could also be interpreted in an orthodox Augustinian light, and this was the interpretation that they petitioned be approved. But in 1653 the bull *Cum Occasione* condemned them as heretical, without demonstrating clearly where in the *Augustinus* they could be found. In its own turn this failure provoked a major crisis of authority which spread to circles hitherto untouched by the Jansenist controversy.

Arnauld and the Jansenists accepted the condemnation and rejected the Five Propositions, but denied that they could be found or were intended in Jansen's book, an interpretation subsequently repudiated by Rome. Arnauld's publication of the *Considerations on the Undertaking*, making it appear that it was the doctrine of St. Augustine himself that was being condemned, followed by another defense of Jansenist ideas, the *Apology for the Holy Fathers of the Church, Defenders of the Grace of Jesus Christ against the Errors which have been Imposed upon Them*, were a gauntlet thrown down in the name of the purity of primitive doctrine against modern interpretations. It is clear from his *Apology for M. Jansénius* that Arnauld canonizes a particular period of church tradition as the acid test for the orthodoxy of later teaching. The interpretation of history also underpins Roman anxieties about Jansenism and its appeal to an ancient authority greater than that of the pope.[18]

---

[18] See Jean Racine, *Abrégé de l'histoire de Port-Royal* (Paris: La Table Ronde, 1994), 95: "The pope, according to the doctrine accepted in France, is only infallible when governing over a council"; and Pascal, *Pensées*, in *Les provinciales, pensées et opuscules divers*, ed. Gérard Ferreyroles and Philippe Sellier (Paris: Librairie Générale Française, 2004), 501; also in *Œuvres complètes*, ed. Louis Lafuma (Paris: Seuil, 1963), 604: "It is now virtually only in France that it is permitted to hold that the council ranks above the pope."

Pascal was a member of the Port-Royal circle. His *Provincial Letters* begin with an assault on the groundless condemnation of the Five Propositions and Arnauld's eviction from the Sorbonne, and a vindication of his doctrinal orthodoxy and thus that of Port-Royal as a whole. In the final two letters, addressed directly to the king's confessor Annat and thus to the king himself, Pascal constructs a vehement and comprehensive denial that Jansenists are heretics in any sense. At the heart of this is not only the particular case of the Five Propositions and their condemnation in *Ad sacram* but the nature of papal authority in matters of fact and doctrine: "knowing well that even the saints and the prophets are open to being surprised." The scientist offers the examples of Galileo and the attempted excommunication by a pope of St. Virgil for believing in the antipodes as proofs that popes can be mistaken in matters of fact, and challenges the Jesuits (and thereby the pope) to a public examination of the *Augustinus* either to prove that it contains errors or to establish that the Jansenists are "without error in points of faith; catholic with regard to the question of right, in the right on the question of fact, and innocent with regard to both."[19]

In 1660 Louis XIV announced his intention to "entirely exterminate Jansenism" for the sake of his conscience, his honor and the good of the state.[20] In 1661 all clergy, religious, and schoolteachers were required to sign the formulary declaring the Five Propositions to be heretical. The nuns and other members of the Port-Royal community tried to protect their consciences by appeal to Arnauld's distinction between "fact" and "right," which agreed that the propositions were heretical but denied that they were, in fact, contained in the *Augustinus*. But in 1664 the new Archbishop of Paris denied the sacraments to the nuns and arrested and imprisoned twelve of them. When four bishops took up the cause of Port-Royal and Clement IX condemned the "Jansenist" translation of the New Testament by the Port-Royal scholar Sacy, the matter escalated into an international conflict with the Gallican liberties of the French church ranged against the growing imperialism of the papacy. It took all the diplomacy of king and pope to avoid schism until the compromise of the "Peace of the Church" was reached in 1668.[21]

There followed a period of apparent calm, a last golden age in which Port-Royal figured as the ancient desert of Thebes, with brilliant solitaries pursuing their studies, nuns living like angels on earth, and all Paris

---

[19] Pascal, *Provinciales*, letter 18, in *Provinciales, pensées et opuscules divers*, 616–17.
[20] René and Suzanne Pillorget, *France baroque, France classique 1589–1715*, 2 vols. (Paris: Laffont, 1995), I, 919–20.
[21] Ibid., I, 923–24.

drawn to the holy simplicity of the liturgies.[22] The spectacular conversions of powerful nobles and the support of literary figures, as well as the publications of Pascal's *Pensées* and Sacy's translation of the Vulgate with commentaries from the Fathers, helped to spread further the influence of Port-Royal.

But Jansenist emphasis on interiority and the autonomy of conscience, coupled with the Richerism implicit in Pasquier Quesnel's *New Testament in French with Moral Reflections on Each Verse*, raised fears of a religiously inspired libertarian movement that were to prove well founded at the end of the next century.[23] Louis XIV gave the death blow to Port-Royal by closing the novitiate, and finally razing it to the ground in 1711. In 1713 he bullied the pope into condemning 101 propositions in Quesnel's *Moral Reflections* in the bull *Unigenitus*. Clerics and parliamentarians rebelled against what appeared to be papal imperialism.[24] The bull raised theological complexities by rendering whole sections of the Catholic population heretical overnight, but more dangerously set the scene for an increasingly strong "political Jansenism" that some see as playing a major role in the French Revolution, the laicization of France, and the ultimate secession of a Jansenist remnant, the "Little Church," from Catholicism in 1871.[25]

It has been argued that while the Jansenists were never heretics in the formal sense, they were pushed into a position of open defiance of church and state authorities by those enemies whose principal task, by whatever means, was to smoke them out into a declaration of open rebellion.[26] If any doctrinal development emerged from the quarrel it was less with reference to the sacraments themselves than to the authority to pronounce on matters of faith and morals and to interpret the true Christian tradition.[27] The notion of an infallibly authoritative voice that could make pronouncements on matters of faith was still in the making, but the disciples of St. Augustine were already pitting patristic authority against that of the pope, so that the definitive break in 1871 between Rome and the Jansenist remnant in Utrecht came as no surprise.[28] At various points in the push to obtain the condemnation of Jansenism in Rome, its enemies

---

[22] Mme. de Sévigné, letter of January 26, 1674, in *Correspondance*, ed. Roger Duchêne, 3 vols. (Paris: Gallimard, 1972), I, 680.

[23] See Edmond Préclin, *Les jansénistes du XVIIIe siècle et la Constitution civile du clergé: le développement du richérisme: sa propagation dans le bas clergé (1713–1791)* (Paris: Gamber, 1929), 1–4.

[24] Pillorget, *France baroque*, I, 1186–88.

[25] Jean-Louis Quantin, "Ces autres qui nous font ce que nous sommes: les jansénistes face à leurs adversaires," *Revue de l'histoire des religions* 212 (1995), 397–417, at 400, 406–07.

[26] Quantin, "Ces autres," 398–99. [27] Ibid., 408.

[28] Quantin, *Catholicisme*, 17, 97–98.

tried to imply that papal pronouncements on the doctrines of Baius or
Jansen carried the obligation of obedience to dogmatic truths.[29] It was a
suggestion that Arnauld was to resist vigorously: "The church would be
courting an unimaginable danger, were it to be permitted for popes to
set themselves up as prophets, pronouncing judgment on every matter
with an infallibility based on enthusiasm."[30] The Jansenists perceived the
Ultramontanist agenda as a modern assault on the eternal truths of orthodox doctrine, lying unassailably within the patristic tradition, while their
enemies attacked as "novelties" the desire for a radical return to the past.[31]

The *Decree of Gelasius* stated that the writings of the Fathers were to
be received as authoritative and not contradicted by one iota.[32] Implicit
in Port-Royal's exaltation of the primitive Christian past was a critique of
certain moral, pastoral, and liturgical aspects of the church of its time. It
became clear that what was in fact at stake was the relationship between
tradition and the magisterium.[33] Moderates argued that in preaching
against the abuses of their times or arguing against heretics, the Fathers
were prone to rhetorical exaggeration that should not be translated into
practical contexts. In the face of differing interpretations of patristic texts,
the authority of the church was more reliable than de-contextualized arguments which their own authors were compelled on occasion to re-explain
or retract, and the vitality of the church lay in more than the exact preservation of its memories.[34]

Both sides in the quarrel took as their model Vincent of Lérins's
Commonitorium.[35] Vincent's criterion for orthodoxy, "what has been
believed everywhere, always and by all," was enthusiastically espoused in
the Tridentine cause by friends and foes of Jansen.[36] What was left open
here was the question as to who might provide an authoritative interpretation of the Fathers, whose works were even more open to multiple

[29] Lucien Ceyssens, "Le Cardinal Jean Bona et le Jansénisme," *Benedictina* 10 (1956), 79–119, at
94–95, 267–327.
[30] Arnauld, letter to anon., January 1664, in *Œuvres complètes*, 42 vols. (Paris: Sigismond d'Arnay,
1775–82), I, 462.
[31] See Pascal, *Pensées*, in *Provinciales, pensées et opuscules divers*, 317; *Œuvres complètes*, 285.
[32] Denzinger, *Sources*, 69 (165).
[33] Bruno Neveu, "Augustinisme janséniste et magistère romain," *XVIIe siècle* 135 (1982), 91–209, at
194–95.
[34] Hervé Savon, "L'argument patristique dans la querelle de la fréquente Communion," *Chroniques
de Port-Royal* 44 (1995), 88–92.
[35] See Quantin, "Fathers," III, 951–86, at 961.
[36] Vincent of Lérins, *Commonitorium*, ed. Reginald Stewart Moxon (Cambridge: Cambridge
University Press, 1915), ch. 2, section 3, lines 6–7. See also Pierre Magnard, "La tradition chez
Bossuet et chez Richard Simon," in Jean-Pierre Collinet and Thérèse Goyet, eds., *Journées Bossuet:
la prédication au XVIIe siècle* (Paris: Nizet, 1980), 375–87 at 384.

understandings than Scripture itself.[37] In the *Augustinus*, in which Jansen effectively subordinates the authority of the church to that of Augustine by claiming that the doctrine of Augustine is that of the church, any rejection of the doctor of grace becomes a rejection of the church itself. Vincent of Lérins's criteria for judging the orthodoxy of a doctrine were applied without exception to the works of Augustine, thus transferring to his person those marks of orthodoxy that after Trent were applied to the church itself. In Arnauld's judgment, support for the infallibility of the pope that overrode the consent of the universal church or council was a denial of the unbroken tradition of the Church, "allowing a man to reign over the truth is to put him in the place of God."[38] It is ironic that anti-Jansenist fears proved a self-fulfilling prophecy, as the gathering profusion of formularies forced otherwise orthodox Catholics into just the sort of entrenched resistance that they were intended to root out.[39]

The Jansenist party was in no doubt that papal pretensions to divinely inspired doctrinal authority posed a grave threat to the church and stood in direct contradiction to the patristic tradition.[40] The eventual publication of the bull condemning the Five Propositions, implicitly claiming infallible judgment on a doctrinal matter in the teeth of Gallican opposition, was accompanied by public prayers and the striking of a medal with the pope's portrait on one side and an image of the Holy Spirit on the other with the words "He renews the face of the earth."

For Arnauld the only true doctrinal authority was that of the competent theologian, "who is not given to the church ... in order to submit slavishly to the enlightenment of others, but to judge matters according to the light which God has given him."[41] The Four Gallican Articles of 1682 confronted papal claims to ultimate authority with a "tradition of the church" firmly established by historical criticism and the example of the African church under Cyprian and Augustine, in which bishops and councils decided on matters of faith, on an equal footing with Rome.[42] The notion of episcopal collegiality, so foundational to the concept of church put forward by Vatican II, was at the heart of Arnauld's ecclesiology. His notion of episcopal autonomy comes alongside a high regard for councils,

---

[37] Yves M.-J. Congar, *La tradition et les traditions*, I: *Essai historique* (Paris: Fayard, 1960), 254–55.

[38] Arnauld, letter to Singlin, September 1, 1663, quoted in *Œuvres*, I, 410. See also his letter to Du Vaucel, October 9, 1686, *Œuvres*, II, 722–30.

[39] Quantin, "Ces autres," 397, 407–08.

[40] Arnauld, letter to M. d'Angers, January 1664, quoted in *Œuvres*, I, 462.

[41] Arnauld, letter to Singlin, September 13–22, 1663, quoted in *Œuvres*, I, 435.

[42] See entries on *Quatre articles* and *Libertés de l'église gallicane* in Pillorget, *France baroque*, II, 964–65, 656–69.

both national and universal, as a source of doctrinal authority over against papal and state power.

The translation of the Scriptures and the reform of the liturgy played a key part in promoting full participation of the church of the laity in an ecclesiology that would find later echoes in Vatican II's Dogmatic Constitution on the church, *Lumen gentium*. Within Arnauld's passion for the pursuit of truth lay also the notion of the freedom of the theologian to exercise his reason and his conscience, submitting not to authority for authority's sake, but to truth, and to authority insofar as it proves to be the guardian of the truth.[43] Jansen's followers clamored for an examination of his accuracy by lay experts, a demand directly challenging the Tridentine concept of privileged papal inspiration in matters of governance and doctrinal truth. The determination of truth being a matter of competence rather than of charism, Arnauld and the Port-Royalists had justifiably little faith in the theological acumen to be found in the Vatican and in papal attitudes to scholars who were not part of the Vatican apparatus. Foreshadowing Vatican II's teaching on the *sensus fidelium*, Arnauld implied that Christians are called not merely to obey ecclesial authorities but to participate also in the pursuit and exposition of doctrinal truth.[44] Yves Congar, a major theologian behind Vatican II, offers a detailed analysis of what was at stake in the censure of the Five Propositions.[45] Implicit in the quarrels over the *Augustinus* and the proliferation of papal bulls that followed were rival claims about who has the authority to establish what is the historically authentic, dogmatically orthodox deposit of faith, handed down via the Scriptures by the apostolic church and the Fathers.

Jansenist enthusiasm for the use of the Scriptures and even, with the exception of the prayers of consecration, the celebration of Mass in the vernacular, the promotion of lay participation in the liturgy, including praying the breviary, and the reading of the canon of the Mass aloud appears both as part of their "primitivism" and as an aspect of the Gallican–Ultramontanist conflict that had political as well as religious implications.[46] The *Regulae indicis* which preceded the *Index librorum prohibitorum* (Index of Forbidden Books) laid out the Tridentine position

---

[43] Arnauld, letter to M.N., June 9, 1661, quoted in *Œuvres*, III, 250 and letter to Du Vaucel, October 5, 1691, *Œuvres*, III, 388.
[44] Grès-Gayer, "Gallicanisme," 38–40.
[45] Yves Congar, *Sainte église* (Paris: Cerf, 1963), 357–73.
[46] See Bernard Chédozeau, *La Bible et la liturgie en français: l'Église tridentine et les traductions bibliques et liturgiques (1600–1789)* (Paris: Cerf, 1990), 123.

on access to the Scriptures for the laity in Rule IV. Favoring the oral tradition, whereby faith through hearing is transmitted from person to person, it stressed that readers should have the capacity to interpret the Bible, as understood according to Catholic tradition, and that this capacity should have been verified by a qualified cleric.[47] Arnauld, echoing Chrysostom, argued that the simple faithful should have a voice in the church and have as much access as possible to the sources of Christian doctrine and holiness.[48] He criticized the papal ban on vernacular translations of the breviary, adding to this critique a comprehensive rejection of the Index and the very notion of forbidding books.

The years 1660–1708 marked the golden era of biblical translation in Port-Royal. In the face of Trent's support for the Latin Vulgate as the authoritative version of the Bible, the laymen of Port-Royal translated directly from the Greek and the Hebrew, producing erudite patristically inspired biblical commentaries, concordances, and histories and the famous *Bible de Sacy,* emphasizing Augustine's pre-eminence as an interpreter of Scripture.[49] Such gestures challenged the clerical hegemony of Trent to an extent that unnerved even the Gallicans among French bishops and theologians.[50] Arnauld's insistence on making the Bible available to all was vindicated in 1757 by a brief of Benedict XIV liberalizing the ban on biblical translation. From his exile in the Netherlands, Arnauld wrote several defenses of the translation of Scriptures, patristic, and liturgical texts, arguing repeatedly, among other points, that it enabled women to have access to these cornerstones of Christian life.[51]

The reform of the liturgy became another power struggle between Port-Royal and Rome. By the mid-seventeenth century, most of the dioceses of France had adopted as normative the Roman missal and breviary of Pius V, but though much reduced, local diocesan usages were jealously guarded, with some clergy refusing outright the imposition

[47] Ibid., 25–29, and Bernard Chédozeau, "Les grandes étapes de la publication de la Bible catholique française," in Jean-Robert Armogathe, ed., *Le grand siècle et la Bible*, VI (Paris: Beauchesne, 1989), 341–60, at 346, 359.

[48] Arnauld, letters to Du Vaucel, October 5 and 12, 1691, quoted in *Œuvres*, III, 388–90.

[49] Bernard Chédozeau, "La publication de l'Écriture par Port-Royal. Première partie: 1653–1669," *Chroniques de Port-Royal* 33 (1984), 35–42, and Bernard Chédozeau, "La publication de l'Écriture par Port-Royal. Deuxième partie: 1672–1693," *Chroniques de Port-Royal* 35 (1986), 195–203.

[50] Chédozeau, "Grandes étapes," 349–50, and Jean Lesaulnier, "Les hébraïsants de Port-Royal," *Chroniques de Port-Royal* 53 (2004), 35–41.

[51] "Défense des versions de' l'Écriture sainte, des offices de l'église et des ouvrages des Pères, et en particulier de la nouvelle traduction du bréviaire, contre la sentence de l'Official de Paris du 10 avril 1688," in Arnauld, *Œuvres*, VIII, 245–54, 684–86: "it is an intolerable error to claim that it is proper to prevent women from reading Scripture simply because they are women."

of Roman reforms on a liturgy originally approved by Charlemagne.[52] The Office of Port-Royal, a translation of the breviary, was inspired by a radicalized Tridentine determination to cleanse the breviary and missal of fanciful medieval accretions in favor of historical realities and the simplicity of the primitive church.[53] It aimed at giving the laity, like the clergy, access to the prayer of the church.[54] In both its preference for the Hebrew text of the Psalms and its encouragement of laity to participate in a prayer generally reserved for priests and religious, it raised a storm of protest.[55] Emphasis on local authority under the patristic flag was not exclusive to Jansenism. The 1685 revision by the anti-Jansenist Archbishop of Paris of the heavily Romanized version of the Paris missal introduced by his predecessor replaces a prayer on the feast of St. Peter referring to Peter holding in person the keys to the kingdom with a reference to a passage from Augustine, where Peter is considered as a symbol for the whole church.[56]

Joseph Voisin's four-volume bilingual missal of 1660, intended to promote greater understanding of and participation in the Mass by the laity, was perceived in Rome as a Jansenist-inspired challenge to the decrees of Trent. A ban by papal decree did little to prevent the missal's huge success, despite its being placed on the Index, where it remained until 1897, and the pope's threat to excommunicate automatically all those involved in producing or using it. In subsequent centuries, several similar attempts were made to combine reform of the liturgy and greater local autonomy in church governance, but this would not come to fruition until Vatican II. Jansenist polemic against "indiscreet" Marian devotion raises an inevitable connection between Jansenist resistance to implicit papal infallibility and Jansenist opposition to the official proclamation of Marian dogmas in the nineteenth century.[57] Pasquier Quesnel's *Moral Reflections* on Sacy's 1665 translation of the New Testament precipitated the bull *Unigenitus* in 1713 and with it the appellant crisis, where bishops, religious, and clergy who appealed against *Unigenitus* and called for

---

[52] Henri Leclercq, "Liturgies néo-gallicanes," in F. Cabrol, ed., *Dictionnaire d'archéologie chrétienne et de liturgie* (Paris: Letouzey et Ané, 1907), IX:2, cols. 1636–729.

[53] See Pascal, *Provinciales*, letter 9, in *Provinciales, pensées et opuscules divers*, 402–04, and Philippe Sellier, *Pascal et la liturgie* (Paris: Presses Universitaires de France, 1966), 92–97.

[54] Nicolas Le Tourneux, *L'office de l'église en latin et en françois contenant l'office des dimanches et des fêtes* (Paris: Le Petit, 1650).

[55] Bernard Chédozeau, *La Bible et la liturgie en français: l'Église tridentine et les traductions bibliques et liturgiques (1600–1789)* (Paris: Cerf, 1990), 117–23.

[56] See Maurice Fréchard, "L'année liturgique dans la liturgie de Paris sous Louis XIV," *La Maison-Dieu* 148 (1981), 123–33.

[57] See Quantin, *Catholicisme*, 503–13.

a general council of the church to arbitrate the matter found themselves fighting a pitched battle on ecclesiological grounds. Owen Chadwick, commenting on the devastating and wide-ranging effects of *Unigenitus*, says:

All the Augustinian doctrines of grace were condemned ... No longer would there be place in the Catholic church for men who thought with Augustine or Aquinas, let alone with Jansen or Luther, if the bull were received at its face value ... The bull released the worst controversy of the eighteenth century; dividing France, troubling Catholic authority, distressing consciences, causing schism within universities, discrediting the authority of the French kings and fostering the power of French unbelief.

Chadwick lays at the door of *Unigenitus* the turning of a controversy of theology into one of jurisdiction with, as a direct consequence, a Europe-wide debate on papal infallibility.[58]

It was the Jansenists' tragedy that they concentrated their claims to exclusive authenticity as interpreters of Augustine on the most extreme expressions of his doctrine of grace. There are significant differences between the tone of the early works after his conversion and that of the *Confessions*.[59] In the thirty years that lay between *On Freedom of the Will* and *On Grace and Free Will* Augustine moved from considerations of the workings of grace and free will to reflections on predestination and the effects of original sin, changing tone and emphasis and giving rise to opposing interpretations of his work in subsequent generations.[60]

For the Jansenists Augustinianism stood as what Gadamer terms a "classic," something that continues down the generations to occupy a central place in thought and "conversation" between the historical context of a text and the contemporary context of its interpreter, working out the dialectic between tradition and understanding in a "fusion of horizons."[61] Modern theologians like David Tracy have developed and sometimes challenged Gadamer's hermeneutical theory, suggesting that if texts are to claim this "classical" status, there can be no definitive interpretation that would effectively close their history.[62] No such theory operated in the seventeenth century, so the drama of the disciples of St. Augustine lay

[58] Owen Chadwick, *A History of the Popes* 1830–1914 (Oxford: Oxford University Press, 2003), 281–84.
[59] Peter Brown, *Augustine of Hippo* (London: Faber and Faber, 1967), 146–57.
[60] André Mandouze, *Saint Augustin: l'aventure de la raison et de la grâce* (Paris: Études Augustiniennes, 1968), 432–44.
[61] Hans-Georg Gadamer, *Truth and Method* (New York: Crossroad, 1975), 256, 267–70.
[62] David Tracy, *The Analogical Imagination: Christian Theology and the Culture of Pluralism* (New York: Crossroad, 1981), 73–75, 135–37 n. 8, n. 16, 115–24.

in being confronted with two apparently incompatible claims to absolute authority, those of tradition and of the papacy.[63]

In his book on the Reformation, Diarmaid MacCulloch observes: "The issues of authority which Jansenism raised are still those that threaten to blow apart the modern Roman Catholic Church. That is reflected in the call back to a vision of papal monarchy, away from the conciliarism of the Second Vatican Council, sounded by Pope John Paul II from 1978."[64] The dominant centralism of the present papacy is a recent phenomenon in church history, making it difficult to enter into the mindset of earlier times when claims to sovereign authority were not met with universal assent among Catholics.[65] France was one of the originators of the late medieval and early modern conciliarist movements, rejecting the Council of Florence's definition of papal power in reaction to the pontifical absolutism increasing since the thirteenth century, and the conciliarist tradition that is constitutive of the very identity of Gallicanism.[66] The implementation of Tridentine reforms in France was largely subject to the hostility or enthusiasm of individual French bishops, who recognized some of the abuses at home, but laid the blame for clerical abuses at Rome's door.[67] The nearer the council came to supporting Gallican preoccupations, the more likely its reforms were to be implemented.[68] The King and bishops of France often had recourse to the principle of reception; French bishops had a strong sense of their status as part of the teaching apparatus of the church and thus received papal decisions in terms of judgment, their consent being an act of authority congruent with their position as doctors of the church.[69]

Chadwick gives a comprehensive list of Jansenism's achievements by the nineteenth century: stronger parish and congregational life, better education of priests, better work in schools, a more congregational liturgy, a love of early Christianity, simplicity, and the Bible, and "the renewal of a quest for the authentic and innermost meaning of Catholicism."[70] The

[63] Richard Gaillardetz, "The Reception of Doctrine: New Perspectives," in Bernard Hoose, ed., *Authority in the Roman Catholic Church: Theory and Practice* (Aldershot: Ashgate, 2002), 95–114, at 100–02.

[64] Diarmaid MacCulloch, *Reformation: Europe's House Divided 1490–1700* (London: Penguin, 2004).

[65] Francis Oakley, *The Conciliarist Tradition: Constitutionalism in the Catholic Church, 1300–1870* (Oxford: Oxford University Press, 2003), 3.

[66] Alain Tallon, *La France et le Concile de Trente (1518–1563)* (Rome: École Française de Rome, 1997), 424, 780.

[67] Ibid., 696–705.

[68] Ibid., 798–807.

[69] Yves Congar, *Église et papauté* (Paris: Cerf, 1994), 249–50.

[70] Chadwick, *A History of the Popes*, 612.

nineteenth century gave names such as "Gallicanism," "Richerism," and "Febronianism" to ideologies connected with Jansenism that have at heart one and the same conciliarist tradition.[71] Saint-Cyran was accused of leading his followers to reject the validity of Trent. Parallel anxieties about the validity of the council that defined papal infallibility were addressed by a number of French bishops to the French prime minister in 1870. The famous remark "I am tradition," attributed to Pius IX, is said to have been circulated by French anti-infallibilist bishops.[72] A number of them left Rome rather than be present at the declaration, although most eventually submitted to it, despite considerable misgiving or restriction of meaning, on the grounds that according to the principle of reception the dogma had been accepted by the majority of the church.[73]

In 1415 the fifth session of the Council of Constance declared in the canon *Sacrosancta* that the pope is subject to the council in matters of faith and the reform of the church in head and members, and that councils should be held on a regular basis. This council was removed from the list of legitimate councils of the church. In the decree *Pastor aeternus* of 1870, which defined papal infallibility, Gallicanism and the remnant of Jansenism received their death blow with the insertion of the phrase that papal definitions are irreformable "of themselves, and not through the consensus of the Church."[74] The present-day "Gallican Catholic Church of France" was founded in 1883 in strenuous opposition to Vatican I's pronouncement of the doctrine of papal infallibility. Permitting married priests and bishops, the feminine diaconate, the remarriage of divorced persons, and freedom in matters of fasting and abstinence, while rejecting obligatory confession, it is a far cry from Port-Royal. Arnauld and Saint-Cyran might warm to the idea of the participation of the faithful in the government of the church, and even the election of bishops by the clergy and faithful, but they would certainly be bemused by the monthly Mass for animals where retired television stars and pretenders to the throne of France are joined in church by an assortment of llamas, Pekingese dogs, Siamese cats, and guinea pigs.[75] There are several fringe movements and

---

[71] August Hasler, *How the Pope Became Infallible: Pius IX and the Politics of Persuasion*, trans. Peter Heinegg (Garden City, NY: Doubleday, 1981), 167–70.

[72] Ibid., 338–40, but see also Congar, *Église et papauté*, 241–42. Hasler's work has been severely criticized, and even accused of being based on Nazi propaganda. Arguments about papal infallibility appear to admit of little moderation to this day.

[73] Ibid., 131–40, 221–23, and Congar, *Église et papauté*, 235–36.

[74] See Hugh Lawrence, "Spiritual Authority and Governance: A Historical Perspective," in Hoose, ed., *Authority in the Roman Catholic Church*, 50–52.

[75] See article and photograph of the Mass (and animals) in the Église Catholique Gallicane de Ste. Rita, Paris, at www.frenchtoutou.com/actualité/reportage8.htm (last accessed February 1, 2010).

sects which trace their origin to Jansenism and whose beliefs and practices tend toward the bizarre and esoteric, but the underlying theological questions which gave rise to the movement are part of the ever-present tensions within Christianity itself.[76]

A modern French scholar describes Jansenism as initially a theological movement, concerned with the doctrine of grace, which "increasingly became an ecclesiology of authority within the church and a ritual for worship. The question was one of how authority should be exercised and how participation in the church should take place."[77] The challenge of "the truth," in this case appropriate participation in church membership and practice, has not disappeared. The time has surely come, however, to give Port-Royal its due. If its interpretation of Augustine was exaggerated and seriously flawed, its insistence on patristic and biblical scholarship laid the foundations for a renewal of Catholicism in the light of long-ignored historical sources. If its assertion of episcopal independence was in some instances questionable, its understanding of the roles of laity, priests, and bishops and their relationship to the papacy harmonizes with the principle of subsidiarity that inspired the reforming conciliar documents of Vatican II, even if subsidiarity failed to have much effect on post-conciliar practice.

Questions about doctrinal authority and ecclesial governance were a central part of the Jansenist and Gallican heritage and resurfaced at the time of both Vatican I and Vatican II.[78] Jansenism can legitimately be viewed, within certain limits, as a thwarted movement for reform, some of whose aspects came to fruition only in Vatican II.

---

[76] Jean-Pierre Chantin, "Les jansénismes tardifs dans la France du XIXe siècle: réflexions et pistes de recherches," *Chroniques de Port-Royal* 54 (2005), 325–37. See also Chantin's interview of 2003 with Bernard Callebat, *Pérennité du mouvement anticoncordataire: deux siècles plus tard, les fidèles de la "Petite Eglise" persévèrent*, at http://religioscope.info/article_231.shtml (last accessed February 1, 2010).

[77] Léo Hamon, ed., *Du jansénisme à la laïcité: le jansénisme et les origines de la déchristianisation* (Paris: Éditions de la Maison des Sciences de l'Homme, 1983), 227.

[78] Jean-Louis Quantin, "The Fathers in Seventeenth-Century Roman Catholic Theology," in Irena Backus, ed., *The Reception of the Church Fathers in the West: From the Carolingians to the Maurists*, 2 vols. (Leiden: Brill, 1997), II, 978–84.

CHAPTER 6

Pius VII: moderation in an age of revolution and reaction

Thomas Worcester

INTRODUCTION

Pius VII was elected pope in 1800, at the end of a century that had seen the papacy challenged by Jansenists, by Gallicans, and by Catholic monarchs; by Enlightenment *philosophes*, and by the French Revolution. But before turning to Pius VII himself, it may be useful to recall briefly the challenges to the papacy that stand out in the later seventeenth century and the eighteenth century. As Gemma Simmonds shows in Chapter 5, Jansenists, taking their initial inspiration from Cornelius Jansen's work on St. Augustine, had emphasized the authority of the Fathers; they had also sought, most especially, to place the authority of Augustine above that of early modern popes. Jansenists appealed not only to patristic authorities such as Augustine, but to the rights of individual conscience, and to the authority of church councils over and against papal claims to supreme and universal authority in matters of doctrine. Pope Clement XI's 1713 bull *Unigenitus* condemned 101 propositions from the works of the Jansenist Pasquier Quesnel. Negative reception of *Unigenitus* was widespread, and was expressed largely through appeals for a future council to have the last word.[1]

Thus, increasingly, conciliarism and Jansenism went hand in hand. The Four Gallican Articles, adopted by the assembly of French bishops in 1682, had been a reaffirmation of longstanding conciliar and royalist ecclesiology. Among the points made in the four articles are these: popes have no temporal authority over kings; and the pope's authority in spiritual matters is not irreformable and may be corrected by a council.[2] The Gallican

---

[1] Favorable reception of *Unigenitus* was, however, not restricted to Jesuits and their sympathizers; see Toon Quaghebeur, "The Reception of *Unigenitus* in the Faculty of Theology at Louvain, 1713–1719," *Catholic Historical Review* 93 (2007), 265–99.

[2] See text reproduced in Klaus Schatz, *Papal Primacy: From its Origins to the Present*, trans. John A. Otto and Linda M. Maloney (Collegeville, MN: Liturgical Press, 1996), 188–89.

articles explicitly mentioned the Council of Constance, the council that had clearly stood above the papacy when it brought the Great Schism to an end.

But Catholic instances of efforts to limit papal authority were not confined to the Jansenists. The Catholic monarchs of Europe were pleased to control episcopal nominations in their kingdoms, but they wanted more than that. By the eighteenth century, kings pushed hard against papal interference in their territories; separation of the church from the state was not the monarchs' goal, but rather the thorough subjection of national churches to kings. Pope Clement XIV suppressed the Jesuits in 1773, under severe pressure to do so from Catholic monarchs who had already expelled the Society of Jesus from their realms. In his history of the popes entitled *Saints & Sinners*, Eamon Duffy calls Clement's implementation of the monarchs' anti-Jesuit agenda "the papacy's most shameful hour."[3] Shameful it may well have been, but surely some historians would offer other examples of even more shameful papal actions. Reception of the suppression of the Jesuits was varied indeed, even among the Jesuits themselves. A recent translation and publication of a history and explanation of that suppression, by Giulio Cordara, SJ (1704–85), offers a good example of a nuanced view by one directly affected by Clement XIV's actions.[4]

Clement reigned in a period difficult for any pope, for not only did heads of state seek to control the churches in their territories, and to minimize any role for the papacy, but Enlightenment culture was hostile to religious traditions that looked to ancient texts as normative. The Enlightenment, unlike the Renaissance, found innovation to be a very positive concept. Heavily influenced by the scientific revolution of the seventeenth century, many eighteenth-century intellectuals saw the past as the realm of ignorance, tradition as blindness, and enlightenment as available through the application of human reason. New and more accurate knowledge was achievable. Progress was change for the better, and it was held back only by those who, like the clergy, gloried in the past.

If Pope Pius VI (1775–99, family name Braschi) looked backward for inspiration, it was as much to popes as patrons of the arts as to anything else. Recent work by Jeffrey Collins shows how Pius VI did in fact succeed

[3] Eamon Duffy, *Saints & Sinners: A History of the Popes* (New Haven: Yale University Press, 1997), 194.
[4] Giulio Cesare Cordara, *On the Suppression of the Society of Jesus*, trans. John P. Murphy (Chicago: Loyola Press, 1999).

in many ways as such a patron.[5] But Pius was confronted with political developments not at all friendly to the papacy. He journeyed to Vienna to try to negotiate peace with Emperor Joseph II, who was keen on reducing if not eliminating altogether any role for papal authority in his domains. The journey – most unusual for a pope in that era – did nothing to modify Joseph's agenda of state control of the church.[6]

The French Revolution and Napoleon seemed for a time to have nearly destroyed the papacy. Pius VI opposed the civil constitution of the clergy in France, and this opposition helped him to earn enduring hostility from the French state.[7] The Papal States were a special target of the French army, deployed, it was said, both to defend the Revolution and to spread its benefits of liberty, equality, and fraternity to other peoples. Eventually, the Papal States were occupied by French troops and stripped of much of their precious artwork; Pius VI died in France, a prisoner of Napoleon.

PIUS VII

The successor to Pius VI was Luigi Barnabà Chiaramonte, a Benedictine monk, bishop, and cardinal. He was elected in a conclave held in Venice, chose the name Pius VII, and reigned from 1800 to 1823.[8] As cardinal and bishop, the future Pius VII was considered a moderate, or at least somewhat open to some of the Revolution's ideals. He had preached a Christmas homily in 1797, in his diocese of Imola, which accepted democracy and a republican civil government as compatible with Christianity.[9] Imola was within the Cisalpine republic that had been set up by the French, and the clergy were under pressure to support the state publicly.

---

[5] Jeffrey Collins, "The Gods' Abode: Pius VI and the Invention of the Vatican Museum," in Clare Hornsby, ed., *The Impact of Italy: The Grand Tour and Beyond* (London: British School at Rome, 2000), 173–94; *Papacy and Politics in Eighteenth-Century Rome: Pius VI and the Arts* (Cambridge: Cambridge University Press, 2004).

[6] On Pius VI and Joseph II, see Duffy, *Saints & Sinners*, 195–99.

[7] On Pius VI and the civil constitution, see Nigel Aston, *Religion and Revolution in France 1780–1804* (Washington, DC: Catholic University of America Press), 142–43, 149–51, 167–68. On Pius VI and the Revolution, see also Gérard Pelletier, *Rome et la Révolution française: la théologie et la politique du Saint-Siège devant la Révolution française (1789–1799)* (Rome: École Française de Rome, 2004). Dale Van Kley argues that Jansenism played an important role in preparing the way for the Revolution: see his *The Religious Origins of the French Revolution: From Calvin to the Civil Constitution, 1560–1791* (New Haven: Yale University Press, 1996); for my review of Van Kley, see *Theological Studies* 58 (1997), 547–49.

[8] See Sergio Baldan, *Il conclave di Venezia: l'elezione di papa Pio VII, 1 dicembre 1799–14 marzo 1800* (Venice: Marsilio, 2000); Giovanni Spinelli, ed., *Pio VII papa benedettino nel bicentenario della sua elezione* (Cesena: Badia di Santa Maria del Monte, 2003).

[9] On the circumstances and content of this homily, see Jean Leflon, *Pie VII: des abbayes bénédictines à la papauté* (Paris: Plon, 1958), 414–47.

Cardinal Chiaramonte sent copies of his homily to his priests as well as to government officials.[10]

But it was in 1814 and beyond, with the restoration of monarchy in France, that this homily gained a new life in France and elsewhere. Its reception in this era was very favorable by those who did not want to see the clock turned back to a marriage of throne and altar as had existed in the Old Regime. Henri Grégoire, the French bishop who was the most persistent clerical champion of the Revolution and its ideals, published a French translation of this homily, which went through various editions.[11] In other words, reception of this homily by clergy and others seeking to promote republican government, and good relations between such government and the church, was very favorable, well into the reign of Pius VII. The homily was eventually published in several languages, and used in several countries by those who sought to promote good relations between the church and a republican state in the decades after the French Revolution.[12]

As Pope Pius VII, Chiaramonte soon agreed to a concordat with Napoleon concerning the church in France. Negotiating on behalf of Pius VII was his secretary of state, Ercole Consalvi. Signed in July 1801, the concordat recognized Catholicism as the religion of the great majority of the French, and included provisions for state-provided salaries for the clergy.[13] In some ways, then, the concordat could be considered a kind of favorable "reception" of Pius VII and the Catholic Church by Napoleon. Yet the concordat also stipulated a good deal of state involvement in governance of the church, including the delineation of diocesan boundaries and the nomination of bishops and pastors of parishes. And in 1802 Napoleon's government unilaterally added Organic Articles to the concordat that severely restricted any papal role in the French church. For example, no papal document could be published or put into effect in France without

[10] Ibid., 443–46.
[11] Ibid., 448–49; see, e.g., Pius VII, *Homélie du citoyen Cardinal Chiaramonti, évêque d'Imola, actuellement souverain pontife Pie VII: adressée au peuple de son diocèse, dans la République cisalpine, le jour de la naissance de Jesus-Christ, l'an 1797*, trans. M. Grégoire (Paris: Baudouin, 1818). On Henri Grégoire there is an enormous literature; for examples of biographies, see Ruth Necheles, *The Abbé Grégoire 1787–1831: The Odyssey of an Egalitarian* (Westport, CT: Greenwood, 1971); Alyssa Goldstein Sepinwall, *The Abbé Grégoire and the French Revolution: The Making of Modern Universalism* (Berkeley: University of California Press, 2005); on Grégoire as a "liberal" Catholic, see Norman Ravitch, "Liberalism, Catholicism, and the Abbé Grégoire," *Church History* 36 (1967), 419–39.
[12] Leflon, *Pie VII*, 450.
[13] See Bernard Ardura, *Le concordat entre Pie VII et Bonaparte, 15 juillet 1801: bicentenaire d'une réconciliation* (Paris: Cerf, 2001). On Consalvi and on how historians have viewed him, see Roberto Regoli, *Ercole Consalvi: le scelte per la chiesa* (Rome: Editrice Pontificia Università Gregoriana, 2006).

state approval. No nuncio or other papal representative could function in France without authorization by the French government. Uniformity within France was also a top priority: there was to be but one form of the liturgy and one catechism in France.[14] Thus Napoleon in 1801–02 sought peace with the Catholic Church, but a peace very much on his terms, and only in part on terms agreed with Pius VII. In the event, the concordat of 1801 far outlasted both Napoleon and Pius VII; indeed, though it was unilaterally abrogated by the French Republic at the beginning of the twentieth century, it still remains in effect in a part of eastern France, in the dioceses of Strasbourg and Metz.[15]

In 1804 Pius VII accepted an invitation to come to Paris for Napoleon's coronation as emperor. Napoleon received him outside Paris, at the castle of Fontainebleau, from November 25 to November 28, 1804, a few days before the coronation at Notre-Dame Cathedral on December 2.[16] One might say that Napoleon's "reception" of the pope was rather mixed for this occasion. Under pressure from Pius VII to regularize their relationship, Napoleon and Josephine were married on the eve of the coronation, though in secret, by Napoleon's uncle, Cardinal Fesch. Pius VII blessed the crowns and other regalia with which the emperor and empress were to be invested, and he anointed both of them with chrism. But Napoleon did not allow Pius to crown him or Josephine, and did it himself.[17]

Pius remained in Paris through the winter of 1804–05, departing for Rome only in April 1805. Even today one may still find commemorative plaques and monuments in French churches, recalling a visit in that period by Pius VII and perhaps a date when he celebrated Mass at a particular altar. The existence and survival of commemorative monuments and the like offer evidence of a favorable view of Pius VII by the Catholics of Paris.[18]

[14] For the texts of the concordat and of the Organic Articles, see Ardura, *Le concordat*, 73–89. On Napoleon and religion, see also Jacques-Olivier Boudon, *Napoléon et les cultes: les religions en Europe à l'aube du XIXe siècle 1800–1815* (Paris: Fayard, 2002).

[15] These dioceses were part of Germany when the concordat was abrogated in France; when they were reincorporated into France after World War I, the French state chose to leave the concordat in place.

[16] See Christophe Beyeler, *Le pape et l'empereur: la réception de Pie VII par Napoléon à Fontainebleau, 25–28 novembre 1804* (Paris: Somogy, 2004).

[17] See José Cabanis, *Le sacre de Napoléon: 2 décembre 1804*, 2nd edn. (Paris: Gallimard, 2007), 182–84, 198–201.

[18] On Pius in the months after Napoleon's coronation, see Margaret O'Dwyer, *The Papacy in the Age of Napoleon and the Restoration: Pius VII, 1800–1823* (Lanham, MD: University Press of America, 1985), 88–89. For the centennial of Pius's visit to a Parisian parish, see Aloys Pottier, *Pie VII à Paris: un centenaire à Saint-Thomas-d'Aquin, 1804 – 26 décembre-1904* (Paris: Dumoulin, 1905).

As Napoleon's domination of Europe intensified, Pius VII sided with the anti-Napoleonic forces, and he refused, in particular, to support Napoleon's blockade of Great Britain. By 1808 the French army once again occupied Rome, and in 1809 took Pius to Savona in northern Italy, and eventually to the castle of Fontainebleau in France.[19] The circumstances of Pius's forced stay at Fontainebleau in 1812–14 were far more menacing to him personally and to the papacy than circumstances had been at the time of his first visit to Fontainebleau in 1804. In early 1813 Napoleon had recently returned, defeated, from Russia; perhaps as a consolation he sought, at least, a victory over Pius VII. Napoleon intimidated Pius to the point where he agreed to a new concordat – sometimes referred to as the Concordat of Fontainebleau – extremely hostile to the interests of the Catholic Church, an agreement Pius soon renounced.[20] The history of Napoleon's treatment of Pius VII – his quite varied "reception" of the pope – is thus a complex and fascinating topic in itself, quite apart from anyone else's reception of Pius VII.

But this pope outlived Napoleon's empire and returned to Rome as a hero in 1814. One of his first actions upon that return was the restoration of the Society of Jesus throughout the world.[21] Francesco Finetti (1762–1842) was a diocesan priest and well-known preacher who entered the Society of Jesus in Rome in the autumn of 1814, just a few months after its restoration.[22] In August 1815 Finetti preached a sermon in St. Peter's Basilica, on the theme of St. Peter in chains, a theme that he used to demonstrate how God's providence was evident in the life and work of Pius VII. Just as Peter was freed from his chains, so Pius was freed from his imprisonment.

Finetti contrasts Pius and Napoleon: Napoleon was a usurper and tyrant; his heart was invaded with rage and furor.[23] In a night of "eternal infamy" Pius, "the most ancient and most legitimate of Sovereigns," was taken prisoner, leaving the Roman church a widow. But God's Providence had been promised to prevail even against the gates of hell; in prison Pius's courage, strength, and virtue ("o coraggio, o fortezza, o virtù")

---

[19] Napoleon did not only seize the Papal States and deport Pius VII; he attacked the church in other ways as well. See, on suppression of religious orders in Italy, Carmelo Naselli, *La soppressione napoleonica delle corporazioni religiose* (Rome: Editrice Pontificia Università Gregoriana, 1986).

[20] Ibid., 112–13. On papal and other Catholic resistance to Napoleon, see Bernard Plongeron, *Des résistances religieuses à Napoléon (1799–1813)* (Paris: Letouzey et Ané, 2006).

[21] See Marek Inglot, "Pio VII e la ricostituzione della Compagnia di Gesù," in Spinelli, ed., *Pio VII papa benedettino*, 381–415.

[22] On Finetti, see Carlos Sommervogel, *Bibliothèque de la Compagnie de Jésus*, 9 vols. (Brussels: Schepens, 1890–1900), III, 740–46.

[23] Francesco Finetti, *Discorso recitato nella basilica di S. Pietro in Vaticano* (Rome: Stamperia de Romanis, 1815), 10.

were manifest. The heart of Pius was saddened and wept more for the dangers facing the sacred bark of the church than for offenses against his person.[24] God's sovereign Providence restored Pius to Rome; the triumph of Pius was the triumph of a just cause and of humanity; sovereign Providence finally abandoned the tyrant to blind ambition; God was the vindicator of Pius and the punisher of his enemies; the tyrant faced a "most just punishing Providence" ("una punitrice giustissima Provvidenza").[25] With Pius's return to Rome, peace was reborn, liberty recovered, dignity reacquired, the rights of peoples and of rulers restored.[26] Finetti concludes by praising Pius as the most worthy father, most worthy prince, and most worthy head of religion; Pius is the most glorious of pontiffs, while Napoleon is the most humiliated of tyrants; Pius's "triumphant return" signals the "most illustrious era" in the history of Roman greatness.[27]

Finetti no doubt exaggerated more than a little. And his enthusiasm for Pius VII and for the restored Society of Jesus was not shared by everyone. Pro-Jansenist sympathy was by no means dead by 1814, and it is no surprise to find negative reactions among Jansenist sympathizers to the papal restoration of the Jesuits. Louis Silvy (1760–1847) is an excellent example. A layman, from a family of magistrates with a long Jansenist tradition, Silvy was a widower from 1809, and he eventually moved to what remained of Port-Royal des Champs, where the abbey most associated with Jansenism had stood, and died there.[28] Among Silvy's works is one published in Paris in 1815, on the Jesuits as they were before their suppression and on why they were suppressed.[29] The last of the book's eight chapters focuses on Pius's bull of restoration for the Jesuits, and on the dangers for France of readmitting the Society of Jesus. Insisting on his "profound respect" for the "common father of the faithful, seated on the chair of St. Peter," Silvy nevertheless does not hesitate both to deplore the silence of Pius VII on why the Society of Jesus was suppressed, and to express his fear that in the matter of restoration of the Jesuits Pius had listened but to "an ardor of precipitous zeal."[30] He expresses his pain in having to recognize in the Holy Father Pius VII one of the greatest adversaries of "our Gallican liberties"

[24] Ibid., 10–13. Here and elsewhere in this chapter, translations are mine unless otherwise stated.
[25] Ibid., 14–15, 11.   [26] Ibid., 6.   [27] Ibid., 16–17.
[28] "Silvy, Louis," in Louis-Gabriel Michaud, ed., *Biographie universelle*, 2nd edn., 45 vols. (Paris: Desplaces, 1843–56), XXXIX, 353–57.
[29] Louis Silvy, *Les Jésuites, tels qu'ils ont été dans l'ordre politique, religieux et moral, ou exposé des causes de leur destruction* (Paris: Adrien Egron, 1815).
[30] Ibid., 245.

ever to occupy the pontifical seat. Recalling how "our fathers" and the bishops of "every country" long fought the Jesuits as the greatest enemies of the episcopate and of royalty, Silvy points out that Pius should have considered the corrupt morals of the Jesuits, their scandalous commerce, their usury, their intrigues, "in a word all the crimes" of which they were convicted.[31] For Silvy, Pius had ignored the best interests of the papacy itself; the Holy See had not had children "more rebellious" to its decrees than the Jesuits. Can one believe that the Holy Father did not engage in "more serious reflection" before re-establishing them?[32] At the very least, argues Silvy, Pius should have sought the agreement of the most important sovereigns of Europe. But instead, Pius speaks of the Jesuits as "robust rowers" in the bark of Peter, even though history shows that no other society has elicited "more storms" against this same bark.[33] Silvy also cautions against what a restoration of Jesuit schools in France would bring. Such schools would be "schools of Ultramontanism" and they would make of the "flower of the nation" anti-Gallicans.[34]

Pius VII presided over an impressive restoration of not only the papacy's temporal authority in Italy, but of papal prestige and influence throughout the Catholic world and far beyond. Cardinal Consalvi represented the Holy See at the Congress of Vienna and obtained restoration of nearly all of the territory that had constituted the Papal States before 1789.[35] On the winning side against Napoleon, Pius VII was highly regarded not only in Catholic states, but in Orthodox Russia and Protestant Britain. For example, the Prince Regent of Great Britain, the future George IV, commissioned a portrait of Pius VII from Sir Thomas Lawrence, one of the best painters of the day. Lawrence journeyed to Rome for this commission; the painting was done in 1819 as part of a series of portraits for the Waterloo chamber at Windsor Castle, a room honoring those leaders who opposed Napoleon. The painting is still in the royal collections (Figure 6.1).[36] Lawrence was neither the first nor the last artist to depict Pius VII. The art historian Roberta Olson has argued that, after Napoleon, Pius "was the most recognized man of his epoch" and a "quasisaint in the eyes of Europeans regardless of faith, except the committed

---

[31] Ibid., 253–55.   [32] Ibid., 255.   [33] Ibid., 255–56.   [34] Ibid., 268.

[35] See John Tracy Ellis, *Cardinal Consalvi and Anglo-Papal Relations, 1814–1824* (Washington, DC: Catholic University of America Press, 1942).

[36] See Michael Levey, "Lawrence's Portrait of Pius VII," *Burlington Magazine* 117 (April 1975), 194–204; and Levey, *Sir Thomas Lawrence* (New Haven: Yale University Press, 2005). On Lawrence see also Douglas Goldring, *Regency Portrait Painter: The Life of Sir Thomas Lawrence* (London: Macdonald, 1951); and Kenneth Garlick, ed., *Sir Thomas Lawrence, Regency Painter* (Worcester, MA: Worcester Art Museum, 1960).

6.1 Sir Thomas Lawrence, *Pope Pius VII*, 1819. The Royal Collection © 2008,
Her Majesty Queen Elizabeth II.

Bonapartists."[37] Olson has explored how, after 1814, many representations of Pius VII celebrated him as a hero of Italian nationalism against the French invaders. Regarded as a "near-martyr" when he returned to Rome, Pius VII was "welcomed by mobs that staged triumphal processions on his behalf."[38] Italian artists who portrayed the post-captivity Pius, in various media, included Tommaso Minardi, Bartolomeo Pinelli, Joseph Grassi, and Vincenzo Camuccini. In some instances, the emphasis was on parallels between Pius and triumphant Roman emperors. Earlier than 1814, too, representations of Pius abounded, in Italy and elsewhere, including France and Britain. Popular images of Pius were disseminated in London during his captivity – presumably to demonstrate the cruelty of the French and their emperor. Pius's image was not missing from the decorative arts either; among extant objects are French dinner plates with his image, embroidered images of Pius at prayer, and a snuff box with an image of him on the cover.[39]

A portrait of Pius VII commissioned by the British monarchy, and from a top artist of the era, does nevertheless stand out amid an abundance of representations of Pius. Lawrence spent several months in Rome working on this portrait, as well as one of the secretary of state Ercole Consalvi; during this time Lawrence actually lived at the Quirinale Palace, along with Pius and Consalvi.[40] Pius was seventy-seven years old when he sat for Lawrence; the artist left notes along with his completed work, and thus we know that he was surprised by Pius's jet-black hair, which was unusual for a man of such an advanced age.[41] Lawrence's portrait shows Pius seated in what appears to be the *sedia gestatoria*, the portable throne on which he would be carried in various ceremonies. The papal ring is prominent in the portrait as well, though the papal tiara is absent. It may be that Consalvi had advised against including the tiara, lest its association with papal claims to judge all Christian rulers offend British Protestant sensibilities.[42] Still, the tiara and the papal keys are in fact in the portrait, above Pius's coat of arms, on each side of the back of his throne. And to Pius's right in Lawrence's portrait is a sculpture gallery, showing in particular the *Laocoön* and the *Apollo Belvedere*, two of the best-known sculptures in

[37] Roberta J. M. Olson, "Representations of Pius VII: The First Risorgimento Hero," *The Art Bulletin* 68 (March 1986), 77.
[38] Ibid., 83–84.   [39] Ibid., 86 n. 32.
[40] See Levey, "Lawrence's Portrait of Pius VII," 201.
[41] Ibid., 197.
[42] See Levey, *Sir Thomas Lawrence*, 229. On Consalvi and papal neutrality after the Congress of Vienna, see ch. 9 below.

the papal collections, works that were looted by the French but, by 1819, had been recently returned to Rome. In Pius's left hand in this portrait is a piece of paper with the name Antonio Canova on it; Canova was the leading sculptor of the time, and the key figure in negotiating on behalf of Pius the return of many works of art to Rome from France.[43] Thus Lawrence highlights in this portrait the role of Pius as patron of the arts, and not only as prince or pastor.

Pius VII's pontificate saw massive expansion of the church outside Europe; many new dioceses were created, especially in North America, and the role of the papacy in the selection of bishops for these new sees would be greater than it had been for most European dioceses.[44] John Carroll (1735–1815) had been a Jesuit in Maryland before Clement XIV's suppression of the Society of Jesus; in 1789 he became the first bishop of Baltimore, the first diocese created in the United States. In April 1808 Pius VII raised Baltimore to the rank of an archdiocese and Carroll to the rank of archbishop and metropolitan for four newly created dioceses: Boston, New York, Philadelphia, and Bardstown.

In Carroll's letters and other papers there are a good number of references to Pius VII, and these offer an example of episcopal support for and defense of Pius. In the same year in which Pius VII created the new dioceses in the United States, he was forcibly removed from Rome by Napoleon's troops. In 1810 Carroll deplored this papal captivity in several of his writings. In a letter of November 11 to the bishops of Ireland, he speaks for himself and for the other United States bishops in affirming "our obedience to Pope Pius VII, who now holds the supreme pontificate. To this man, whom we cannot adequately commend, we submit ourselves, and we adhere to him as members to our head."[45] Carroll points out that if all suffer when one member suffers, "how much more should the bitter suffering of the very head entail great suffering to all of the members." He declares that "we are righteously indignant" and find it "shocking that an old man should be driven from his residence and native country," and "that the Church should be despoiled of her patrimony; and that a pontiff who merits well of all should be so harassed with indignities."[46] In a

---

[43] Levey, *Sir Thomas Lawrence*, 230. On Canova's success in obtaining the return of looted art to Rome, see Christopher M. S. Johns, *Antonio Canova and the Politics of Patronage in Revolutionary and Napoleonic Europe* (Berkeley: University of California Press, 1998), 171–94.

[44] See James Hennessey, "Rome and the Origins of the United States Hierarchy," in Bernard Cooke, ed., *The Papacy and the Church in the United States* (New York: Paulist Press, 1989), 79–97.

[45] *The John Carroll Papers*, ed. Thomas Hanley, 3 vols. (Notre Dame: University of Notre Dame Press, 1976), III, 125.

[46] Ibid., III, 125.

pastoral letter dated November 15, 1810, signed by Carroll as well as the
bishops of Boston, Philadelphia, and Bardstown and sent to their dioceses,
similar themes are developed. Pius was "forcibly dragged away from the
Chair of St. Peter and the sacred ashes of the Apostles." God's providence
has "permitted him to drink of that cup, and share in those sufferings, of
which … St. Peter" had a large portion. In order that "our chief Pastor"
may be delivered from the hands of his enemies, pastors of parishes should
recite Psalm 120, on Sundays and feast days, either immediately before
Mass or before the sermon.[47]

In July of 1814, shortly after Pius's return to Rome, Carroll sent a pastoral letter to his diocese, ordering a Te Deum "of praise and thanksgiving"
to be sung or reverently read on Sunday, July 10. Though enemies had predicted the downfall of the apostolic chair of Peter, "the faithful disciples of
Jesus Christ" had "constantly renewed" their acknowledgement of Pius as
"Supreme pastor of the Church … because the Son of God invested him
as the successor of St. Peter, with a Supremacy of honour and jurisdiction
over his whole Church."[48] Carroll states that in the return of Pius VII to
Rome one should see "a manifest confirmation of the promises of Christ
for the perpetual protection of his Church" and a "splendid interposition
of heaven for the maintenance of the Apostolical See of St. Peter."[49]

In 1817 a Spanish and English version of Cardinal Chiaramonte's 1797
Christmas homily was published in Philadelphia. The title page includes
a statement making clear what kind of "reception" of Pius VII's ideas was
intended by this edition: the Philadelphia version is to be a reply "to a
Letter of the same pope in behalf of Ferdinand VII against the insurgents
of the … Spanish colonies."[50] In other words, Cardinal Chiaramonte's
homily of some twenty years earlier is proposed as contradicting the
reactionary stance of Pope Pius VII regarding independence for Latin
American nations from the Spanish monarchy. A preface declares that this
edition of the 1797 homily is "addressed to the sons of Columbus who are
contending … for their independence and liberty against the religious and
political despotism of Spain."[51] The homily is said to show that "popular
government is so far from being repugnant to Christianity, that it is the
most conformable to that equality, liberty, and brotherhood recommended
by the gospel." But a recent "letter from the same Pontiff" was "not at all
agreeable to sentiments declared in the homily … but very conducive to

[47] Ibid., III, 129.   [48] Ibid., III, 280–81.   [49] Ibid., III, 282.
[50] Pius VII, *Homily of Pope Pius VII Directed to the People of his Diocese in the Cisalpine Republick in 1797. Translated by a Citizen of Venezuela* (Philadelphia: J. F. Hurtel, 1817).
[51] Ibid., v.

the regeneration of the age of Alexander the 6th."[52] The preface also compares and contrasts insurgents in North and South America: the former, against George III, have not been condemned as sinful, so why should sin "be imputed" to the latter, "when we are so much more in the right as we are fifty times over more tyrannized then they?"[53]

On January 30, 1816 Pius VII had issued an encyclical, *Etsi longissimo*, calling on both secular and religious clergy to oppose revolution against the King of Spain.[54] The 1817 Philadelphia edition of the 1797 homily appends this encyclical, thus showing the extent to which it is at odds with the earlier sentiments of Cardinal Chiaramonte. In this encyclical, at least as published in Philadelphia, Pius denounces the "fatal discords of tumults and seditions" and the "terrible and incalculable mischiefs of rebellion."[55] Pius exhorts his readers to "the obedience and fidelity due to your king."[56] Yet Pius was not deaf to unfolding events; the revolution of 1820 brought an anti-clerical government to Spain, and Pius moved to a neutral policy regarding developments in Latin America. After Pius's death on September 28, 1823, his successor, Leo XII, adopted a more intransigent position in opposition to independence for Spanish colonies.[57] Among the issues of great interest to both Pius VII and his successors was the question of how bishops would be chosen in newly independent states; would the patronage rights enjoyed by the Spanish king pass to new heads of state, or not? This was a complex and important question, and one that would engage several pontificates beyond that of Pius VII.[58]

In an age of restoration of monarchical authority in Europe, Ultramontanists not only sought to restore the pope's authority to what it had been before what they saw as the horrors of the eighteenth and early nineteenth centuries, but wanted the pope to play a greater and more direct role as head of the church than had ever been the case. Joseph de Maistre (1754–1821) was a Savoyard count, lawyer, and diplomat; born in Chambéry, he did his studies in Turin. An opponent of the French Revolution, he found refuge in Lausanne and other places from the

---

[52] Ibid., vii, ix.   [53] Ibid., xv.
[54] See Leslie Bethell, *The Independence of Latin America* (Cambridge: Cambridge University Press, 1987), 228.
[55] Pius VII, *Homily*, 69.   [56] Ibid., 71.
[57] Bethell, *Independence*, 228–29.
[58] See Ondina and Justo González, *Christianity in Latin America: A History* (Cambridge: Cambridge University Press, 2008), 136–37; Robert Schwaller, "The Episcopal Succession in Spanish America 1800–1850," *The Americas* 24 (January 1968), 207–71; and an older, but still useful article, J. Lloyd Mecham, "The Papacy and Spanish American Independence," *The Hispanic American Historical Review* 9 (1929), 154–75.

advancing French army. From 1802 to 1817 he was ambassador in St. Petersburg, and it was in this period that Maistre became a prolific writer. His best-known work from his St. Petersburg years is his *Du pape*, first published, in 1819, in Lyons.[59] This work would enjoy a long life in the nineteenth century and beyond, in many editions and translations, as an apology for an Ultramontanist understanding of papal authority.[60] It included a dedication to Pius VII.[61]

Maistre also published, in 1821, a work entitled *De l'Église gallicane dans son rapport avec le souverain pontife*, in which he denounced Gallicanism and Jansenism as injurious to the Catholic Church.[62] Dividing the work into two books, Maistre first examines what he calls the "spirit of opposition nourished in France against the Holy See," and then he considers the "Gallican system" and the Four Articles of 1682. "By contemplating itself too much," Maistre asserts, the Gallican Church sometimes did not recall, or did not recall adequately, that it "was but a province of the Catholic empire."[63] Those who spoke of the "liberties" of the Gallican Church did so even though its prelates submitted to secular authority; to speak of liberties of that church was an "immense absurdity."[64]

Calling Jansenism but a "phase" of Calvinism, Maistre points out that the Calvinists, at least, were openly declared enemies of the Catholic Church, while the Jansenists stabbed the church in the back. Jansenism had "the incredible pretension" of being Catholic "despite" the Catholic Church.[65] The Jansenist convent of Port-Royal "divided the church; it created a space of discord, defiance, and opposition to the Holy See." The literary reputation of Port-Royal was a false one, as every writing from there was announced in advance as prodigious and as a "literary meteor."[66] "Unshakeable obstinacy in error" and "invincible and systematic scorn for authority" are the "eternal character of this sect." But the one who does not know how to "bend under authority" ceases to belong to the Catholic Church.[67]

Maistre finds the Four Articles adopted in the 1682 assembly of the French clergy to have severely undermined ecclesiastical authority. Colbert, Louis XIV's minister, he identifies as having been the true

[59] "Maistre, Joseph-Marie de," in Michaud, ed., *Biographie universelle*, XXVI, 174–82.
[60] For a critical edition see Joseph de Maistre, *Du pape*, ed. Jacques Lovie and Joannès Chetail (Geneva: Droz, 1966).
[61] Ibid., 11–13.
[62] Joseph de Maistre, *De l'Église gallicane dans son rapport avec le souverain pontife* (Lyons: Rusand, 1821).
[63] Ibid., 3.   [64] Ibid., 5.   [65] Ibid., 9, 18–19, 27.
[66] Ibid., 41, 48–49.   [67] Ibid., 93, 98.

author of these propositions, while the bishops remained passive. Maistre contrasts strongly the assembly of 1626 with that of 1682; the former, he asserts approvingly, had affirmed papal infallibility.[68] Responding to the conciliarist ecclesiology of the Four Articles, and completely ignoring the early councils which were neither called by nor attended by popes, Maistre claims that if there can be an ecumenical council without a pope, as the articles affirm, there is no longer any church.[69] These articles are useful only for making a pastor "suspect to his flock," for spreading division in the church, for "releasing the pride of innovators, for rendering the government of the church difficult or impossible."[70]

The eighteenth century finds, in Maistre's estimation, little or nothing positive. The assembly of the clergy held in 1700, Maistre regrets, sought to condemn Jesuit moral theology, claiming that its advocacy of probabilism led to laxism. To such claims Maistre responds, arguing that probabilism had been taught by the order of St. Dominic well before it was taught by the Society of Jesus.[71] The eighteenth century Maistre summarizes as a "perverse and frivolous century" and one in which the French clergy found itself in a servile relationship to temporal power.[72] The "pretended liberties" of the Gallican Church were but a conspiracy of the temporal power to "despoil" the Holy See of its legitimate rights.[73] As a particularly damning proof of the destructiveness of the Four Articles, Maistre draws a close link between them and the French Revolution. The day will come, he asserts, when it will be universally agreed that "the revolutionary theories" were but "a rigorously logical development" of the principles behind the articles.[74]

In Maistre's version of history, Napoleon was most certainly not the liberator of Europe; on the contrary, he infringed upon liberty, ecclesiastical and other. The Four Articles of 1682 "were very dear to the terrible usurper who formerly put all the liberties of Europe in peril."[75] This same Napoleon was the "odious jailer of the sovereign pontiff."[76] Maistre's apparently unlimited confidence in papal authority went hand in hand with a critique of limits placed on such authority by temporal or episcopal

[68] Ibid., 127–32. On the history of the assemblies of the clergy, see Pierre Blet, *Le clergé du grand siècle en ses assemblées (1615–1715)* (Paris: Cerf, 1995).
[69] Maistre, *De l'Église gallicane*, 142.
[70] Ibid., 238.
[71] Ibid., 257. On this point of historical development, Maistre is correct. For a history of Jesuits and probabilism, see Robert Maryks, *Saint Cicero and the Jesuits: The Influence of the Liberal Arts on the Adoption of Moral Probabilism* (Aldershot: Ashgate, 2008).
[72] Maistre, *De l'Église gallicane*, 285.   [73] Ibid., 296, 303.
[74] Ibid., 156.   [75] Ibid., 238.   [76] Ibid., 238.

powers. Maistre praises the "moderation of the Holy See," and argues that
popes "walk with a scrupulous circumspection, and condemn only as a
last resort."[77] This may well have been true for Pius VII, who had been
pope for some twenty years when Maistre wrote this work, but would it be
true for Pius's successors in the nineteenth century?

An important example of an Ultramontanist a generation or two later
than Maistre is Nicholas Patrick Wiseman (1802–65), Cardinal Archbishop
of Westminster. Wiseman's memoir, *Recollections of the Last Four Popes*,
first published in 1858, begins with Pius VII. Wiseman had studied in
Rome for some years shortly after Pius's 1814 return. He recounts an audience that he and other students from the English College had with the
"good and holy Pius VII"[78] at the Quirinale Palace. The "amiable" pontiff
gave them a "fatherly reception" and praised the English clergy for their
"fidelity to the Holy See."[79] This audience with the "illustrious Pius VII,"
Wiseman explains, formed a tie "not to be broken, but rather strengthened
by every subsequent experience."[80] Wiseman does not in fact limit himself to recalling his personal contacts with popes, but also recounts their
life stories. Pius VII's imprisonment by the French he compares with St.
Paul's imprisonment; Pope Pius VII "bore his captivity … as became his
high dignity and noblest inheritance, and in the character and spirit of an
apostle."[81] Wiseman insists that Pius, who was a Benedictine monk, per-
manently retained monastic traits: "Pius had been educated in the rough
habit, and with the plain diet of the monk, in fastings often, and in watch-
ings, and in many trials of subjection and obedience."[82] He argues that just
as "a painter never forgets how to sketch," so "the monk, in his simplicity
and habits of endurance, had lived in Pius through episcopacy, cardinalate, and papacy."[83] Like Finetti, Wiseman can barely contain himself in
lauding Pius VII.

But not every nineteenth-century proponent of a restoration of
Catholicism was as uncritical of Pius VII as Wiseman was. Viscount
François-René de Châteaubriand (1768–1848) promoted a Romantic version of what he called the "genius" of Christianity.[84] In his memoirs, first
published in 1847–48, Châteaubriand reproached Pius VII for his weakness in dealing with Napoleon: in 1809 when Napoleon decreed that
Rome was henceforth a part of the French Empire, Pius VII issued an

---

[77] Ibid., 334.
[78] Nicholas Patrick Wiseman, *Recollections of the Last Four Popes and of Rome in their Times* (Boston:
Donahoe, 1858), 24.
[79] Ibid., 28.   [80] Ibid., 29.   [81] Ibid., 48.   [82] Ibid., 45.   [83] Ibid., 45.
[84] See François-René de Châteaubriand, *Génie du christianisme*, rev. edn. (Paris: Vermot, 1859).

excommunication of those who despoiled the church. But he did not mention Napoleon by name; the circumstances called for "thunder claps" and
"lightning for lightning" and yet Pius VII did not do all he could against
Napoleon.[85] Châteaubriand recalls the conflict between Pope Gregory VII
(1073–85) and Emperor Henry IV, and suggests that Gregory would not
have failed to go further than Pius did in countering Napoleon.[86]

CONCLUSION

In conclusion: in both what he did, and in how he and his pontificate
were received, Pius VII was a bridge between the papacy prior to the
French Revolution and the papacy as it developed in the nineteenth century. Pius VII was a prince, a pastor, as well as a patron of the arts. He
outlived Napoleon's domination of Europe and put the Papal States back
on the map of Europe, with the support of the allied powers that had
defeated the French army. As a patron of the arts, Pius was surely not as
significant as Julius II (1503–13), but neither was he negligible in that role.
The return to Rome of many of the papacy's greatest artistic treasures
that had been stolen by the French was no small accomplishment, and
one with long-lasting consequences for the Vatican museums and for the
pope as patron of these priceless collections. As a pastor, Pius VII inspired
Catholics and others by his fortitude under persecution, and he presided
over a major expansion of the Catholic Church outside Europe, in some
ways anticipating the world church that has since developed. A political
moderate, who as bishop had accepted the compatibility of democratic
states with Catholicism, Pius VII sought accommodation when possible,
with a variety of regimes. The concordat of 1801 pointed forward to the
kinds of arrangements popes would make with heads of state, including
Mussolini and Hitler, in the twentieth century.[87] Pius VII's restoration of
the Jesuits was both a kind of return to an earlier era and an authorization for the Society of Jesus to operate in the new world after the French
Revolution, after Napoleon, and after the American Revolution. Cardinal
Wiseman's encomium of Pius VII points forward to the Ultramontanist
devotion to the pope that has been prominent in Catholic culture since at
least the reign of Pius IX (1846–78).

[85] François-René de Châteaubriand, *Vie de Napoléon* (Paris: Éditions de Fallois, 1999), 154.
[86] Ibid., 154.
[87] See Frank Coppa, ed., *Controversial Concordats: The Vatican's Relations with Napoleon, Mussolini, and Hitler* (Washington, DC: Catholic University of America Press, 1999).

Wiseman emphasized Pius VII's Benedictine training and experience. Over the centuries, many members of religious orders had been elected pope: monks of various kinds, Franciscans, Dominicans. But Pius VII reigned near the end of the eras of popes from religious orders. The last monk or any kind of religious to be elected pope was Mauro Capellari, a member of the Camaldolese order, who became Pope Gregory XVI and reigned from 1831 to 1846. In 1799, after Pius VI had been taken prisoner by the French, Capellari had published a work entitled *The Triumph of the Holy See and of the Church against the Attacks of Innovators* (*Il trionfo della Santa Sede et della chiesa contro gli assalti de' novatori*).[88] Gregory XVI would be more conservative and certainly more intransigent than Pius VII, and is remembered, among other things, for opposing the construction of railroads in the Papal States. With a wordplay in French, he is reported to have condemned the new means of transportation: the *chemin de fer* was but a *chemin d'enfer*: the railroad was but the road to hell.[89] Though Gregory was the immediate predecessor of Pius IX, recent precedents for Pius IX to consider surely included the long and very eventful pontificate of Pius VII.

[88] Mauro Capellari, *Il trionfo della Santa Sede et della chiesa contro gli assalti de' novatori ...* (Rome: Stamperia Pagliarini, 1799).

[89] J. N. D. Kelly, "Gregory XVI," in *The Oxford Dictionary of Popes* (Oxford: Oxford University Press, 1986), 307.

CHAPTER 7

Pius IX: pastor and prince

Ciarán O'Carroll

The pontificate of Pius IX (1846–78) impacted greatly on the universal church. It witnessed the victory of Ultramontanism over Gallicanism. It was an era of liturgical and structural reform – of devotional revolution and theological Romanization, of renewed and assertive, hierarchical self-confidence. Pius IX's pontificate was one which witnessed the diminution of the temporal power of the church with the loss of the Papal States but one which asserted spiritual authority with the proclamation of papal infallibility at the First Vatican Council and with Pius's assertion of the pope's immediate universal pastoral jurisdiction over the church. Reception of Pius IX tended to be either very favorable or very unfavorable, depending on the location. This chapter will pay special attention to the case of Ireland because of the considerable influence that Irish clergy exercised throughout the English-speaking world, to which they traveled widely as enthusiastic apostles of Ultramontanism.

BIOGRAPHY

The difficult and turbulent pontificate of Pius IX began at a critical time for the church. He was born Giovanni Maria Mastai-Ferretti in Sinigaglia into a noble family, that of Girolamo dei Conti Ferretti, on May 13, 1792. As a child he suffered noticeably from epilepsy. He was educated at the Piarist college in Volterra and in Rome. As a theology student in Sinigaglia he met, in 1814, Pope Pius VII (reigned 1800–23) on his return from French captivity. In 1815 he entered the papal noble guard but was soon dismissed after an epileptic seizure. Despite health challenges, Pope Pius VII decided to support Mastai-Ferretti's continued theological studies. Following ordination in April 1819 he worked initially as the Rector of the Tata Giovanni Institute in Rome. Shortly before his death Pope Pius VII sent him as auditor to Chile and Peru in 1823 and 1825 to assist the apostolic nuncio Mgr. Giovanni Muzi in the first mission to post-revolutionary

South America, which had the objective of mapping out the role of the Catholic Church in the newly independent South American republics. He was to be the first pope ever to have experienced South America. When he returned to Rome, the successor to Pius VII, Pope Leo XII, appointed him head of the hospital of San Michele in Rome (1825–27) and canon of Santa Maria in Via Lata.

In 1827 Pope Leo XII appointed him as Archbishop of Spoleto. There he gained a reputation as a liberal and an effective organizer of relief and charity following an earthquake. In 1832 he was moved to the more prestigious diocese of Imola and was made a cardinal *in pectore* in 1839. In 1840 he was publicly announced as cardinal priest of Santi Pietro e Marcellino. As in Spoleto, among his episcopal priorities in Imola were the formation of priests through improved education and the promotion of charities.

On June 14, 1846, two weeks after the death of Gregory XVI, a conclave consisting of some fifty cardinals assembled in the Quirinale Palace, Rome. The cardinals at the conclave divided into two factions; the conservative faction favored a continuance of absolutism with respect to the temporal government of the church, while the liberal faction advocated moderate political reforms. On the fourth vote, on June 16, 1846, Cardinal Mastai-Ferretti, the preferred liberal candidate, received a surplus of three votes beyond the required majority. Ardent and emotional, with a gift for friendship and a reputation for generosity, he chose the name of Pius IX in honor of Pope Pius VII. His pontifical coronation took place in St. Peter's Basilica on June 21, 1846. The election of Cardinal Mastai-Ferretti was greeted with considerable enthusiasm in Europe and elsewhere despite his limited curial experience. As pontiff he had a daily schedule which was frugal and almost monastic. He was assiduous in prayer and in charity and was noted as an eloquent preacher. He was also the last pope to rule over the Papal States as they had been constituted following the French Revolution.

At the outset of his pontificate Cardinal Mastai-Ferretti was hailed as an ardent reformer. Upon election as pontiff, as civil head of the Papal States, he was immediately confronted with the secular challenge of their administration. The unyielding and intransigent attitudes of both his immediate predecessor, Gregory XVI, and the then secretary of state, Cardinal Lambruschini, to repeated calls for domestic political reform had resulted in considerable political unease in the Papal States. In response to the calls for political reform, Pius granted a general amnesty to political exiles and prisoners a month after his election, on July 16, 1846. The amnesty was greeted with considerable, though not universal, enthusiasm by the citizens of the Papal States. While the move was attacked by some who denounced the new pontiff as being in league with freemasons and the Carbonari, some of those released under the amnesty program used their new-found liberty to further their revolutionary ideas.

Partly in response, Pius IX demonstrated his opposition to radical political philosophies in an encyclical, *Qui pluribus*, on November 9, 1846. In this encyclical he condemned those who oppressed the interests of the Catholic Church or who fomented sectarian bitterness and intrigues against the Holy See. He continued, however, to grant numerous political and administrative reforms. He initiated the construction of railroads in the Papal States and the installation of street lighting throughout Rome. He improved agricultural technology and productivity through agricultural educational programs in newly created scientific agricultural institutes. He repealed the rule requiring Jews to attend Catholic services and opened the papal charities to non-Catholics in need. Numerous administrative political reforms were advanced. On April 19, 1847, for example, an announcement was made advising the pontiff's intention to establish an advisory council (the Consulta di Stato). This was to be composed of members of the laity from various provinces within the Papal States. Later that same year, on July 5, 1847, he announced the establishment of a civic guard, and, before the close of the year, on December 29, the establishment of a cabinet council.

Initial political and administrative reforms by Pope Pius IX served to further demands by the revolutionary independent Young Italy movement for greater political freedom. Demands were made for the establishment of a purely lay and constitutional government, along with an express public declaration of open hostilities between the Papal States and Austria. In response to continued intense agitation and active political unrest in February and March 1848, the papal administration promised further political reforms including the establishment of a constitution. In opposition to popular demand, however, on April 29, 1848 the pope proclaimed that, as the Father of Christendom, he could never declare war against Catholic Austria.

A popular uprising greeted this declaration. Pius IX was denounced as a traitor, and in the violence that ensued the Prime Minister of the Papal States, the liberal Pellegrino Rossi, was assassinated. Following this an angry and violent crowd attempted to besiege the pope in the Quirinale Palace, and during disturbances a papal prelate was shot. Under pressure from revolutionaries to promise further democratic reforms in the Papal States, with the help of the Bavarian and French ambassadors, Pius fled the Quirinale Palace in disguise. He traveled south to Gaeta, in the kingdom of Ferdinand II of the Two Sicilies, where he was joined by many of the cardinals. Meanwhile in Rome supporters of the Young Italy movement seized political power. On February 9, 1849 in the name of a democratic republic the temporal power of the pope was declared to have been abolished. This republic was demonstrably and openly hostile to the Catholic Church, celebrating Good Friday with huge fireworks on St. Peter's Square and desecrating St. Peter's Basilica on Easter Sunday. Following reports of a series of violent incidents in Rome, Pius appealed to France, Austria, Spain, and Naples for support to suppress the republican Young Italy administration. On June 29, 1849, French troops under General Oudinot restored order to the Papal States. Several months later Pius returned to Rome in triumph, as popular opinion swung once more in his favor. He was received amid cannon thunder and the pealing of church bells while sizeable tumultuous crowds greeted him joyously along his route home.

The violent and anti-clerical nature of the 1849 revolution profoundly affected the future political stance of Pope Pius IX. Following his return to Rome, political reforms and constitutional improvements continued, if less radically than previously. He did, however, continue to reform the governmental structure of the Papal States on September 10, 1850, and its finances on October 28 in the same year. Under the terms of such reforms the financial administration was increasingly put in the hands of the laity with financial expertise. Under their management new fiscal policies were introduced whereby the difficult financial burden that Pius encountered on assuming office was greatly alleviated. On an economic front Pius made systematic efforts to improve both trade relations and manufacturing in the Papal States. This was achieved through actively promoting domestic producers of wool, silk, and other materials destined for export and establishing trade relations with numerous foreign states. The transportation system within the Papal States was radically improved through the construction of roads, viaducts, bridges, and sea ports. Significantly, a series of new railroad links connected the Papal States to northern Italy.

During Pius IX's pontificate numerous efforts were undertaken to restore historic walls, fountains, streets, and bridges in the Papal States. Substantial financial investment was directed to archeological projects such as the discovery of Christian catacombs. A new archeological commission was established in 1853. Pius also oversaw the restoration of Etruscan and ancient Roman monuments in a variety of cities in the Papal States. Administratively he divided the states into provincial units and communities. However, these reforms, while important, did not have the liberal flavor of his activities prior to the 1848 revolution. The cardinal secretary of state to Pius IX, Giacomo Cardinal Antonelli, exerted a paramount political influence on the pontiff and on his policies throughout the pontificate, and following Pius's return from Gaeta, Cardinal Antonelli headed a cabinet which included members of the laity. Despite this, one of the accusations against the regime continued to be focused on its overly clerical nature, as many influential positions within the administration were exclusively reserved for members of the clergy.

Pius IX's relationship with the Jews was ambiguous. In the Papal States, with respect to issues of governance, all non-Catholics, most notably Protestants and Jews, were excluded from various social circles, roles, and responsibilities. However, as pontiff Pius repealed legislation that prohibited Jews from practicing certain professions and rescinded laws requiring them to attend conversion homilies several times a year. Early in his pontificate, in 1847, Pius personally welcomed and baptized four Roman Jews into the Catholic Church. At the outset of his pontificate he opened up the Jewish ghetto area of the city of Rome. Following the experience of the Roman Republic, however, he reinstated the ghetto and promulgated a series of anti-liberal measures. In 1858, in a case which was widely publicized, Edgardo Mortara, a six-year-old Jewish child, was taken from his parents by the police of the Papal States. It was reported that he had been baptized by a Catholic servant of the family when he fell ill, and, since legislation of the day prohibited Christians from being reared by Jews, the child was removed from his family circle. Pius steadfastly refused to release the child into the custody of his parents despite appeals for such a move from various heads of state. Later, in 1870, Edgardo Mortara was ordained a priest, and as Don Pius Mortara he entered a monastery in Poitiers, France.

Pope Pius IX was deeply revered by many Catholics worldwide, although attacked by revolutionary nationalists. As pontiff he promoted the inner life of the church by means of many important liturgical regulations and especially by an unprecedented number of beatifications, canonizations, and jubilee celebrations. His was the longest pontificate in the history of the papacy, lasting almost thirty-two years, and in 1871 he celebrated his twenty-fifth and in 1876 his thirtieth anniversary as pope. At the fiftieth anniversary of his episcopal consecration, his golden episcopal jubilee, people from all parts of the world came to see the pontiff between April and June 1877. Such jubilees were celebrated with impressive public devotions which drew large crowds of pilgrims. Pius also publicly commemorated several jubilees of significant events in the history of the church, such as the 300th anniversary of the Council of Trent. Another major event was the eighteenth centenary anniversary of the martyrdom of the Apostles Peter and Paul on June 29, 1867, which he celebrated with over 500 bishops, 20,000 priests, and 140,000 laity in Rome. In 1875 Pope Pius IX declared a Holy Year, which was celebrated throughout the Catholic world. More than his predecessors Pius IX used the papal pulpit to address the bishops of the world. In 1862, for example, some 300 bishops accepted his invitation to attend the canonization of twenty-six martyrs of Japan. The repeatedly large attendance of prelates, priests, and laity from various parts of the globe testified to the popularity of the pontiff and the growing international assertiveness of the Catholic religion.

Pius IX did not achieve equal popularity throughout Italy. On a national level his temporal reign over the Papal States, up to the seizure of the city of Rome itself in 1870, was one of continuous struggle. Politically the pontificate after 1848 was faced with revolutionary movements not only in Italy but also throughout Europe. The Pope's political difficulties regarding the Papal States were further augmented by the strategic maneuvering of Napoleon III and later the defeat of Austria at Magenta on July 4, 1859. This defeat resulted in the withdrawal of the Austrian troops from papal legations. The insurrection in some cities of the Romagna resulted in a demand for the annexation of Romagna to Piedmont in September 1859. On February 6, 1860 Victor Emmanuel demanded the annexation of Umbria and the Marches. Pius rejected this demand, and a military campaign ensued. After the defeat of the papal army at Spoleto, Castelfidardo, and Ancona in September 1860, the Papal States were radically reduced in size, having lost all their possessions with the exception of Rome and its immediate vicinity. This remnant of the Papal States continued to come under increased pressure from anti-papal nationalists over the course of the ensuing decade. On September 20, 1870 Italian unificationists seized Rome and declared it the capital of a united Italy. A law of guarantees was passed in May 1871 which accorded the pope the rights of a sovereign, including the right to send and receive ambassadors along with an annual remuneration and acceptance of extraterritoriality for numerous papal palaces in Rome. Pius IX officially rejected this offer in his encyclical *Ubi nos*, of May 15, 1871, maintaining his claim to all the conquered territory. He denounced the law of guarantees and refused to accept the financial offer of Italian monthly stipends. Although he was not prevented from traveling as he wished, he called himself "a prisoner in the Vatican." It was a status he retained to his death.

WORLDWIDE PASTOR

Foreign policy during the pontificate of Pope Pius IX was continually strained, and the church experienced a variety of challenges to papal authority and influence in numerous countries. A policy of establishing or maintaining concordats with various countries had mixed impact. In Piedmont the concordat of 1841 was dismantled: tithes were abolished, secular education was introduced, monasteries were suppressed, church property was confiscated, religious orders were expelled, and prelates who objected to anti-ecclesiastical legislation were imprisoned or expelled. Pius objected to such moves publicly in his allocutions of 1850, 1852, 1853, and 1855. He also publicized numerous injustices which he asserted the Piedmontese government had committed against the church.

At the outset of Pius IX's pontificate in 1846 the church in France was divided between moderates and intransigents. The former faction was led by Charles Forbes René de Montalembert, the latter by Louis Veuillot. In his encyclical *Inter multiplices* Pius addressed the French bishops and appealed for unity. Despite ecclesiastical divisions, French religious life experienced a significant revival during his pontificate. Ultramontanism thrived, as the widespread support from French bishops for a decree on papal infallibility in 1870 indicated.

In Spain, by the time of the accession of Pius IX to the pontificate a series of anti-Catholic governments had been in power since 1832. Their executive actions had decreed the expulsion of various religious orders, the closure of convents, Catholic schools and libraries, and the seizure and sale of churches and religious properties. The church was also restricted in its ability to appoint bishops to episcopal sees as they fell vacant. In 1851 Pius successfully concluded a concordat with Queen Isabella II under the terms of which any unsold ecclesiastical properties were to be returned to the church, while the church agreed to renounce its claim on properties which had already changed hands. The church was also accorded renewed freedom in the field of religious education in schools and seminaries.

During the pontificate of Pius IX the Catholic population of the United States rose, largely because of an influx of Catholic immigrants from Ireland, Italy, and Germany. The Catholic population increased from 4 percent at the beginning of the pontificate to 11 percent in 1870, while the number of clergy rose from 700 priests to some 6,000. Pius fostered church growth through his innovative foundations of new ecclesiastical regions, the summoning of regular diocesan synods, and the making of some remarkable and noteworthy episcopal appointments. He renewed the structure of the church in the United States through the establishment of numerous archdioceses and dioceses, including the dioceses of Portland in Maine, Springfield in Illinois, Burlington, Cleveland, Columbus, Galveston-Houston, Providence, Fort Wayne–South Bend, Kansas City in Kansas, St. Paul and Minneapolis, San Francisco, Seattle, and San Antonio.

The United States established formal diplomatic links with the Holy See on April 7, 1848, although the Holy See never sent an ambassador to Washington, owing to the refusal of successive United States administrations to accept a Catholic priest as a papal nuncio. In 1867, when relations with the Holy See were closed for a period, considerable pressure arose. Diplomatic tensions increased during the American Civil War, when Union Catholics turned to the Archbishop of New York while Confederate Catholics looked to the Archbishop of New Orleans for support. Pius IX promoted the establishment of an American College in Rome, charged with training future American priests, and promised personal financial support for the venture. A college was founded in 1859 under the Rev. John McCloskey. Following pressure from Abraham Lincoln, on March 15, 1875 Pius IX elevated John McCloskey to the College of Cardinals, in which he was the first American.

In Germany, as in other countries, the pontificate of Pius IX was to witness a growth and development of the church after the 1848 revolution. His pontificate was to witness the establishment of a variety of movements and organizations which pledged fidelity to the pope and the teachings of the church. In November 1848 the German hierarchy established a Catholic bishops' conference which met annually. In 1850 the Prussian constitution guaranteed complete freedom to the Catholic Church.

A concordat with the government in Württemberg was negotiated but never implemented, and a concordat with the Grand Duchy of Baden in 1859 was later abolished on April 7, 1860. Following the definition of papal infallibility at Vatican I, both Protestant and liberal Catholic fears of possible papal interference in German affairs increased. Otto von Bismarck promoted a _Kulturkampf_ which effectively restricted Catholic Church involvement in the areas of education, evangelization, clerical formation, and episcopal administration. Five of the eleven Prussian bishops were incarcerated for a period, and several religious congregations were proscribed, with members of the Society of Jesus expelled from the country by law in July 1872. Active discrimination took place against Catholics throughout the _Kulturkampf_ era. By 1878 two-thirds of the Catholic bishops had been forcefully removed from their positions and over 1,000 parishes were without priests. The German government expropriated churches in an attempt to weaken the Catholic faith further. In Baden the ruling duchy claimed the right to nominate all prospective episcopal and clerical appointments and to oversee the formation of clerical students for the priesthood. After Archbishop Hermann von Vicari refused to accept government restrictions on his ministry, he was tried and was placed under twenty-four-hour state supervision while members of his clergy were imprisoned, exiled, or fined. Despite such restrictive moves by the civil authorities, however, Catholicism in Germany continued to thrive under Pope Pius IX. Following his death in 1878 moves promoting a rapprochement between church and state were actively pursued by von Bismarck. Finally, on May 27, 1887, the successor to Pius IX, Pope Leo XIII, acknowledged the formal ending of the *Kulturkampf.*

In Austria-Hungary the 1848 revolution had some positive outcomes with respect to the internal governance of the church. During his pontificate, for example, Pius was able to create new episcopal sees throughout the Austro-Hungarian Empire. In 1866 Austria nullified several legal provisions in areas of religion regarding education and marriages. In 1870 the previous 1855 concordat with the Holy See was revoked by Emperor Franz Joseph I under pressure from anti-Catholic political movements. Responding to anti-Catholic legislative moves in the empire, Pius, following a series of failed diplomatic interventions, demanded educational and religious freedom for Catholics in an encyclical, *Vix dum a nobis,* on March 7, 1874.

In the year after his pontificate commenced Pius IX came to an arrangement with Russia under the terms of which the Holy See was empowered to fill vacant episcopal sees of the Latin rite in both the Baltic countries and the Polish provinces of Russia. Aspects of this agreement were quickly undermined by personal and political tensions within rival Orthodox Church communities. Polish independent political activism, often based in church property and communities, coupled with the brutality of imperial Russian suppression of dissenting groups, posed challenges for the successful implementation of the agreement. Pius initially attempted to negotiate a middle way through diverse factions, strongly opposing revolutionary independence movements while appealing for more church freedom. Following the failure of the Polish uprising in 1863, he publicly sided with the persecuted Poles, thereby alienating the Tsarist regime. The civil authorities retaliated by severing relations with the Holy See, expatriating whole Catholic communities to Siberia, exiling priests, condemning many to labor camps, abolishing Catholic dioceses, and suppressing all Catholic episcopal sees by 1870.

On September 29, 1850, with the bull *Universalis ecclesiae*, Pope Pius IX re-established the Catholic hierarchy in England by erecting the Archdiocese of Westminster with twelve suffragan sees: Beverley, Birmingham, Clifton, Hexham, Liverpool, Newport and Menevia, Northampton, Nottingham, Plymouth, Salford, Shrewsbury, and Southwark. The British government reacted strongly to the restoration of the English Catholic hierarchy. In Protestant Britain the restoration was strongly denounced as yet another encroachment on the rights of both the established church and the civil authority by the Roman Catholic Church. The result was that "furious no popery agitation" erupted.[1] So strong was the reaction that the Liberal prime minister, Lord John Russell, whose anti-Roman Catholic tendencies were already known, denounced the papal decision to restore the Roman Catholic hierarchy and introduced the Ecclesiastical Titles Bill, which would make illegal the assumption by Catholic prelates of titles taken from any place in the United Kingdom.[2]

Stimulated by an Irish episcopal appeal urging nonviolent resistance to the Ecclesiastical Titles Bill, a series of mass public protests, modeled on Daniel O'Connell's "monster meetings" of earlier decades, took place all over Ireland. By March 1851 the widespread extent of the meetings was such as to cause concern to the British authorities in Ireland. The chief secretary for Ireland, William Somerville, wrote in alarm to the prime minister of the manifest strength and size of the groundswell of opinion against the bill, warning how "accounts from Ireland lead me to believe that the agitation against the bill in its present form is only commencing."[3] This movement was undoubtedly influential in ensuring that the impact of the Ecclesiastical Titles Bill was more symbolic than real.

THE PAPAL MAGISTERIUM

Pius IX was both aware and convinced of his role as the highest teaching authority in the church. In a record total of thirty-eight encyclicals he took a position on church issues, which helped to assert identity and confidence in the church. Pius IX was the first pope to popularize encyclicals

---

[1] Cullen to Kirby (Rector, Irish College, Rome), December 3, 1850, Irish College Archives, Rome, New Collection, III, 1, 2, no. 60.

[2] In "Relazione sullo stato generale della religione cattolica in Inghilterra ed Irlanda," February 15, 1848, Russell is described as "un nemico manifesto della nostra Santa Religione." Archivio Segreto Vaticano, Vatican, Rome, Pio IX, Oggetti Vari, no. 440.

[3] Somerville (chief secretary Ireland) to Russell (prime minister), March 4, 1851, National Archives, Kew, PRO, 30/22, no. 9.

on a large scale. On a theological front he fought against what he viewed as false liberalism, which he believed threatened to destroy the very essence of faith and religion. In his encyclical *Quanta cura* of December 8, 1864, for example, he condemned sixteen propositions relating to the errors of the age. This encyclical was accompanied by the "Syllabus of Errors" – a table of eighty censured propositions bearing on pantheism, naturalism, rationalism, indifferentism, socialism, communism, free-masonry, and various kinds of religious liberalism. In this "Syllabus of Errors," highly controversial at the time, Pius IX stood up against what he considered heresies of secular society. This condemnatory approach to perceived intellectual and societal enemies to Catholicism was reflected in Ireland in the condemnation of the revolutionary nationalist Fenian organization in 1870.

After a lengthy series of deliberations by preparatory commissions, Pius opened the First Vatican Council in St. Peter's Basilica on December 8, 1869. It was the twentieth ecumenical council of the Catholic Church and the first ecumenical council to be convened in over three centuries. Nearly 800 church leaders representing every continent attended, although the European members held a clear majority. A disproportionate percentage of the English-speaking bishops who attended, for example, were Irish or of Irish descent. The council passed two constitutions, *Dei filius* and *Pastor aeternus*. Undoubtedly the most important theological legacy of Pope Pius IX lies in the decrees of Vatican I. From the outset of the council the question of infallibility dominated discussion. A vocal and vigorous minority opposed the doctrine both on theological and historical grounds and as being inopportune. Nonetheless, on July 18, 1870, in the constitution *Pastor aeternus* the council solemnly accepted the proposition that when a pope speaks *ex cathedra* on faith or morals he does so definitively with the supreme apostolic authority. Although this was controversial, once it had been passed numerous bishops who had argued that proclaiming the definition was inopportune accepted it. Numerous members of the council effectively abstained in the ultimate vote on the draft constitution by leaving Rome on the day before the vote. Shortly after the vote on infallibility, the Franco-Prussian War and the ultimately successful invasion of the Roman state by the Italian army abruptly ended the council. Vatican I marked the climax and triumph of the movement of Ultramontanism yet also helped stimulate a renewed wave of anti-clericalism in several European states. It also contributed significantly to a strengthening and centralization of the Catholic Church throughout the world.

Pope Pius IX professed and practiced a deep devotion to the Virgin Mary and ensured that Marian doctrines and devotions were actively promoted. Responding to various petitions requesting the dogmatization of the Immaculate Conception, in 1848 Pius appointed a theological commission to analyze the possibility of a Marian dogma. He proclaimed the doctrine of the Immaculate Conception as a dogma of the church on December 8, 1854 by means of the bull *Ineffabilis Deus*, in the presence of over 200 bishops. Theologically this declared the preservation of Mary from every stain of hereditary sin from the first moment of her conception, as a divinely revealed truth which demanded universal acceptance. While it had been a traditional belief for many centuries, the declaration ranks among the more significant theological acts of Pope Pius IX. Throughout his pontificate Marian devotion was actively encouraged throughout the Catholic world. Marian altars and statues proliferated and were established in many Catholic churches, schools, hospitals, institutions, and homes.

IRELAND

Throughout Ireland the pontificate of Pius IX was marked by a noticeable expansion of a church building program. His pontificate also witnessed a renewed focus on Ultramontane theological formation in Ireland. With the growth in numbers studying for the priesthood and religious life came an increase in formation programs and seminaries. Dublin Archdiocese, for example, opened its own seminary, Holy Cross College, in 1859, which taught a theological program in accordance with a theology of the pontificate of the day. In Ireland the new self-confidence of the Catholic Church under Pius IX was seen in the establishment of the Catholic Defence Association of Great Britain and Ireland on August 19, 1851[4] and the foundation of the National Association in December 1864.[5]

The era of Pope Pius IX witnessed the foundation of many institutions to cater for the spiritual, medical, social, and educational requirements of Catholics in Ireland. Numerous hospitals administered by a variety of religious orders were established. Likewise many secondary schools providing for the educational needs of Catholics opened under the auspices of various religious congregations. No fewer than thirty-nine significant religious foundations were opened in Dublin, and a wide variety of religious orders, both male and female, established or expanded their mission in Ireland. Alongside the increase in vocations and the establishment and

---

[4] *Freeman's Journal* (August 20, 1851).   [5] Ibid. (December 30, 1864).

development of religious orders, the pontificate was to witness a marked increase in church building in Ireland.

The influence of Pius IX was seen universally in his episcopal appointments. Whenever a diocesan vacancy occurred, a policy was followed of appointing Ultramontane bishops to sees previously occupied by recognized or perceived Gallican ones. The appointment of Ultramontane coadjutor bishops also became popular. Historically Pius's most significant episcopal appointment to Ireland was that of Paul Cullen to Armagh in 1849. Paul Cullen had by then served as Rector of the Irish College in Rome and Professor and Rector of the Congregation for the Propagation of the Faith. Ordained Archbishop of Armagh in Rome on February 24, 1850, he was also appointed apostolic delegate to Ireland.[6] In 1852 he transferred to the See of Dublin, and in 1866 he was named as Ireland's first cardinal – all marks of the pontiff's confidence in Cullen. With the approval and blessing of Pope Pius IX Cullen set about a program of reform that was to leave a lasting mark on the Irish church for many decades.

Pope Pius IX's interest in Ireland featured from early in his pontificate. Conscious of the devastating effects of the Great Famine, he issued an encyclical, *Praedecessores nostros*, on the topic in 1847 in which he appealed for prayers and for charity. This model of response was to be followed many times in the face of economic plight later in his pontificate. The Irish hierarchy adopted the same approach when tackling the question of national poverty.[7] They kept the Holy See fully informed of the economic plight of people in Ireland, and while they attacked the structures that created or contributed to this poverty,[8] the theology preached was the acceptance of suffering.[9]

During the pontificate of Pius IX the Irish hierarchy grew increasingly assertive, concerning itself not only with theological questions but also with contemporary social, economic, and political issues, particularly those deemed to involve morality. Pius IX repeatedly called for episcopal unity in Ireland, and he personally dedicated considerable time, effort, and energy to the issues that confronted the Irish church. His pontificate also

[6] Archivio Segreto Vaticano, Secretaria Brevium 5172, fol. 59.

[7] "The Synodical Address of the Fathers of the National Council of Thurles 1850," in P.F. Moran, ed., *The Pastoral Letters and Other Writings of Cardinal Cullen* (Dublin: Browne and Nolan, 1882), I, 44.

[8] See Cullen to the Congregation for the Propagation of the Faith, September 22, 1852, Archives of the Congregation for the Propagation of the Faith, Vatican, Rome, "Scritture riferite nei congressi, Irlanda," vol. 31, fol. 249.

[9] See ibid., fol. 248v; see also Cullen to Smith, September 22, 1852, Benedictine Archives, Rome, Smith Papers.

witnessed greater attendance of bishops at Rome. All four archbishops, for example, attended the declaration of the Immaculate Conception, and Irish episcopal participation was significant at Vatican I. In the years following the commencement of the pontificate Ireland was named as "the poorest country that one can know."[10]

By the time of the death of Pope Pius IX the Irish church had been restructured; the clergy had become more disciplined; the numbers of religious and clergy increased; the educational and social outreach of the church expanded; the numbers of Catholic churches and institutions vastly expanded; the hierarchy was more unified; the liturgy was reformed; and the Catholic populace was better catechized and more assertive and self-confident. Along with its material poverty and a wide range of social, health, and educational challenges, ecclesiologically the Irish church was disorganized and overall poorly administered at the dawn of Pius IX's pontificate, lacking many fundamental structures. Pastoral care and preaching were sometimes fitful, attendance at Eucharistic celebrations was irregular, and the administration of the other sacraments was often erratic. The pontificate of Pope Pius IX was to witness a restructuring of the Irish church emerging from an era of penal legal discrimination, weak organizational frameworks, and the social impact of repeated hunger and national famine. Encouraged by Pius IX, great use was made of the summoning of regular synods, national, provincial, and diocesan, in Ireland and other countries, and in Ireland the pontificate was to witness a convening of the episcopal conference at regular intervals. The Irish episcopal synods initiated during Pius's pontificate served to assert publicly the Irish hierarchy's expressions of both power and influence; they marked an important stage in the rising confidence of the Catholic Church and its leaders and shaped Irish Catholicism for well over a century after Pius's death. Not only was the convening of synods a significant innovation in establishing a post-penal model of church, but their frequency was also noteworthy. They were often summoned to address pressing issues such as the appropriateness or otherwise of active political involvement by priests. However, the fact that a synod might direct or prohibit any particular clerical activity did not result immediately in universal compliance in every diocese. Nowhere was this more evident than in the field of priests in politics.

---

[10] "Relazione riguardo al proselitismo protestante nell'occidente d'Irlanda. Suo successo e mezzi adoperati," no date, Archivio Segreto Vaticano, Pio IX, Oggetti Vari, no. 993. Here and elsewhere in this chapter translations are mine unless otherwise stated.

In accordance with the mind of Pope Pius IX, the strategy of enacting change through synodal decree was adopted by Paul Cullen as apostolic delegate. Cullen was an Ultramontanist. He believed that the church in Ireland should follow the Roman model in teaching, practice, and discipline. He was opposed to many local popular religious beliefs and spiritual expressions and was determined to replace them with theologically acceptable devotions such as forty-hour Eucharistic devotions, missions, and parish retreats. Such initiatives transformed the devotional religious face of Ireland. The Synod of Thurles, held from August 22 to September 9, 1850, marked the beginning of this process in aiming to reform the institutions of the Catholic Church. This was the first national synod of the Catholic hierarchy held in Ireland since the Middle Ages and the most significant one of the nineteenth century. Along with succeeding synods, it achieved this end by a variety of means, such as standardizing administrative and sacramental practices, introducing uniform liturgical norms, and outlining behavioral standards for members of the clergy. The synods that took place during the pontificate of Pius IX initiated a process of introducing new regulations and norms which impacted radically on the Catholic Church in Ireland.

This is true in particular in relation to the administration of sacraments. During the era of the penal laws the sacraments of baptism, marriage, and reconciliation were celebrated mostly in private homes, and these practices continued into the mid-nineteenth century. During the pontificate of Pius IX an expansion in church building resulted in a change of religious liturgical custom. The celebration of the sacraments of marriage and baptism in private residences was forbidden and was normally restricted to churches. Marriage and baptismal registers were mandated for every parish. Marriages between Catholics and non-Catholics were actively discouraged, and the church's disapproval of such unions was demonstrated by its withholding from the ceremony much of what was contained in the normal marriage ritual.

The pontificate of Pius IX witnessed the emergence of a more disciplined clergy. By synodal regulation, priests were instructed to attend retreats and to keep themselves theologically informed. Restrictions were imposed on their lifestyle. Each parish was mandated to provide a parochial house for the parish priest. Priests were prohibited from denouncing individuals from the altar, or from celebrating Mass after noon. They were instructed not to engage in public disputes with members of other religions. Ecumenical dialogue was also restricted.

Prior to the pontificate of Pius IX deep divisions remained among the Irish hierarchy, clergy, and people on the issue of the university question.

With respect to the controversial issue of third-level education, under Pope Pius IX the so-called Queen's Colleges were condemned. From early in his pontificate the Irish hierarchy repeatedly published rescripts from Rome which prohibited clerics from holding office in the colleges. During his pontificate he took several strides – not always successful – to resolve the disputes and mandate a single policy about university education for Catholics. With the direct encouragement of Pope Pius IX the Irish hierarchy attempted to establish a Catholic university, but it proved to be a controversial, contentious, expensive, and short-lived project.

Under Pope Pius IX church attendance among Catholics in Ireland increased dramatically. This renewed devotion was helped by the increase in religious vocations, the expansion of church building since the 1840s, and the decline of the Irish population resulting from the Great Famine. In the two decades following Cullen's arrival in Ireland as apostolic delegate of Pope Pius IX the number of priests and religious increased appreciably. Under the impetus given by Pius IX the Irish Catholic laity had greater access to clergy and churches than at any other time for generations past. The renewal in devotion was accompanied by an evident increase in religious vocations. The Ultramontane Catholic Church created in Ireland under Pius IX had a powerful influence on education, health care, public morality, and national politics, though it professed to be non-political.

Pope Pius IX and his apostolic delegate Paul Cullen are still acknowledged as the influential figures that made Catholic Ireland what it remained for over a hundred years. The structures established during the era of Pius IX in the areas of health care and education endured for a similar length of time. Religious dominance in these authoritarian systems of care, however, facilitated the development of a structure which was inherently flawed, in that those in care had no voice and remained invisible in the event of injustice or cruelty or abuse.

The popular depth of affection and dedication of the Irish church to the Catholic faith in general and Pope Pius IX in particular can be seen in the manner in which the bishops and people responded to the Italian political crisis of 1859–60. At this time the Irish church launched a campaign to assist the beleaguered pope in defense of his territorial possessions against the forces of the Italian Risorgimento. This initiative would result in a prayer campaign for the pope, financial collections for him, and the formation of a 1,200-strong military Battalion of St. Patrick, popularly referred to as "the Irish Papal Brigade."[11]

---

[11] *Battersby's Catholic Directory, 1860* (Dublin: W. J. Battersby, 1860); Edward Lucas, *The Life of Frederick Lucas, MP*, 2 vols. (London, 1886), 138.

It is interesting to speculate why so many volunteered for military service: there were undoubtedly many who could honestly claim that their sole motive was to defend the rights of the church and to fight for the pope.[12] These volunteers went to the Papal States with the strongest feelings of devotion to the Holy Father and without any other motive.[13] Indeed, they viewed the cause as a noble one,[14] a holy cause, a sentiment exemplified by the volunteer who resigned from his employment by sending his employer a telegram announcing "Rome being threatened – I hasten to her defence."[15] All of this demonstrated the public popular appeal of Pope Pius IX. The Irish brigade served in military engagements in Perugia, Spoleto, Castelfidardo, and Ancona, but in all these encounters it was on the losing side. Three members of the brigade lost their lives in Spoleto, and it is estimated that in the entire campaign, the Irish sustained some sixty-five casualties.[16] Across Ireland the defeat of the papal armies brought an outpouring of sympathy for Pope Pius IX.[17] Large crowds, composed in the main of the lower social orders, according to *The Irish Times*,[18] hailed the returned volunteers as men conquered but not disgraced.[19] After defeating the papal army in various engagements, in September 1860 Victor Emmanuel took all of the papal territories except Latium with Rome. On September 20, 1870 he seized Rome as well, making it the capital of a new united Italy. With the end of the Papal States in 1870, popes no longer held temporal powers.

The pontificate of Pius IX witnessed a growth of social influence in the Catholic Church in Ireland. The church expanded and flourished. It became more assertive and grew in consciousness of its identity, especially in opposition to the Protestant churches. The pontificate also marked an important stage in the rising confidence of the Catholic Church in Ireland and its leaders, and helped shape Irish Catholicism for well over a century to come. Pius's leadership of the church contributed to an ever-increasing centralization, with Rome and the papacy as the center of the Catholic Church. The Catholic Church in Ireland gained during this era an increasingly powerful influence on education, public morality, and social life. Irish missions and migrants began to export this type of Catholicism to the English-speaking

[12] Narrative of Brother Aloysius Howlin, National Library of Ireland, Dublin, MS 13282, file G.
[13] *The Cork Examiner* (November 27, 1929).
[14] O'Carroll to O'Carroll, June 27, 1860, National Library of Ireland, MS 21522.
[15] O'Connell to Berkeley June 19, 1911, National Library of Ireland, MS 13284.
[16] Cf. G. F. H. Berkeley, *The Irish Battalion in the Papal Army of 1860*; Lucas, *Life of Frederick Lucas*, 242.
[17] *The Irishman* 3:15 (October 20, 1860).   [18] *The Irish Times* 2:472 (November 5, 1860).
[19] W. to Quinn, October 25, 1860, Dublin Diocesan Archives, 333/3.

world – to Britain, the British Empire, and the United States. While his political views and policies caused controversy, Pius's personal lifestyle was above any criticism.

Pope Pius IX's pontificate marks the beginning of the modern papacy. The art of photography was developed, and he was the first pope to be photographed, mainly in his later years. He also was artistic, and was the composer of one of Italy's favorite Christmas carols. He was beatified by Pope John Paul II on September 3, 2000. His reforms and Vatican I, which he convened, were considered milestones not only in his pontificate but also in church history.

Pope Pius IX died on February 7, 1878. Throughout his lengthy pontificate he succeeded in provoking deep emotions – both negative and positive. Even after his death the procession with his remains for interment was attacked by some who attempted to disrupt the funeral cortege. In his lifetime he lost temporal power in the Papal States, but the gain in spiritual authority as a pastor is exemplified by the popularity for generations in Ireland of a hymn, "Faith of our Fathers," that was sung by the Irish Papal Brigade in 1860 before one of the failed military ventures, the Battle of Spoleto. This became a rallying cry not only for religious festivities in Ireland but also on cultural and sporting occasions in Gaelic Athletic Association stadia, where Irish nationalists sang with pride:

> Faith of our fathers burning still
> We will be true to thee till death
> We will be true to thee till death.

CHAPTER 8

The social question in the papacy of Leo XIII

Thomas Massaro

This chapter explores the distinctive contribution of Pope Leo XIII (1810–1903, reigned 1878–1903) to the contemporary understanding and practice of papal pastoral leadership. The central focus will be on how Leo exercised the papal teaching office in new ways that corresponded to the unprecedented challenges of his time. After a brief review of how Leo utilized the genre of papal encyclicals to advance his agenda as a universal pastor, particularly by treating political and cultural issues of his time, the chapter will assess the significance and legacy of the 1891 encyclical *Rerum novarum*. This pioneering social teaching document placed the church on the side of workers in their struggle for labor justice and ushered in a new era of social concern on the part of the worldwide church. The strength and vitality of Catholic social teaching and its advocacy of social justice that we take for granted today derive from this landmark encyclical.

When Gioacchino Vincenzo Pecci became Pope Leo XIII in 1878, nobody could have imagined the bewildering changes that lay in store for the church and the world during his reign. Ahead lay one of the very longest papacies in history, one that would stretch well into the twentieth century. Few would have expected a pope elected in his late sixties, having served over three decades as the Archbishop of Perugia, to lead the church for another quarter-century.

Yet the sheer length of Leo's papacy, which ended with his death in 1903, was more than matched by the remarkable achievements of this papacy. Chief among the initiatives of Pope Leo XIII was a deliberate enhancement of the formal teaching role of the Bishop of Rome. In many and frequent ways, Leo signaled his intention to broaden and deepen this pastoral dimension of the office that he held. The papal encyclical emerged as the favored medium for communicating new (and, of course, sometimes not so new) teachings to the faithful on an astonishingly wide range of subjects. The encyclical (or circulating letter) is a vehicle well suited for highly authoritative and well-developed papal pronouncements. Unlike many other types of papal documents, addresses, and occasional writings, encyclicals are often of considerable length, surpassing on occasion the 10,000-word mark. Although this genre demonstrates considerable variability in length, tone, content, and intended audience, it is fair to say that in issuing an encyclical a pope is indicating a highly deliberate intention to serve as a teacher and pastor to all who will read and ponder the topics treated in this sophisticated document.

THE ENCYCLICALS OF LEO XIII

By the time of Leo's election, the genre of the modern encyclical had been employed for over a century, ever since Benedict XIV issued *Ubi primum* in 1740. The eight popes who reigned from 1740 to 1846 promulgated thirty-nine encyclical letters in all. Leo's immediate predecessor, Pius IX, nearly matched that total output, issuing thirty-eight during his own long papacy (1846–78). But it was Leo XIII who set the still-current record, producing eighty-six encyclicals and easily surpassing the total output of his nine predecessors in total number of words and pages. Even John Paul II, the only pope since Leo to hold office for over twenty years, was responsible for just a small fraction of the number of encyclicals that Leo contributed.[1]

What messages do the encyclicals of Leo XIII offer? The topics treated in the teaching corpus of Leo resist brief summary, for this pontiff deliberately utilized the genre of encyclicals to cover the full range of concerns that occupied his papacy. For example, a number of his encyclical writings are dedicated to promoting the theology of St. Thomas Aquinas, a favorite of Leo as well as of his brother, a Jesuit priest who taught for many years as a seminary professor. Most notable among these documents is *Aeterni Patris*, published in 1879 as the third encyclical of Leo's papacy (and, at nearly 7,000 words, one of the longest). Here, the pope praises the Christian philosophy of this thirteenth-century doctor of the church and lays out a programmatic strategy to encourage the teaching of Aquinas

[1] For a comprehensive accounting of papal encyclicals, including full texts of the entire corpus translated into English, see Claudia Carlen, IHM, ed., *The Papal Encyclicals, 1740–1981*, 5 vols. (Raleigh, NC: Pierian Press, 1981). Leo XIII is the only pope whose encyclicals occupy an entire volume of this five-volume set. As a supplement to a reprinting of the set in 1990, Carlen has also edited a two-volume set of additional papal pronouncements in other genres, such as papal addresses that constitute less formal teaching, *Papal Pronouncements: A Guide, 1740–1978* (Ann Arbor, MI: Pierian Press, 1990), but the present analysis considers only the single genre of papal encyclicals.

in seminaries and Catholic institutions of higher learning.[2] The legacy of Pope Leo's support of the Thomistic revival has continued right up to the present.

Not every encyclical of Leo contained messages of such universal importance and scope. Dozens are directed at local Catholic communities and their leaders, usually the bishops of a given country or region. Thus we encounter encyclicals on Christian education in England (*Spectata fides*, 1885), on Italian immigration into the United States (*Quam aerumnosa*, 1888), and on the morality of economic boycotts in Ireland (*Saepe nos*, 1888). Many others (usually among the shortest in length) take on the modest tasks of announcing jubilees or commending pious practices, such as the recitation of the Rosary or devotion to particular saints. Some initiatives that occupy Leo's encyclicals strike the contemporary ear as unnecessary or even amusing attempts at micro-managing the moral lives of Catholics around the world. For example, Leo issued an encyclical on the morality of dueling (*Pastoralis officii*, 1891) and another on the controversy regarding which language should serve as the official spoken tongue in Bohemia (*Reputantibus*, 1901). More typical, however, are the many Leonine encyclicals that offer encouragement and religious guidance to Catholic leaders and laity or that seek to inspire energy for missions abroad or fidelity to the ordinary tasks of maintaining a vibrant local church community.

THE POLITICAL WRITINGS OF LEO XIII

Besides these instructions for social mores and for the internal life of the church, Leo often took up topics that clearly held weighty implications for the relations between church and world, and often specifically for the Catholic Church in a given political environment. This concern for the political conditions faced by Catholics in many parts of the globe is a hallmark of Leo's papacy, and indicates much about his understanding of himself as teacher and pastor. At times, it appears that Leo was indirectly appealing to certain parties outside the Catholic ecclesial community, such as diplomats, legislators, and heads of state, whatever their religious commitments, to heed his advice on points of diplomacy and international relations. Although encyclicals of this era were still presented

---

[2] For an assessment of Pope Leo XIII's project to revive the study of St. Thomas Aquinas, see Serge-Thomas Bonino, OP, "Le fondement doctrinal du projet léonine: *Aeterni Patris* et la restauration du thomisme," 267–74, and Philippe Capelle, "Le retentissement d'*Aeterni Patris* en philosophie et en théologie," 275–84: both in Philippe Levillain and Jean-Marc Ticchi, eds., *Le pontificat de Léon XIII: renaissances du Saint-Siège?* (Rome: École Française de Rome, 2006).

as *ad intra* (or in-house) documents, Leo clearly expected these outsiders to be "looking over the shoulders" of bishops and other church officials, to whom the encyclicals are in most cases formally addressed. Emerging from such Leonine encyclicals as *Immortale Dei* ("On the Christian Constitution of States," 1885), *Libertas* ("On the Nature of Human Liberty," 1888), *Sapientiae christianae* ("On Christians as Citizens," 1890), and *Graves de communi re* ("On Christian Democracy," 1901) is a rather sophisticated theory of church–state relations. Leo evidently thought it his mission, precisely as pontiff (a title that derives from the Latin word for "bridge"), to address a wide variety of audiences, directly or indirectly. He did not allow previous constraints upon the encyclical genre to limit the scope and audience of his message. Encyclical letters could serve purposes that transcended the utility of intramural messages; when they took note of developments in the extra-ecclesial world, it could be for purposes other than issuing anathemas or condemnations.

These observations about Leo's *ad extra* concerns are nevertheless compatible with this reminder to the converse. Even the most political of Leo's encyclicals remain at heart religious documents, concerned above all about matters of faith and the conditions related to living out a vibrant faith in a complex world. To John Courtney Murray goes credit for discerning in these writings of Leo the seeds of transition to something new. As this influential American Jesuit noted in his seminal analysis of the political writings of Leo XIII, these encyclicals represent an attempt to stand firm on core principles derived from the Christian tradition of reflection on life in human society.[3] However, Leo is doing more than merely repeating past ecclesial formulations regarding political justice and the shape of correct public order. He addresses political life in a way that grapples profoundly with the bewildering challenges presented to the institutional church by the radically new social, political, and economic order of the late nineteenth century. Whether the topic is the introduction of democracy to new cultural contexts or the imperative of abolishing slavery in lands colonized by European powers, Leo XIII utilizes the encyclical genre to accomplish two goals. First, he seeks to commend the preservation of what is best in past practices. Second, Leo is eager to offer his assessment of the wisdom of proposed reforms that might foster the attainment of constructive social change.

---

[3] John Courtney Murray, SJ, "Leo XIII: Two Concepts of Government," *Theological Studies* 14 (1953), 551–67, and, "Leo XIII: Two Concepts of Government, II: Government and the Order of Culture," *Theological Studies* 15 (1954), 1–33.

It is crucial in this regard to recall that the papacy of Leo XIII commenced at almost the precise midpoint between the French Revolution and the Second Vatican Council. This pope's encyclicals on political topics reflect this reality, looking both forward and backward as they do. The church had not yet overcome its posture of extreme defensiveness and suspicion regarding the modern liberal order, as the long hangover of the French Revolution era had not yet dissipated. However, Catholicism in the Leonine papacy was evidently beginning to grope its way toward a renewed and more positive stance toward church–world relations, something that would eventually be reflected in the Vatican II document *Gaudium et spes* ("Pastoral Constitution on the Church in the Modern World") of 1965. On the specific topic of politics in these years, John Courtney Murray demonstrates how Leo's approach to government may be interpreted as a bridge to twentieth-century Catholic political thought. By commenting on where Christians stood vis-à-vis core principles of political justice in the closing decades of the nineteenth century, Leo's political writings prepared the ground for change and thereby positioned the church to face the coming challenges of a new century, as unpredictable as these developments would prove to be.

To characterize Leo XIII as a bridge figure in this way is to acknowledge at least two aspects of his contribution. On the one hand, Leo's accomplishments are extremely valuable in themselves, as his political writings analyzed with keen insight the political situation of his day, at least the conditions that obtained in Europe and North America and the possibilities that these conditions contained for religious communities and their members. On the other hand, Leo's guidance remains fundamentally transitional in nature. That is to say, Pope Leo XIII stands self-consciously in the line of eighteenth- and nineteenth-century popes who were forced to come to grips, often in wrenching ways, with the fallout of the French Revolution and subsequent events that stripped the Catholic Church of so much of its power in Western Europe. It is easy for twenty-first-century observers to forget that some of this power had been temporal in nature, involving large landholdings and financial interests. Indeed, Leo XIII was the first pope to come into office without the advantage of controlling the Papal States. These were the swaths of territory in central and southern Italy that had been removed from papal control during the Italian national unification that culminated during the reign of Leo's predecessor, Pius IX. The wounds to the prestige and power of the Catholic Church were still raw, and the effects of the resultant backlash must not be underestimated. Nineteenth-century church leaders found themselves in the position of actively seeking to redefine the public role of the church in a liberalizing and secularizing world.

It is thus not surprising to see in Leo's political writings repeated denunciations of the secularizing trends of his day, and particularly of what traditional Catholics perceived as virulent forms of laicism that were most evident in Continental Europe. Successive popes throughout this era engaged in the Sisyphean task of reasserting their authority however they could. What ended this quest was the eventual collective realization that this authority could no longer be construed as directly political, but must now be primarily moral in nature. Even the most Ultramontane of observers had to face up to changed social and political conditions that were redefining the scope and features of papal power. Church leaders were learning to drop all pretense of exerting direct control over worldly events in favor of acknowledging a more modest role within a sharply differentiated area of competence: a restricted sphere best described, in common theological parlance, as consisting of "faith and morals." In his study of the encounter of Catholicism and liberalism, sociologist Gene Burns traces the arc of how the church gradually embraced the mantle of "moral advocacy" in a world that had come to deny direct political power to religious authorities.[4] In conducting this "boundary work" that aimed at specifying the role, but also at determining the limits, of the church's influence, Leo and subsequent popes adopted new strategies and even came to recognize new allies in their efforts to develop a social doctrine that would protect and promote key values in the context of a new world order.

LEO XIII AND THE CATHOLIC CHURCH IN THE UNITED
STATES: A CASE STUDY IN CATHOLICISM WITHIN
NEW LIBERAL CONSTITUTIONAL ORDERS

In the political realm, the key questions facing Catholics of Leo's time related to the standing of the Catholic Church within the newly established secular republics of Europe and other regions of the world. The United States, with its national constitution enshrining a formal prohibition of religious establishment, was a pioneer in this regard. By the time Leo assumed the papacy in 1878, the United States Constitution had experienced nine decades of remarkable success. Not to be overlooked was the fact that the Catholic community in the United States had worked

---

[4] Gene Burns, *The Frontiers of Catholicism: The Politics of Ideology in a Liberal World* (Berkeley: University of California Press, 1992), 201.

out a favorable *modus vivendi* with the legal arrangements of the republic. Indeed the small but growing Catholic Church in the United States was most evidently thriving in a uniquely pluralistic setting that featured extensive religious freedom and a completely voluntary principle regarding religious affiliation and church support. As such, the vitality of the American Catholic community demonstrated that a regime of religious neutrality could be a favorable environment for Catholics. It was certainly superior to situations where Catholic minorities found themselves persecuted, barely tolerated, or severely restricted in their religious practices. Compared with the situation of Catholics in Great Britain, the mother country of what came to be the United States, American Catholicism enjoyed greater freedom.

But, it was conversely argued, the Catholic Church in the United States did not enjoy the distinct advantages available in situations where Catholicism was the favored or formally established religion. These advantages might include government support for Catholic education, hospitals, and social services among other institutions, as well as many other prerogatives and privileges long enjoyed in southern and western Europe. Such throne-and-altar arrangements still functioned as the point of reference for papal pronouncements on the subject of church–state relations. Indeed, Leo's 1895 encyclical *Longinqua*, an assessment of the religious scene in the United States addressed to the United States bishops, expressed the sentiment that the Catholic Church there "would bring forth more abundant fruits if, in addition to liberty, she enjoyed the favor of the laws and patronage of the public authority."[5] Questions regarding the appropriate Catholic stance toward the legal status of religion would, of course, persist until Vatican II's Declaration on Religious Freedom (*Dignitatis humanae*, 1965). There the council fathers took a strong stand in favor of American-style liberty of conscience, portraying it as more than a grudging concession to pluralism, but as truly a permanent guiding principle of Catholic social thought.

Well beyond the scope of this chapter lies a comprehensive assessment of how Leo XIII and his successors dealt with the general matter of the status of Catholicism within pluralist contexts, or even more specifically the resolution of problems regarding church and state facing the Catholic community in the United States. There is in fact some disagreement among historians about the extent to which such matters were in serious dispute

---

[5] From the text of the 1895 encyclical *Longinqua*, quoted in Chester Gillis, *Roman Catholicism in America* (New York: Columbia University Press, 1999), 65.

or ever constituted a "crisis" at all. In an insightful essay surveying Leo's dealings with his American flock, Gerald Fogarty, SJ, offers an account of this era that downplays the various conflicts pertaining to the legal status of Catholicism on United States shores.[6] But even the most irenic account cannot completely overlook the frictions that led Leo to address the United States bishops in the famous 1899 apostolic letter *Testem benevolentiae.* This document was occasioned by the so-called "Americanist heresy." At issue was a supposed set of propositions that threatened to drive a wedge between United States Catholics and Rome on matters of local church autonomy and the basic framework of church–state relations. One accusation was that anyone with an exaggerated regard for American culture and democratic mores was in danger of compromising key tenets of the Catholic faith, or at least of indiscriminately grafting on cultural accretions that did not properly fit with a Catholic worldview. Wrapped up in the position that was labeled offensive was excessive zeal for adapting Catholicism to American culture, including an overly high regard for lay participation in ecclesial matters, extending to the practice of lay trusteeship of Catholic parishes and institutions.

The prevalence of anything resembling Americanism is in dispute, and many contemporary historians concur that its extent has been greatly exaggerated. Some even call it a "phantom heresy," the central tenets of which were held by extremely few Catholics or perhaps nobody at all.[7] In any case, the nuanced letter promulgated by Leo XIII employed indirect enough language that it succeeded in quelling any lingering tensions and misunderstandings in this sensitive situation. This gave United States church leaders an easy path to reaffirming what they all wanted anyway: amicable relations with the Roman authorities, based on the commonly held principle that strong church unity was not to be compromised. Whatever furor the controversy had kicked up quickly died down. The topic of Americanism would surface again in earnest just once more. This was when Leo's successor, Pius X, included Isaac Hecker, the American priest who founded the Paulists, in the list of potentially dangerous modernist thinkers reprimanded in the 1907 document *Pascendi dominici gregis.*

As mentioned above, John Courtney Murray portrays Leo XIII as providing a crucial bridge for Catholic thought between the era of the *ancien*

---

[6] Gerald P. Fogarty, SJ, "Leo XIII and the Church in the United States," in Levillain and Ticchi, eds., *Le pontificat de Léon XIII*, 351–68.

[7] See, e.g., the characterization of Americanism in Charles R. Morris, *American Catholic* (New York: Viking Books of Random House, 1997), 108–12.

régime (indeed, an era of nostalgia for the medieval order that obtained before the Reformation and Enlightenment) and the contemporary world we know. In one of his last publications before his untimely death, an article assessing the treatment of church-and-state issues at Vatican II, Murray credits Leo as providing the inspiration for much of what the council fathers said about the relationship between church and world. But as much as Leo's political writings laid the foundation, the world also awaited, as Murray puts it, "the development of doctrine beyond its Leonine stage."[8] Although the pontiff never fully repudiated the notion of church–state unity, he did plant the seeds for later doctrinal development on this neuralgic issue. Leo's contribution to establishing a proper relationship between ecclesial and political authority ran parallel to his effort to forge a just relationship between workers and owners in a new industrial order, and to that contribution we now turn.

THE ECONOMIC TEACHINGS OF LEO XIII:
RERUM NOVARUM

Noted above are many aspects of the reign and activity of Leo XIII that surprised or even shocked Vatican watchers. Eclipsing all the foregoing was the appearance of his 1891 social encyclical *Rerum novarum*. Even well into his pontificate, nobody could have predicted that Leo's most noteworthy encyclical would focus on economic realities in general, and the question of worker justice specifically. No previous pope had addressed matters of ethics as applied to the social order in such detail. By presenting his support for just resolution of labor issues as an outgrowth of Catholic social philosophy, Leo expanded the portfolio of authentic papal pastoral concerns. The agendas of practically all subsequent popes would include what would henceforth be referred to, somewhat idiosyncratically, as "the social question."

Released on May 15, 1891, *Rerum novarum* was the twenty-seventh of Leo's eighty-five encyclicals. At 11,250 words, it was the second longest encyclical that he would ever produce. While it does treat some of the same topics (specifically, the evils of socialism) as Leo's much shorter 1878 encyclical *Quod Apostolici muneris, Rerum novarum* reveals to the reader a side of Leo's thought and concerns barely glimpsed before. The church's engagement with the conditions of civilization was now expanded to

---

[8] John Courtney Murray, SJ, "The Issue of Church and State at Vatican II," *Theological Studies* 27 (December 1966), 580–606, at 582.

include commentary and moral judgments about the industrial order, specifically its shortcomings and injustices. Leo's consistent efforts at encouraging orderly relationships were being extended to include new fields of human endeavor, specifically the sphere of production, distribution, and employment, which now emerged as legitimate, indeed urgent, areas of ecclesial concern and papal leadership.

Rendering an account of why and how *Rerum novarum* came to be written turns out to be a rather complicated task. As is the case with most papal encyclicals, the text of *Rerum novarum* flowed from the pens of others besides the pontiff who promulgated it. Recent scholarly research has amply documented a multi-stage writing and redaction process that produced several drafts before the final text of *Rerum novarum*. Contributors evidently included the Jesuit neo-Thomist Matteo Liberatore, several monsignors (including Volpini, Boccali, and Antonazzi) close to Leo, at least two cardinals (Zigliara and Mazzella), and others who worked in the papal curia.[9] Aside from the question of who was responsible for the actual words that comprised the encyclical, the initiative for *Rerum novarum* undoubtedly sprang from Pope Leo XIII himself, who solicited information on the topic of industrial relations and oversaw the writing process. In the final accounting, despite whatever facts emerge about ghostwriting and editing, Leo must be considered the author of this document. Two key questions for historical inquiry are these: (1) what prompted Leo in the first place to take on the project of producing a statement on economic justice, and (2) precisely what courses of action does Leo propose in this document?

The first of these questions, regarding the motivation behind the first-ever social encyclical, is rather difficult to answer with certainty. While we have no direct access to the internal workings of the mind of a figure who died more than a century ago, several clues point us toward at least partial answers to questions about the impetus behind *Rerum novarum*. First, although the central Italy that Gioacchino Vincenzo Pecci and the later Leo XIII knew as home for most of his life was only in the incipient stages of industrialization, the future pope had served for three years (1843–46) in Brussels, as papal nuncio to Belgium. There he experienced his most prolonged contact with a highly advanced industrial society, and his observations of the horrifying plight of the low-paid workers there made a distinct

[9] An excellent summary of what can be known about the drafting process appears in Thomas A. Shannon, "Commentary on *Rerum novarum*," in Kenneth R. Himes, OFM, et al., eds., *Modern Catholic Social Teaching: Commentaries and Interpretations* (Washington, DC: Georgetown University Press, 2005), 127–50, at 133–34.

and lasting impression upon him. The new factory-based system of mass production trapped this new class of the proletariat into a cycle of dire poverty, one compounded by frequent injury from industrial accidents, substandard housing, and poor sanitary conditions in urban slums. Brief trips to London, Paris, and the German Rhineland may have confirmed the future pope's judgment that the church could not long ignore these social conditions.[10] If simple pastoral concern for souls reduced to grinding urban poverty and industrial exploitation were not enough to prompt Leo to go on record as an advocate of employment reforms, perhaps the familiar motive of defending the church against enemies had something to do with his papal initiative. During the decades that preceded the publication of *Rerum novarum*, Catholics and even certain high church officials had repeated the warning that the church was rapidly "losing the working classes" to socialism.[11]

However imprecise and difficult to document was this admonition, the fear of an ascendant socialist or communist menace surely sent shivers down the spines of Catholic officials in rapidly industrializing Europe. Even in the United States, where the specter of serious strife between workers and employers was just heating up in the post-Civil War decades, members of the church hierarchy began asking hard questions about ways to support workers in their struggles. Though generally quite conservative men, the United States bishops breached the topic of industrial relations in their deliberations beginning with the Third Plenary Council of Baltimore in 1884. One prelate in particular, Cardinal James Gibbons (1834–1921), Archbishop of Baltimore, went to extraordinary lengths to advocate official church recognition of the Knights of Labor, a pioneer American labor union. When he failed to receive the requisite unanimous approval of his fellow bishops in the United States, Gibbons took his case directly to Rome. On the same 1887 voyage to the Eternal City during which he received his cardinal's red hat, Gibbons submitted two memorials (letters of report and inquiry) to the Holy See. The first, appealing for approval

[10] T. F. Casey, "Pope Leo XIII," in *The New Catholic Encyclopedia*, 2nd edn. (Detroit: Thomson Gale, in association with the Catholic University of America, Washington, DC, 2003), VIII, 490–93, at 491.

[11] Paul Misner characterizes the pro-labor advocacy of Ketteler as motivated by precisely these concerns. "Pastorally, it was of the greatest moment for the church to bestir itself. Inaction was tantamount to abandoning vast numbers of the working masses to a 'proximate occasion of sin.' To preach other-worldly rewards while not lifting a finger to help the working masses would lead predictably to mass alienation from Christianity. Already they were turning to other sources of support that were indifferent to Christianity or hostile to it." *Social Catholicism in Europe: From the Onset of Industrialization to the First World War* (New York: Crossroad, 1991), 144.

of the Knights of Labor, was successful. The second asked Pope Leo not to condemn Henry George (1839–97), a populist socialist thinker whose writings (especially the 1879 volume *Progress and Poverty*) had inspired the growth of the organized labor movement in the United States, including the Knights of Labor. When it became clear to Gibbons that his second request would not be granted, the cardinal proposed the issuing of a papal encyclical on the general topic of industrial relations, that is, the rights of capital and labor.

Because Leo XIII greatly admired Cardinal Gibbons, this request no doubt played some role in creating momentum for *Rerum novarum*, which would appear less than five years later. But how accurate is it to say that this episode placed labor and social justice questions on the agenda of Leo XIII? One commentator reports matter-of-factly that Gibbons's intervention was "a proposal that ultimately resulted in Leo XIII's *Rerum Novarum*."[12] Despite the kernel of truth here, there is ample evidence, when the full story is told, that other factors contributed earlier and more significantly to persuading Leo to address economic questions. For one, the pope had been in regular contact with a group of scholars called the Fribourg Union. Led by Geneva Bishop Gaspard Mermillod (1824–92) and the French nobleman René de La Tour du Pin (1834–1924), this exclusive Catholic economic study group had provided Leo XIII with voluminous reports of its annual meetings. The topics on which it forwarded recommendations to the pope included many of the same items that showed up in the text of *Rerum novarum*: the suffering of impoverished industrial workers, great concentrations of wealth and associated abuses within the capitalist system, the dangers of untrammeled markets, and the need to establish a more equitable social equilibrium.[13]

The Fribourg Union may have been the single most influential group of its type in influencing Leo XIII, but it was by no means unique in seeking to fashion a distinctive Catholic response to the unfolding process of industrialization. For much of the nineteenth century, European Catholics had been engaged in a number of initiatives in order to understand and to improve the emerging order of industrial society, first in their particular national contexts and eventually on an international level. This very loose and diverse movement came to be labeled Social Catholicism, and notably tapped lay energies as well as clerical leadership, often with considerable support from the local church hierarchy. Prominent bishops such as Wilhelm Emmanuel von Ketteler (1811–77) of Mainz, Germany,

---

12 Fogarty, "Leo XIII," 356–57.   13 Misner, *Social Catholicism*, 203–04.

and Cardinal Henry Edward Manning (1808–92) of Westminster gained high profiles for their pioneering support for struggling workers. But a multitude of lay leaders and participants accounted for the true vitality of the movement as it struggled to forge an adequate response to new economic and social conditions. Some initiatives proceeded according to familiar models of direct charitable service, such as the social assistance organization founded by the French layman Frédéric Ozanam (1813–53) that grew into the St. Vincent de Paul Society. The budding Christian labor movement (in which the collaboration of Catholics with Protestants was long eyed with suspicion) also went beyond works of charity to identify and champion structural reforms in order to foster social justice. In many countries of Europe, Catholics founded an array of sodalities, workers' associations, education and self-improvement societies, periodicals, and study groups that advocated and enacted social reform, but which represented a self-conscious alternative to socialist organizations espousing some of the same goals.

Pope Leo XIII was familiar with the full array of these endeavors of Social Catholicism. If nothing else, he frequently received visits and granted formal audiences to organized pilgrimage groups of workers and volunteers who journeyed to Rome from industrialized regions of northern Europe, particularly France. He also received advice from the academic community, including the Roman Committee for Social Studies, a group whose activities roughly paralleled those of the Fribourg Union. Typical of many such initiatives that fell under the umbrella term "Social Catholicism" was a powerful combination of general and specific foci: a simultaneous interest in general features or even theoretical aspects of the emerging social and economic realities and an abiding concern about the concrete victims of rapid industrialization. Over several decades preceding the publication of *Rerum novarum* in 1891, committed Catholics worked hard to articulate and respond to many difficult questions regarding the relation of faith to the new economic order.

It is advisable, then, to imagine Leo XIII as responding to a number of stimuli as he decided to commission the writing of *Rerum novarum*. Espousing the multi-factor model suggested by the above analysis, Thomas A. Shannon invokes the image of "several streams of influence coming together" to motivate and inform Leo, and ultimately to account for the final text of *Rerum novarum*.[14] Even the most cursory glance at the text of

---

[14] Thomas A. Shannon, "Commentary on *Rerum novarum*," in Himes et al., eds., *Modern Catholic Social Teaching*, 133.

the encyclical demonstrates that Leo was surely responding above all to the sheer enormity of the suffering of factory workers of Europe, a social condition that constituted the premier economic sign of his times. The litany of misery is familiar: hasty urbanization as formerly rural populations flocked to newly crowded cities, disruptions in familiar patterns of family and community life, high unemployment, and meager subsistence wages for those who could find work in the new factory-based system of mass production. In the absence of adequate health care or safety regulations, employment was dangerous and degrading, as long hours and unsanitary working conditions simply wore down the overworked unskilled employees. Industrial accidents, child labor, workplace harassment – the list of abuses and modes of exploitation could go on, as any reader of Dickens's novels will confirm. And the only thing worse than one's treatment on the job was the threat of having no work at all, as the existence of a veritable "surplus army of labor" not only kept wages impossibly low, but also meant that industrialists and factory managers could intimidate employees with impunity.

Leo XIII addresses the plight of the workers by establishing certain principles of proper social order and then suggesting some rather concrete labor reforms that will enact these principles. Among the ethical principles Leo articulates in the opening paragraphs of *Rerum novarum* are many imperatives that are familiar to the ears of contemporary people of faith, but were novel or at least disputed in the late nineteenth century. Extreme inequality is not desirable. Workers have certain rights and must be treated with respect. The economy is chock-full of moral significance and ethical obligations. Deep poverty is neither God's will nor is it inevitable, for we are not to imagine ourselves captive to a set of impersonal and inflexible economic laws. Before the reader turns the first page of the encyclical, "the misery and wretchedness which press so heavily at this moment on the large majority of the very poor" is contrasted with "the concentration of so many branches of trade in the hands of a few individuals, so that a small number of very rich men have been able to lay upon the masses of the poor a yoke little better than slavery itself."[15] Leo reserves a major role in any program of social improvement, of course, to the church and those who follow its moral guidance. *Rerum novarum* is punctuated with reminders that "no practical solution of this question

---

[15] *Rerum novarum*, no. 2. All translations of the original Latin texts are taken from David J. O'Brien and Thomas A. Shannon, eds., *Catholic Social Thought: The Documentary Heritage* (Maryknoll, NY: Orbis Books, 1992).

will ever be found without the assistance of religion and the Church," for "the church provides the remedy."[16]

If the role of the church in addressing the social question is here emphasized in a full-throated manner, it is on the role of the state that the encyclical equivocates. In the early paragraphs of *Rerum novarum*, Leo signals his rejection of socialism by reminding the reader of the distinction between state and society ("Nor must we, at this stage, have recourse to the state. Man is older than the state"[17]). But soon it becomes clear that, however much voluntary or church-based action might be preferable in Leo's opinion, private initiatives will not be sufficient to address the problems associated with the new industrial economy. The letter breaks new ground in proposing an inevitable resort to government action (termed "public remedial measures" in no. 31) to restore proper social order. Ultimately, the pope knows he is on solid ground in invoking traditional Catholic (and, all to the better, Thomistic) social theory, in which public authorities are charged specifically with promoting the common good. The moral imperative of protecting workers from degradation and even extinction justifies significant government activism and regulation in the interest of achieving labor justice.

Rerum novarum winds up signaling approval for a relatively ambitious (for the times) program of interventions into the economy, and specifically into the ambit of labor relations that shape the condition of workers. These proposals remain measured responses to great needs that can be met in no other way, not a mandate for rampant centralization of state power over the economy. Leo encourages "workingmen's associations" (no. 36 recommends that "the artificer's guilds of a former day ... should be adapted to the requirements of the age in which we live") that will have the power to engage in collective bargaining. He devotes nos. 31 to 34 to enumerating a list of worker rights and protections (limitation of hours, Sabbath rest and regular vacations, regulation of child labor, resort to strikes, and above all the right to a living wage) that are to be ultimately guaranteed by government.

The notable innovations justified here by Leo are nevertheless wrapped in a sturdy blanket of conservative sentiments that observers of this pope would have come to expect. Leo repeatedly voices his suspicion of the forces of abrupt or sweeping change. His predilection to favoring a static social order, the preservation of a hierarchical class structure, and

---

[16] *Rerum novarum*, nos. 13 and 22. See also nos. 18 and 42, among others that emphasize this point.
[17] Ibid., no. 6.

traditional gender roles and family patterns culminates in his warning: "Humanity must remain as it is. It is impossible to reduce human society to a level. The socialists may do their utmost but all striving against nature is vain."[18] But this essentialistic view of social reality that Leo hastens to attribute to the very laws of nature does not prevent him from siding with a new class of laborers in advocating innovative measures to address new social problems. All the backward-looking aspects of *Rerum novarum* – its tendency to lapse into an other-worldly spirituality of resignation, its rigid defense of nearly absolute rights to private property, a nostalgia for medieval institutions, a restorationist brand of ecclesiology that grates on contemporary ears – are eclipsed by this one remarkable development. A nineteenth-century pope had adopted a surprisingly sophisticated structural view of economic forces responsible for the exploitation of millions, and urged both church and state to act as agents of social justice and economic reform on behalf of the poor. While the encyclical remains cautious in tone and exhibits a fair dose of clericalism and paternalism in denying a thorough program of empowerment to the poor, it is nevertheless a stunning breakthrough.

What, precisely, did Leo XIII think he was doing in issuing *Rerum novarum*? While it might be possible to impute some manner of cynical motives to the pope, this initiative was neither a public relations ploy nor an attempt at strategic positioning to bolster the power and influence of the universal church. This first of the great social encyclicals was at its heart a pastoral intervention to protect and benefit the hard-pressed workers of Europe. It is crucial to remember that *Rerum novarum* is above all a religious document, concerned with the faithful, their earthly welfare and supernatural well-being. It is neither a free-floating treatise on economics nor an exercise in political posturing. The attentive reader will note how often Leo justifies his policy recommendations with direct reference to the will and plan of God. For example, the pope interrupts his rather specific list of worker rights with this appeal to divine order and the afterlife: "No one may outrage with impunity that human dignity which God himself treats with reverence, nor stand in the way of that higher life which is the preparation of the eternal life of heaven."[19] These are not the admonitions of a political economist or even of a diplomat. They are the earnest entreaties of a universal pastor.

---

[18] Ibid., no. 14. See no. 16 for a similar formulation. Leo had rejected the leveling impulse in the earlier encyclicals *Quod apostolici muneris* and *Humanum genus*.

[19] *Rerum novarum*, no. 32.

THE RECEPTION AND LEGACY OF *RERUM NOVARUM*

Immediate reaction to the encyclical was decidedly positive but rather mixed, both within and beyond Catholic circles. The various European parties with the greatest stake in the social question (socialists, liberals, reactionaries) struck predictable postures, praising *Rerum novarum* for its support for their favorite projects and interests and criticizing Leo's words when they appeared to concede too much to their enemies.[20] The encyclical set off particularly fierce debates within highly industrialized Belgium, where its strong defense of the rights of poor workers sparked disputes among industrialists, labor unions, political parties, and local clerics, who interpreted Leo's teachings in various ways.[21]

The task of evaluating the reception of *Rerum novarum*, however, far transcends recording any such short-term reactions to the encyclical. Leo's teaching set off long-lasting ripple effects in the institutions of church and society. No effect of the encyclical was more important than the encouragement that Leo's words gave to labor unions. By legitimizing Catholic participation in organized labor, *Rerum novarum* veritably "opened the door to the union movement, particularly in the United States."[22] It would be hard to overestimate the momentous significance of the pope's support for the bourgeoning practice of collective bargaining, which came to shape the entire landscape of industrial relations in much of the world. It took longer for Leo's reasoning about the ethical obligation for employers to pay a "family wage" or "living wage" to win enactment, but minimum wage legislation did eventually spread to all the major industrialized economies to protect the same values that Leo advocated for the well-being of his flock.[23]

The enactment of public policies favoring labor is, of course, at most an indirect measure of the influence of this or any papal teaching, as church advocacy interacts with many other factors that shape legislation in a given political setting. A more direct way of measuring the lasting impact of *Rerum novarum* is to chart the trajectory of social justice teaching and practice within the Catholic Church itself, across various contexts around the world. The United States again provides a particularly good case study in the legacy of Leo's contribution. The inaugural social

---

[20] Lillian Parker Wallace, *Leo XIII and the Rise of Socialism* (Durham, NC: Duke University Press, 1966), 296; Shannon, "Commentary on *Rerum novarum*," 146.
[21] Misner, *Social Catholicism*, 224–25.
[22] Shannon, "Commentary on *Rerum novarum*," 147.
[23] The first minimum wage laws in the United States, for example, were enacted by Massachusetts in 1912.

encyclical emboldened the bishops of the United States to take an increasingly activist stance regarding economic justice. Barely a quarter-century after *Rerum novarum*, at the conclusion of World War I, the American bishops took the unprecedented step of publishing an advocacy document, the 1919 Bishops' Program of Social Reconstruction. The man most responsible for the publication and success of this 1919 document (as well as many successor documents) was Mgr. John Augustine Ryan, whose entire career in academic and ecclesial circles on the national level was dedicated to applying to the United States context the principles of distributive and worker justice found within *Rerum novarum*.[24] Walking this same path was a plethora of lay activists, academics, and even "labor priests" (including the legendary Mgr. George Higgins) whose efforts in the field of labor relations were inspired, directly or indirectly, by the landmark encyclical of Leo.

It remains important not to think of *Rerum novarum* as an isolated and discrete contribution of a single pope, however important in itself, but rather to situate it in a tradition of social teachings with certain predecessor and successor documents, understandings, and practices. At least two astute commentators upon the tradition of Catholic social teaching, Michael Schuck and Joe Holland, portray Leo's work as such a landmark that they divide all church social thought into pre-Leonine, Leonine, and post-Leonine eras.[25] Nevertheless each maintains the requisite appreciation for the continuity of the tradition to which Leo contributed. Schuck explicitly identifies as a half-truth the notion that *Rerum novarum* was an "Urtext" that can be understood without reference to what came before it.[26] Holland similarly resists the temptation to portray *Rerum novarum* as a "big bang" that eclipses and overshadows in importance all social teaching that came before or after. Even the brightest stars in the galaxy must remain in proper context.

However, in assessing the legacy of this important encyclical, it remains true that no pope before Leo produced anything like the message contained in *Rerum novarum*. All the popes who have served since Leo have in some way addressed "the social question" according to the way he defined

---

[24] Besides the original texts of Ryan, see the very informative Robert G. Kennedy et al., eds., *Religion and Public Life: The Legacy of Monsignor John A. Ryan* (New York: University Press of America, 2001).

[25] Michael J. Schuck, *That They Be One: The Social Teaching of the Papal Encyclicals, 1740–1989* (Washington, DC: Georgetown University Press, 1991); Joe Holland, *Modern Catholic Social Teaching: The Popes Confront the Industrial Age, 1740–1958* (New York: Paulist Press, 2003).

[26] Michael J. Schuck, "Early Modern Roman Catholic Social Thought, 1740–1890," in Himes et al., eds., *Modern Catholic Social Teaching*, 99–124, at 100.

it. Pius X (1903–14) and Benedict XV (1914–22) may each have focused on quite different matters from those that affected Leo, owing to the circumstances and pressing issues of their times, but the lead given by Leo in *Rerum novarum* was an impetus to them also to address the main social questions of their own day. The next chapter will explore how Benedict XV, who became pope in the year in which World War I began, attempted this in relation to the question of peace.

CHAPTER 9

The perils of perception: British Catholics and papal neutrality, 1914–1923

Charles R. Gallagher

Among the major scholarly studies of Catholics and World War I, vast attention has been drawn to papal personalities, geopolitics, peace diplomacy, intelligence studies, and wartime curial affairs.[1] Little to nothing has been written about how ordinary Catholics perceived and received the strategic position of the Holy See and the wartime papacy. This chapter aims to begin that examination using British Catholics as a test case. It hopes to show that under the surface, a momentous cultural and religious tussle was taking place in connection with how lay British Catholics related to the papacy. Such wrestling in the pews was precipitated by the Holy See's adoption of a relatively new diplomatic doctrine which it called absolute impartiality. It was a policy which was agreed upon within the upper tier of the Holy See's diplomatic corps, but one which went unexplained to the average Roman Catholic, and even to local bishops themselves.

THE BRITISH CATHOLIC MOMENT

'Liquid Protestantism' was a term coined by G. K. Chesterton to describe, in part, the impact that World War I had on British Protestantism in general. For Chesterton, by 1929 Protestantism no longer represented a monolithic cultural wall in British life. British Protestantism was composed, rather, of multiple liquid lava streams searching for their geographic base. While anti-Catholicism surely lingered in Britain, Chesterton saw the period from 1900 to 1923 as providing sufficient religious fluidity for the emergence of a larger cultural stream of thought.[2] The cordiality, popular

---

[1] On many of these topics see the Bibliography.
[2] This period proffered, for Chesterton, what the late American theologian Richard John Neuhaus described as a "Catholic moment" of moral ascendancy. Richard John Neuhaus, *The Catholic Moment: The Paradox of the Church in the Postmodern Era* (New York: Harper & Row, 1987), 283.

domestic British acceptance, and parliamentary political approval of King Edward VII's visit to Pope Leo XIII at his Vatican apartments on April 29, 1903 seemed to bear out the first flush of Chestertonian ebullience.[3] It marked the first face-to-face encounter between a British monarch and the pope since the Reformation.

According to the historian James Obelkevich, in the period leading up to 1914 no other church in Britain, "neither the Anglican nor its Protestant rivals, changed as profoundly as Roman Catholicism."[4] From barely 100,000 adherents in 1780, the Catholic population of Britain had climbed to over 2 million by 1914. In Scotland, over 15 percent of the population was Catholic, urban, and working-class. The legacy of Newman and Manning etched itself into the educated classes. "Up to the outbreak of war, there was a continual expansion of churches and religious houses in the new suburban areas all over England."[5]

Even by the early decades of the twentieth century there was no true monolithic character to the British Catholic Church. "More than half were of Irish blood, the rest were of English blood, and a few were of Cornish or Welsh blood," the popular writer Daniel Sargent concluded in his breezy interwar survey of British Catholics.[6] The distribution of Catholics was uneven, Birmingham and Liverpool being considered strongholds, whereas Catholics were fewest in the west midlands, Norfolk, and Suffolk. "Catholics were pocketed here and there like strange minerals," Sargent remarked.[7]

The historical theologian Adrian Hastings has argued that by the early twentieth century, the presence of the upper-class English Catholic recusant families was helping to bridge the divide between Protestant elites and Roman Catholic clerical authorities. These were Catholic aristocratic families possessing "all the proper qualities of the British establishment ... utterly reliable as senior citizens of the Empire."[8] Chief among them was the line of Roman Catholic (recusant) Dukes of Norfolk, the premier dukedom in the peerage of England.[9] In the first decade of the

[3] B. J. C. McKercher, *Esme Howard* (Cambridge: Cambridge University Press, 2006), 34.
[4] James Obelkevich, "Religion," in F. M. L. Thompson, ed., *The Cambridge Social History of Britain* (Cambridge: Cambridge University Press, 1993), 335.
[5] Dennis Gwynn, "Growth of the Catholic Community," in G. A. Beck, ed., *The English Catholics* (London: Burns & Oates, 1950), 423.
[6] Daniel Sargent, "The Catholic Church in Contemporary England," *Catholic Historical Review* 18 (1932), 60.
[7] Ibid., 61.
[8] Adrian Hastings, *Church and State: The English Experience* (Exeter: University of Exeter Press, 1991), 42.
[9] Ibid., 43.

twentieth century, British Catholics were consolidating modest gains
and beginning to come of age.

BACKDROP TO A CRISIS: PAPAL CENTRALIZATION
AND BRITISH ULTRAMONTANISM

The upturn in British Catholic collective self-assurance happened to
coincide with another dramatic change at the center of Catholicism. "By
the end of the reign of Pius X in August 1914," John F. Pollard has argued
about the end of a decades-long consolidation campaign within the papacy, "the construction of the modern papacy was virtually complete."
New mechanisms of authority were finally in place. They included formal declarations of papal infallibility, the "Romanization" of the British
bishops through their education in Rome, the centralization of decision-
making, and the use of papal nuncios and encyclicals to enforce the
teaching authority of the church. Most importantly for Pollard, by 1914
"the cult around the personality of the reigning pontiff had been fully
developed."[10]

In the history of Roman Catholicism in Britain, such papal consolidation
on the international plane worked only to redouble an already heightened
sense of allegiance to the papacy. In Britain, the term "Ultramontanism"
was "used to describe that tendency within the Catholic Church which
would centralize authority in the Roman See."[11] After the First Vatican
Council (1870) and its promulgation of papal infallibility, this posture
became more prevalent in English Catholicism.

Complex social developments were taking place within both institutional Roman Catholicism and British Catholicism by the time the first
shots of World War I were fired. British Catholics were making neat
social gains while trimly swimming through Chesterton's pool of liquid
Protestantism. British nationalism spiked with entry into the war, and
Catholics naturally sped to show their allegiance to their government's
policy. At the same time, Pope Benedict XV fastened onto a program of
neutrality. But as the war dragged on, and as casualties and "atrocities"
increased, papal neutrality would prove a terribly thorny problem for loyal
and socially upward British Catholics.

---

[10] John F. Pollard, "The Papacy," in Hugh McLeod, ed., *World Christianities* (Cambridge:
Cambridge University Press, 2006), 29.
[11] J. Derek Holmes, *More Roman than Rome: English Catholicism in the Nineteenth Century* (London:
Burns & Oates, 1978), 14.

THE LEGACY OF PAPAL NEUTRALITY

Most papal historians locate the arrival of the papacy's neutrality program with Pope Pius IX, his pronouncements, and his actions as Italian nationalists wrested control from the Habsburgs in the revolutionary year of 1848. But designs to move the papacy to a position of neutrality began much earlier, nearly as soon as the Congress of Vienna was concluded in 1815. In Rome, Pope Pius VII and his masterful assistant in world affairs, Ercole Cardinal Consalvi, concluded that Metternich's new international system suggested that a neutral position for the pope might be the best way for an increasingly marginalized papal state to find relevance in a new system of bloc state power relationships.[12]

In order to do this, the viability of neutrality as a mode of operating on the international plane had to be bolstered. Up until the nineteenth century, lip service was rendered to a neutrality which was "frequently ignored in practice."[13] The thorniest issues involved the recruitment of troops in neutral states and the transfer of war materiel.[14] Stricter codes of behavior needed to be asserted. The first opportunity for the Holy See to stiffen its posture of neutrality and put its new perspective down in writing came during the Neapolitan revolt of 1821.

Although only a small draft among the European revolutionary winds, when the position of papal neutrality vis-à-vis Naples and Austria was formalized by Cardinal Consalvi in 1821, it offered perhaps the first modern formulation of the Holy See's neutrality policy. "The Holy Father," Consalvi wrote in his "notification," "because of his position as the Visible head of the Church, and as an essentially peaceful sovereign, will continue to maintain … a perfect neutrality toward all nations."[15]

The Holy See's perceived neutrality was a key element for the rising diplomatic hopes of Gioacchino Vincenzo Pecci, Pope Leo XIII, who was elected to the papacy in 1878. At age twenty-seven, Pecci entered the diplomatic service of the Holy See, and while unimpressive in his early diplomatic career as a nuncio in Brussels, as pope he hoped to use Christian diplomacy to increase the prestige of the Holy See internationally.[16] Leo's

[12] Eamon Duffy, *Saints & Sinners: A History of the Popes*, 3rd edn. (New Haven: Yale Nota Bene, 2006), 272.
[13] Ibid., 272.
[14] J. H. W. Verzijl, *International Law in Historical Perspective* (Leyden: A. Sijthoff, 1968), 154.
[15] Joseph H. Brady, *Rome and the Neapolitan Revolution of 1820–1821: A Study in Papal Neutrality* (New York: Columbia University Press, 1937), 13, 108.
[16] James E. Ward, "Leo XIII: 'The Diplomat Pope,'" *The Review of Politics* 28 (1966), 49. While Ward's article is dated, it foreshadowed in part the current historiographical debate regarding

idea was to infuse European Great Power diplomacy with the Christian vision which was severed from it during the years of European revolution. These principles harked back to the medieval idea of Europe as the original *communitas christiana* – a grouping of states whose moral rules and customs were ultimately grounded in faith.

For the first time in modern history, the idea of the Holy See as a great moral power began to emerge.[17] Mediation, arbitration, and Christian brokerage of disputes would take on deep new significance for Vatican diplomats. As the papal diplomatic historian Vincent Viaene has stated, "the Vatican's attempt to take on the role of mediator … became an important test for its success in overcoming international isolation."[18]

Of course, papal isolation began shortly after the Austro-Italian War of 1859 and the annexation of the Papal States to the Kingdom of Italy. This was the beginning of the so-called "Roman Question," which forced the Holy See to configure how exactly it would relate to an Italian government which it considered an unjust occupier. Regardless of such obstacles, Leo longed to have the Holy See play the role of respected Christian arbiter.

The great signal of this arrival back in the world diplomatic arena occurred in 1885, when Germany's "Iron Chancellor," Otto von Bismarck, enlisted the good offices of the Holy See to resolve a new crisis in the Caroline Islands. In this dispute, which nearly led to war between Germany and Spain, Pope Leo hammered out a decision whereby he awarded sovereignty of the islands to Spain while granting Germany essential trading rights. In his settlement of the Caroline Islands dispute, Pope Leo catapulted the Holy See back into the role of international arbiter and mediator, a position it had not held since 1631, when Pope Urban VIII concluded the Treaty of Ratisbon.

Two years removed from this diplomatic triumph, in 1887, Pope Leo XIII's secretary of state, Mariano Cardinal Rampolla, brought Mgr. Giacomo della Chiesa (1854–1922) to Rome to act as his personal assistant. Over the course of the coming years, della Chiesa would improve himself as an administrator and diplomat. As under-secretary of state to Rampolla, "one Italian observer paid him the highest compliment, [calling him] … 'a new Consalvi.'"[19]

Leo's papacy as either religiously "prophetic," and spiritually successful, or simply "political," and diplomatically engaged with varying results.

[17] The argument here is taken from Vincent Viaene's excellent introduction and his edited work in *The Papacy and the New World Order: Vatican Diplomacy, Catholic Opinion and International Politics at the Time of Leo XIII, 1878–1903* (Leuven: Katholieke Universiteit Leuven, 2005), 10.

[18] Viaene, *Papacy and the New World Order*, 14.

[19] Michael P. Riccards, *Vicars of Christ: Popes, Power, and Politics in the Modern World* (New York: Crossroad, 1998), 72.

Consalvi's earlier formula of papal neutrality may have stuck with della Chiesa as he assumed the papacy on September 3, 1914. As war broke over Europe, della Chiesa, now Pope Benedict XV (reigned 1914–1922), offered himself as a "shepherd to peoples in both camps."[20] He would still play the role of universal pastor, but would recalibrate Consalvi's neutrality plan as a means to stave off division within the worldwide church.

When war broke across Belgium in early August of 1914, Benedict acted quickly. Remarkably, he broke with "the established custom of the Roman Pontiffs at the beginning of their apostolate" of writing a weighty and extensive encyclical letter to all the bishops – a process which could take months.[21] Instead he issued a short apostolic exhortation, *Ubi primum*, on September 8, 1914. Largely unstudied by historians, it is important because it ranks as Benedict's first utterance on the war.[22]

In *Ubi primum*, Benedict saw the war in the West as a war among Christians – and Christian nations. This was a war in which the papacy, by its very nature, should have its voice heard.[23] Benedict was "filled with horror and inexpressible grief … by the sight of … so great a part of Europe reddened by Christian blood, devastated by fire and sword." Theologically aligning his own pastoral duties with those of Christ, the Good Shepherd, he embraced "with paternal love all the lambs and sheep of his flock."[24]

Not long afterward, the Catholic press in Britain began aping secular press accounts in publishing stories of "German atrocities" committed in Catholic Belgium. An entire historiographical debate has emerged concerning the real extent of German atrocities in Belgium.[25] For Catholics in Britain, the question was why Benedict – who vigorously protested the deportation of refugees in the aftermath of invasion – refused to condemn either the German invasion or the purported atrocities in Belgium during August 1914. *L'osservatore romano*, the official news organ of the papacy, laid out the church's position on how Catholics ought to view the actions of the Holy See in wartime: "From the very beginning of the present

[20] Carl Eckhardt, *The Papacy and World Affairs: As Reflected in the Secularization of Politics* (Chicago: University of Chicago Press, 1937), 241.

[21] "The Pope and the War," *The Tablet* (September 26, 1914).

[22] Benedict XV, apostolic exhortation *Ubi primum*, September 8, 1914, *Acta apostolicae sedis* 6 (1914), 501.

[23] Puzzlingly, given the intense focus on Benedict's wartime conduct, *Ubi primum* has been missed by all of Benedict's major biographers.

[24] Benedict XV, "Exhortation of Pope Benedict XV to all Catholics of the World," *L'osservatore romano* (September 10, 1914).

[25] John N. Horne and Alan Kramer, *German Atrocities, 1914* (New Haven: Yale University Press, 2001); Larry Zuckerman, *The Rape of Belgium* (New York: New York University Press, 2004), 171.

crisis ... the Holy See has always wished and wishes to maintain the most absolute and complete neutrality."[26]

QUIET REVOLUTION: THE ARRIVAL
OF ABSOLUTE IMPARTIALITY

"Absolute impartiality" would now become the guiding concept through the war. Such a concept would preserve the institutional authority of the pope, it was thought, while allowing the church to minister religiously behind the lines. The Holy See's adoption of the absolute impartiality doctrine marked a conceptual revolution in how the papacy operated in the world of international affairs. The new move toward absolute impartiality was a rejection of the previously prevailing secular view of neutrality espoused by Hugo Grotius, the Christian jurist and sixteenth-century international relations theorist.

Although Grotius is often called "the father of international law," the British political historian G. R. Elton has asserted that he understood himself largely as a theologian.[27] While his writings on the legal duties of neutrals were inchoate, Grotius did provide a starting point for the behavior of neutrals during wartime. "The primary duty of those not involved in a war," the Grotian scholar Yasuaki Ōnuma has argued, flows "from Grotius' just-war doctrine: one must give assistance to the party waging the just war."[28] Grotius "made the neutral state into a judge of justice or injustice of the war."[29] For Grotius, the neutral state was to pronounce upon the aims of the belligerent and could rightfully play the role of moral arbiter.[30]

But while European diplomatic elites looked to him for guidance on such matters, the Holy See eschewed Grotius. Since Grotius was a Protestant, the Holy See viewed his work as nothing more than a Protestantization of natural law ethics – the final excision of St. Thomas Aquinas and Roberto Bellarmino from international relations. When his *De jure belli et pacis* (*On the Law of War and Peace*) was published in 1625, professionals quickly

---

[26] *L'osservatore romano*, quoted in *The Tablet* (October 24, 1914).

[27] L. C. Green and Olive P. Dickason, *The Law of Nations and the New World* (Edmonton: University of Alberta Press, 1993), 54; G. R. Elton, *Political History: Principles and Practice* (New York: Basic Books, 1970), 44.

[28] Yasuaki Ōnuma, *A Normative Approach to War: Peace, War, and Justice in Hugo Grotius* (Oxford: Oxford University Press, 1993), 111.

[29] T. J. Lawrence, *The Principles of International Law* (London: Macmillan, 1910), 590.

[30] Nicolas Politis, *Neutrality and Peace*, trans. Francis Crane Macken (Washington, DC: Carnegie Endowment for International Peace, 1935), 28.

considered it the foundational treatise of modern international law.[31] But since Grotius included the proposition "even were we to accept that God did not exist," the Holy See promptly placed it on its Index of Forbidden Books.[32] Because the Holy See turned its back on Grotius so early, it failed to consider his theological and natural law claims about the role of moral deliberation for neutrals in wartime.

At the same time urgently seeking to enhance its prestige at the table of world leaders, the Holy See began to accept diplomatic innovations which, though thoroughly secular, remained in harmony with the general contours of Christian diplomacy. By the early twentieth century, one of the more secular codicils which the Holy See added to its foreign relations agenda was the new concept of "absolute impartiality" – "a nicety and distinction understood by few."[33] Much under-studied, absolute impartiality was not just a passing concept or a short-lived experiment. For the Holy See, it would become the means by which the papacy would enhance and project its prestige both within the chancelleries of Europe and in the world.

On top of this, and more important still, "absolute impartiality" was more than simply a tightened concept of neutrality, although many commentators subsequently would place the two in the same category. Absolute impartiality distinctly forbade public moral determinations by non-belligerent states. This was a piece of the puzzle which the Holy See rarely explained as it took up its new mantle. And it was the one element which would cause the Holy See so much misunderstanding. For British Catholics in World War I who were looking for public moral clarity from the papacy, this lack of moral content created a perilous mix of doubt and dissatisfaction.[34]

The legal theorist who did the most to formulate the concept of what would later be called absolute impartiality was the eighteenth-century Swiss diplomat and legal philosopher Emmerich de Vattel. Vattel's system exercised "great influence on the subsequent development of international

[31] Michael P. Zuckert, *Natural Rights and the New Republicanism* (Princeton: Princeton University Press, 1998), 119; Hedley Bull, Benedict Kingsbury, and Adam Roberts, eds., *Hugo Grotius and International Relations* (Oxford: Oxford University Press, 1992), 77.
[32] Oliver O'Donovan and Joan Lockwood O'Donovan, *From Irenaeus to Grotius: A Sourcebook in Christian Political Thought, 100–1625* (Grand Rapids, MI: William B. Eerdmans, 1999), 788.
[33] Frank J. Coppa, *The Papacy, the Jews, and the Holocaust* (Washington, DC: Catholic University of America Press, 2006), 134, 186.
[34] As late as World War II, Pope Pius XII enshrined "absolute impartiality" in his 1943 encyclical *Mystici corporis*, indicating that Catholics of warring countries looked "to the Vicar of Jesus Christ as to the loving Father of them all, who, with absolute impartiality" took up the cause of charity and peace.

law," and as late as 1924 one commentator urged that even though his name was not easily recognizable, "his system still dominated the thought of Latin Europe."[35]

"The principal point in Vattel's teaching, which distinguished him from [all] previous writers ... and marks the beginning of the modern theory of neutrality," the British historian V. M. S. Crichton wrote within a decade of the conclusion of World War I, was "his insistence on the absolute impartiality and abstention of all interference on the part of the neutral states."[36] Vattel argued that what was formerly known as neutrality ought now to be transformed into "an impartial attitude so far as war is concerned, and that the neutral people abstain from furnishing help ... or anything ... of direct use in war."[37] Easily accessible in his writing style, Vattel relied on positivist cases and empirical evidence in his examples of international political relations. Surprisingly, one of his greatest fans was Cardinal Consalvi, who "cited [Vattel] copiously and approvingly in [his] diplomatic submissions" as Vatican secretary of state.[38]

By the early twentieth century, neutrality was becoming newly scrutinized under the theories of Vattel. In 1899 the Hague Peace Conference began to draw up articles and points relating to neutrals in wartime. Pope Leo XIII and Cardinal Rampolla both hoped that the conference might create "a Christian legal constituency as a panacea for a world which had made self-interest and brute force prevail over notions of justice and charity."[39] But Pope Leo XIII was not invited to the conference, a snub by the world community which embittered Leo and compelled his successors to redouble their efforts toward proving their own competence in international relations.[40]

Because of the so-called "Roman Question," Italy protested vigorously against inviting the pope. Interestingly, an obscure point of the Italian protest was that the Holy See still refused to take Grotius's *De jure belli et pacis* – and its support, based on natural law, for neutrals as

[35] Charles G. Fenwick, *International Law* (London: George Allen & Unwin, 1924), 55.
[36] V. M. S. Crichton, "The Pre-War Theory of Neutrality," in *The British Year Book of International Law* (London: Royal Institute of International Affairs, British Institute of International Affairs, 1928), 102.
[37] William Edward Hall, *A Treatise on International Law* (Oxford: The Clarendon Press, 1904), 585.
[38] Timothy J. Hochstrasser, *Natural Law Theories in the Early Enlightenment* (Cambridge: Cambridge University Press, 2000), 182.
[39] Arthur Eyffinger, *The Hague Peace Conference: "The Parliament of Man and the Federation of the World"* (The Hague, London and Boston: Kluwer Law International, 1999), 78.
[40] David J. Alvarez, "The Holy See and the First Hague Peace Conference," *Archivium historiae pontificiae* 26 (1988), 437 n. 29.

moral arbiters in diplomacy – off the Index.[41] It was at the Second Hague Peace Conference in 1907 that the notion of "absolute impartiality" was introduced into the formal lexicon of international relations. "It is, for neutral Powers, an admitted duty to apply … rules impartially to the several belligerents," the Thirteenth Hague Convention asserted in its preamble.[42]

What was emerging in international affairs was a specified procedural path for the maintenance of absolute impartiality. The Hague rules meant that now a neutral's moral claim against a military aim or operation on either side might be considered as "hostile" in perspective.[43] Thus, by the time Pope Benedict XV took the papal throne in 1914, the Holy See was well on its way toward integrating the doctrine of absolute impartiality outlined at The Hague. For some, this new position of absolute impartiality was nearly untenable. "To maintain … absolute impartiality as an immutable principle of neutrality," the famed international lawyer Hersch Lauterpacht wrote, "betray[s] an imperfect knowledge of the history of international law."[44]

Regardless of the perilous potential of this new doctrine, within the first two months of the war the Holy See strained to emphasize that absolute impartiality would be the mainstay of its international position. "The common duty of Catholics of every land," *L'osservatore romano* outlined, "in unison with the wishes and intentions of the Holy See … wishes to maintain the most absolute and complete neutrality."[45] The Holy See presumed that a neat Vattelian formula would allow it to stay above the fray and present opportunities for it to act as an international partner among the community of nations. Yet it became clear, over the course of bloodier and bloodier battles, that the world wanted an arbiter which could clearly delineate right from wrong on the moral plane. Adding to the difficulty for the papacy was that "absolute impartiality" was a technical diplomatic concept – one particularly complex, nuanced, and not easily explained to the Catholic laity. As war started, ordinary Catholic observers and critics in Britain became bewildered by the position of the Holy See.

---

[41] Hedley Bull, "The Importance of Grotius in the Study of International Relations," in Hedley Bull, Benedict Kingsbury, and Adam Roberts, eds., *Hugo Grotius and International Relations* (Oxford: Oxford University Press, 1990), 77.

[42] Politis, *Neutrality and Peace.* 28.

[43] Frederick Smith, *International Law* (London and Toronto: J. M. Dent & Son, 1918), 293.

[44] Hersch Lauterpacht, *International Law: Collected Papers,* V: *Disputes, War and Neutrality* (Cambridge: Cambridge University Press, 2003), 700.

[45] *L'osservatore romano,* quoted in "The Pope and Peace," *The Tablet* (October 24, 1914).

PAMPHLET WARS: THE PAPACY AND PUBLIC VOICES

The first criticisms of papal absolute neutrality emerged during a fierce "pamphlet war" over the question of the Holy See's neutrality in wartime.[46] While the Church of England's own pamphlet war has been studied well, there is currently no examination of this arguably more spirited Roman Catholic tussle.[47] Conducted amid an explosion of patriotism, the pamphlet war over absolute impartiality created a new situation for Catholics in Britain. For centuries Catholics had been forced to defend faith-based doctrines from Rome to which they readily assented. Absolute impartiality, however, now forced Catholics to defend a papal policy which was largely non-theological, aped its secular counterpart, rested on the authority of the papal office alone, and admitted no room for movement.

Within six weeks of his first encyclical, and about five months from the opening of hostilities, Pope Benedict set forth one of his most important instructions on war when on January 22, 1915 he gave a consistorial address to gathered Roman cardinals and prelates. Historians to this point have assessed the address in relation to Benedict's insistence that he would condemn injustice on both sides of the conflict "by whatever side it has been committed."[48] But an overlooked aspect of the address was that Benedict used it in large part to explain his new policy of absolute impartiality (Figure 9.1).

In his allocution, after indicating to the cardinals that he would condemn injustice anywhere and unreservedly, Benedict suddenly switched gears. He pointed out to the cardinals, the regional leaders, that in denouncing wartime injustice there was "no need to involve the pontifical authority in the controversies of the belligerents." To do so would be "neither suitable nor useful" ("neque conveniens foret nec utile"), an eyebrow-raising development which one contemporary academician argued "was not without danger."[49]

The Holy See would monitor "the frightful conflict" with great attention, but in the end the pope was "bound to a complete impartiality."

[46] Peter H. Sutcliffe, *The Oxford University Press* (Oxford: Oxford University Press, 1978), 172.
[47] Albert Marrin, *The Last Crusade: The Church of England in the First World War* (Durham: Duke University Press, 1974), 48.
[48] John F. Pollard, *The Unknown Pope: Benedict XV (1914–1922) and the Pursuit of Peace* (London: Geoffrey Chapman, 1999), 94; Franz Coetzee and Marilyn Shelvin Coetzee, *Authority, Identity, and the Social History of the Great War* (Providence, RI: Berghahn Books, 1995), 128; W. H. Peters, *The Life of Benedict XV* (Milwaukee: Bruce Publishing, 1959), 121.
[49] George F. La Piana, "From Leo XIII to Benedict XV," *The American Journal of Theology* 21 (1917), 188.

9.1 Auguste Rodin, *Head of Pope Benedict XV*, 1915. Bronze, cast no. 8, Georges
Rudier Foundry. Iris and B. Gerald Cantor Art Gallery Permanent Collection, College
of the Holy Cross, 1978.01. Photo by John L. Buckingham.

Unknowingly, the British press for the most part translated Benedict's
insistence on "absolute impartiality" as "absolute neutrality," placing
the pope in the same old categories as before and making it more difficult to show British Catholics that a sea change had occurred in papal
policy.[50]

For ordinary British soldiers, as well as for the consistorial cardinals, the
nuance of impartiality was hardly noticed. But there was one theologian

---

[50] *The Tablet* mistranslated the wording "ha da mantenersi perfettamente imparziale" as "must preserve the most absolute neutrality." See "The Pope and the War: Allocution at the Consistory,"
The Tablet (January 30, 1915).

who looked askance at such fine distinctions. An old nemesis of Pope Pius X's consolidation program was the modernist – and by then excommunicated – French theologian Alfred Loisy. Loisy ranks as the first observer to notice Benedict's distinction between "neutrality" and "absolute impartiality." For Loisy, impartiality needed to be "consonant with the moral claims of a universal Christianity."[51] But since Benedict refused to make such a claim as an impartial observer of war, Loisy considered his position bereft of moral worth.

"His Holiness," Loisy's pamphlet began, "ignores or mistakes the proper meaning of the word *impartiality* (italics are Loisy's), which he seems to identify here with the term *neutrality*." For Loisy, the terms differed drastically in moral weight: "Impartiality and neutrality are quite different things: in fact they are incompatible with one another in the sphere of morals; for no one has any right to be neutral in moral questions."[52] Reviewing Loisy's pamphlet in *The Church Quarterly Review*, Arthur C. Headlam counted the pope's neutrality as one of the great questions of the war in the religious sphere and "a matter which has stirred many minds very deeply."[53]

The Loisy pamphlet jolted British Catholics. It was Loisy's assertion that "no one has any right to be neutral in moral questions" which struck at the heart of the matter for many observers. Decades later, some even referenced Loisy's tract when assessing Pope Pius XII's public attitude and lack of forthright speech amid what would later become known as the Holocaust.[54]

FROM BATTLEFIELD TO BISHOP'S HOUSE: EXPLAINING
ABSOLUTE IMPARTIALITY

On the World War I battlefields, however, ordinary Allied soldiers scrambled to assert that the sympathies of the Vatican were on their side. In May of 1915 the British army chaplain John Strickland, SJ, was asked to preach at a frontline Mass in Belgium and offer some words on the papacy and the war. Moving quickly, Strickland reached back fifty years and told an anecdote about a British officer who, while at an audience with Pope Pius IX, "asked the Vicar of Christ to bless his sword in order that he should

---

[51] Alfred Loisy, *The War and Religion*, trans. Arthur Galton (Oxford: Basil Blackwell, 1915), 46, in the London Library, 14 St. James's Square, London, Montefiore Pamphlet Collection, M359.

[52] Ibid.

[53] Arthur C. Headlam, "The War and Religion," *The Church Quarterly Review* 83 (1917), 105.

[54] Pierre Van Paassen, *The Forgotten Ally* (New York: Dial Press, 1943), 41.

never unsheathe it, except in defence of religion or justice."[55] Strickland indicated to the gathered soldiers that they could be assured that the Vicar of Christ similarly would bless their arms, "because the Allies have a just cause."[56] But such quick historical refitting was difficult to keep up on the frontline.

When Britain's bishops grasped the possibility that the Holy See's absolute impartiality doctrine might rupture the ordinary British Catholic soldier from his allegiance to the papacy, it was one step too far. Trickier for the English bishops was that after a papal encyclical, and an allocution to the cardinals of the church, "the attitude of the Holy See was still just so incomprehensible to most people in England."[57] With much at stake, in the summer of 1915 London's Cardinal Archbishop of Westminster, Francis Bourne, decided to take on the problem. In the June 5 edition of *The Tablet*, Britain's foremost journal of Catholic opinion, Bourne wrote a piece entitled "The Pope and the War," which was quickly reprinted by London's Catholic Truth Society as a "penny pamphlet."

Bourne was, in the words of one historian, "the leader and public face of English Roman Catholicism throughout the Great War."[58] He was successful in raising the profile of Catholicism and harmonizing it with the war aims of the Allies, "thus allowing considerable integration … in a society with a long history of anti-Catholic feeling."[59] There is no question but that Bourne believed that the Allies' war effort was just. In writing of the pope in wartime, however, he was greatly nuanced and even sardonic. He argued that those English who had up until 1915 disparaged the church had no right to beg the pope for a moral pronouncement on the war. It was a "wonderful spectacle," Bourne began, "that those who have been the first to reject … the Holy See, should now, in this time of stress, come to invoke the power of the Holy See on the side of England."[60] The issue was "extraordinarily complex," but Catholics who "accused the Holy Father of silence" were "certainly guilty of rash, if not false witness."[61]

---

[55] Rev. J. Strickland, SJ, diary entry for May 11, 1915, in "Our Army Chaplain's Experiences," *Letters and Notices* (Roehampton: Manresa Press, 1916), 168.

[56] Ibid.

[57] Denis Gwynn, *The Vatican and the War in Europe* (London: Burns, Oates, and Washburn, 1940), 2.

[58] J. M. Bourne, *Who's Who in World War One* (London: Routledge, 2001), 33.

[59] Ibid.

[60] Francis Cardinal Bourne, *The Voice of Belgium: Being the War Utterances of Cardinal Mercier* (London: Burns & Oates Ltd., 1917), vii.

[61] Ibid., 14.

At the same time as his pamphlet was published, Bourne was confronted with the publication of a privately published short book by the pseudonymous writer Francis Tyrrell. Bourne was aware of Tyrrell's *The War and the Holy See: The Silence of Benedict XV* as being "lately exposed for sale on the bookstalls," but was unaware that it sold 20,000 copies in its first printing.[62] Moreover, Tyrrell's short book seems to have been the first modern examination of a wartime pope to use the word "silence" in connection with the papacy's obligation to pronounce on wartime moral issues.

Inflammatory, rhetorical, and polemical, Tyrrell called papal impartiality "only another name for moral cowardice."[63] Benedict's position was "an ugly position" which "justly caused grave searchings of hearts amongst hundreds of thousands of thinking Catholics" in Britain.[64] Writing in 1957, one historian called Tyrrell's work "a grandiloquent indictment of the Pope's apparent indifference to the war ... which enjoyed large sales."[65]

With Tyrrell's book creating a stir, it was becoming clear to the Catholic hierarchy that Cardinal Bourne's speech provided no resolution to the papal neutrality issue. Someone else needed to step up and explain the pope's position. Acting quickly, the Bishop of Northampton, Frederick William Keating, was designated to set the record straight. In his pamphlet entitled *The Neutrality of the Holy See*, London's Catholic Truth Society printed an initial run of 14,000 copies. This figure provides an indication of the gravity with which British Catholics viewed the Holy See's absolute impartiality doctrine. Up to 1910 the Catholic Truth Society's top-selling pamphlet was *The True Story of Maria Monk*, which registered 89,000 copies – but that pamphlet had been in print for nearly twenty-five years![66]

"The Holy See has not deviated one hair's breadth from the path of strict neutrality," Keating stated authoritatively in his opening phrase.[67] "Even some of the faithful, overheated by patriotism," he wrote ambivalently, "have caught the infection, and grumble about the Pope's 'silence'

[62] Ibid., 9.
[63] Francis Tyrrell, *The War and the Holy See: The Silence of Benedict XV* (London: Hampden Press, 1915), 4, in the Western European Theatre Collection, box 14, folder "Tyrrell, Francis," Public Policy Papers, Department of Rare Books and Special Collections, Princeton University Library.
[64] Ibid., 8.
[65] Douglas Eldridge, "Pope Benedict XV and World War I," in *King's Crown Essays: Columbia College Journal of Social Sciences* 4 (1957), 15.
[66] Christopher Ralls, *The Catholic Truth Society: A New History* (London: Catholic Truth Society, 1993), 10.
[67] Frederick Keating, *The Neutrality of the Holy See* (London: Catholic Truth Society, 1914), 1: Historical Archives of the Catholic Truth Society, Harleyford Road, London, reference no. 2746, code DO57.

being 'significant,' or even 'guilty.'"[68] But Keating was fuzzy about the distinction between absolute impartiality and neutrality.

Keating's defense of Benedict was somewhat muddled and reliant on weak argumentation. Belgian atrocities still loomed large in British thinking, yet "even those who would welcome a papal utterance on the atrocities, would receive it, not as a statement of God's Law, but as a declaration on one side [or] ... a triumph of diplomacy in securing a pope."[69] "The atmosphere of war is *not* congenial to the exercise of growth of moral influence" (italics are Keating's).[70] Absolute impartiality was sacrosanct.

British observers found it just as hard to warm to Keating's argument as to Cardinal Bourne's. "Bulgaria and Switzerland may make the same claim," chimed the *Review of Reviews*, a journal which printed excerpted material in larger and more popular mass-circulation magazines, "but the world does not identify the government of those countries with the guardianship of morality."[71]

THE GERLACH AFFAIR AND BRITISH CATHOLIC PERCEPTIONS

According to the political philosopher and founder of the Partito Popolare Italiano, Don Luigi Sturzo, the "Gerlach affair" was one of the greatest "political troubles" ever faced by any of the four popes from Pius IX in 1846 to Benedict XV in 1917.[72] Briefly stated, in the spring of 1917 – the very time when Benedict was aiming to project an image as worthy and impartial – a Mgr. Rudolph Gerlach was arrested and accused of leading an Italian espionage ring with links to German and Austrian intelligence. Gerlach conducted his intrigues during the period of Italian neutrality in 1914 and 1915. The historian David Alvarez, who has written the most comprehensive study of the Gerlach affair, indicated that while for testimonial reasons the espionage charge was somewhat unclear, "the case was still compelling."[73]

The Gerlach affair was so devastating from the standpoint of public perception of the pope's "absolute impartiality" that it forced British Catholic defenders to move from a position of friendly persuasion to one of

[68] Ibid., 2.   [69] Ibid., 10.   [70] Ibid., 11.
[71] "The Pope's Dilemma," *Review of Reviews* 52 (1915), 139.
[72] Luigi Sturzo and Angeline Helen Lograsso, "The Roman Question Before and After Fascism," *The Review of Politics* 5 (1943), 497.
[73] David Alvarez, "German Agent at the Vatican: The Gerlach Affair," *Intelligence and National Security* 11 (1996), 354.

straight-backed surprise and aggressive defence. *The Tablet* retreated to the age-old cover of Catholicism as a persecuted and misunderstood minority religion. "It was perhaps scarcely to be expected," one writer claimed, "that the opportunity afforded by such an upheaval would be allowed to pass without an outburst of the enemies of the Papacy."[74] The "charges hurled at the occupant of the chair of Peter" were so much of the same: "silence taken as connivance," the wish to "get into the Peace Conference," and "an ambition for the restoration of the Holy Roman Empire."[75]

The difficult point about the Gerlach situation in Britain was that it thrust claims of papal absolute impartiality directly back into the public eye. All the gains made since the end of the "pamphlet war" in 1915 seemed to be dissipating with each report of Mgr. Gerlach's spying adventures. The dogged issue of the pope's absolute impartiality spilled over into even more ink with the publication of *No Small Stir: What the Pope Really Said about the Great War* by the pseudonymous writer "Diplomaticus."

The pseudonymous author noticed that at the beginning of the war, many tracts appeared linking the Holy See in alliance with the Central Powers. But these pamphlets were mere literary curiosities. Later, by 1917, the perception of Benedict XV as "the old 'triple tyrant' … in the service of the enemy" was rife.[76] "Diplomaticus," an able and emotive writer, took as his task a firm defense of the impartiality of the Holy See. What was extraordinary about *No Small Stir* was that it was not written by a Roman Catholic at all. Its publisher, the Society of SS. Peter and Paul, touted its claim as "Publisher to the Church of England." The author, an Anglo-Catholic, showed that the neutrality issue was leaking over into Protestant areas of concern.

WAR'S END: THE TRIUMPH OF
ABSOLUTE IMPARTIALITY?

In August of 1917 Benedict put forward his famous Peace Note, one which the British public met with a skeptical eye. Its popular reception was conditioned by Benedict's absolute impartiality doctrine.

Indeed, Benedict's opening line in his letter "To the Heads of the Belligerent Peoples" stressed that his primary aim throughout the war had been "to maintain perfect impartiality toward the belligerents, as becomes

---

[74] "The Pope and his Critics," *The Tablet* (August 11, 1917).   [75] Ibid.

[76] "Diplomaticus," *No Small Stir: What the Pope Really Said about the Great War* (London: Society of SS. Peter and Paul, 1917), 6.

him who is the common father and who loves all his children with equal affection."[77] As in the Caroline Islands dispute, the Peace Note then listed a number of areas weighing on the papacy, from territorial adjustment to freedom of the seas and the "full evacuation of Belgium." In contrast with Leo's free invitation into dispute resolution in 1885, this time Benedict found a skeptical if not hostile Allied reception.

"The Papal Note has been received with universal respect," the normally staid British editors at *International Law Notes* opined in August of 1917, "but undoubtedly has had a 'Bad Press' in all the countries, somewhat curiously including that of the Central Powers."[78] The lawyers, while "purposely abstaining in detail from criticizing the note," nevertheless offered their observations – primarily those dealing with the absolute impartiality doctrine.[79] "It is, we think, a matter of common knowledge that the attitude of the Vatican has been ... the source of deep regret to many Catholics."[80] This reading so insinuated itself into the Catholic consciousness that *The Tablet* was forced to write a long editorial showing that Benedict's Peace Note was "not of Austro-German Inspiration."[81]

It was as if the neutrality question never seemed to be able to go away. In January of 1918, *The Birmingham Daily Post* published a series of articles accusing Benedict of being pro-German and silent about the Belgian atrocities. Birmingham's newly elevated Archbishop John McIntyre responded with a hastily arranged lecture to the Birmingham Reunion. In a talk of the same title as Cardinal Bourne's three years earlier, "The Pope and the War," McIntyre equated the Holy See with other neutral states who also failed to speak out.[82] "To single out in that silent crowd the Holy Father, who had no hand in making the international law which had been violated," McIntyre advanced, "was a piece of mean and dastardly bullying." His talk was immediately published in pamphlet form by the Catholic newspaper *The Universe* – with an astonishing first printing of 20,000.

By February of 1918, the Holy See had become so weary of the criticism of its absolute impartiality that Benedict authorized the collation of primary source documents to create a *libro bianco*, or "White Book," meant

[77] *Official Statements of War Aims and Peace Proposals, December 1916 to December 1918* (Washington, DC: Carnegie Endowment for International Peace, 1921), 129.
[78] "The Pope's Proposals for Peace," *International Law Notes* 117 (1917), 118.
[79] Ibid.   [80] Ibid.
[81] "The Pope's Peace Note," *The Tablet* (September 1, 1917).
[82] Most Rev. John McIntyre, *The Pope and the War: Full text of Archbishop McIntyre's Address to the Birmingham Reunion, Monday, January 14, 1918* (London: Associated Catholic Newspapers, 1918), 1–8.

to answer critics of the papal position.[83] Almost a year later, there was still little headway on the White Book. *The Tablet* remained under great pressure to deal with the issue and urged its readers to go back to the original wartime statements of the pope. If others had "taken the trouble" to do so, it would "thus save [us] many erroneous disquisitions on the neutrality and impartiality of the Holy See."[84]

As the diplomatic historian John Zeender has pointed out, Benedict would suffer possibly his most painful defeat in the winter of 1918–19.[85] When he was excluded from the Paris Peace Conference, he was precluded from playing the role which Cardinal Consalvi played in 1814 at the Congress of Vienna. Although his exclusion was orchestrated by the Italian government in connection with the vexatious Roman Question, this was certainly a crushing blow for the touted efficaciousness of absolute impartiality.

CONCLUSION

Writing in 2001, the Vatican legal historian Robert John Araujo, SJ, cited Bishop Keating's 1915 *The Neutrality of the Holy See* to show that the Holy See's neutrality policy in World War I was "poles asunder from cold indifference," and instead allowed the papacy to work for world peace, arranging "mutual concessions on behalf of all victims of war without distinction."[86] As John F. Pollard has pointed out, beginning with his small inspiration to aid prisoners of war, Benedict XV ushered in a whole host of humanitarian concerns.[87] Later in the war, Benedict would make great strides in helping to alleviate the suffering of displaced war children. One could argue that the entire modern professional apparatus of the Holy See's humanitarian direct-action aid programs – Caritas and Catholic Relief Services – had their start in the mind and heart of Pope Benedict XV. As Pollard indicates, Benedict got little recognition for his remarkable humanitarianism during the war, and instead "was attacked by all sides."[88] This was because the Holy See's publicity of papal aid was poor, and because the persistent problem of absolute impartiality skewed

---

[83] Coppa, *The Papacy*, 139.
[84] "A Forthcoming White Book," *The Tablet* (November 23, 1918).
[85] John Zeender, review of Pollard, *Unknown Pope, Catholic Historical Review* 87 (2001), 78.
[86] Robert John Araujo, SJ, "The International Personality and Sovereignty of the Holy See," *Catholic University of America Law Review* 50 (2001), 306 n. 65.
[87] Pollard, *Unknown Pope*, 112.   [88] Ibid., 116.

the public discourse.[89] Lack of appreciation of Benedict's true role in helping humanity was one of the final casualties of the absolute impartiality doctrine.

Regardless, many historians believe that the Holy See's experience in World War I allowed it to exercise diplomatic deftness, maintain its unique status in the midst of the Roman Question, and raise the international profile of the papacy during world conflict. While that may have been the case for the papacy, within the local Roman Catholic churches of Britain a historic level of questioning emerged. The popular questioning and the debate centered on how British Catholics viewed themselves in relation to the papacy during time of war. For British Roman Catholics, a relationship formerly weighted with Ultramontanism became deeply confused and strained. G. K. Chesterton's enthusiasm for a social "Catholic moment" was overplayed.

In May of 1923 King George V and Queen Mary were scheduled to pay a visit to Pope Pius XI at the Vatican as they concluded an Italian sojourn. By this time, prominent British Catholics were pushing the royal visit as "final proof that Great Britain regards Catholics no longer as enemies, but as co-guardians of her safety."[90] But inside the church, it was still the wartime record of Benedict XV which needed to be clarified and defended. In a two-column article entitled "Pope Benedict & the Kaizer," the *Birmingham Catholic News* was still busy clearing Benedict's position of absolute impartiality.[91] Later that year, in an article entitled "The Vatican and War," the *Birmingham Catholic News* again was forced to debunk further reports of Benedict's partiality.[92] Nearly five years after the end of hostilities, Benedict's absolute impartiality doctrine was still a major stress point in popular British Catholicism. Echoes of the doctrine still reverberated up to the eve of World War II.

---

[89] In research for this chapter, the paucity of articles on and notices of papal relief efforts during the war was telling, and was completely overshadowed by the neutrality question. It was not until after the war had concluded that the Holy See began to draw attention to its own outstanding aid efforts.

[90] *The Times* (May 10, 1923).

[91] *Birmingham Catholic News* (May 5, 1923), 6.

[92] "The Vatican and War," *Birmingham Catholic News* (October 23, 923).

CHAPTER 10

Electronic pastors: radio, cinema, and television, from Pius XI to John XXIII

John F. Pollard

INTRODUCTION

The announcement in late January 2009 that Pope Benedict XVI had decided to make himself accessible on YouTube is a reminder that most of the modern popes have adopted new inventions as a means of furthering their ministry to the church and the world. In the era of mass-circulation newspapers from the early nineteenth century onward, the Holy See had encouraged the development of the Catholic press as a weapon against liberal and anti-clerical foes,[1] and in the late nineteenth century, despite the warning of their predecessor Gregory XVI that "chemin de fer, che-min d'enfer!" ("the railroad is the road to hell!"), Popes Pius IX and Leo XIII exploited the spread of railroads and steamships to facilitate mass pil-grimages of the faithful to Rome.[2] Photography also helped facilitate the development of a papal "cult of the personality," and Leo XIII was the first pope to appear on a moving film, though the Vatican was diffident about the use of the cinema for some time to come.

This chapter will consider the use made of radio, cinema, and televi-sion by the papacy in the mid-twentieth century: how the sounds and images of successive popes projected by these media were received by Catholics and non-Catholics alike, and how they helped develop the pro-file of the Roman Catholic Church throughout the world. The chapter is based on archival material held in the Vatican and Italian state archives,

---

I wish to thank Peter James, Rob Bricheno, and Eric Marcus for explaining various technical issues to me, Dr. Claudia di Giovanni of the Filmoteca del Vaticano, and Dr. Andrea di Stefano, who did some vital research for me in Rome.

[1] See V. Viaene, "'Wagging the Dog': An Introduction to Vatican Press Policy in an Age of Democracy and Imperialism," in Vincent Viane, ed., *The Papacy and the New World Order: Vatican Diplomacy, Catholic Opinion and International Politics at the Time of Leo XIII, 1878–1903* (Leuven: Katholieke Universiteit Leuven Press, 2005), 322–48.

[2] John F. Pollard, *Money and the Rise of the Modern Papacy: Financing the Vatican, 1850–1950* (Cambridge: Cambridge University Press, 2005), 58–59.

sight of various films in the Vatican film library (Filmoteca del Vaticano), newspaper sources, and some key secondary sources.

THE ADVENT OF VATICAN RADIO

Radio was the first of the new media to be wholly embraced by the papacy, though strangely, the founder of Vatican Radio, Pius XI, disliked using the telephone. There is evidence that a radio station was part of the pope's plan all along for the State of the Vatican City, which emerged from the February 1929 Lateran Pacts that concluded the sixty-year "Roman Question," the conflict between the Holy See and the Kingdom of Italy over ownership of Rome and the surrounding territory.[3] Vatican City, the hundred-acre sovereign state, then on the western edge of Rome, was equipped with almost all the accoutrements of statehood, including separate postal and telegraphic services.[4] The Vatican radio station was established two years after the signing of the pacts in order to provide radiotelegraphy and radiotelephone facilities entirely independent of the Italian authorities.[5]

The technical design of the radio station was entrusted to Guglielmo Marconi, who was brought in to view possible sites for transmitters in Vatican City as early as June 1929, when the Lateran Pacts were being ratified by both sides.[6] The management of Vatican Radio was entrusted to the Jesuits, perhaps because they were under the direct orders of the pope and perhaps also because they contained a number of scientists in their ranks – the Vatican astronomical observatory was also run by a Jesuit, Fr. Gianfranceschi, SJ, a scientist and the Rector of the Gregorian University, who had been on a Polar expedition in 1929; he was named Director-General of Vatican Radio in 1930.

---

[3] See John F. Pollard, *Catholicism in Modern Italy: Religion, Society and Politics since 1861* (London: Routledge, 2008), 85–91.

[4] Pollard, *Money*, 150–53.

[5] During World War I, the Holy See's diplomatic efforts were hindered by the fact that its telephonic and telegraphic communications with the outside world were provided by the Italian authorities, who intercepted its traffic. This was the result of Pius IX's rejection of the Italian parliament's law of papal guarantees of 1871, which, though it denied papal sovereignty over the Vatican City, would have allowed the Holy See independent telephone and telegraph facilities. See John F. Pollard, *The Unknown Pope: Benedict XV (1914–1922) and the Pursuit of Peace* (New York: Geoffrey Chapman, 1999; reprinted London: Continuum, 2005), 77.

[6] F. Bea, *Qui Radio Vaticana: mezzo secolo della radio del Papa* (Vatican City: Edizioni Radio Vaticana, 1981), 19. Here and elsewhere in this chapter, translations are mine unless otherwise stated.

The radio station was inaugurated by Pius XI on February 21, 1931, and his first message, which was given in Latin and was then repeated in other languages, talked appropriately about "the secrets of an omnipotent and Divine Providence."[7] The historic event was filmed by Paramount News, a Hollywood "newsreel" company, and shown in the United States.[8] February 1931 also saw the first broadcast of a papal audience, with large numbers of listeners in Italy, including enclosed convents of nuns in Turin and Venice, in France, and in Britain. According to London's *News Chronicle* of February 13, 1931, 3,500 people heard the broadcast in Westminster Cathedral,[9] and it was relayed to the United States, where, according to *The New York Herald* of February 14, Cardinal O'Connell said he could hear it perfectly in Boston.[10] Mgr. Angelo Roncalli (later Pope John XXIII) also heard it in Sofia, where he was apostolic delegate, and even Australian Catholics heard it, thanks to a link-up with the Australian Broadcasting Corporation.[11]

It is noticeable that in the first few years of its existence, Vatican Radio *broadcast* very little. In this period it seemed to have been largely used for radio telephone and radiotelegraph purposes. It is likely that the Vatican secretariat of state was afraid that regular broadcasting might upset the authorities in fascist Italy, who would consider it "foreign propaganda," like broadcasts from Radio Moscow and Radio Luxembourg, and some French radio stations which hosted interviews with Italian anti-fascist exiles, which were jammed. The Vatican avoided talking about *radiodiffusione* (radio broadcasting), and thus in July 1931 *L'osservatore romano* actually published a statement from Vatican Radio which said:

The Administration of Vatican Radio wishes to announce that it has received requests from various quarters for a schedule of our broadcasts. It needs to be understood that we are not making nor will we be making radio broadcasts. Our transmissions are used for the giving of news and information, and for reading news and letters from the missions.[12]

The statement was almost certainly prompted by the ongoing crisis in relations between Italy and the papacy at that time.[13]

At the World Congress of Radio Organizations in Madrid in 1932, Gianfranceschi stressed that Vatican Radio was a "radio telegraph and

---

7   "L'inaugurazione della Radio Vaticana 1931," Filmoteca del Vaticano, Vatican, Rome, coll. 1.
8   Bea, *Qui Radio Vaticana*, 30.   9   Ibid., 54.   10   Ibid.   11   Ibid., 55.
12   As quoted in ibid., 65.
13   See Pollard, *The Vatican and Italian Fascism, 1929–1932: A Study in Conflict* (Cambridge: Cambridge University Press, 1985), ch. 6.

radio telephone service."[14] In 1933 the International Telecommunications Union gave agreement for Vatican Radio to have radiotelephone links with Spain, France, Germany, Austria, Poland, and the United States, with extensions to Canada and Central and South America. This would tally with the fact that by then the apostolic nunciatures and delegations in various countries had all been given radio receivers, and a short-wave radio station had been established at Castelgandolfo, the papal summer residence in the hills outside Rome.

But transmissions increased in 1933, when Vatican Radio broadcast some of the celebrations for the extraordinary Holy Year which Pius XI had designated to commemorate the passion and death of Jesus Christ. Vatican Radio also came into its own as a means of broadcasting the pope's messages to the Eucharistic congresses organized in various parts of the world – Dublin, September 1932; Buenos Aires, October 1934; Melbourne, December 1934; Lourdes, April 1935; Cleveland, Ohio, September 1935; Lima, September 1935; Manila, February 1937; New Orleans, October 1937; Madras, December 1937; and Budapest, 1938. This was very important. These regional assemblies of Catholics were equivalent to the "pilgrim" journeys of Popes Paul VI and John Paul II, with a profound impact upon local Catholics, giving them a stronger sense of belonging to the universal church and of their closeness to the pope, now intensified by actually hearing his voice in their own countries.

If the emergence of new, electronic means of communication required the Roman Catholic Church to use them to ensure that its voice would be heard in the world, then the rise of the totalitarian dictatorships made it absolutely imperative. The threats posed by atheistic communism, German Nazi neo-paganism, and, to a lesser extent, Italian fascism, not to mention the on-going threat from anti-clericalism, the latter usually perceived in Catholic circles as a "masonic plot," all required a response. There were requests from India, Australia, the Philippines, China, Canada, and Spain for a "Catholic information service" which would no longer be dependent on the Reuters news agency, which was regarded as not being very sympathetic to the church.[15] Matelski's claim that the Catholic information service instituted by Pius XI in 1938 was "created solely to attack the atheistic propaganda coming from Germany, Italy, Japan and Russia" may therefore have some grounding in fact.[16]

[14] As quoted in ibid., 76. [15] Ibid., 101.
[16] Marilyn J. Matelski, *Vatican Radio: Propaganda by the Airwaves* (Westport, CT: Praeger, 1995), xvii.

In 1935 some Latin American correspondents asked that Vatican Radio broadcast "programmes of a social character, aimed at countering Nazi and Soviet propaganda," and some German bishops also came to the conclusion that Vatican Radio could have an anti-Nazi function: according to Bea, they wanted more regular broadcasts on religious matters.[17] The initial technical capacities of Vatican Radio were hardly designed for such purposes, and so between 1931 and 1937 the idea that the radio station should become the core of an international Catholic broadcasting *network* was ventilated both inside and outside the Vatican.[18] When the issue of an international Catholic radio station was first raised in 1931, Pius XI was all in favor but Gianfranceschi advised caution, pointing out that it would be expensive to build and maintain and might be heavily dependent upon the good will of the Italians.[19] In April 1932 a commission to examine the question of establishing "a Radio Station in the Vatican or utilizing the existing station for radio broadcasts" was set up.[20] Four years later Cardinal Villeneuve, Archbishop of Quebec, wrote to the secretary of state, Cardinal Pacelli, advocating a plan for radio transmitters around the world which would use the same programs on disks to reach various categories of Catholics, with the stations positioned on the properties of religious orders.[21] Pacelli's response was to say that it was a good idea, but too ambitious.[22] Then in 1936 there were consultations with the Bureau Catholique International de Radiodiffusion which brought together Catholic radio stations from all over the world, including the Catholic radio station in the Netherlands, where Catholic broadcasting had been an essential and important part of efforts to sustain the minority Catholic community in that nation since 1925.[23] But, in the end, the idea of an international Catholic radio network came to nothing, and no more was heard of it after 1937.

In the meantime, important developments had taken place in the Vatican's radio station. 1936 marked a crucial turning point when the International Radio Union meeting in Geneva formally permitted both the League of Nations and the State of the Vatican City to have "radio

---

[17] Bea, *Qui Radio Vaticana*, 96–97.
[18] Archivio Segreto Vaticano, Vatican, Rome, Affari Straordinari Ecclesiastici, Quarto Periodo, busta 472, fascicoli 473–74, 1931–37, Ente Radiofonico Cattolico.
[19] Letter of Fr. Gianfranceschi to the pope, October 29, 1931, ibid.
[20] Unsigned memorandum of April 13, 1932, ibid.
[21] Cardinal Villeneuve to Pacelli, February 1, 1936, ibid.
[22] Pacelli to Villeneuve, no date but numbered 727/35, ibid.
[23] Memorandum of Fr. Dito, OP, August 28, 1936, about Radio Catholique aux Pays-Bas (the Catholic radio station of the Netherlands), and Dito to Pizzardo, March 17, 1937, ibid.

stations," broadcasting without any geographical limitation. As has been seen, there had for a while been spontaneous pressure for Vatican Radio to increase its broadcasts: eventually, by mid-1936, following growing Vatican exasperation with the Nazis' repeated violations of the *Reichskonkordat* of 1933, another Jesuit, the anti-Nazi, Swiss German Fr. Muckermann, was enlisted to make more regular broadcasts in German.[24] In April 1937 the station broadcast in various languages the text of *Mit brennender Sorge*, the papal encyclical which explicitly condemned Hitler's violations of the *Reichskonkordat* and implicitly aspects of Nazi ideology, including its racialism, paganism, and "statolatry" as well.[25] We do not know how the average German received this particular broadcast, because the Nazis may already have been jamming Vatican Radio, but it infuriated the Nazi leadership, resulting in formal protests by the German ambassador at the Vatican, von Bergen. The latter protested again when Muckermann broadcast an explicitly anti-Nazi talk in May 1937, and there were further protests when Vatican Radio broadcast a program which attacked Cardinal Innitzer, Archbishop of Vienna, for the cordial welcome he had extended to Hitler when German armies invaded Austria and effected the *Anschluss*, or union with Germany.[26] So, already before the outbreak of World War II, Vatican Radio was regarded as an "enemy radio" by the Nazis, and the irony of all this was that the new, more powerful, transmitter installed in 1937 was supplied by Telefunken, a German company![27]

Another crucial development was the establishment of a Catholic news center in Vatican Radio with the nucleus of a team of journalists and editors.[28] Significantly, it too was largely drawn from the ranks of the Jesuit order and was closely linked to its secretariat for combating atheism, based in the Russicum, the college which had been founded to train priests for perilous missionary work in the Soviet Union.[29]

Pius XI's most important, and last, radio broadcast came in September 1938, on the eve of the Munich conference at which Britain, France, Germany, and Italy decided the fate of Czechoslovakia. Talking to Mgr. Domenico Tardini, Vasco de Quevedo, Portugal's minister to the Vatican, explained how he and his wife, daughter, and brother-in-law had

[24] Bea, *Qui Radio Vaticana*, 96–97.   [25] Ibid., 102–03.
[26] A. Rhodes, *The Vatican in the Age of the Dictators, 1922–1945* (London: Hodder & Stoughton, 1973), 151–52.
[27] On the other hand, this probably made it easier for the Germans to jam Vatican Radio.
[28] Bea, *Qui Radio Vaticana*, 150.
[29] For the role of the Jesuits in the battle against communism pre-1939, see G. Petracchi, "I gesuiti e il comunismo fra le due guerre," in Vincenzo Ferrone, ed., *La Chiesa Cattolica e il totalitarismo* (Florence: Leo S. Olschki Editore, 2004), 123–52.

all listened to the pope's speech and wept at his pleas for peace: many Italians must have had the same experience, for there was a great fear of war in Italy at that time.[30] By now, Pius XI was at odds with Mussolini over the introduction of the racial laws against the Jews into Italy, and Italian fascism was spared a stinging criticism of its shortcomings in the pope's eyes only by the latter's death the day before he was due to deliver the speech.[31]

The pope's life drew to a close a few months after his last radio broadcast, in February 1939. Medical bulletins were broadcast by Vatican Radio, and at 6.30 a.m. on the ninth of that month the news of his death. Three days later, Tardini read the pope's obituary.[32] These broadcasts and those of the funeral, as well as the conclave which elected his successor, Pius XII, and the latter's coronation on March 12, 1939, impacted upon Catholic sentiments worldwide, as is demonstrated by the flow of letters to Vatican Radio and to leading newspapers.[33] So, for the first time in the history of the papacy, the death of a pope and the election and coronation of his successor became a major media event, raising the worldwide profile of the Roman Catholic Church as a result.

VATICAN RADIO AND WORLD WAR II

Though Cardinal Pacelli was supposedly the "designated 'dauphin'" of Pius XI, when the latter died in 1939 and Pacelli was elected his successor as Pius XII, the Vatican's policy toward the fascist dictators changed. The encyclical which Pius XI had commissioned against Nazi and fascist racialism – *Humani generis unitas* – was "hidden" on the orders of the new pope, and the papacy adopted a policy of studied impartiality between the democracies and dictatorships.[34] Papal diplomacy was now employed in a desperate effort to prevent the outbreak of war, and thus Pius XII's first broadcast as pope, made on September 24, was a plea for peace: "The danger is imminent, but there is still time. Nothing is lost with peace. Everything can be lost with War. Men must seek to understand one another. They must

[30] Diario di S. E. Mons. Tardini dal 27 settembre al 29 ottobre 1938, entry of September 29, 1938, Archivio Segreto Vaticano, Affari Straordinari Ecclesiastici, Quarto Periodo, Stati Ecclesiastici, 560, 592.
[31] For the last, tormented months of Pius XI's reign see E. Fattorini, *Pio XI, Hitler e Mussolini: la solitudine di un papa* (Turin: Einaudi, 2007), chs. 7, 8.
[32] Bea, *Qui Radio Vaticana*, 116.   [33] Ibid., 117.
[34] For the text of the encyclical see G. Passelecq and B. Suchecky, *The Hidden Encyclical of Pius XI: The Vatican's Lost Opportunity to Oppose Nazi Racial Policies that Led to the Holocaust*, trans. Steven Rendall (London: Harcourt, Brace and Company, 1997).

resume negotiations."[35] Of course, it had no effect. World War II began a few days later with Hitler's invasion of Poland.

Inevitably, the tragic fate of Catholic Poland was one of the dominant concerns in the Vatican during the "phoney war" between September 1939 and April 1940, when Hitler launched his *Blitzkrieg* in the West (the other was the danger of Italian intervention in the conflict because Mussolini had remained neutral at the outbreak of the war). In September 1939, Cardinal Hlond, the Primate of Poland now in exile, made an emotional speech on Vatican radio:

> Martyred Poland, you have fallen to violence while you fought for the sacred cause of freedom ... Your tragedy arouses the conscience of the world ... On these radio waves, which run across the world, carrying truth from the Vatican hill, I cry to you. Poland, you are not beaten! By the will of God you will rise with glory, my beloved, my martyred Poland.[36]

It is not absolutely clear whether Pius XII authorized this speech, but the fact that the Father-General of the Jesuits, Ledóchowski, was a Pole may explain why Vatican Radio broadcast it. Owen Chadwick in his *Britain and the Vatican during the Second World War* says that "Nothing like this broadcast was ever allowed to happen again,"[37] but in fact the Nazis would have reason to object to Vatican Radio broadcasts on many more future occasions. As he himself also says, there were further broadcasts about the appalling German atrocities in Poland during the winter of 1939–40, and because they were in both English and French they had a wider and more powerful impact than they would have had if confined to a single language.[38]

The broadcasts of the Belgian priest Fr. Mistiaen, which criticized the Nazis directly, prompted a protest from Herr Menshausen of the German embassy to the Holy See on January 27, 1940.[39] There is a sense in which, during World War II, Vatican Radio had become a pawn in the struggle between the Axis and the Allied powers. Chadwick, for example, says that Mistiaen "became for Osborne the most important person at Vatican radio ... and made no pretence of neutrality."[40] Sir D'Arcy

---

[35] *Allocuzioni e radiomessaggi di S.S. Pio XII, con commento degli scrittori della* Civiltà cattolica (Rome: Edizioni della Civiltà cattolica, 1943), 59.
[36] As quoted in O. Chadwick, *Britain and the Vatican during the Second World War* (Cambridge: Cambridge University Press, 1986), 80–81: in April 1940, the station also broadcast the pastoral of the Dutch bishops against the Nazi party; see Pierre Blet, Angelo Martini, and Burkhart Schneider, eds., *Actes et documents du Saint-Siège relatifs àla Seconde Guerre Mondiale*, 11 vols. (Vatican City: Libreria Editrice Vaticana, 1965–67), IV, 514.
[37] Chadwick, *Britain and the Vatican*, 143.   [38] Ibid.   [39] Ibid.   [40] Ibid., 141.

Osborne, Britain's minister to the Holy See, was immured within the Vatican itself between June 1940 and the Allied liberation of Rome four years later. Whenever Vatican Radio was told to tone down its broadcasts or remove a particular broadcaster, like Mistiaen, from his post, Osborne and other Allied diplomats inside the Vatican protested.[41] According to Adler, "Mistiaen's criticisms of the persecution of the Catholic Church in Germany, Poland and Alsace-Lorraine was one issue that Germany was not prepared to tolerate."[42] Even worse, in a broadcast in January 1941 Mistiaen declared: "the Church will never submit to the claim that might is right. There is an order of slavery and death, quite unsuitable for the whole of humanity. Is that what those who talk about the *new orders* mean?"[43] Listeners could have had little doubt that these criticisms were aimed at the "New Order" which Germany had installed in Europe following its military victories of 1939 and 1940. Following protests from the German foreign office and threats of reprisals, Mistiaen was taken off the air between May 1941 and the end of the year.[44]

But Mistiaen's broadcasts were effective. They provided the material for much Resistance literature that was circulated clandestinely in both Nazi-occupied France and the territory of Marshal Pétain's Vichy France. They were transcribed by members of the Dominican order in Marseilles (where the Vatican Radio signal was especially strong), and then distributed among French Catholics in the form of a magazine, *La voix du Vatican*, by young activists in Catholic action organizations.[45]

Broadcasts were also made on Vatican Radio for the American people. A very effective critic of the Germans was the American Jesuit Fr. J. E. Coffey, who broadcast in English primarily for North America. In one broadcast he described the conditions with which the Nazis treated the people of Poland: "Jews and Poles were herded together in separate ghettoes, hermetically sealed, with miserably inadequate means of economic sustenance provided for those who had to live inside."[46] Chadwick makes the point that broadcasts like these "helped nauseate the British and French" and that "Between the outbreak of the war and the end of April 1941 the Foreign Office in London valued Radio Vaticana as one of the

[41] Ibid., 147–48.
[42] Jacques Adler, "The 'Sin of Omission'? Radio Vatican and the Anti-Nazi Struggle, 1940–1942," *Australian Journal of History and Politics* 50:3 (2004), 402.
[43] Ibid. [44] Ibid., 402.
[45] David Alvarez and Robert Graham, SJ, *Nothing Sacred: Nazi Espionage against the Vatican 1919–1945* (London: Frank Cass, 1997), 142–43.
[46] As quoted in R. Graham, SJ, "La Radio Vaticana tra Londra e Berlino: un dossier della guerra delle onde: 1940–1941," *La civiltà cattolica* 127 (1976), 139.

most useful instruments on their side in the struggle to influence European and American opinion."[47] Another anti-German broadcast was made by an American secular priest working in the Roman curia, Mgr. Hurley, in July 1940. Hurley had been close to Pius XI, whose messages and radio broadcasts he had translated into English. After the election of Pius XII, Hurley found himself out of sympathy with the new policy and out of favor in the Vatican. Yet, somehow, he managed to give a speech entitled "The Duty to Fight" which contained the statement that "The Church is no conscientious objector" and was specifically directed at Catholic isolationists in the United States, and so was totally out of line with Pius XII's "impartiality."[48] The impact of the speech can be judged by the headline in *The Times* of July 5, "Voice of the Vatican: Duty to Fight for the Right."[49] Within a few weeks Hurley was banished from the Vatican and sent as bishop to the obscure, poverty-stricken see of St. Augustine, Florida.[50] The broadcast of another American Jesuit, Fr. Vincent McCormick, in October 1940 on the persecution of the church in Poland triggered another German protest. Its content was exaggerated by the BBC and also by the American press, and so Ledóchowski told Fr. Soccorsi, Gianfranceschi's successor, to be more careful and reduce the number of broadcasts.[51]

Indeed, by the autumn of 1940 Vatican Radio was in serious trouble. Already under mounting pressure from German diplomats, after Mussolini's declaration of war against Britain and France in June it faced a threat from much closer to home. Its precarious position was a reflection of that of the State of the Vatican City itself, completely surrounded as the latter was by the territory of an Axis belligerent, Italy, and wholly dependent upon the good will of that country for the provision of the basic elements of survival – food, power, and other utility services.[52] The Italian authorities subjected the Vatican to intense surveillance, particularly after the British, French, and other Allied ambassadors were forced to take up residence there, infiltrating spies into many parts of its administration. Vatican Radio, and especially Soccorsi and Mistiaen, were subject to close surveillance: both were regarded as hostile to Italian fascism and German National Socialism.[53] Even the official in Vatican Radio responsible for

[47] Chadwick, *Britain and the Vatican*, 143–44.
[48] C. Gallagher, SJ, *Vatican Secret Diplomacy: Joseph P. Hurley and Pope Pius XII* (New Haven: Yale University Press, 2008), 98.
[49] Ibid.   [50] Ibid.
[51] Chadwick, *Britain and the Vatican*, 146.   [52] Ibid.
[53] Archivio Centrale dello Stato (henceforth ACS), Rome, Ministero dell'Interno (henceforth MdI), Polizia Politica, busta 71, fascicolo "Radio Vaticana – Varie"; see the detailed report of September 7, 1940.

processing the enciphered radiograms of the secretariat of state was an agent of the Italian police.[54]

The Italians also supported the diplomatic efforts of their German ally to silence the criticisms by Vatican Radio of the Nazi "New Order," that is, their brutal subjugation and oppression of the territories which they had occupied in Europe. MinCulPop, the fascist propaganda ministry, carefully monitored Vatican Radio and was thus very much aware of these attacks. Attolico, Italian ambassador to the Holy See, repeatedly warned Mgr. Montini, the Vatican's substitute secretary of state, of the perilous course which Vatican Radio would be taking if it continued to criticize the occupation policies of Mussolini's ally.[55]

These protests from the Germans raised an important issue: who controlled Vatican Radio? When pressed by von Bergen, the German ambassador, on the question of responsibility for Vatican Radio broadcasts, Mgr. Domenico Tardini, Vatican under-secretary of state, denied that there was direct secretariat of state control over the station, implying that it was in some sense a "private" undertaking.[56] That was being disingenuous to say the least. Though it is true that, while *L'osservatore romano* was directly answerable to the secretariat of state, Vatican Radio was not; everyone in the Vatican knew that it was ultimately answerable to the pope, *via the Father-General of the Jesuits, Ledóchowski.* The Vatican was thus playing a dangerous game. Whatever comments were made about the policies of national governments, whether they were approved by the pope or not, they would be deemed to be so, and in wartime this was a serious issue. Chadwick has argued that "Vatican Radio [was] believed to be the direct mouthpiece of the Pope. Actually it has as much independence from the Pope as the BBC had from the British government."[57] The BBC's independence *in wartime* was probably not, in any case, as great as Chadwick imagines, but more important than this is the fact that, in the last resort, the pope could and did intervene directly in the operations of Vatican Radio via the Jesuits, the only Catholic religious order directly answerable to him. While it is true that the Vatican is not, and never has been, the internal power monolith that has often been assumed, nevertheless, the papacy is an absolute monarchy in which the sovereign's will is literally the law. It simply suited the Vatican or, rather, Tardini, Montini, and Cardinal Maglione, the secretary of state, to *pretend* that Vatican Radio

[54] Alvarez, *Nothing Sacred*, 152.   [55] Chadwick, *Britain and the Vatican*, 132.
[56] Blet, Martini, and Schneider, eds., *Actes et documents*, III:1, 208–09.
[57] Chadwick, *Britain and the Vatican*, 106.

was independent, at least of their office, in their endless battles with the German and Italian ambassadors.

The role of Vatican Radio during the course of the war is a matter of great significance in the on-going debate about "Hitler's Pope," that is, the controversy over Pius XII's response to the Holocaust and other fascist genocides, like the mass murder by the Croatian Ustasha of gypsies, Jews, and Serbs.[58] As has been seen, there is very clear evidence that whether it was acting on the pope's orders or not, the broadcasts of the radio station were extremely critical of Nazi occupation policies and accordingly aroused the Germans' wrath. But the radio station rarely singled out Jewish victims of Nazi atrocities, even when, by mid-1942, the full extent of the Holocaust taking place in those parts of Eastern Europe occupied by the Germans was becoming evident. There was, however, "An unnamed speaker" who said in 1940, "In Germany the Jews are killed, brutalized, tortured."[59]

Pius XII broadcast on Vatican Radio more than his predecessor, and when he did, it usually caused a stir in both belligerent camps. His next major broadcast following his appeal for peace in September 1939 was his Christmas Eve broadcast of that year, in which he enunciated his "Five Peace Points":

1. The independence of all nations, large and small
2. General disarmament
3. Rebuilding international institutions
4. Recognizing the rights of ethnic minorities
5. Recognition of the rule of law.[60]

The message had a powerful impact, prompting a joint letter from the Archbishops of Canterbury, Westminster, and York and the Moderator of the Free Church Council to the London *Times*, urging that the five principles form the basis of a possible peace with Nazi Germany.[61]

Pius XII's Easter message on April 13, 1941, which contained a plea to the occupying powers to exercise humanity, evoked a furious response from Goebbels because only Germany and its ally the Soviet Union were

---

[58] J. Cornwell, *Hitler's Pope: The Secret History of Pius XII* (New York: Viking, 1999); the best survey of the controversy as a whole is to be found in J. Sanchez, *Pius XII and the Holocaust: Understanding the Controversy* (Washington, DC: Catholic University of America Press, 2002); on Yugoslavia, see S. Alexander, *Church and State in Yugoslavia since 1945* (Cambridge: Cambridge University Press, 1979), 29–40.

[59] As quoted in Adler, "The 'Sin of Omission'?," 404.

[60] P. Blet, SJ, *Pius XII and the Second World War: According to the Vatican Archives*, trans. Lawrence J. Johnson (Hereford: Gracewing, 1999), 30.

[61] J. Derek Holmes, *The Papacy in the Modern World, 1914–1978* (New York: Crossroad, 1981), 124.

occupying territory in Europe at that time. The German propaganda minister exclaimed that "The Vatican continues to attack us through the Radio" and insisted that Vatican Radio had to be silenced.[62] As on previous occasions, there were formal German and Italian protests to the secretariat of state, and the pope told Vatican Radio to stop talking about Germany and persecution; and, as usual, Osborne protested. On the other hand, the message was well received in the British and American press. *The New York Times* printed the message in full with a photograph of the pope, and in its editorial it argued that, "Despite the impartiality imposed upon him as the head of a Church with congregations in every warring nation, Pope Pius XII gave the world an Easter message which could be of small comfort to the Nazis."[63]

The pope's Christmas message in 1942 evoked a similar response. In it he declared, "Humanity owes this vow to those hundreds of thousands who, without any fault of their own, sometimes only by reason of their nationality or race, are marked down for death or gradual extinction."[64] Fr. Vincent McCormick was critical of the speech, describing it as "much too heavy, ideas not clean cut and obscurely expressed."[65] The Christmas message also came in for a lot of criticism for the vagueness of the pope's statement, such that it prompted an official complaint on the part of the Belgian, British, Polish, and Brazilian ambassadors to the Holy See.[66] Nevertheless, the Germans were predictably furious about its content, seeing, quite rightly, that the message was "virtually accusing the German people of injustice towards the Jews and [the pope] makes himself a mouthpiece of the Jewish war criminals," provoking threats of retaliation from their ambassador, von Bergen.[67]

Another important aspect of Vatican Radio's wartime role was strictly humanitarian: the seventy or so broadcasts which it made each week, for twelve to thirteen hours a day, asking for information about missing persons, civilian and military, and prisoners of war on behalf of the Ufficio Informazioni, a Vatican office which employed various monsignori and priests of the Roman curia plus other religious, male and female. Between 1940 and 1945 it broadcast 1,240,728 messages.[68] Modeled on

---

[62] *Goebbels' Diaries, 1939–1941*, trans. and ed. Fred Taylor (London: Sphere, 1983), 332, entry for April 25, 1941.

[63] *The New York Times*, April 15, 1941, 3.

[64] As quoted in Adler, "The Sin of Omission'?," 397.

[65] James Hennessey, "American Jesuit in Rome: The Diary of Vincent McCormick, S.J., 1942–1945," *Mid-America*, 56:1 (1974), 36.

[66] Rhodes, *The Vatican*, 272.   [67] SS report of January 1943, as quoted in ibid., 273.

[68] Bea, *Qui Radio Vaticana*, 134.

the organization set up by Benedict XV during World War I, the Ufficio succeeded in bringing together, physically or via mail, hundreds of thousands of people who had been displaced and scattered by the war.[69] Bea claims that Vatican Radio was also used in this endeavor to enter into direct communication with nuncios and delegates to collect information, for instance with Mgr. Panico, apostolic delegate in Sydney on August 30, 1940.[70] Even these broadcasts aroused the wrath of the Italian government, which claimed that they were revealing details of the Italian order of battle by mentioning the location of ships, submarines, planes, and army units to which Italian prisoners of war had belonged.[71] It put pressure on the Vatican secretariat of state to prevent information being disclosed which might be of harm to the German or Italian war effort.[72]

Summarizing the impact of broadcasting by Vatican Radio during World War II is difficult. There is little evidence that its broadcasts actually reached Germany, where it was effectively jammed by the Nazi authorities, or Poland and other parts of Nazi-occupied Eastern Europe, where it was also jammed but where, in any case, it was often barely audible. Nevertheless, those caught listening to Vatican Radio, or even suspected of doing so, were severely punished and even executed.[73] On the other hand, members of the British propaganda machine regarded Vatican Radio as a godsend: they repeated its descriptions of Germany's brutal occupation policies and atrocities, often embellishing and exaggerating them.[74] They even went so far as to establish a fake radio station of their own, "Radio Christ the King," which purported to be an emanation of the Vatican, and broadcast anti-Nazi propaganda in its name, prompting the real Vatican radio station to disavow it. According to Alvarez:

Each broadcast began with a selection of classical and religious music and a brief prayer by the announcer, a refugee Austrian priest, who then spoke at length about the Nazis' contempt for law and morality, citing such examples as the Regime's persecution of the Jews, its attacks against religious institutions, and its policies in the area of euthanasia and eugenics.[75]

The foreign office in London was in no doubt about the propaganda value of Vatican Radio to the Allied cause. In May 1940 a report stated,

[69] C. Falconi, *The Popes in the Twentieth Century* (London: Weidenfeld & Nicolson, 1967), 262–64.
[70] Bea, *Qui Radio Vaticana*, 134.
[71] Report of September 10, 1940, ACS, MdI, Polizia Politica, busta 71.
[72] Letter from the Ministry of Foreign Affairs, January 11, 1941, ACS, MdI, Direzione Generale della Pubblica Sicurezza.
[73] Graham, "La Radio Vaticana," 132.   [74] Ibid.
[75] Alvarez, *Nothing Sacred*, 144.

"The independent position assumed by Vatican radio is of the greatest importance for our propaganda in general and for our appeals to the German Catholic population in particular," and Sir Alec Randall, later British minister to the Vatican, declared, "Vatican Radio has been of the greatest use to our propaganda and we have exploited it to the full."[76] When the Vatican finally bowed to pressure in the spring of 1941 and effectively discontinued its broadcasts about conditions in Nazi-occupied Europe, Osborne protested on behalf of the British government, claiming that the Vatican had allowed Axis pressure to compromise its independence.[77]

THE POPES, RADIO, CINEMA, AND
TELEVISION AFTER 1945

After 1945 the advent of the Cold War and in particular the persecution of the Catholic Church in Eastern Europe prompted Vatican Radio to turn its attention to an anti-communist crusade. Throughout the period, Vatican Radio transmitted a regular program, *La chiesa del silenzio* (*The Church of Silence*), edited by Jesuits, and from 1957 onward *Radiogiornale* (*Radio News*), which was directed especially at Eastern Europe.[78] In October 1957, during his solemn opening of the new and bigger Vatican radio transmitter at Santa Maria della Galeria, north-west of Rome, Pius XII broadcast to the world, being linked up to radio stations in Italy, France, Ireland, Monaco, the Netherlands, Germany, Canada, and the United States, and to Radio Free Europe. Radio Free Europe was, of course, an American propaganda initiative (funded by the CIA) and directed at the peoples of the communist states of Eastern Europe.[79] Again, it is difficult to know just how effective these broadcasts during the Cold War were. The American bishop Joseph Hurley, who in 1947 had been sent as Vatican envoy to Tito's Yugoslavia, complained to his friend Archbishop Mooney of Detroit about the "the sepulchral ineptitude and incompetence of Vatican radio" during the early Cold War era in the battles versus communism.[80] Its broadcasts almost certainly had a

[76] As quoted in Graham, "La Radio Vaticana," 148 and 150.

[77] Blet, Martini, and Schneider, eds., *Actes et documents*, IV, 234–35, 258.

[78] Bea, *Qui Radio Vaticana*, 196; see A. Rhodes, *The Vatican in the Age of the Cold War, 1945–1980* (Norwich: Michael Russell, 1992), 118, where he says that in 1951 Mgr. Beran, the Archbishop of Prague imprisoned by the communists, used Vatican Radio to send messages to his parochial clergy.

[79] Bea, *Qui Radio Vaticana*, 189–92.

[80] Letter to Mooney of December 12, 1949, as quoted in Gallagher, *Vatican Secret Diplomacy*, 191.

deeper impact on the peoples of the West than they did on those living behind the Iron Curtain, if only because of jamming by the communist authorities.

The battle for the "Church of Silence" was not the only major preoccupation of Vatican Radio during the reign of Pius XII. He also used it on the occasion of major festivals and anniversaries to reach out to the Catholic populations of countries as far apart as Portugal and Colombia, Spain, Mexico, and Argentina for the promotion of Catholic spirituality.[81] The end of Pius XII's reign in 1958 was treated in the same way by Vatican Radio as it had treated that of his predecessor nineteen years earlier. Fr. Francesco Farusi gave regular medical bulletins about Pius XII throughout his eight-day terminal illness, and when Mgr. Tardini celebrated Mass *pro infirmo* in the pope's private chapel, next to his bedroom, this was also broadcast to the world.[82]

PASTOR ANGELICUS AND OTHER FILMS

In 1942 the Vatican embarked upon an important, unprecedented venture in the use of the media: it decided to make a film about the pope. Hitherto, the Vatican had shown a certain diffidence toward the film industry. Even though Vatican money had been heavily invested in Cineas, a very successful film production company in Rome in the early 1900s, the ecclesiastical authorities remained extremely suspicious of the new medium and in a series of decrees forbade priests from going to see even "sacred films."[83] In 1930 the Vatican published its first official warning to the world's Catholics about the dangers posed by films,[84] and two years later Pius XI published a full-blooded encyclical, *Vigilanti cura*, on the motion picture industry.[85] Addressed in the first instance to the bishops of the United States, *Vigilanti cura* was also intended to demonstrate to the Catholic bishops of the world the efficacy of American Catholic arrangements for the censorship of films, especially the workings of the League of Decency, in which not only Catholics, but also

---

[81] See *Allocuzioni e radiomessaggi*; owing to the closure of the Vatican library, the author could not access all the volumes of *Discorsi e radiomessaggi* and thus was unable to chart all the papal broadcasts down to 1958.

[82] Bea, *Qui Radio Vaticana*, 194.

[83] F. Traniello and G. Campanini, eds., *Dizionario storico del movimento cattolico in Italia*, 3 vols. (Turin: Marietti, 1981), I:1, 304.

[84] *Acta apostolicae sedis* 22 (1930), 82, *Divini illius magistri*, no. 90.

[85] For the text, see Claudia Carlen, IHM, ed., *The Papal Encyclicals, 1740–1981*, 5 vols. (Raleigh, NC: Pierian Press, 1981), III, 217–23.

Jews and Protestants participated.[86] Pius XII would modify and relax the very strict guidelines of the League of Decency in *Miranda prorsus* ("On the Entertainment Media") in 1957.[87]

The 1942 film *Pastor angelicus* was not the first in which Eugenio Pacelli had "starred": already in May 1938 the Hungarian company Magjar had filmed the Eucharistic congress held in Budapest, in which he had played the central role as papal legate.[88] Pacelli's visit to Budapest and others to France, the United States, and Latin America were intended by Pius XI as a means of showing his designated successor to the Catholic world. *Pastor angelicus*, on the other hand, was entirely dedicated to Pacelli, on the twenty-fifth anniversary of his episcopal ordination. After brief footage of the Vatican during the last days of Pius XI, his funeral, and the conclave, the eighty-minute film showed scenes from the early life of Pacelli, his daily routine, and then the key moments of his three-year pontificate, including his first radio speech on September 25, 1939.[89] The film was initially shown in Rome and Italy, and Vincent McCormick, an astute American Jesuit observer of Roman life during World War II, said of its reception: "Here in Rome it only ran for a few days, and was ordered off the screen by the civil authorities. [The] Pope became too popular, it is said: it occasioned shouts for peace. It is now on the Rome circuit [*sic*] and may return to Rome later."[90] This confirms what one might well have surmised: during the last, increasingly difficult year of the fascist regime (it fell in July 1943), Mussolini was extremely unhappy about any public manifestation of the papal charisma. Mussolini's own "cult of the Duce" always had to compete with two rivals: that still lingering around the Italian monarch, Victor Emmanuel III, and the other around the pope. *Pastor angelicus* effectively prepared the ground for Pius XII's emergence as the key personality in Italy after Mussolini's fall. Already, in July 1943, while Mussolini was at Feltre in northern Italy conferring with Hitler, the pope was able to upstage him after the American bombing of the San Lorenzo district of Rome, where he quickly appeared among the ruins, bringing moral and financial succor to the victims.[91] Pius XII then strove to establish and maintain Rome's status as an "open city," thus sparing it further aerial bombardment, as well

---

[86] See G. Black, *The Catholic Crusade against the Movies: 1940–1975* (Cambridge: Cambridge University Press, 1997).

[87] Ibid., 177–78.

[88] *Congresso eucharistico di Budapest*, Filmoteca del Vaticano, titolo 34.

[89] *Pastor angelicus*, 1943, Centro Cinematografico Cattolico, ibid.

[90] Hennessey, "American Jesuit in Rome," 37.

[91] Report for the Duce of July 19, 1943, ACS, MdI, Direzione Generale della Pubblica Sicurezza, Capo della Polizia.

10.1 Piazza Pio XII, Rome, 2008. Photo by Pamela M. Jones.

as street fighting. This, and the Vatican's work to provision Rome in 1943 and 1944, as well as the hospitality given to thousands of escaped prisoners of war, Jews, and members of the anti-fascist resistance, earned him the title of *Defensor Civitatis*, defender of the city of Rome. This title appears prominently today on the street sign of the piazza named after him in that city (Figure 10.1).[92]

McCormick is probably right to suggest that the fascist authorities were wary about the impact of *Pastor angelicus*, though a report of February 1943, barely three months after the release of the film, to the secret police from a "confidential Vatican source" claimed that "Catholic circles have been perplexed and upset by the public's rather cold reception of the film *Pastor Angelicus* ... their only hope is America and other foreign countries, but in Italy it has been a complete flop."[93] As far as Italy was concerned, the secret police informant was ultimately proved quite wrong: between the end of 1942 and first three months of 1947, the film made over 5,000,000 lire at the box office, not a bad success for a film on general release in Italy at that time.[94] Some of its success undoubtedly came about thanks to the network of hundreds of little parochial cinemas which had been developed by the church during the fascist period and which were supplied by several specifically Catholic film-making

[92] See U. Gentiloni Silveri and M. Carli, *Bombardare Roma: gli alleati e la "citta aperta" (1940–1944)* (Bologna: Il Mulino, 2007).
[93] Report of February 13, 1943, ACS, MinCulPop.
[94] ACS, MinCulpop, Direzione Generale del Cinema, busta 7, fascicolo 154, *Pastor angelicus*, lists box office receipts in 1944–45 according to whether it was north or south of the front line, and then quarterly for the whole country for the period 1943–47.

companies.[95] *Pastor angelicus* later played an important role in mobiliz-
ing the Catholic vote against the threat of a Communist–Socialist victory during the campaign for the 1948 Italian general elections, when it
"was projected from cinematic cars donated by the Vatican."[96]

Another film in which Pius XII "starred" was *Anno santo 1950*, a record of the celebrations which accompanied the jubilee year of 1950.[97] All
of the major ceremonies, which included the opening and closing of the
holy doors of the major basilicas, the canonization of Maria Goretti,
and the pope's proclamation of the dogma of the Assumption of Mary,
Mother of God, into heaven on October 31, were filmed. An especial
feature of the film was the treatment of scenes of the journeys and arriv-
als of pilgrims from all over the world, emphasizing the universality of
Catholicism. Arguably, 1950 marked the high point of absolute papal
power: as Spinosa has claimed, Pius XII "was the last real pope."[98] It was
appropriate, therefore, that the last scene showed the pope receiving the
vows of obedience of representatives of the church – cardinals, bishops,
priests, and religious. *Anno santo* will undoubtedly have been shown in
the church's network of parochial cinemas in Italy. We have little information about the reception accorded to it either in Italy or elsewhere,
but it seems likely that the showing of the film to the faithful would
have helped consolidate their sense of Catholic identity and their loyalty
to the pope, so the success of films like *Pastor angelicus* suggests that the
Vatican should have made use of motion pictures as a propaganda tool
much earlier.

TELEVISION

The papacy entered the television "age" at Whitsun (Pentecost) in 1954,
when Pius XII's blessing, *urbi et orbi* ("to the city and the world"), was
broadcast to eight countries via the newly established Eurovision link.[99]
Following his death in October 1958, the funeral procession from the
papal summer residence at Castelgandolfo and then through the city of
Rome was broadcast live by Italian television (RAI), and relayed through
other national television stations.[100] The ceremonies accompanying

---

[95] Jonathan Dunnage, *Twentieth Century Italy: A Social History* (London: Longman, 2002), 99.
[96] O. Logan, "Pius XII: *romanità*, Prophesy and Charisma," *Modern Italy* 3:2 (November 1998), 241.
[97] *Anno santo 1950*, 1951, Filmoteca del Vaticano.
[98] A. Spinosa, *L'ultimo papa* (Milan: A. Mondadori, 1992), 153.
[99] *The Tablet* (October 11, 1958).
[100] There is even a suggestion that, thanks to Pius XII's personal physician, Dr. Galeazzi-Lisi, televi-
       sion cameras penetrated into the dying pope's sickroom: see Falconi, *The Popes*, 303.

the election at the end of October, of his successor, Cardinal Angelo Roncalli, Patriarch of Venice, as Pope John XXIII and the subsequent coronation were, in the latter's own words, "communicated to the whole world" as television brought the scene into millions of homes around the globe.[101]

In fact, the beginning of John XXIII's reign marked an even broader change in the papacy's relationship with the media than merely the fact that his coronation was the first to be televised. The pope's first blessing from the balcony of St. Peter's on October 28 was also televised, and whereas previous popes had set out the "mission statements" of their pontificates in their first encyclical – Benedict XV in *Ad beatissimi* (November 1914), Pius XI in *Ubi arcano Dei* (December 1922), and Pius XII in *Summi pontificatus* (October 1939) – John XXIII chose to do so in a broadcast to the whole world ("Hac trepida hora," "In this Moment of Trepidation") on Vatican Radio on the first day of his pontificate, October 29.[102] He followed this innovation with an even more remarkable break with papal tradition by holding a "press conference" two days after his coronation. The impact on the Roman and international press corps was impressive; it established his image as "good Pope John" for ever. "After the gravely hieratic and austere Pius XII," a fat and genial "brother pope" was astonishing: moreover, the spontaneity of his approach meant he was constantly unpredictable, and therefore "newsworthy."[103] As Hebblethwaite implies, there was nothing *casual* about this event: it was part and parcel of an effort on the new pope's part to appeal to Catholics and the rest of the world over the heads of the Roman curia, which must have seemed in the first few months of his pontificate to have constituted a kind of gilded cage.[104] The opening ceremony and some sessions of the Second Vatican Council which John called were televised, as was his signing of the key encyclical *Pacem in terris*.[105] In this way, John XXIII inaugurated a completely new era in the history of the papacy's relations with the media that would be brought to its apogee during the pontificate of John Paul II, the charismatic pope from Poland who had been an actor in his youth.

[101] As quoted in P. Hebblethwaite, *John XXIII: Pope of the Council* (London: Geoffrey Chapman, 1984), 295.

[102] Ibid., 292–93.   [103] Ibid., 297.   [104] Ibid.

[105] See Andrea di Stefano, "Stati-Uniti-Vaticano: relazioni politiche e aspetti diplomatici, 1952–1984," thesis for the *dottorato di ricerca* in the Faculty of Political Sciences, University of Teramo, Italy, academic year 2007–08, 58.

CONCLUSION

Roosevelt's fireside chats, the broadcasts and films of the Nuremberg and other rallies of Hitler and the Nazi Party, and the broadcasts of Churchill and Stalin's wartime speeches were all very important in "making" the history of the twentieth century, in particular in the era of totalitarianism that ran from the outbreak of World War I in 1914 to the first major break in Cold War tensions in the 1960s. What then was the overall impact of the radio broadcasts and the film and television appearances of successive popes in this same period of history?

If Pius IX was the first pope whose image was known to millions of Catholics thanks to photography, then Pius XI was the first pope whose voice was heard by millions of Catholics, Pius XII was the first pope seen on moving film by millions of the faithful, and John XXIII the first to be seen regularly on television. While much of the activity of Vatican Radio did not involve the popes themselves, nevertheless, many of its broadcasts were essentially projections of the magisterium, the teaching authority of the papacy. This was particularly important during World War II. Then, Pius XII had the opportunity to speak out against the evil of the Holocaust and other genocides, and the horrors of modern warfare more generally. Whether or not he used Vatican Radio to sufficient effect in that endeavor is a matter that has to be left to historiography.

On the other hand, the Vatican's ventures into film and the early coverage on television were almost entirely focused on the popes themselves. In this sense, the media became for the papacy another way of developing the "cult of the personality" around the pope. While it could be argued that the *institution* of the papacy is itself charismatic, given its allegedly divine origins, its infallible spiritual authority, and its long historical procession of successors of St. Peter, the personality of each individual pope was crucial to the projection of his image. Though the voice of Benedict XV would have passed muster on Vatican Radio, his physical appearance would have been a disaster on film or television. Pius XI's charisma, on the other hand, was potent because of his robust physical presence and his strong, imperious personality. The charisma of his successor was rather different: Pius XII was tall and thin with a hieratic, ascetic, and withdrawn demeanor. Yet he was, nevertheless, as successful as Pius XI in projecting his personality on screen. Finally, John XXIII was an absolute television "natural," whose warm personality conquered the hearts of viewers. Thus, while viewers of film and television worldwide would have been impressed by the splendor of the papal court and the majesty of pre-Vatican II Catholic ritual, especially that presented in St. Peter's Basilica, what really mattered were the images of the pope himself. They were or became Catholicism for the watching masses. No matter what the reality of Catholicism was on the ground, in each locality, in each parish, its image in this period was increasingly fashioned by the way in which it was presented in the media – radio, cinema, and television – which made the papacy accessible to millions of people, Catholic and non-Catholic alike.

CHAPTER 11

Mixed reception: Paul VI
and John Paul II on sex and war

Linda Hogan

what was forbidden became lawful (the cases of usury and marriage); what was permissible became unlawful (the case of slavery); what was required became forbidden (the persecution of heretics)[1]

John Noonan's by now classic articulation of how the church's moral doctrine developed highlights the complexity of the question of reception. Whether one examines the church's teaching on marriage, on divorce, on abortion, on slavery, on human rights, on conscientious objection to war, or on religious freedom, one encounters an always evolving, often inconsistent, and occasionally contradictory body of thought. Previously unquestioned positions have been abandoned and substantial innovations have occurred. Moreover, not only have the conclusions about the morality of certain practices changed, but the ethical frame within which many practices are evaluated has also been transformed. The scope of the teaching too has undergone significant development, as has its relationship with the other sciences. Its evolution can thus be seen not only in terms of its content, but also in terms of its nature, its scope, and the entire subject-matter with which it is expected to deal. Of course it would be wrong to overstate the trajectory of change in the evolution of the moral tradition, for it is precisely as *tradition* that it has evolved. Thus the church's moral teaching is best understood as a discursive tradition forged through an ambiguous dynamic of continuity and change.

This recognition that the church's moral tradition is discursive rather than unchanging inevitably shapes how questions about its reception are framed and pursued. Not only do we need to ask whether reception takes different forms within this multi-layered and highly differentiated teaching tradition and what the hallmarks of a teaching that has been received

---

[1] John T. Noonan, Jr., "Development in Moral Doctrine," in James F. Keenan and Thomas A. Shannon, eds., *The Context of Casuistry* (Washington, DC: Georgetown University Press, 1995), 194.

might be, but we need also to attend to the questions of to whom the church's moral doctrine is directed, and by whom reception is expected. Thus as one reflects on the reception of the changing and changeful tradition that is the church's moral teaching it is important to problematize the concept of reception. Moreover as one reflects on the reception of specific aspects of the church's moral teaching in the late twentieth century it is important to note that in the last two centuries there has been a significant shift globally in how citizens relate to authorities, whether they be political, scientific, or religious. Democratization, globalization, and access to education have created an expectation that citizens will participate in decision-making on critical issues. Within this context of changed expectations the language of reception appears oddly passive. Moreover in the church the changes wrought by the Second Vatican Council have had an impact on how the faithful relate to the teaching function of the hierarchy. Pre-conciliar texts like Pius X's *Vehementer nos*, which suggests that "the only duty of the multitude is to allow themselves to be led, and, like a docile flock, to follow the pastors,"[2] are utterly unfamiliar. Although the "docile flock" metaphor may not then have had the pejorative connotations that it has today, nonetheless the starkly hierarchical model of church and the posture expected of the faithful in respect of the reception of church teaching finds little resonance in the post-Vatican II church.

The focus of this chapter is on the reception of the church's moral teaching in two discrete fields, namely sexuality and war, during the papacies of Paul VI (Giovanni Battista Montini, 1963–78) and John Paul II (Karol Wojtyla, 1978–2005). Except for a brief interlude of thirty-three days, during the papacy of Pope John Paul I (Albino Luciani), these two pontiffs shaped both the mode and the content of the church's interaction with the modern world in the late twentieth century. Socially, politically, and economically this was a period of great change. In the spheres of life with which we are concerned, namely sex and war, the late twentieth century was a time both of innovation and of turmoil. Technological developments in each sphere raised new moral questions and rearticulated the old ones in a different register. Moreover the renewed ecclesiology of Vatican II created a sense of expectation among Catholics that they not only had permission, but also had a duty, to discuss and debate the morality of the new questions which they encountered. This expectation was particularly pronounced in respect of sexual ethics since it was here that a

[2] Pius X, *Vehementer nos* (encyclical on the French law of separation. February 11, 1906), no. 8, in C. Carlen, IHM, *The Papal Encyclicals, 1740–1981*, 5 vols. (Raleigh, NC: Pierian Press, 1981), III, 48.

significant majority experienced both the possibilities and the limitations of new technologies. However, the desire for engagement was also strong in respect of social and political issues, as witnessed in the significant role that Catholics played in the global campaign for nuclear disarmament and in the various anti-war movements.

SEXUAL ETHICS: THEMES AND TRENDS

Central to the church's teaching on sexual ethics has been a concern to articulate the proper relationship between the unitive and procreative dimensions of human sexuality. Whether the issue in question is contraception, *in vitro* fertilization, premarital and extramarital sex, or homosexuality, the critical factor is the relationship between what the tradition called "the ends of marriage." Historically the church's teaching on sexuality has evolved, although the centrality of procreation has been a constant theme.[3] Nonetheless, over the centuries, there was a change in the way in which the role of procreation was understood, with a move away from speaking of the primary and secondary ends of sex (procreation, mutual help, and the alleviation of concupiscence) to the language of the equal ends of love and procreation. In the background of course were other developments, without which this positive evaluation of the unitive role of sexuality could not have occurred. Of particular importance was the personalism of Häring and Doms, which instituted a new paradigm in moral theology.[4] This new paradigm reinterpreted the traditional ethical categories within a more biblically based person-centered framework; ascribed an important role to historical consciousness in ethics; focused on the moral significance of intentions and circumstances rather than on "the moral act"; and took steps to re-evaluate the tradition's longstanding suspicion of the body. Its impact was especially significant in respect of sexuality, which had, for many centuries, been pursued exclusively through the idiom of natural law; had been focused on acts rather than contexts; and was characterized by an essentially negative approach to the human body. The fact that this new paradigm had been promoted during the council was significant, and its impact on how the ethics of sex might have developed can be seen especially in *Gaudium et spes*.

[3] John T. Noonan, *Contraception: A History of its Treatment by the Catholic Theologians and Canonists*, enlarged edn. (Cambridge, MA: Belknap Press of Harvard University Press, 1986).
[4] See Bernard Häring, *The Law of Christ*, 2 vols. (Cork: Mercier Press, 1961 and 1963) and *Free and Faithful in Christ*. 3 vols. (Slough: St. Paul Publications, 1978–81). See also Herbert Doms, *The Meaning of Marriage* (London: Sheed and Ward, 1939).

Paul VI's *Humanae vitae* (1968) was issued into this context of renewal and cast a long shadow on its progress. Despite the findings of the papal commission *Humanae vitae* reiterated the ban on contraceptive methods that interrupted or altered biological processes with the purpose of preventing conception. Paul VI also appealed to public authorities worldwide, imploring them not to "tolerate any legislation which would introduce into the family those practices which are opposed to the natural law of God."[5] Despite the decades of debate engendered by the promulgation of *Humanae vitae*, Pope John Paul II strongly defended the encyclical, elaborating more fully its personalist theology and explaining why it should be seen as an expression of, rather than a contradiction of, the personalism of Vatican II. In idealized language that is characteristic of John Paul II's theology of sexuality, he insists that the use of artificial forms of contraception leads to "a falsification of the inner truth of conjugal love."[6] He also actively pursued *Humanae vitae*'s public policy agenda, not only through the encyclical *Evangelium vitae*,[7] but also in the run-up to the 1994 Cairo World Conference on Population and Development, during which a global campaign to influence world leaders, international agencies, and non-governmental organizations (NGOs) was mounted.

This determination to hold together the unitive and procreative elements of each and every sexual encounter is also evident in all other aspects of Catholic teaching on sexual ethics. Within this period the contours of the church's contemporary debate about the ethics of homosexual activity were established. A critical component of the later theology was articulated by the Congregation for the Doctrine of the Faith during Paul VI's papacy in the 1975 declaration *Persona humana*.[8] Herein, for the first time, a distinction was drawn between "the homosexual condition or tendency and individual homosexual actions," thereby, arguably, allowing for a more compassionate and pastoral approach to homosexual persons. Notwithstanding its conceptual limitations, the 1975 declaration did, for the first time, allow for the development of a less condemnatory discourse about the ethics of homosexual desire. However, within a decade the Congregation for the Doctrine of the Faith, apparently concerned about what was regarded as an overly benign interpretation of this distinction

---

[5] Noonan, *Contraception*, 23.

[6] *Familiaris consortio*, no. 32.4, available at www.vatican.va (last accessed February 2, 2010).

[7] *Evangelium vitae*, (1995), in J. Michael Miller, CSB, ed., *The Encyclicals of John Paul II*, rev. edn. (Huntington, IN: Our Sunday Visitor, 2001), 681–762.

[8] *Declaration on Certain Questions concerning Sexual Ethics* (December 29, 1975), available at www.vatican.va/roman_curia/congregations/cfaith/documents/rc_con_cfaith_doc_19751229_persona-humana_en.html (last accessed February 4, 2010).

between homosexual persons and acts, issued its *Letter to the Bishops of the Catholic Church on the Pastoral Care of Homosexual Persons*. Herein Catholics were reminded that "although the particular inclination of the homosexual person is not a sin, it is a more or less strong tendency ordered towards an intrinsic moral evil; and thus the inclination itself must be seen as an objective disorder."[9] Moreover, with this text, the question of the ethics of homosexual sex moved from being a marginal concern for the church (witness the very low profile that this question had for the previous millennium) to being one of the most controversial and contested issues today.

This preoccupation with holding the unitive and procreative dimensions of sex in a seamless unity also impacted on the manner in which the church responded to the reproductive possibilities afforded to infertile couples. The question was first addressed by the Holy See in 1897, when artificial insemination of wife by husband was declared illicit.[10] This position was reaffirmed routinely by various popes, and especially by Pius XII in his 1951 address to the Italian Union of Midwives.[11] Technological advances in the late twentieth century created new possibilities, including third-party involvement in the processes of procreation, complicating further the moral questions to be considered. The intensity and subtlety of the public debate that surrounded *in vitro* and other technological interventions in human reproduction suggest that there is an appreciation of the ethically significant nuances associated with the different interventions. However, although the debate among theologians mirrored this nuanced approach, the papacy maintained an unambiguous condemnation of all interventions. Within the period the most significant teaching was the Congregation for the Doctrine of the Faith's 1987 *Instruction on Respect for Human Life it its Origin and on the Dignity of Procreation*. Although it marshaled a number of different arguments against various interventions (especially against the increasingly popular *in vitro* fertilization), its central argument continued to be about the inseparability of the unitive and the procreative, which became the sole lens through which the ethics of sex came to be evaluated.

Of importance too for the church's teaching on sexuality was Pope John Paul II's interpretation of the personalism that had emerged from the

[9] Congregation for the Doctrine of the Faith, *Letter to the Bishops of the Catholic Church on the Pastoral Care of Homosexual Persons*, no. 3 (October 1, 1986), at www.vatican.va (last accessed February 4, 2010).
[10] *Acta apostolicae sedis* 29 (1896–97), 704.
[11] *Acta apostolicae sedis* 43 (1951), 835–54.

1950s onward. Through texts like *Mulieris dignitatem, Familiaris consortio,* and *Veritatis splendor,* as well as in his theological writings, the distinct-iveness of the pontiff's personalist theology was established. Herein one could discern a far more positive appreciation of the body than had been common in Catholic theology heretofore. However, it displayed a number of limitations, not least an excessive physicalism and an uncritical adop-tion of the principle of complementarity. In *Veritatis splendor* (1993), Pope John Paul II articulated a theology that responded to what he regarded as "the crisis of truth" that engulfs the world today. Developing a strongly anti-relativist argument, the encyclical defends a natural law approach to ethics in which "the universal and permanent validity of its precepts"[12] are recognized and argues that "the Church has the right always and every-where to proclaim moral principles, even in respect of the social order, and to make judgments about any human matter ... "[13] It is within this framework that the faithful too are to understand their role as interpreters of the moral life. In the sections on conscience (nos. 54–64) the encyclical follows the tradition in insisting that the judgment of the individual con-science has an imperative character and that the maturity and responsibil-ity of its judgments are measured by "an insistent search for truth and by allowing oneself to be guided by that truth in one's actions."[14] Alongside this narrative, however, there is an insistence that "the Magisterium does not bring to the Christian conscience truths which are extraneous to it; rather it brings to light the truths which it ought already to possess." In fact it contends that "the Church puts herself always and only at the *ser-vice of conscience* ... helping it ... to attain the truth with certainty and to abide in it."[15] Quite where that leaves those who, in conscience, find that they disagree with what is taught, on sexual and other matters, is however unclear.

SEXUAL ETHICS: RECEPTION

History has shown that these two dimensions of the moral life cannot be as easily harmonized as *Veritatis splendor* would have us believe. Moreover, nowhere are the serious disagreements more in evidence than in the reception of the church's teaching on sexual ethics. Indeed in the four decades since the promulgation of *Humanae vitae* the church has expe-rienced an unprecedented failure of reception of its teaching on sexual

---

[12] *Veritatis splendor* (London: Catholic Truth Society, 1993), no. 4, p. 8.
[13] Ibid., no. 27, p. 24.   [14] Ibid., no. 61, p. 93.   [15] Ibid., no. 64, p. 98.

ethics. Primarily this failure of reception has been associated with the encyclical's ban on the use of artificial contraception, although recent decades have shown that the core claim of the inseparability of the unitive and procreative dimensions of sex has also been challenged. The scale of the international reaction to the encyclical is evident in the documentation gathered by Dr. Leo Alting von Geusau for the interdenominational Center for International Documentation on the Contemporary Church.[16] By May 1969 the center had received over 4,000 reactions to the encyclical. These came from a variety of geographical regions and included responses from demographers, economists, medics, and theologians, as well as from a range of denominational perspectives. The responses from episcopal conferences worldwide varied. Most were supportive, but others were aware of the difficulties it would present.[17] The public policy impact, especially in the developing world, was also the subject of debate. Concern about population growth had dominated international politics for a number of years, and while analysts were divided on whether the critical issue was numbers or impact, nonetheless it was recognized that the earth could not sustain unlimited population growth.[18] Research on the encyclical's reception among clergy and laity suggests a complex and evolving picture. In the first two decades the negative reaction to the encyclical dominated, except in Africa, where the deeply ingrained desire for large

---

[16] F. V. Johannes, Humanae vitae: *dossier delle reazioni* (Milan: Mondadori, 1969), Eng. trans. as *The Bitter Pill: Worldwide Reaction to the Encyclical* Humanae vitae (Philadelphia, PA: Pilgrim Press, 1970).

[17] See discussions in Johannes, *The Bitter Pill*. See also John Horgan, ed., Humanae vitae *and the Bishops* (Shannon: Irish University Press, 1972). In his "International Reaction to the Encyclical *Humana vitae*" Leo Alting von Geusau summarizes the reaction thus: "In countries where many bishops, government officials, and public opinion were in favour of the Encyclical, the conferences came out with clear statements. Conferences in black Africa, the Philippines, as well as in Concordat countries such as Spain and Portugal, came out with favourable statements. Bishops behind the Iron Curtain, as well as conferences in some Asian countries such as India, Vietnam, and Korea, also announced support (although in some cases support conflicted with the government's policy). Reactions in western countries were different. The Dutch bishops were the first to react with a statement to their priests on August 4, 1968: 'In the formation of the conscience an authoritative role should be given to the word of the magisterium, even if in this case of *Humanae Vitae* we are not faced with an infallible teaching. The priests and the faithful have therefore to study the document carefully, giving however, the last word to the individual conscience.' This became the pattern of reaction of the German, Belgian, Austrian, Canadian, Swiss, British, Irish, Indonesian, Australian, South African, Scandinavian, and the United States Catholic Conferences … The Latin American bishops generally approved the papal statement. However, the Chileans raised the issue of the question of conscience. In a continent-wide congress in Medellín, Colombia, in August 1968, to which Pope Paul paid a visit, they approved a document expressing concern about the population problem and emphasizing the importance of education to responsible parenthood." *Studies in Family Planning* 1:50 (February 1970), 9.

[18] See Alting von Geusau, "International Reaction," 9.

families predominated. This negative reaction was accompanied by what Keely calls a benign neglect of the teaching for the remainder of Paul VI's papacy, when there was no longer any sustained effort to influence the family planning policies of governments worldwide. Neither was there any serious effort to silence dissent or to curtail debate.[19] Benign neglect was replaced by a more vigorous defense of *Humanae vitae* during the papacy of John Paul II. A detailed analysis of this trend, which had far-reaching educational, ecclesial, and political ramifications, is beyond the scope of this chapter. What is evident, however, is that the diversity of opinion of the first post-*Humanae vitae* decade has hardened into two distinct camps, with adherence to the hierarchical magisterium's position on sexual ethics being the critical factor in the maintenance of the division.

Although the intensity of the reaction to *Humanae vitae* has not been replicated in respect of later developments in sexual ethics, the pattern itself has. With the HIV and AIDS pandemic the church's ban on the use of prophylactics became a major public health issue. In the face of scientific evidence that public health initiatives which use an "ABC" approach (abstain, be consistent, use contraception) are successful, the church continues to insist on an abstinence-only approach,[20] and refuses to use the principle of double effect to allow individuals to protect themselves from infection.[21] Some Catholic development organizations have struggled to work within the existing framework and instead have adopted a more nuanced approach to prevention.[22] The reception of the teaching that sanctions any engagement with reproductive technologies is more difficult to gauge. Anecdotal evidence, especially in Europe, North America, and Australia, suggests that Catholics take up this option as frequently as non-Catholics, and while many may opt for processes that fertilize and implant only one ovum (so as to ensure that no supernumerary embryos are created), the majority do not have difficulties with the technical processes that involve a separation of unitive and procreative dimensions of sexual intercourse. The reception of the church's teaching on homosexuality is even

---

[19] Charles B. Keely, "Limits to Papal Power: Vatican Inaction after *Humanae vitae*," *Population and Development Review* 20 (1994), supplement: *The New Politics of Population: Conflict and Consensus in Family Planning*, 220–40.

[20] The position continues to be articulated by Pope Benedict XVI, most recently on March 18, 2009 in his address to journalists enroute to Cameroon; see www.vatican.va/holy_father/benedict_xvi/travels/2009/index_camerun-angola_en.htm (last accessed February 4, 2010).

[21] See David Kelly, *Critical Care Ethics* (Kansas City: Sheed & Ward, 1991), 204–09, and Mark Johnson, "The Principle of Double Effect and Safe Sex in Marriage: Reflections on a Suggestion," *Linacre Quarterly* 60 (1993), 82–89.

[22] See www.cafod.org.uk/press-centre/hiv/cafod-response (last accessed February 4, 2010).

more complex and is perhaps best assessed through a multi-generational lens. More than any other teaching, the condemnation of homosexual activity has mirrored the views of populations throughout the world, at least, that is, until very recently. However, the limited empirical evidence that does exist suggests that there has been a significant generational shift, so that in the Western world homosexuality is either tolerated or seen in positive terms by a majority of those aged under thirty-five.[23]

Of course many Catholics accept and defend these teachings on sexuality. Indeed in recent years there have been significant catechetical and other initiatives designed to explain and promote the teaching.[24] The dissenting voices and practices, however, have been more frequent and have become so engrained in the modern Catholic psyche that the real danger for the church in this context is that it becomes irrelevant as individuals contend with their moral questions. In summarizing why the reception has failed to such a degree one must first note that the teaching has been found to be unconvincing. In the four decades since its promulgation the central premise that the unitive and procreative dimensions of sexual intercourse are inseparable has consistently been rejected as both overly physicalist and counter-experiential. Moreover its implausibility has been accentuated when its impact on both the treatment of infertility and the approach to HIV prevention is understood. Other elements of the teaching are also called into question. For example, the validity of the distinction between a person's sexual orientation and the expression of that orientation is frequently criticized, both because it is in a fundamental contradiction with the personalist theology of the tradition and because it is regarded as improbable.

While the content of the teaching has been the primary cause of its failed reception, its tone has also been problematic. At a somewhat superficial level the fact that *Humanae vitae* is addressed to "Honored Brothers and Dear Sons," and to "venerable brothers, the patriatrchs, archbishops, bishops and other local ordinaries, ... the clergy and faithful ... and to all men of good will" illustrates the relentlessly exclusive nature of the idiom and the mindset. However, this exclusive language is but a reflection of a deeper patriarchal approach to sexuality. Critics have also often stressed

---

[23] There are numerous sociological studies affirming this change in attitude. See Jeni Loftus, "America's Liberalisation in Attitudes towards Homosexuality 1973–1998," *American Sociological Review* 66 (October 2001), 762–82, and Jacqueline Scott, "Changing Attitudes to Sexual Morality: A Cross-National Comparison," *Sociology* 32 (1998), 815–845.

[24] The establishment of John Paul II institutes in many countries worldwide is evidence of this desire to explain and defend the pope's position on marriage and family.

the harsh tone of the language of condemnation, especially in relation to homosexuality. The church's contribution to the public debate in this regard is especially problematic since its language of condemnation can leave the church open to charges of homophobia and discrimination. And although the hierarchical magisterium may be increasingly sensitive to the negative impact that this language may have, it has not yet found a way of mitigating the negative social consequences of that language or of limiting its corrosive effect on the norms of civility in public life.

WAR AND PEACE: THEMES AND TRENDS

While the conflicting positions on sexual ethics within the Catholic Church are well known, less well known is the manner in which the church's teaching on war and peace has also undergone substantial change. Indeed the question of whether Christians should ever have recourse to war has been debated from the earliest centuries. Moreover it is accepted that for the first three centuries Christians followed Jesus' prophetic denunciation of violence and adopted what we now call a pacifist stance. However, as Christianity was legitimized and became ever more closely associated with the civil authority (initially with Constantine in the fourth century), it began to reconsider the absolutist pacifist position and developed a set of principles that would allow for the defense of the innocent against unjust aggression in certain restricted circumstances. Thus began the just war tradition, initially developed by Ambrose and Augustine and later elaborated by Aquinas, di Vittoria, and Suárez, which quickly eclipsed the pacifist trajectory of the early church. Moreover the emergence, between the sixteenth and eighteenth centuries, of specific churches that were committed to a principled pacifism further distanced the major denominations, including the Roman Catholic Church, from pacifism, so that the just war tradition became the primary means by which the church engaged with this question. By the time Pope John XXIII addressed the issue of modern warfare the landscape had changed so significantly that there was a growing recognition that in the atomic age war is no longer a "suitable way to restore rights which have been violated."[25] *Pacem in terris* (1963) also reoriented discussions about how the morality of waging war was to be appraised, asserting that the individual conscience has primacy above political authority.[26] *Gaudium et*

---

[25] *Pacem in terris*, no. 127, in Carlen (ed.), *The Papal Encyclicals*, V, 121.
[26] *Pacem in terris*, no. 51, in Carlen (ed.), *The Papal Encyclicals*, V, 21.

spes (1965) continued in this vein, both in denouncing the massive and indiscriminate destruction that had been visited on populations and cities, and also in terms of recognizing the primacy of the individual conscience in the determination of ethical assessments about the legitimacy of participating in war.[27] Thus the teachings of both Pope Paul VI and John Paul II are best understood within this evolving context, and although it is difficult to provide a comprehensive analysis of this teaching, three themes predominate, namely: (1) a rearticulation of the nature of peace as involving a commitment to a just international order; (2) a focus on the role of international institutions as a means of resolving conflicts; and (3) a response to the nuclear threat, the arms race, and the policy of deterrence.

Paul VI's *Populorum progressio* (1967) was primarily concerned with the then current international economic order, identifying the principles of Catholic social teaching that could be brought to bear on global inequality. It had a major impact on Catholic responses to economic disparity and foregrounded justice, rather than charity, as the mode of engagement. However, the signature phrase of the encyclical, namely "development is the new name of peace,"[28] has had an equally important impact on how the church's teaching on war and peace was subsequently framed. Of course traditional discussions of just war principles had already foregrounded the duty to do justice. However, during the twentieth century there was an increasing recognition that structural and intergenerational injustices required a different sort of economic and political analysis, and as a result the "duty to do justice" acquired a more institutional and systemic focus. *Populorum progressio* was sensitive to the changing nature of conflict worldwide and saw that "excessive economic, social and cultural inequalities among peoples arouse tensions and conflicts, and are a danger to peace."[29] Moreover it argued that the most appropriate way to mitigate conflict is to ensure that all have access to the material resources necessary for authentic human development. Throughout his papacy, and especially in his addresses on World Day of Peace, Paul VI insisted on the essential link between justice and peace and spoke consistently about the obligations of political authorities to ensure a just and equitable economic order. Yet there was a degree of unease with the potential political

---

[27] *Pastoral Constitution on the Church in the Modern World*: *Gaudium et spes*, no. 80, in Walter M. Abbott, SJ (general ed.), *The Documents of Vatican II* (London: Geoffrey Chapman, 1966), 293–94.

[28] *Populorum progressio*, no. 87, in Carlen (ed.), *The Papal Encyclicals*, V, 199.

[29] *Populorum progressio*, no. 76, in Carlen (ed.), *The Papal Encyclicals*, V, 197.

ramifications of this rhetoric, especially in respect of revolutionary movements. This is very evident in Paul VI's *Evangelii nuntiandi* (1975), wherein the destructive dimensions of seeking justice through violence were highlighted. Moreover, as this theme was developed by Pope John Paul II the ambivalence became even more pronounced. Pope John Paul II was acutely aware that a genuinely peaceful society is premised on a just economic and political order. Recurrent themes include the centrality of justice and human rights, of solidarity and development, and of reconciliation in the task of building a culture of peace.[30] Moreover as the phenomenon of military humanitarian intervention became more frequent John Paul II became a strong supporter (under certain conditions). Indeed, speaking on the fiftieth anniversary of the Geneva Conventions in 1999, he commented on "the need to find a new consensus on humanitarian principles and to reinforce their foundations to prevent the recurrence of atrocities and abuse."[31] Yet as liberation theology movements began to act on these principles and occasionally to support revolutionary movements, the papacy began to reassert the role of nonviolent action as a means of political change and warn about the seductiveness and the destructiveness of violence.

The establishment of the United Nations in 1945 and the gradual expansion of its remit is a critical context in which to understand the second of the themes with which the two papacies were concerned, namely their focus on the role of international institutions. The United Nations Charter asserts in its preamble that its purpose is to save succeeding generations from the scourge of war, and already by 1963, when Paul VI took office, the United Nations had a set of precedents within which a state's obligations under the United Nations Charter were interpreted. Chapter 7 of the charter provided a new context for the application of just war principles, and although the charter did not impair the right of self-defense,[32] nonetheless members agreed that the security council would decide what measures would be taken to maintain or restore international peace and security.[33] The dissolution of Cold War politics during the papacy of John Paul II (and in which he played a critical personal role) allowed the United Nations to take a more active role internationally. *Centesimus annus* (1991) acknowledged that the United Nations had not yet succeeded in establishing

[30] http://vatican.va/holy_father/john_paul_ii/messages/peace/index.htm (last accessed February 4, 2010).
[31] Pope John Paul II, general audience on the fiftieth anniversary of the Geneva Conventions, August 11, 1999.
[32] *Charter of the United Nations*, ch. 7, article 51. [33] Ibid., article 39.

alternatives to war,[34] but nonetheless asserted that adherence to principles of international law is the only remedy for war, "which destroys the lives of innocent people, teaches how to kill, throws into upheaval even the lives of those who do the killing and leaves behind a trail of resentment and hatred, thus making it all the more difficult to find a just solution of the very problems which provoked the war."[35]

The destructive capacity of nuclear weapons challenges, in a fundamental way, the limitations on which just war doctrine is based. Both *Pacem in terris* and *Gaudium et spes* noted that in the modern period scientific weapons cause destruction "far exceeding the bounds of legitimate defense,"[36] and Paul VI and John Paul II continued to be vocal critics of a host of strategic and policy positions adopted by the major powers in this regard. Paul VI did not address the nuclear threat very frequently, but when he did so he was highly critical of both the use and the possession of nuclear weapons. Indeed he described the possession of these armaments as "an act of aggression which constitutes a crime for even when they are not used, by their cost alone armaments kill the poor by causing them to starve."[37] John Paul II also insisted that any use of nuclear weapons would be disproportionate, and followed Paul VI in making a negative assessment of the arms race and of the policy of deterrence (which had escalated to epic proportions). At the United Nations in 1982 Pope John Paul II suggested that deterrence should not be an end in itself but, "as a step towards a progressive disarmament, may still be judged morally acceptable".[38] During his papacy John Paul II was a vocal and consistent voice for peace. With the exception of his growing support for military intervention in supreme humanitarian emergencies, the pope's messages seemed to restrict more and more the contexts in which a state might legitimately resort to force. He was an outspoken critic of the First and Second Gulf Wars and has been to the fore in resituating the role of just war within Catholic thinking. Indeed from Paul VI's address to the United Nations in 1965, during which he insisted "Jamais plus la guerre," to John Paul II's forceful condemnation of particular wars one can see that the duty to engage in peace-making and conflict resolution is more prominent now than it has been for seventeen centuries.[39]

[34] *Centesimus annus* (London: Catholic Truth Society, 1991), no. 21, p. 16.
[35] Ibid., no. 52, p. 37.
[36] *Gaudium et spes*, no. 80, in Abbott (ed.), *The Documents of Vatican II*, 293–94.
[37] www.vatican.va/holy_father/paul_vi/letters/1978/index.htm (last accessed February 4, 2010).
[38] John Paul II, *Message to the Second Special Session of the United Nations on Disarmament* (1982) no. 8, at www.vatican.va/holy_father/john_paul_ii/speeches/1982/june/documents (last accessed February 4, 2010).
[39] Drew Christiansen, "Whither the Just War?" *America* 118:10 (March 24, 2003), 7–11.

WAR AND PEACE: RECEPTION

Within the period with which we are concerned the church's teaching on war and peace has undergone considerable change, especially in terms of emphasis. While prior to *Pacem in terris* just war doctrine was central, its dominance has begun to wane somewhat. There is no doubt that Paul VI and John Paul II had an influence on this development. Through their continued stress on the role of the individual conscience in respect of participation in war, they contributed to the dislodging of just war theory as the church's primary mode of engagement with issues of political violence. Moreover, and perhaps more importantly in terms of assessing the reception of the church's teaching, in foregrounding the individual conscience they also provided an impetus for the growth of Catholic peace movements and ultimately for the support of conscientious objection as a legitimate posture within a democratic state.

Although conscientious objection to war has long been something individuals have chosen, it is only in recent decades that it has been recognized as a legitimate way of expressing one's civic responsibilities. That this was also the case for Catholics is evident from the 1956 Christmas message of Pius XII. Reflecting the culture of the time, Pius XII declared that the Catholic citizen "cannot invoke his or her own conscience in order to refuse to render the services and perform the duties established by law."[40] Nonetheless both *Pacem in terris* and *Gaudium et spes* reoriented this discussion significantly, recognizing that although a war may be declared to be just, individual citizens may legitimately come to a different conclusion. Moreover in the subsequent decades, although neither pontiff addressed this issue very frequently, they each adopted this position. However, the role of lay Catholics in this change of emphasis cannot be overestimated. Throughout Europe and the United States in particular there was a vibrant, often difficult public debate about the responsibilities of Catholics vis-à-vis the democratic state. Through the 1970s and 1980s European countries gradually accepted as legitimate the decisions of citizens to refuse to go to war, while in the United States Roman Catholics were among those who gave witness to conscientious objection during the Vietnam War. The gradual acceptance of the legitimacy of conscientious objection was strongly related to the activism of Catholics in movements such as the Catholic Worker Movement and Plowshares. The prophetic witness of Dom Helder Camara in Brazil also gave an impetus to the

---

[40] Pius XII, Christmas message 1956, in *Acta apostolicae sedis* 49 (1957), 5–22, at 19.

resurgence of pacifist positions within Catholicism, as indeed did the nonviolent activism of the church in the Philippines. Each context experienced a combination of severe poverty, radical injustice, and political repression, yet the moral leadership provided by the church stressed the need for nonviolent revolution. Inevitably in Brazil and the Philippines, as well as in El Salvador and Argentina, there was a diversity of views among Catholics. Nonetheless, without compromising the denunciation of the structural violence visited on the people, one of the consistent messages of this period was that Christians were challenged to engage in revolution through nonviolent means. Although it is difficult to determine precisely what role these two pontiffs had in the prioritization of peace activism over just war positions, it is clear that from the 1960s the church became ever more reluctant to endorse wars between nations, and became a powerful supporter of and advocate for nonviolent approaches to conflict resolution. Indeed Kenneth Himes notes the statement of Archbishop Renato Martino, head of Justitia et Pax, who has suggested that war, like capital punishment, is permissible, but in practice neither should receive support.[41] Moreover the significance of peace activism and the voices of Catholic pacifists have never been stronger.

This departure from the assumption that Catholics have a duty to support their governments in their pursuit of wars of defense has had its critics. Controversial too, in some quarters, has been the Vatican's increasing support for conflict resolution in specific contexts (as in, for example, the invasion of Iraq by the United States and its allies in 2003), and its endorsement of the role of international institutions, especially the United Nations, in the resolution of international conflicts. Although John Paul II was clear that he was not a pacifist, his condemnation of virtually every war waged during his papacy led critics to suggest that the strength of his presumption against war effectively made him one.[42] Both George Weigel and Michael Novak were vocal critics of the direction taken on this matter by John Paul II. Arguing against the position that the presumption against war is *the* defining feature of Catholic teaching, Weigel insists that the obligation to defend

---

[41] Quoted in Kenneth Himes, "Intervention, Just War and National Security," *Theological Studies* 65:1 (March 2004), 157.

[42] There are notable exceptions to John Paul II's condemnation of specific wars; however, these fall within the categories defined in the document *Responsibility to Protect*, namely genocide, crimes against humanity, and other supreme humanitarian emergencies. See www.iciss.ca/report-en.asp (last accessed February 4, 2010), for the document, initially prepared for the United Nations by the International Commission on Intervention and State Sovereignty, and adopted by the United Nations General Assembly in 2000.

a country's security is stronger than the presumption in favor of non-violent means of resolving conflict. Weigel was particularly troubled by John Paul II's assessment that the invasion of Iraq did not meet the criteria of just war doctrine. Michael Novak too took this line when he made the United States administration's case for war to the Vatican early in 2003. He did so without success. Weigel and Novak are but two examples of a minority, yet influential, strand of Catholic thought worldwide, which resists the change in emphasis heralded in *Pacem in terris* and continued with vigor by Paul VI and John Paul II. Of concern to such critics has been the strengthening of the presumption against violence; the expectation that Catholics would maintain a critical rather than uncritical stance vis-à-vis their nation's wars; and the unambiguous support for international institutions.

The reception of *Populorum progressio*'s insistence that "development is the new name of peace" is interesting. Judging from how it has become a cornerstone of the work of Catholic NGOs, one can confirm that it has been received, appropriated, interpreted, and enacted. One simply has to examine the programs of the Catholic Agency for Overseas Development (CAFOD), the Comité Catholique contre la Faim et pour le Développement (CCFD), Cordaid, the Jesuit Refugee Service, Misereor, and the myriad indigenous NGOs working in Africa, Asia, and Latin America to observe that they are premised on the conviction that there will be no peace until institutional injustices are addressed. Moreover it is increasingly recognized that conflict resolution practices need to be structured into specific development programs, if the seemingly inevitable recourse to violence is to be resisted. Theologians from Africa, Asia, and South America have been to the fore in developing this perspective, and in ensuring that the depth of this challenge is understood.[43] The support of Catholic NGOs by the laity worldwide is another indication that this particular teaching has been successfully received. That these NGOs are frequently consulted by governments, regional bodies, and international organizations indicates that their values have an appeal that is broader than the church. Their appeal is evident too in the success of the "Jubilee 2000" campaign, an initiative that was rooted in theological discourse but that acquired a global and pluralist complexion. The more difficult question is that of whether they have been effective in terms of reducing

---

[43] See David Hollenbach, ed., *Refugee Rights, Ethics, Advocacy, and Africa* (Washington, DC: Georgetown University Press, 2008) and essays by Yáñez, Tarimo, and Hinga in Linda Hogan, ed., *Applied Ethics in a World Church* (Maryknoll, NY: Orbis, 2008).

conflict through promoting justice. This is a complex question to answer, in the main because of the challenge of identifying criteria for judging the success of preventative measures in contexts wherein intergenerational political, economic, and ethnic grievances exist. However, this question of efficacy, although relevant, is subsequent to and dependent on that of reception.

The reception of the teaching on nuclear ethics has been affected by a debate about the relationship between the view that nuclear war is inherently disproportionate and the limited acceptance of deterrence as an interim measure. In some cases national episcopal bodies shaped the manner in which the teaching was received and elaborated. Of signal global significance was the United States bishops' 1983 pastoral letter *The Challenge of Peace*. Arguing that it is neither tolerable nor necessary for human beings to live under the threat of nuclear war, the bishops addressed the American people, reminding them that they are citizens of the only country to use atomic weapons, and insisting that they refuse to legitimate the idea of nuclear war.[44] In relation to their use, the pastoral "ruled out counter-population use absolutely, opposed first-use on the basis of prudential judgment, and acknowledged a very narrow permissibility for second strike, counter-force, retaliation."[45] Although John Paul II's limited acceptance of deterrence was noted, the pastoral highlighted the prophetic challenge of taking more resolute steps to actual bilateral disarmament and peace-making.[46] The bishops consulted extensively and garnered significant support among clergy and laity worldwide. Moreover, in its articulation of the moral hazard of nuclear deterrence as a political strategy it gave an impetus to the growing disarmament lobby (which counted Catholics among its most influential activists). In developing the papacy's critical appraisal of deterrence, the American pastoral went further than other episcopal interventions, especially those of some of the Europeans. Hehir's analysis of the differences in emphasis discernible in the French and West German pastorals is illuminating, highlighting as it does the manner in which political contexts can shape both the tenor and the character of reception.[47] Developing countries too had their own particular concerns, focused primarily, to use the words of *Gaudium et spes*,

[44] The National Conference of Catholic Bishops, *The Challenge of Peace: God's Promise and Our Response* (Washington, DC: US Catholic Conference, 1983), no. 131.
[45] J. Bryan Hehir, "Catholic Teaching on War and Peace: The Decade 1979–1989," in Charles E. Curran, ed., *Moral Theology, Challenges for the Future: Essays in Honor of Richard A. McCormick, SJ* (New York: Paulist Press, 1990), 368.
[46] *The Challenge of Peace*, no. 198.   [47] Hehir, "Catholic Teaching," 364–69.

on "the utterly treacherous trap" that is the arms race, "which injures the poor to an intolerable degree."[48]

This challenging teaching on war and peace in the second half of the twentieth century has caused Catholics worldwide to reappraise how they stand in relation to the nation state. The Constantinian assumptions that had shaped the tradition's approach have been gradually fractured as the two pontiffs witnessed to the destructive allure of war. Moreover as its prophetic dimensions have become more pronounced, its reception has increased, and while dissent is in evidence, there is an increased commitment to nonviolent means of resolving conflict, an acceptance of conscientious objection as a legitimate stance for Catholics within the state, and a recognition that structural injustice must be addressed if peace is to be achieved. Inevitably one must question the teaching's efficacy, given that it has been promulgated during what Jonathan Glover observes has been the most brutal century in history.[49] However, precisely why this is the case is beyond both the scope of this chapter and the competence of this author.

CONCLUDING REMARKS

The changeful nature of the church's moral tradition raises questions not only about the reception of particular teaching but also about what reception can mean for a church that is *semper reformanda*. There is no doubt that the creation of tradition involves a dynamic of teaching and reception, with the magisterium and faithful each playing a role in both aspects. When a teaching resonates with the lived experience of the faithful, when it is developed in a collaborative manner, or when it is refined in a dialogical process, its reception is likely to be successful. When it fails to resonate with the moral discernment of serious and faithful Catholics it is unlikely to be received. As the role of the papacy has evolved from prince (and often its closely associated role of patron) to (universal) pastor, so too has the nature of its moral teaching as well as its relationship with the faithful. As the laity have embraced a form of participation in community life (including church life) that recognizes the depth and variety of human experience, our relationship with teachers and teaching has changed. Whether reception is an adequate description of a process that requires

[48] *Gaudium et spes,* no. 81, in Abbott (ed.), *The Documents of Vatican II,* 293–94.
[49] See Jonathan Glover, *Humanity: A Moral History of the Twentieth Century* (London: Jonathan Cape, 1999).

understanding, appropriation, interpretation, revision, and development has yet to be properly discussed. However, the emergence of alternative ways of thinking about the relationships involved and the articulation of categories like "creative fidelity" are promising. Specifically they give hope because they capture the dynamism that is at the heart of inhabiting an evolving and sometimes prophetic tradition.

CHAPTER 12

John Paul II: universal pastor in a global age

James Corkery

INTRODUCTION: JOHN PAUL II – SEEN EVERYWHERE, BEEN EVERYWHERE

When, in October 1978, Cardinal Karol Wojtyla of Krakow (1920–2005) was elected pope, taking the name of John Paul II, he seemed poised, in his relative youth (he was fifty-eight), his boundless energy, and, above all, his commanding presence, to take the world by storm; and he did. Images of this new pope were quickly relayed around the world and in no time this "man from a far country," the first non-Italian pope in 455 years, was a household name and a face recognized by all. With his actor's instincts and his capacity to captivate both the crowds and the media, John Paul II unleashed on the world a succession of arresting images that placed the papacy before the eyes of all at a time when the Catholic Church was already struggling to maintain its membership, certainly in its traditional strongholds. John Paul II seemed a law unto himself – universally favorably received even as the church that he led was battling to remain at the forefront – and images of the new pope kissing the ground in foreign lands, hugging children, charming enormous crowds, and making bold pronouncements[1] ensured his indelible etching on the psyches of all. He became an overnight superstar, an iconic figure, a world personality.

Predecessors of John Paul II, like Pius XI and Pius XII in their use of radio, and Paul VI, portrayed widely on television, managed to impress the world in new and effective ways by means of these newly available

---

[1] An example, from his very first trip abroad (to Latin America, from January 25 to February 1, 1979), is this extract from his address to the Third Conference of Latin American Bishops gathered at Puebla: "We cry out once more: Respect man! He is the image of God! Evangelize, so that this may become a reality; so that the Lord may transform hearts and humanize the political and economic systems, with man's responsible commitment as the starting point!" (part III, no. 5). Quoted from www.vatican.va/holy_father/john_paul_ii/speeches/1979/january/documents/hf_jp-ii_spe_19790128_messico-puebla-episic-latam_en.html (last accessed February 5, 2010).

communications media,[2] but none was as gifted as John Paul II at using the means of communication to make an impact on whole peoples through his presence and his message. An editorial in the United States lay Catholic journal *Commonweal*, reflecting on his visit in 1995 to the United States and, above all, on "the centerpiece of his trip," his address to the United Nations, referred to John Paul II's "mastery of the media event, a celebrity-driven spectacle that he himself might dismiss as a symptom of the 'culture of death' in other contexts."[3]

The same *Commonweal* editorial quickly went on to advise – in line with the thinking of John Paul II himself – getting "beyond the pomp and the glitz to the substance of things."[4] There can be no doubt that the message John Paul II sought to communicate, through his sophisticated use of modern communications media and on the 104 international journeys of his papacy (not to mention his 145 trips within Italy),[5] was indeed substantial, but whether "the pop star-style packaging that often surrounds a papal tour"[6] was always accompanied by a genuine hearing and heeding of this pope's message by his target audiences is a matter for further reflection.

The present chapter aims to carry out some of this needed reflection. When he became pope, Karol Wojtyla adopted the title "Universal Pastor of the Church"[7] and, from the very beginning, made it clear that his intent was to be a pastor first and foremost; and he would be a pastor for the entire world. To achieve this, he built on strengths he already possessed – an actor's sense of presence and a deep appreciation of the diversity of human cultures and peoples – to become a presence in the world both electronically, through the communications media, and in person, by means of unprecedented travel. Thus his image was relayed around the globe and he was seen, physically, by more people than any other human

[2] See ch. 10 above (by John F. Pollard).

[3] Editorial "The Pope at the UN," *Commonweal* 122:18 (October 20, 1995), 5–6, at 5.

[4] Ibid.

[5] See United States Conference of Catholic Bishops, "Pope John Paul II's Travels: Journeys Outside of Italy," http://www.usccb.org/pope/travels.htm (last accessed April 16, 2007); also Caroline Pigozzi, *Pope John Paul II: An Intimate Life. The Pope I Knew So Well* (New York: Faith Worlds and Hachette Book Group USA, 2008), 108.

[6] John L. Allen, Jr. uses this phrase to point to a "frequent objection" made by critics of papal tours. See his article "23-Year Odyssey: For Good or Ill, John Paul II's Road Show has Revolutionized the Papacy," *National Catholic Reporter* 38:36 (August 16, 2002), 3–6, at 4.

[7] See Gerard Mannion, "Introduction: The Challenges of Discerning the Legacy of Pope John Paul II," in Gerard Mannion, ed., *The Vision of John Paul II: Assessing his Thought and Influence* (Collegeville, MN: Liturgical Press, 2008), 1–9, at 2.

being – ever![8] By the end of his twenty-six-year papacy, he had been almost everywhere and his face had been seen everywhere. Furthermore, the press coverage following his death on April 2, 2005 was mostly positive, displaying remarkable appreciation for the life of this religious leader who had become something of an international superstar.[9]

CONTINUITY AND DISCONTINUITY
WITH HIS PREDECESSORS

Although it had been the custom for the papacy to make use of emerging communications media – the Vatican newspaper *L'osservatore romano* had been founded under Pius IX in 1861, Pius XI had started Vatican Radio, Pius XII had developed this and also made use of film technology – it was not until the papacy of John XXIII (1958–63) that the pope began to move outside the Vatican and to make use of modern means of travel. John XXIII, a frail man elected at age seventy-eight, made just two trips, both within Italy. But Paul VI (1963–78) made several apostolic journeys outside Italy. The journalist Caroline Pigozzi quotes him as promising on the first day of his pontificate (June 30, 1963): "I shall travel in order that a great fire of faith and love shall pass over the entire world and engulf all men of good will."[10] Paul VI was the first pope to address the United Nations, in New York in 1965. He undertook many other journeys also, across several continents, intent on spreading the Gospel.[11]

Pope John Paul II was following in the footsteps of Paul VI when he chose to be a traveling pope. And the motivation of the two popes was similar: each traveled to evangelize. Of John Paul II the story is told that, on his first journey abroad – to Latin America, in January 1979 – he prayed before an image of the Virgin Mary in Mexico City and understood, from that time, that his was to be a pilgrim papacy:

He saw that he would become a pilgrim with the whole world as his destination. He would tour the globe much as a parish priest might tour his parish. Like that

---

[8] See George Weigel, *Witness to Hope: The Biography of John Paul II* (New York: Cliff Street Books, 1999), 4. See also Chicago Tribune, *John Paul II: The Epic Life of a Pilgrim Pope* (Chicago: Triumph Books, 2005), iii.

[9] For just one example, see Phil McCombs, "The People's Pope: John Paul II, Happy to Serve God and Layman," *The Washington Post* (April 3, 2005), D01.

[10] Pigozzi, *Pope John Paul II*, 96.

[11] See Avery Cardinal Dulles, SJ, "John Paul II and the New Evangelization: December 4–5, 1991," in *Church and Society: The Laurence J. McGinley Lectures, 1988–2007* (New York: Fordham University Press, 2008), 87–102, at 89.

priest, he would inspire and comfort and teach and admonish. He would do this not just as head of the church speaking remotely from the Vatican, but as the church's living, breathing manifestation, a physical presence at the eye of the storm of attention that surrounded him.[12]

John Paul II took the mandate "Go and make disciples of all nations" (Matthew 28:19) with consummate seriousness, seeing it as arising not only from the words of Jesus "but also from the profound demands of God's life within us."[13] According to one of his biographers, George Weigel, he was first and foremost a disciple; this image of him, Weigel has argued, is the best one for understanding John Paul II from the inside.[14] It refers to how he was, above all, a man of faith – with a message to proclaim to the ends of the earth. He was – and saw himself as – an evangelizer: "I am a pilgrim-messenger who wants to travel the world to fulfill the mandate Christ gave to the apostles when he sent them to evangelize all men and all nations," he said in Santiago de Compostella in 1982, in just the fourth year of his papacy.[15] His first international trip, just over three months after his election as pope, was to the meeting of the Conference of Bishops of Latin America (CELAM), the theme of which was "Evangelization at Present and in the Future of Latin America," and, according to Cardinal Avery Dulles: "Beginning with the Puebla conference, John Paul II has made himself the principal evangelizer in the Catholic Church."[16] He traveled with a purpose, not as a tourist.

As John Paul II's papacy unfolded, the connection between his evangelical zeal and his use of modern means of communication and air travel emerged with greater clarity. In the introduction to his encyclical letter *Redemptoris missio* (December 7, 1990), he repeats the famous cry of St. Paul ("Woe to me if I do not preach the Gospel" – 1 Corinthians 9:16) and states: "From the beginning of my Pontificate I have chosen to travel to the ends of the earth in order to show this missionary concern."[17] A little further on in the same document he lists among the new opportunities for mission "the opening of frontiers and the formation of a more united world due to an increase in communications."[18] Furthermore, in his apostolic exhortation on the laity *Christifideles laici* (December 30, 1988), he

[12] Chicago Tribune, *John Paul II*, 32.
[13] John Paul II, encyclical letter *Redemptoris missio*, no. 11.5, in J. Michael Miller, ed., *The Encyclicals of John Paul II* (Huntington, IN: Our Sunday Visitor, Inc., 1996), 503.
[14] See Weigel, *Witness to Hope*, 7–8; also 9–10 and 13.
[15] Quoted in Allen, "23-Year Odyssey," 4.
[16] Dulles, "John Paul II and the New Evangelization," 90.
[17] *Redemptoris missio*, no. 1.2 (see also 1.1), in Miller, ed., *The Encyclicals of John Paul II*, 494.
[18] *Redemptoris missio*, no. 3.3, in Miller, ed., *The Encyclicals of John Paul II*, 496.

exhorts them "to make use of new media of communication to proclaim the Gospel that brings salvation."[19]

What did Pope John Paul II mean by "evangelize," and what was the essential content of the message he delivered both in person and over the airwaves? He distinguished between primary and secondary evangelization, the former referring to what is "called for in regions where Christ and the gospel are not yet known" and the latter, also called a "re-evangelization," referring to what is "required in areas where large groups of Christians have lost a living sense of the faith and no longer consider themselves members of the Church."[20] In *Redemptoris missio*, Dulles points out, the expression "new evangelization" seems to refer more to the re-evangelization of areas that were once Christian; nonetheless there is not a rigid demarcation between so-called primary and secondary evangelization.[21]

From an examination of John Paul's writings, especially his encyclicals, the themes of human dignity, human freedom, opening up to Jesus Christ, entering into solidarity with one another, and Christianity unity – the list is not exhaustive – can be seen to be central. These themes are rooted in his own biography as a twentieth-century Pole who lived, first, under Nazi dictatorship and, subsequently, under communist rule. Neither respected the dignity of the human person; John Paul II emphasized this throughout his papacy. Neither respected human freedom, above all freedom of worship; he championed this all through his papacy. On his first – electrifying! – trip to Poland in 1979, the year after he became Pope, he stood in Warsaw's Victory Square proclaiming that "Christ cannot be kept out of the history of man."[22] He declared this because the authorities held the opposite; and it became a constant refrain of his papacy. The theme of "solidarity" – with its implied critique of the excesses of both communism and capitalism – becomes increasingly central in his writings, certainly in his great social encyclicals; and this occurs in tandem with the growth, and triumph, of the *Solidarność* (Solidarity) movement that proved ultimately instrumental, always with the support and encouragement of John

---

[19] Dulles, "John Paul II and the New Evangelization," 92; the relevant paragraph in *Christifideles laici* is 44 (latter part). See *The Lay Members of Christ's Faithful People – Christifideles laici*, Vatican trans. (Boston, MA: Pauline Books & Media, 1988), 115–16.
[20] Dulles, "John Paul II and the New Evangelization," 92.
[21] Ibid.   [22] See Allen, "23-Year Odyssey," 3.

Paul, in overthrowing the system of communism in Poland (and elsewhere in Eastern Europe). Yet another recurrent theme is unity, John Paul being convinced that a disunited Christianity is an obstacle to mission and evangelization, and to rendering the Gospel credible.[23]

The central themes of John Paul II's teachings bear the marks of the intellectual (cultural, philosophical, and theological) formation that the student, seminarian, and academic Karol Wojtyla received. Gerard Mannion mentions "how, under the totalitarian regimes of first the Nazis and then the pseudo-communists, he developed a philosophical and theological outlook that has been described as Christian humanism or personalism."[24] Avery Dulles speaks about John Paul's "prophetic humanism" as a theme that "permeates his teaching as a whole."[25] The humanism and personalism took early root through his exposure to the literature of his Polish culture, not least the poetry of the nineteenth-century Romantic Adam Mickiewicz, who, himself writing at a time when Poland was partitioned, gave hope to the young Wojtyla at the time of Poland's occupation by the Nazis.[26] Through his participation in clandestine Polish theatre, keeping alive his nation's culture at a time when the Nazi occupiers were attempting to efface "Polish-ness" from history, Wojtyla saw the power of a people's culture to shape and maintain their identity.[27]

In philosophy and theology, too, Karol Wojtyla's training, first in Thomism and later in phenomenology, furnished him with a realist metaphysical outlook coupled with a deep appreciation of human experience; and he developed a kind of "Thomistic personalism" that undergirded his own humanism and anthropological concerns.[28] His experience at the Second Vatican Council, especially his work on the draft text of *Gaudium et spes* and his involvement in the debates surrounding the Declaration on Religious Freedom (*Dignitatis humanae*), remained with him and is

---

[23] See Pigozzi, *Pope John Paul II*, 139; see also *Redemptor hominis*, no. 11.4 and 5, in Miller, ed., *The Encyclicals of John Paul II*, 61; see John Paul II's encyclical *Ut unum sint*, nos. 98 and 99 (Miller, ed., *The Encyclicals of John Paul II*, 973–74), pointing out how unity among Christians supports evangelization – and how its absence impedes it; and see *Ut unum sint*, no. 71.2 (Miller, ed., *The Encyclicals of John Paul II*, 958), where John Paul II states that some of his journeys have "a precise ecumenical 'priority.'"

[24] Mannion, "Introduction," 2.

[25] Avery Cardinal Dulles, "The Prophetic Humanism of John Paul II," in Dulles, *Church and Society*, 142–56, at 142.

[26] See Edward Stourton, "John Paul II: The Man and his Ideas," in Gerald O'Collins and Michael A. Hayes, eds., *The Legacy of John Paul II* (London: Burns & Oates, 2008), 17–30, at 27–28.

[27] Ibid., 28.

[28] See Ronald Modras, "Karol Wojtyla the Philosopher," in Mannion, ed., *The Vision of John Paul II*, 29–44, esp. 32–36.

reflected in the emphasis that he placed on human dignity and freedom through all the years of his pontificate.[29] The message he preached was the man he was, the circumstances he had lived in, and the conviction that had become part of him. To sum it up in a single concern: it was a passion for the human person created by God as a transcendent being and redeemed by Christ from sin and for love. He was certain that closeness to Christ took nothing from the dignity and freedom of the human being. He was passionate about the transcendental character of the human person and opposed all philosophies that denied this. And he knew about sin, but also about redemption – and the price Christ had paid to "buy us back." This came out strongly on "one of the very rare occasions when John Paul II lost his cool in public" because a journalist referred, in his presence, to the cost of his travels. Caroline Pigozzi reports him as saying:

I do not consider it something to account for when you remember that we humans were bought for a price beyond measure. There is no way to calculate that. It is stupid. People talk about cost as a way of trying to stop the Pope. People say that he costs more than the queen of England. That is just as well, for the message he carries is of transcendental value.[30]

It may seem odd to quote this angry remark here but I do so because, as is often the case with anger that is expressed suddenly, real feelings and beliefs emerge. Here one is made aware of what the central concern of John Paul II was and why he traveled to the ends of the earth to express it. It was that human beings are valuable beyond any and every measure because we are created transcendent – made for and "open to" what is beyond us – and redeemed in a love that is itself beyond measure. This, the love of God really, is what makes us great; and this is the core of the message John Paul wished to convey to the whole world. And it is evident everywhere. It is found in the first encyclical of his pontificate, *Redemptor hominis* (March 4, 1979), where it is stated that the human being "is the primary route that the Church must travel in fulfilling her mission: *he is the primary and fundamental way for the Church*, the way traced out by Christ himself, the way that leads invariably through the mystery of the Incarnation and the Redemption."[31] It is also found in an address, from very early on in John Paul's pontificate too, to the Diplomatic Corps Accredited to the Holy See (on January 14, 1980), in which he speaks of the

[29] On Vatican II's significance for John Paul II, see Paul McPartlan, "John Paul II and Vatican II," in Mannion, ed., *The Vision of John Paul II*, 45–61, esp. 47–51.
[30] Quoted in Pigozzi, *Pope John Paul II*, 126.
[31] *Redemptor hominis*, no. 14.1, in Miller, ed., *The Encyclicals of John Paul II*, 66.

church as both "the sign and the safeguard of the transcendental dimension of the human person" (*Gaudium et spes*, no. 76.2) and states that, since Jesus Christ has united himself with every person and the solicitude he has for each person he has redeemed "has become that of the Church," there is nothing regarding human welfare that is not the church's concern and nothing that threatens human welfare to which the church can remain insensible (cf. *Redemptor hominis*, no. 13).[32] The human person, because of John Paul II's faith, his history, and his personal inclination, stands at the center of the message he proclaimed throughout his twenty-six-year reign. Avery Dulles said in 2003:

> As the literary output of Pope John Paul II has accumulated, expanding almost beyond the assimilative powers of any one reader, and as he celebrates the silver jubilee of his pontificate, I have been asking myself, as I am sure that many others have: What lies at the very heart of his message? Is there some one concept that could serve as a key to unlock what is distinctive to this pope as a thinker? My thesis will be: the mystery of the human person. As pope, he is of course bound to the whole dogmatic heritage of the Church, but he presents it in a distinctive way, with his own emphases, which are in line with his philosophical personalism.[33]

At the very heart of John Paul II's message lies the mystery of the human person. Thus all that concerns the welfare of human persons becomes his concern: respect for human dignity and life; freedom, especially freedom of worship; justice for the poor; peace among nations and peoples; bringing faith and human culture(s) into fruitful dialogue. John Paul promoted these concerns by using modern means of communication fully and by availing himself copiously of modern means of travel. In what follows, I shall examine his manner of using each. In a subsequent section, I shall reflect on how effective he was in communicating his message and on how he and his words were received.

A GREAT COMMUNICATOR: PRESENT TO ALL THROUGH TRAVEL AND MEDIA

There is no doubt that Pope John Paul II, not unlike the United States actor-president, Ronald Reagan, with whom he enjoyed a close relationship, was,

---

[32] Pope John Paul II, "Address to the Diplomatic Corps, 14 January 1980 n. 4 [858]," in André Dupuy, *Pope John Paul II and the Challenges of Papal Diplomacy: Anthology (1978–2003)* (Vatican City: The Pontifical Council for Justice and Peace, 2004, and New York City: The Path to Peace Foundation, 2004), 5.

[33] Avery Cardinal Dulles, "John Paul II and the Mystery of the Human Person, October 21, 2003," in *Church and Society*, 414–29, at 414.

like Reagan himself, a "great communicator." John Paul, a gifted actor with "cinematic good looks," a master of the dramatic gesture and the quick-witted response, a speaker of many languages, could gain people's attention and win their admiration.[34] If it could be argued that his papacy was one of important teachings (fourteen weighty encyclicals, not to mention his many other writings and speeches), of doctrinal and disciplinary consolidation, of diplomacy and statesmanlike contributions to the peace and unity of the world, it must be added that it was all these things *in a new way*: a way that availed itself of the spectacular opportunities through which persons, by means of jet air travel, and images, by means of increasingly sophisticated electronic media, could be "transported" at record speed around the entire globe. Even the teachings are most readily and instantly available – and at no cost – on the internet, at the recently developed Vatican website: www.vatican.va. John Paul II's was a papacy that managed to make itself at home in the computer and internet age. Indeed there is a photograph from 2001 that shows him using a laptop bearing the papal seal to send a message to bishops, the first such use of the internet by a pope, it is claimed.[35]

As well as finding his way in the internet age, John Paul II was a master of jet-age travel. The statistics on his journeys abroad are staggering: over a hundred trips, covering mileage that would have taken him to the moon, back to earth, and out to the moon again. In the opening pages of his biography of John Paul II, George Weigel has written:

> John Paul II has also been, indisputably, the most visible pope in history. In fact, a case can be made that he has been the most visible human being in history. He has almost certainly been seen by more people than any man who ever lived. When one adds the multiplying impact of television to the equation, the breadth of his reach into the worlds-within-worlds of humanity becomes almost impossible to grasp.[36]

Weigel is insightful in putting John Paul II's trips and television images together. Both have to do with being *seen*, with impacting on people universally. John L. Allen has stated: "In any analysis of his papacy, the trips loom as one of its most original and important features."[37] The two went together – the travels *and* the sophisticated use of electronic media – and they made this particular papacy entirely different from every papacy

---

[34] See John Cornwell, *Breaking Faith: The Pope, the People, and the Fate of Catholicism* (London and New York: Viking, 2001), 55–56; also Pigozzi, *Pope John Paul II*, 110.
[35] See Chicago Tribune, *John Paul II*, 120.
[36] Weigel, *Witness to Hope*, 4. See also Cornwell, *Breaking Faith*, 1.
[37] Allen, "23-Year Odyssey," 4.

preceding it. He was a "relentless traveller."[38] He was "a pilgrim, in the original sense of a religious traveller, and his witnessing of the Christian faith in 129 nations, comprising almost all of the 1 billion Roman Catholics on earth."[39]

Integral to the travels – and to generating memorable images as John Paul showed up in country after country – were his unforgettable gestures. Caroline Pigozzi says: "As a young man, Karol Wojtyla was a great lover of the theatre, and he retained his belief in the importance of a gesture."[40] Bending to kiss the ground in each new country he visited, kissing babies, tenderly touching the sick (vividly portrayed, for example, on television during his visit to the Marian shrine of Knock in Ireland in 1979), revealed a pope who had genuine affection for people. John Cornwell notes that "he was particularly impressive when he greeted and blessed old people, the sick and the young."[41] Also, his presence on stage was dramatic. During a meeting with youth in California in 1987, he wore a wireless microphone and, in the style of a talk-show host, conversed with the young, interspersing his prepared remarks with spontaneous ones and looking, through it all, quite relaxed – appearing, in fact, to enjoy himself.[42] He appealed to men and women of violence at Drogheda, in the Irish Republic near the border with Northern Ireland, to turn from their violent ways, saying "On my knees I beg you." On visiting Australia, he was photographed endearingly holding a koala bear. Rugged, even pained, images of him clutching his cross in various parts of the world, for example in Maribor, Slovenia, in 1999, remain unforgettable.[43] Images of him kneeling in prayer in many different places, in Auschwitz, for example, and in countless Marian shrines throughout the world, are still vivid. I recall a photograph of him standing beside Cuba's Fidel Castro in Havana's José Martí airport in 1998, with Castro dressed in civilian clothes and each of them apparently checking the time on his watch.[44] And no one could forget the historic picture of him, in 2000, placing a prayer in Jerusalem's Western Wall.[45] And then, in his final, ailing days, pictures of the pope slumped forward during liturgical ceremonies and, eventually, the image of him waving to

---

[38] Mannion, "Introduction," 4.
[39] Pigozzi, *Pope John Paul II*, 105. Pigozzi, in a book that is an altogether favorable portrait of John Paul II bordering on a kind of adulation of his person, includes an entire chapter on his travels: "Around the World 29 Times: Inside Secrets of the Travelling Pope," 105–47.
[40] Ibid., 111.   [41] Cornwell, *Breaking Faith*, 2.
[42] "John Paul Stars in Hollywood.(Main)," *Albany Times Union (Albany, NY)* (September 16, 1987), *HighBeam Research,* at http://www.highbeam.com/doc/1G1-158417939.html (last accessed August 23, 2009).
[43] Chicago Tribune, *John Paul II*, 15.   [44] Ibid., 43.   [45] Ibid., 94–95.

people from his sick window showed the world how a person, although suffering and infirm, could still contribute to life. Images such as these have stamped the world's memory and won, for John Paul II, universal affection and appeal. By his travels, and through his media coverage, he indeed became the universal pastor.

A penultimate image – I recall it vividly! – from John Paul's funeral in April 2005 is that of a stunning array of heads of state and heads of government, some craning their necks like schoolchildren to catch a glimpse of the final obsequies of a person who had – and this *must* have impressed them – commanded a prominent place on the world stage for more than a quarter of a century.[46] And a final image, provided not by John Paul II himself but by his devoted mourners, is of a group of them carrying signs bearing the demand *santo subito*, or "saint immediately," effectively calling for a waiving of the requirement that five years must pass after a person's death before his or her canonization process can be set in motion (Figure 12.1).

John Paul II's papacy, by appealing with a panoply of arresting images to the image-drenched cultural circumstances of its times, ensured its impact and, to a considerable extent, got across its message. There are over 14,500 photographs of him on the Vatican website, made available there by (and under copyright to) the official Vatican newspaper, *L'osservatore romano*, founded in 1861 just after the defeat of the papal troops at Castelfidardo on September 8, 1860 and the proclamation of the Kingdom of Italy on March 17, 1861.[47] This newspaper was founded to defend and promote the pope and it does so still, now in several parallel editions in different languages and, as just noted, with the best of digital photography. Pictures of John Paul, relayed all over the world by means of the internet and television, depict him and his journeys and activities in countless and memorable ways. If "a picture speaks a thousand words," what do thousands of them speak? John Paul's papacy did not lag behind in the use of communications media. As he himself pointed out to entertainment industry and news media leaders in 1987 in Los Angeles, the church has "promoted the media and been in the forefront of the use of new technology."[48]

---

[46] See Michael Walsh, "From Karol Wojtyla to John Paul II: Life and Times," in Mannion, ed., *The Vision of John Paul II*, 10–28, at 27.

[47] See "The Origins of 'L'osservatore romano'" at www.vatican.va/news_services/or/history/hI_eng.html, 1 (last accessed June 16, 2009).

[48] John Paul II, "An Immense Spiritual Power" (Address to 1,600 policy makers in television, radio, motion pictures and the print media, Registry Hotel, Los Angeles, September 15), in *John Paul II in America: Talks Given on the Papal Tour September 1987* (Boston, MA: St. Paul Books & Media, 1987), 174–80, at 179 (no. 8).

12.1 Postcards for sale, Rome, 2008. Photo by Pamela M. Jones.

In 1984 John Paul chose Joaquín Navarro-Valls, medical doctor and journalist, Spaniard, and numerary of Opus Dei, as director of the Holy See's press office. Of this man, it is said that he is

believed to have had a determinant hand behind the scenes in ensuring that John Paul's natural starlike persona shined to maximum effectiveness. Whether fielding press questions on thorny theological or political issues, issuing medical bulletins or making sure cameras were set up at the best angle, Navarro-Valls helped move the papacy to the forefront of the modern media age.[49]

In 1982, less than four years into his papacy, John Paul II decided to set up the Vatican Television Center (CTV). It was "established to produce audiovisual materials of a religious nature for worldwide broadcast consumption ... [and it] now possesses and controls the largest archive of images of the pope in the world."[50] John Corry said of it in 1987: "CTV is not so much a television station as a production agency, charged with filming everything the Pope does in public, whether saying a Rosary in Rome or addressing multitudes in Africa, Central America or Eastern Europe. Then the film is distributed, sometimes in the form of documentaries for third world countries."[51] CTV has developed since then. Today it posts, on the Vatican website, a list of events that are to be broadcast in the immediate future. For example, as I consult it in July 2009, it lists the audience of Pope Benedict XVI with the President of the United States, Mr. Barack Obama, to be broadcast between 3.45 and 5.00 p.m. on Friday, July 10.[52] Vatican Radio has continued to develop also. It can now be heard on the web ("Web Audio Live" is how the Vatican website presents it) on five channels, some of them in a dozen languages or more, broadcasting to Rome itself and to many far-flung regions of the world. Since the development of the Vatican website, the documents, events, pronouncements, images, and myriad activities of the pope (and of those around him) have all become available in a single place. This is an access to the papacy hitherto inconceivable and, for those who manage it, an opportunity to present the papacy at all times, in a very favorable light, to the entire world.

Audiovisual materials grew, through the activities of CTV, to become an important avenue through which, during John Paul II's papacy, the

[49] Elizabeth Guider and Nick Vivarelli, "People's Pontiff was Pop Icon," *Daily Variety* (Monday, April 4, 2005), 1 and 22, at 22.
[50] Ibid.
[51] John Corry, "The Pope, The Media, The Drama," *The New York Times* (September 6, 1987), H21.
[52] See www.vatican.va/news_services/television/multimedia/live_en.html (last accessed July 9, 2009).

man and his message were communicated. The pope also found time to write several books, most memorable among them being *Crossing the Threshold of Hope*, a collection of written responses to questions from the Italian journalist Vittorio Messori, and, to celebrate his golden jubilee as a priest in 1996, *Gift and Mystery*, which first appeared in English in 1997.[53] John Paul II published in just about every medium. In 1994 *Time* magazine chose him as its "Man of the Year," and in the cover story of its December 26 issue, referring to how "a CD featuring him saying the rosary – in Latin – against a background of Bach and Handel" was at that time rising in the charts in Europe, suggested that "the only conceivable reason" for this was charisma.[54] By means of his charisma – and the communications and travel technologies that spread it – John Paul made an impact on the world. A critical examination of this impact follows.

RECEPTION OF A GLOBE-TROTTING AND MEDIA-FRIENDLY POPE

The Vatican learned well, during the John Paul II era, to capitalize on this pope's media skills and to hone its own with dramatic effect.[55] It could be said that this pope's easy and appealing style made him a media star. It could also be said that his media apparatus – and, indeed, much of the world's media – built on his persona to "package" him as a superstar, an icon, a "hot item," much as had occurred with figures such as Michael Jackson or Diana, Princess of Wales, in the 1980s. The Vatican makes its stars just as others do. Not all of this is questionable; John Paul II used this celebrity status to proclaim the rich message about the human person that has already been presented. Yet a question can be raised as to whether he might have been differently "packaged" to greater effect. For his traveling and appearing in the image of a kind of pop star, while often "electric" in its initial impact, may not have been lasting in its eventual results.

[53] See His Holiness John Paul II, *Crossing the Threshold of Hope*, ed. Vittorio Messori, trans. Jenny McPhee and Martha McPhee (New York: Alfred A. Knopf, 1994, reprinted 2008). See also Pope John Paul II, *Gift and Mystery: On the Fiftieth Anniversary of My Priestly Ordination* (New York: Doubleday, 1997).
[54] See Paul Gray; Thomas Sancton and Greg Burke; Joseph Ngala; and John Moody and Richard N. Ostling, "John Paul II: Empire of the Spirit," *Time* (December 26, 1994), opening paragraph, at www.time.com/time/magazine/article/0,9171,982043.00.html (last accessed August 23, 2009).
[55] David Carr, in "The Media and the Vatican: Opposing Goals," *The New York Times* (April 23, 2005), B9, refers to Diane Winston, professor of media and religion at the University of California, as pointing to the Vatican's and to John Paul's skills in using the media.

Young people in Galway, Ireland, in 1979 danced and cheered for four-teen full minutes after John Paul told them: "Young people of Ireland, I love you." But evidence for a strong take-up of, and adherence to, the values that he put before them on that visit is not easy to find in the Ireland of subsequent years, during which trends in Catholic life and practice went rather in the opposite direction. The Archbishop of New York (and for-merly Milwaukee), Timothy M. Dolan, for whom Pope John Paul II is a major role model, is quoted in a newspaper article on the day of his death as saying: "The paradox that everybody mentions is that, while he is a tower-ing personality and has tremendous popularity, they will say people will not obey him." Dolan adds: "To use one phrase, 'They like the singer. They don't like the song.' I don't know how true that is."[56] John Cornwell observes that, while "the Pope remains at the very heart and centre," nevertheless "the papacy has for some decades now been subject to an ever-widening gap between its teaching and the faithful's adherence."[57] There is evidence that John Paul's impact, being of the pop-star, crowd-mesmerizing kind, was often dramatic, but did not always go deep, thus provoking initial, but not lasting, responses. The parable of the sower comes to mind – the fate of the seed falling on shallow ground (Luke 8:6, 13).

The year following John Paul II's visit to Ireland saw a 20 percent rise in applicants for the priesthood there,[58] a trend, however, that later turned in the opposite direction and had certainly done so by the end of his pap-acy, during which most of Ireland's seminaries closed. John Cornwell reflects on the "mass enthusiasms" of gatherings of youth with John Paul on occasions such as "Youth Day in Rome during the Jubilee Year," stating that "these passing displays are no indication of the true state of affairs: in France, for example, only 7 percent of the young ever attend church."[59] Hans Küng acknowledges that Pope John Paul, as a charismatic communi-cator and media star, had a strong effect on youth, but argues that he relied, above all, on the new ecclesial movements of Italian origin and on Opus Dei. Küng suggests that, under the care and direction of the hierarchy and of the new lay movements (Focolare, Communione e Liberazione, Sant' Egidio, Regnum Christi) hundreds of thousands of young people, many of them of good will, too many of them devoid of a critical sense, were drawn to the World Youth Days, but that, ultimately, the attraction of

---

[56] Tom Heinen, "Pope John Paul II, 1920–2005: At Peace," *The Milwaukee Journal Sentinel* (April 3, 2005): *HighBeam Research*, at http://www.highbeam.com/DocPrint.aspx?DocId=1P2:6335015 (last accessed June 22, 2009).
[57] Cornwell, *Breaking Faith*, 33.   [58] See Allen, "23-Year Odyssey," 5.
[59] Cornwell, *Breaking Faith*, 3.

the shared event and of what radiated from "John Paul Superstar" proved mostly more important than the content he proclaimed.[60]

Some images remain from John Paul II's travel and media appearances that reveal a negative reception of him, as well as an inability on his part to deal with a critical public. If he captivated the wider world, which was not, of course, bound by his teachings as Roman Catholics were, he often dismayed sections of his own church. Indelible as an image is how he publicly wagged his finger at the Sandinista government minister Father Ernesto Cardenal in Nicaragua in 1983, telling him to put in order his situation with the church.[61] During the same visit, he shouted "silencio" three times at those who, during his homily asking Catholics to heed their bishops and not the Sandinistas, called for a church that stood with the poor and protested that between Christianity and the revolution there was no contradiction.[62] John Paul II was frequently experienced as authoritarian (a word his unflagging supporters metamorphose to "authoritative"). In John Cornwell's words: "His benign appearance before the masses, however, concealed a sterner presence behind closed doors," as American, French, German, and African bishops could testify on the basis of the admonitions they received from him.[63] His championing of theological orthodoxy and his pursuit – through the Congregation for the Doctrine of the Faith under its prefect (and eventual successor), Cardinal Joseph Ratzinger – of theologians who dared to question any teachings of the magisterium remains an image – for many theologians a specter – of his papacy.[64]

During the years when John Paul II was pope and Joseph Ratzinger was the Prefect of the Congregation for the Doctrine of the Faith, the media-savvy Vatican sought to conduct its business with theologians away from the public eye. "Dissent" was essentially defined as *public* disagreement with the magisterium, the church's teaching authority. In the *Instruction on the Ecclesial Vocation of the Theologian* in 1990 from the Congregation for the Doctrine of the Faith, recourse of any kind to the media by theologians was rejected, and no recognition was given to the sheer inevitability of media interest and involvement in situations of dissent in the modern era.[65] Despite

---

[60] Hans Küng, "Pontifikat der Widersprüche," *Der Spiegel* (March 26, 2005), 107–10, at 109–10.
[61] The incident occurred in Managua in 1983. A picture of it is available in Chicago Tribune, *John Paul II*, 40.
[62] Allen, "23-Year Odyssey," 5.   [63] Cornwell, *Breaking Faith*, 56.
[64] Ibid., 18–21 (esp. 20); also Mannion, "Introduction," 5.
[65] See Sacred Congregation for the Doctrine of the Faith, *Instruction* Donum veritatis *on the Ecclesial Vocation of the Theologian* (May 24, 1990), esp. paragraphs 30, 32–33, and 39, at www.vatican.va/roman_curia/congregations/cfaith/documents/rc_con_cfaith_doc_19900524_theologian-vocation_En.html (last accessed August 23, 2009); Francis A. Sullivan, SJ, "The Theologian's

both Cardinal Ratzinger's and John Paul II's frequent use of the media themselves – Ratzinger gave three book-length interviews during his years as the prefect of the congregation, in 1985, 1996, and 2002 respectively – they considered the media off-limits for theologians who had any disagreement with them. For this reason, among others, the Swiss theologian Hans Küng wrote, just a week before Pope John Paul II's death, in Germany's frontline news magazine, *Der Spiegel*, about how his papacy was one of contradictions. He had supported human rights *ad extra* but had withheld them *ad intra* – from bishops, theologians, and women, above all. He had blocked reform within the church, refused dialogue, and set as his goal absolute Roman rule.[66]

John Cornwell writes also of John Paul as a pope of contradictions, pointing out that he "has taken the Church in the direction of hardline conservatism, but he has regularly exploited the media to give the opposite impression."[67] James Voiss observes how, "in the practical realm, some have experienced John Paul's actual leadership as conflicting with his articulated ideals."[68] While, in the abstract, he had a vision of the church as a communion of persons in which dialogue was to play a key role, in the concrete, when doctrine and church life intersected, he fell short of this ideal.[69] For example, his statements regarding artificial contraception and the inadmissibility of women to priestly ordination were directed toward ending discussion, even though many theologians considered that, in these areas, important questions remained unresolved.[70] During his long papacy, increasingly, bishops were appointed who would unswervingly hold his line; and appointments occurred in a manner that did little to consider the wishes of the local clergy. It was the voice of Rome that counted. During the John Paul II era, decision-making in the church became ever more centralized,[71] aided and abetted by access to media and travel that enabled the pope to be seen and heard instantly and everywhere, in a manner unthinkable in any previous era.

John Cornwell, writing toward the end of John Paul II's papacy, said of it that "Catholicism has become a one-man show: the Vatican's publicity machine and large sections of the Catholic media ensure that

Ecclesial Vocation and the 1990 CDF Instruction," *Theological Studies* 52 (1991), 51–68; and James Corkery, SJ, *Joseph Ratzinger's Theological Ideas: Wise Cautions and Legitimate Hopes* (New York and Mahwah, NJ: Paulist Press, and Dublin: Dominican Publications, 2009), 85–89.
[66] Küng, "Pontifikat der Widersprüche," 108.
[67] Cornwell, *Breaking Faith*, 16 (see also 15).
[68] James Voiss, SJ, "Understanding John Paul II's Vision of the Church," in Mannion, ed., *The Vision of John Paul II*, 62–77, at 69.
[69] Ibid., 66–69.   [70] Ibid., 69.   [71] Ibid.

his voice and words, his opinions and verdicts, are broadcast daily and amplified throughout the world."[72] His copious writings, and those of the Congregation for the Doctrine of the Faith led by Cardinal Ratzinger, have managed, over a quarter of a century, to touch on every significant area of theology, indicating the boundaries to be observed and the preferred directions to be followed. Furthermore, all these writings were, and are still, available at the click of a button, free of charge, on the well-stocked Vatican website. These two men's attempts to set, and to direct, the church's theological agenda has been very focused, so much so, indeed, that it has left many theologians hardly offering this pope a ringing endorsement but, at best, according him an ambiguous reception. This is the case particularly in the areas of moral theology, liberation theology, and John Paul II's brand of feminism (sometimes referred to as "the new feminism").[73] Despite his stating that women shared equally with men in the dignity of being human, John Paul failed again and again – and not only because of his position that they could not be ordained priests – to assure them that the church was really seeking to listen to their voices and include them in its decision-making. Even in the language used in papal texts, their "invisibility" visibly continued.[74]

John Paul's trips also, and often, stressed loyalty to Rome and obedience. These emphases have been ascribed by some to an overstated desire for unity, as well as to a model of church owed to his Polish background, when dissent would have been "a dangerous luxury" capable of easy exploitation by forces outside, and hostile to, the church.[75] Gerard Mannion, reflecting on his experiences of totalitarian regimes and their effects, speaks about John Paul as both *rebel* and *dissident* and raises the question as to whether this background of rebellion *ad extra* and unity *ad intra* might be related to John Paul's demanding an unswerving allegiance to the magisterium by theologians.[76] The question remains, however, as to whether this was the best and the most effective attitude to bring to

---

[72] Cornwell, *Breaking Faith,* 15.
[73] See Charles E. Curran, "The Sources of Moral Truth in the Teaching of John Paul II," 128–43; Mario I. Aguilar, "John Paul II and Theologies of Liberation," 144–58; Susan Rakoczy, IHM, "Mixed Messages: John Paul II's Writings on Women," 159–83; and Gemma Simmonds, CJ, "John Paul II and the Consecrated Life," 200–14: all in Mannion, ed., *The Vision of John Paul II.* See also Lawrence S. Cunningham, Joseph A. Komonchak, Dennis M. Doyle, Charles E. Curran, Janet E. Smith, Lisa Sowle Cahill, Stanley Hauerwas, and Anne E. Patrick, "*Veritatis splendor,*" *Commonweal* 120:18 (October 22, 1993), 11–18.
[74] See Cahill, in Cunningham et al., "*Veritatis splendor,*" 16, in paragraph beginning "Finally, the sexist language." See also Rakoczy, "Mixed Messages."
[75] Stourton, "John Paul II: The Man and his Ideas," 26; and Pigozzi, *Pope John Paul II,* 138.
[76] See Mannion, "Introduction," 4; also Stourton, "John Paul II: The Man and his Ideas," 26.

governance of the church worldwide, beyond the circumstances of Nazi-occupied and (later) communist Poland.

Through his mode of self-presentation on his travels and by means of media, John Paul II quickly became the object of a *personality cult*: "a personality cult of hitherto unprecedented global adoration and adulation."[77] Catholic Ultramontanist devotion to the person of the pope had already existed since at least the nineteenth century, and this already provided a basis for focusing on the person of the pope. However, it grew enormously in strength and effect when it encountered the present age's penchant (and technology) for creating larger-than-life figures, for fashioning "superstars." The question arises, however, as to whether the creation of such "icons" facilitates reflective assimilation of a message about how to live, or just provides an occasion for celebrating in the presence of a "man of the moment."

CONCLUDING OBSERVATIONS

Before ending, the question should be asked: what of the other two papal roles which are discussed in this book but hardly touched on in relation to John Paul II, who fulfilled the third – that of universal pastor – so energetically? Was he in any sense a prince-pope? He was, at least indirectly, because his international diplomacy was immense, and he acted as an advocate for justice and peace and was listened to even by those who did not agree with him – or act upon his advice, as was the case with the two Presidents Bush in the United States with regard to the wars they fought in the Middle East. He was in a sense a world leader, a political as well as a moral figure; it is no accident that Weigel casts him in the role of *statesman*.[78]

Was John Paul II in any sense a patron-pope? He was, indirectly. For it was during his papacy that the Sistine Chapel and other Vatican and ecclesiastical treasures were restored. Also, he told entertainment and media leaders in Los Angeles how the church had always supported the arts – and now supported, and used, the media arts. This linking, by him, of the arts and the media was creative, enabling him to praise what the entertainment chiefs and news-makers were doing, calling attention even to its beauty (the beauty of art), but inviting them, also, to be aware of their awesome responsibilities as practitioners of these arts because of the influence they had on people around the globe.

[77] See Mannion, "Introduction," 2; also John Cornwell, *Breaking Faith*, 15–16.
[78] See Weigel, *Witness to Hope*, 13.

Given his time in history and the opportunities open to him, Pope John Paul II was first and foremost a pastor, a universal pastor, in a highly visible way. He was effective in this role, through which he influenced world events also, even to the extent of contributing to communism's collapse in Eastern Europe. At times he impressed people beyond his church more than people within it. His rich message about the dignity and sacredness of the human person found an echo with many, although it did not always lead to them following the path he indicated, and at times his own manner of treating people within his church made the discrepancy between what he was saying and how he was acting difficult to take. Scholars of his papacy will have to probe further the reasons for this if memory of him is not to remain blighted within the church.

Conclusion

James Corkery and Thomas Worcester

As this book on the papacy since about 1500 – from Julius II (1503–13) to John Paul II (1978–2005) – comes to a close, reflection is prompted along two lines. First, was the lens through which the contributors examined the papacy a fruitful one? That is, did the focus on papal roles (prince, patron, pastor) and on the factors leading a pope to emphasize a particular role (or roles) during his papacy and on how the exercise of the different roles was undertaken and received yield perspectives on the papacy throughout the past 500 years that a general history, or a mere chronological account, would not have provided? Second, what does such a lens or focus suggest for the papacy of the future, unfolding from that of Benedict XVI?

To explore the first of these two lines of thought, it is necessary to recall where the book's interpretative lens came from originally and to highlight some of the perspectives that resulted from looking at the modern papacy by means of it. First, the origins of the focus itself. The editors happened to be teaching, at the same time and in the same place, two separate undergraduate courses that involved the papacy. Thomas Worcester, a historian, was presenting a course in the modern papacy, and James Corkery, a theologian, was offering a module in theological anthropology engaging, in particular, with the writings of late twentieth-century German theologians, Joseph Ratzinger among them. At the same time he was also writing a book about the theological ideas of the (then recently elected) pope, Joseph Ratzinger (Benedict XVI). The point of common interest of the historian and the theologian was the papacy in its historical context. Worcester's investigations had made him increasingly conscious of the extent to which factors external to the papacy influenced how popes actually exercised their office; and he had seen how, at particular times, popes had acted predominantly in certain roles – those of prince, patron, and pastor in particular – more in response to circumstances external to themselves than as a result of any personal views on the papacy that they might have held. Thus, contrary to a perspective that would ascribe the

243

shaping of a papacy principally to what popes themselves thought and did, Worcester and his students came to see how factors such as politics, technology, economic and social conditions, the prevailing conditions of war and peace, and a variety of cultural developments determined, to a large extent, how any given papacy unfolded and how the papacy itself, over a 500-year period, had evolved in a complex, non-linear fashion.

The complex, non-linear manner of evolution of the papacy suggested that, if one were to appreciate it fully, an interdisciplinary focus would be required. Not only historians, but also theologians and art historians, would need to be called upon. Noting also the growth in the papacy's international character during the period under examination, it seemed essential that the expertise drawn upon would be not only interdisciplinary, but also international, in character. These interdisciplinary and international perspectives would ensure an exploration of the papacy not so much from a "great men" point of view as through the lens of what *shapes* popes and papacies. It was recognized that all papacies have their own *Sitz im Leben* that influences their possibilities and that affects, also, how what popes undertake is received and what developments are likely to result from it. Thus it was that factors shaping the papacy and affecting its reception became the main interest of this book, which seeks to grasp how the papacy as it is today came to be a reality quite different from what it was 500 years ago under Julius II.

In order to highlight what emerged from applying the book's lens to the development of the papacy in the modern era, it is necessary to reflect on at least some of the key changes that occurred in it during the time-period investigated in the book. In our introduction, it was stated that the book places special emphasis on the evolution of two roles of the pope, those of prince and pastor, with a third role – that of patron of the arts – receiving some attention also. In our conclusion, we bring to the fore how the papacy, whose incumbents acted variously (in accordance with their circumstances) in the roles mentioned – culminating in the present-day emphasis on the pope being a kind of universal pastor – has undergone shifts that might have been noticed less if the lens of this book had not been applied to it. The first of these shifts marks the change in the pope from warrior to peace-maker; the second highlights how the papacy has moved from being less central to being more central in the life of the church; and the third shows how the papacy became more focused *ad extra*, turned toward the world, than *ad intra*, as it had been in earlier times.

First, a significant development occurred between the pontificate of the sixteenth-century Julius II and the twentieth-century pontificates of

Benedict XV and (later on in that century) Paul VI and John Paul II. Julius II, in addition to being a renowned patron of the arts, was a warrior of note. During his papacy, the Swiss Guards, whose role today is to provide security for the pope and the Vatican,[1] engaged in military campaigns, fighting to defend the pope and his interests. Military preoccupations also played a dominant role in other sixteenth-century papacies. Clement VII, who took office in 1523, just ten years after the death of Julius II, found that his commitment to the liberty of the Italian peninsula, which was so necessary for maintaining his own political autonomy, involved him in costly military engagements – forced on him by a series of political alliances that he entered into, between the Spanish and the French sides – that left him without resources either for patronage of the arts or for reform and pastoral care in the church. Of Pius V, also a sixteenth-century pope, it cannot however be suggested that he was impeded in his pastoral role by the battles that engaged him; certainly Sixtus V, portraying Pius's military successes as the result of his prayer for divine intervention, and Clement XI, depicting him as a warrior who was also prayerful and pastoral, are not suggesting that the energies he devoted to battle lessened what he was able to achieve in implementing the reforms of the Council of Trent (1545–63). Yet in due time the "holy warrior" image of papal sanctity passed. When the papacy had ceased to be a temporal power, being a warrior was not required. Gradually popes' pastoral possibilities came more to the fore and created, indeed, a space for pontiffs to speak about war and peace in an entirely new manner.

Twentieth-century popes, Paul VI (1963–78) and John Paul II (1978–2005) especially, have distinguished themselves not on the battlefield but as apostles of peace, the former appealing to the United Nations in 1965 to end all war, and the latter reiterating that appeal in a subsequent address to the same body. This marks a significant change, made possible by the fact that the papacy, in the centuries that are covered in this book, has passed from being a powerful entity with influential temporal powers to having these increasingly eroded by the secular powers of the day until eventually, in the nineteenth century, it lost all of them. This occurred not so much through some dramatic new insight into what the papacy was, or even should be, as through events – including the exiling and imprisoning of a pope (Pius VII), not to mention the ignominious defeats of the papal army in nineteenth-century battles over the Papal States – that forced

---

[1] See Angela Ambrogetti, "Swearing-In Ceremony for the Swiss Guards," *Inside the Vatican* (June–July 2009), 29; also, in the same issue, Micaela Biferali et al., "Vatican Watch," 42–43, at 42.

the papacy, as it were, to "re-group." Without temporal powers, military involvement made little sense; popes no longer needed to go to war; and if the papacy was to remain a force to be reckoned with, it had to achieve this in other ways. Thus it adapted and changed; and if it diminished in temporal importance, it gained in spiritual influence in the wake of that loss, and to a large extent it has continued to do so ever since, at least insofar as the kind of Roman centralism and papal absolutism that evolved in the latter part of the nineteenth century are still very much in the picture.[2]

Second, during the modern era, the papacy has come, increasingly, to be situated at the center of the Catholic Church's life. This development was also complex, arising not only from what the papacy, no longer a temporal power, was unable to do, but also from the presence of challenges from other quarters that it had to take into account. There was a serious challenge to papal absolutism from Jansenism in the seventeenth century; and this continued through the conciliarism that it promoted and that prospered in the eighteenth century. Thus it was not just its demise as a worldly power that led the papacy to assert itself as a spiritual power; it did so also because it was under a certain threat from within the church. The Ultramontanism that triumphed mightily in the nineteenth century grew in response not only to temporal losses but also to threats to the papacy's spiritual and political significance from within Catholicism. At the same time, a development occurred that facilitated it in acquiring greater prominence and centrality in the church as a whole: it became increasingly internationalized.

The increased international stature of the papacy enabled popes to acquire pre-eminence in a church that was spreading worldwide so that, in spite of the challenges from Jansenism and from the prevalence of conciliarist attitudes, papal absolutism gradually won the day. Furthermore, this did not happen only during the papacy of Pius IX. In the two quarter-century-long papacies that have occurred since his, those of Leo XIII and John Paul II, centralization of the papacy and papal exercise of the universal pastor role (through encyclicals in Leo's case, and through encyclicals plus travel and communications technology in John Paul's case) have continued to grow to the present day. These developments have been accompanied also by the papacy itself becoming an object of conscious reflection and change: at the First Vatican Council, through the pronouncement of

---

[2] See Thomas P. Rausch, *Pope Benedict XVI: An Introduction to his Theological Vision* (New York and Mahwah, NJ: Paulist Press, 2009), 3, where Rausch writes that John Paul II "recentralized power and decision making in Rome."

papal infallibility and also through the assertion of the pope's immediate universal pastoral jurisdiction over the entire church; and later, through John Paul II's invitation, in his 1995 encyclical letter, *Ut unum sint*, to all Christians to help him to reflect anew on papal primacy – even if he did not find the reflections subsequently offered by the retired Archbishop of San Francisco, John Quinn, particularly welcome.[3]

Third, the "to the world" (or *orbi*) dimension of the papacy grew with the development of the encyclical teaching genre from Pius IX onward, followed by the founding of the Vatican State in 1929 and, in due course, by radio, television, global travel, and the explosion in communications technology. Pius IX, author of some thirty-eight encyclicals,[4] taught on a variety of subjects and had an impact worldwide through his letters. Leo XIII, Pius's successor, achieved, by means of a staggering use of the encyclical genre – he penned eighty-six of them in all – an influential teaching authority not only within but also outside the church. His encyclical on the rights and conditions of workers, the famous *Rerum novarum* (1891), started a tradition of Catholic social teaching that has continued unabated in Catholicism ever since, with several "anniversary encyclicals" addressing economic and social conditions of their times in pertinent ways. Principles for the regulation of social, political, and economic life have been developed in this tradition of social teaching over the years, so that there is consistency over time and subtle development with respect to prevailing conditions at each time of writing.[5]

Popes have continued the tradition of Catholic social teaching begun with Leo XIII, not least because of the hearing – and largely positive reception – that his *Rerum novarum* was granted. Continuing its social teaching has meant an on-going orientation, on the papacy's part, to the world: to the concrete political, economic, and social circumstances in which particular popes have found themselves. Thus it was that Benedict XV (1914–22), the first pope to exercise the office during a world war, attempted, with his policy of "absolute impartiality," to foster peace. He was largely unsuccessful, but not, at least, because – as was seen earlier in this book in the case of Urban VIII (1623–44) – he had a temporal stake in the war that rendered a policy of neutrality on his own part impracticable. Benedict XV's manner of attempting to influence events during World War I constituted another development in the way in which popes

[3] See John Cornwell, *Breaking Faith: The Pope, the People, and the Fate of Catholicism* (London and New York: Viking, 2001), 258–60.
[4] See www.papalencyclicals.net/all.htm (last accessed August 7, 2009).
[5] See Editorial "Towards a More Humane World," *The Tablet* (July 11, 2009), 2.

did things and sought to exercise their universal pastorate in responsible and creative ways. His poorly received efforts may have left him personally weary; Rodin seems to have captured very well this weariness in his 1915 sculpture of Benedict (see above, Figure 9.1). Yet without Benedict's contribution it might have been more difficult for the subsequent prophetic stances of Paul VI and John Paul II before the United Nations to win the approval that they did.

Benedict's XV's successor, Pius XI (1922–39), during whose reign the Vatican State as we know it today was created, became able, through its creation, to function as a head of state (even if, territorially, the state that he headed was largely insignificant) and so to be a voice for peace among the nations. Thus a tradition, prophetic in character, slowly came about in the twentieth century that enabled popes to become champions of world peace. Pontiffs subsequent to the arrival of radio and television on the scene had greater influence regarding matters of war and peace, as the almost universally positive reception of the teaching of Paul VI and John Paul II on these topics indicates. Significantly, the present pope, Joseph Ratzinger, recalls Benedict XV's peace-making efforts (in addition to the heritage of Benedict of Nursia) when seeking to explain why he chose the name Benedict on being elected pope on April 19, 2005.[6]

Above all others, one single factor can be highlighted that explains what shaped papacies subsequent to that of Benedict XV and what enabled the twenty-six-year-long papacy of John Paul II in the late twentieth century to propel the pope to superstardom: technology. Electronic communications technology – radio, television, satellite broadcasting, and, in due course, internet technology and the cellphone – facilitated a centrality and dominance by the papacy for which the Ultramontanists of the nineteenth century would happily have died, but of which they could scarcely have dreamt. Dr. Joaquín Navarro-Valls, the chief Vatican spokesman for almost twenty years of the papacy of John Paul II, is reported as having said, not long after he assumed his role, that "one of the Pope's major goals in travelling was to extend his personal authority and that of the papacy."[7] There have been gains and losses from this. Certainly the papacy enjoys a stature in the world today that it could never have acquired without the modern means of communication. However, its use of these has also made it so central, and so centralizing, a force in Roman Catholic life that its

[6] See Rausch, *Pope Benedict XVI*, 5.
[7] Roberto Sura, "Papal Visits Viewed as Special Exercises in Vatican Strategy," *The New York Times* (6 September, 1987), 1 and 30, at 30.

gains *ad extra* are matched by losses *ad intra* as more and more Catholics – from bishops to ordinary believers, not to mention women, theologians, homosexuals, and victims of sexual abuse by clergy and religious – find themselves increasingly alienated from a centralized church that has forgotten that Rome is not the only player.[8] Why did the church become thus and the papacy under John Paul II become so unyielding that even *discussion* of disputed elements of papal teaching was outlawed? Was it perhaps the negative reception of the 1968 encyclical *Humanae vitae* prohibiting the use of artificial means of regulating birth that caused Paul VI to write no further encyclicals but that led John Paul II to pen them with vigor? Throughout his papacy, he promoted *Humanae vitae* passionately. He also defended the church's teaching that women cannot be ordained priests to the (unenforceable) point of pronouncing that the matter should not even be discussed.

History, however, never stands still. If the papacy of John Paul II was marked by the kind of centralizing (and absolutism) just described, with its accompanying legacy of problems, a different approach, although hardly different positions, will most likely be taken by his successor, Benedict XVI. Are there any signs of this? Yes. Benedict XVI certainly seems to downplay the kind of personality cult that has grown up around the pope ever since the nineteenth century and that flourished beyond all imagining through fashioning John Paul II into a superstar of remarkable proportions. His behavior in relation to crowds is markedly different from that of his predecessor. When he went to Australia for World Youth Day in 2008, he did not travel widely but confined his appearances to a limited number of locations, focusing instead on the message he wished to communicate; and he acted quite similarly in Brazil in 2007.[9] In general, he cultivates a style that differs from that of his predecessor, with which he did not always agree and to the criticisms of which he is sensitive.[10] Thus the reception of John Paul II is already affecting the behavior of his successor. Benedict's inclination is to dampen down audience applause and to discourage a focus on himself. According to Sandro Magister, "John Paul II dominated the stage. Benedict XVI is careful to direct attention towards something beyond himself."[11] This

---

[8] See Rausch, *Pope Benedict XVI*, 3.

[9] See James Corkery, SJ, *Joseph Ratzinger's Theological Ideas: Wise Cautions and Legitimate Hopes* (New York and Mahwah, NJ: Paulist Press, and Dublin: Dominican Publications, 2009), 137.

[10] Ibid., 140–42.

[11] See Sandro Magister, "Benedict XVI, a Pope Armed with 'Purity,'" 2, at http://chiesa.espresso. repubblica.it/articolo/103921?&eng=y (last accessed August 10, 2009). See also Corkery, *Joseph Ratzinger's Theological Ideas*, 140.

is the case during Vatican liturgical ceremonies and also during events when he travels. Liturgically, he directs the focus of the people to the words and actions of the celebration. His *motu proprio* permitting the use of the Roman missal promulgated in 1962 by John XXIII,[12] as well as his writings pointing out that priest and people together should face east, serves also to limit the undue attention given to the personality of the celebrant that Ratzinger considers became the tendency following Vatican II's liturgical changes and the virtually exclusive use of the liturgical books approved in 1970 by Paul VI.

In contrast to John Paul II's *ad extra* approach, his world focus, in exercising his papacy, Benedict XVI's governance as pope is quite focused *ad intra*. He takes a crisper, leaner, "essentials of the faith" approach, whereas the phenomenologist John Paul focused on the world of wider human experience.[13] Benedict's first two encyclicals were addressed to members of the church. His focus on liturgy is also quite an internal church matter. He has built up the Roman curia, the Vatican administration, but with people with whom he is comfortable, who share his views, and with many of whom he has worked in times past;[14] and he seems to consult only a circle very close to him – particularly his secretary of state, Cardinal Tarcisio Bertone – but not to consult relevant others, such as his fellow German, Cardinal Walter Kasper, President of the Pontifical Council for Promoting Christian Unity, who was not consulted in the unforgettable case of Benedict rescinding the excommunication of Bishop Williamson, the member of the St. Pius X Society who questioned the very fact of the Holocaust. Benedict XVI can be almost too focused on what he himself desires. He attends to ecclesiastical administration more than his predecessor did, and he is administratively more efficient and decisive than John Paul II also. His meetings are said to begin on time and to end early; and he grasps thorny nettles. One example is the case of Fr. Maciel, LC, founder of the Legionaries of Christ, against whom accusations of sexual abuse of his young recruits had been brought. During John Paul II's papacy, when Ratzinger, as Prefect of the Congregation for the Doctrine of the Faith, would have had this case in his files, it seems that it was not possible for him to bring it to a satisfactory conclusion, for whatever

---

[12] See Benedict XVI, Motu proprio *Summorum pontificum* on the "Roman Liturgy Prior to the Reform of 1970," July 7, 2007, at www.vatican.va/holy_father/benedict_xvi/motu_proprio/index_En.htm (last accessed August 15, 2009).

[13] See Corkery, *Joseph Ratzinger's Theological Ideas*, 139.

[14] See the feature article of Robert Mickens, "All the Pope's Men," *The Tablet* (August 8, 2009), at www.thetablet.co.uk/article13277 (last accessed August 10, 2009).

reason; but, on becoming pope himself, he saw to the swift and judicious handling of the matter.[15]

On becoming pope, Benedict XVI said he had no program of his own, merely a desire to implement the policies and texts of John Paul II.[16] This seems to suggest a seamless relationship between the two with regard to the interpretation of the Second Vatican Council; with regard to doctrine and theology; and with regard to the matter of change itself. Thus continuity seems indicated. Nevertheless, as has been shown in the previous paragraph, there were differences; and changes are occurring as a result of these and also as Benedict is impinged upon from without by events such as the current economic crisis and his attention to that in his third encyclical, *Caritas in veritate* (June 29, 2009). Thus this papacy is developing also in response to events external to it and in response to the reception of the previous papacy no less than because of the initiatives of its particular incumbent. So it is impossible to predict its future accurately without being able to predict *the* future accurately. A "great men" approach to the history of the papacy may suggest otherwise. But it has been the contention of this present book that the papacy evolves in large measure through how it responds to historical events and through how its responses are received. Surprises, therefore, and major changes, can still be expected.

[15] In 2006, with the approval of Pope Benedict XVI (but without a formal trial due to Maciel's advanced age and poor health), the Congregation for the Doctrine of the Faith directed that he live a life of penitence and prayer and relinquish all public ministry. This is the typical penalty imposed on aged priests found guilty of sexual abuse.

[16] Quoted in David Gibson, *The Rule of Benedict: Pope Benedict XVI and his Battle with the Modern World* (San Francisco: HarperSanFrancisco, 2006), 248.

Select bibliography

Note: This bibliography is a selection of the most important works cited in the book, as well as a selection of other works significant for understanding the development of the papacy from 1500 to the present.

Abbott, Walter M., general ed. *The Documents of Vatican II*. London: Geoffrey Chapman, 1966.

Acta apostolicae sedis: commentarium officiale, vols. 1– (1909–).

Adler, Bill. *Pope Paul in the United States*. New York: Hawthorn, 1965.

Alberigo, Giuseppe. *A Brief History of Vatican II*. Maryknoll, NY: Orbis, 2006.

Alberigo, Giuseppe, general ed., and Komonchak, Joseph A., ed. of English version. *History of Vatican II*. 5 vols. Maryknoll, NY: Orbis, and Leuven: Peeters, 1995–2006.

Alvarez, David. "The Professionalization of the Papal Diplomatic Service, 1909–1967." *The Catholic Historical Review* 75/2 (April 1989), 233–48.

Spies in the Vatican: Espionage and Intrigue from Napoleon to the Holocaust. Lawrence: University Press of Kansas, 2002.

Aubert, Roger. *Le pontificat de Pie IX (1846–1878)*. Paris: Bloud & Gay, 1952.

Baumgartner, Frederic J. *Behind Locked Doors: A History of the Papal Elections*. New York: Palgrave Macmillan, 2003.

Bedini, Silvio. *The Pope's Elephant*. Nashville: Sanders, 1998.

Bernstein, Carl, and Politi, Marco. *His Holiness: John Paul II and the History of our Time*. New York: Doubleday, 1996.

Bertrams, Wilhelm. *The Papacy, the Episcopacy, and Collegiality*. Westminster, MD: Newman Press, 1964.

Blet, Pierre. *Pius XII and the Second World War: According to the Archives of the Vatican*. Trans. Lawrence J. Johnson. Hereford: Gracewing, and New York: Paulist Press, 1999.

Blouin, Francis, ed. *Vatican Archives: An Inventory and Guide to Historical Documents of the Holy See*. New York: Oxford University Press, 1998.

Bock, Angela. *Die Sala Regia im Vatikan als Beispiel der Selbstdarstellung des Papsttums in der zweiten Hälfte des 16. Jahrhunderts*. New York: Olms, 1997.

Boorsch, Suzanne. "The Building of the Vatican: The Papacy and Architecture." *The Metropolitan Museum of Art Bulletin, new series*, 40:3 (Winter 1982–83), 1–2 and 4–64.

Braaten, Carl, and Jenson, Robert. *Church Unity and the Papal Office: An Ecumenical Dialogue on John Paul II's Encyclical* Ut unum sint. Grand Rapids, MI: W. B. Eerdmans, 2001.

Braunsberger, Otto. *Pius V. und die deutschen Katholiken.* Freiburg im Breisgau: Herdersche Verlagshandlung, 1912.

Broderick, John F., ed. *Documents of Vatican Council I, 1869–1870.* Collegeville, MN: Liturgical Press, 1971.

Büchel, Daniel and Reinhardt, Volker, eds. *Modell Rom? Der Kirchenstaat und Italien in der frühen Neuzeit.* Cologne: Böhlau, 2003.

Buckley, Michael J. *Papal Primacy and the Episcopate: Towards a Relational Understanding.* New York: Crossroad, 1998.

Burke, Peter. *The Historical Anthropology of Early Modern Italy: Essays on Perception and Communication.* Cambridge: Cambridge University Press, 1987.

Burkle-Young, Francis. *Passing the Keys: Modern Cardinals, Conclaves, and the Election of the Next Pope.* Lanham, MD: Madison Books, 1999.

Burton, Katherine. *Leo the Thirteenth, The First Modern Pope.* New York: D. McKay Co., 1962.

Cahill, Thomas. *Pope John XXIII.* New York: Viking, 2002.

Calvez, Jean-Yves. *The Social Thought of John XXIII:* Mater et magistra. Trans. George J. M. McKenzie. Chicago: H. Regnery Co., 1965.

Carlen, Claudia, IHM, ed. *The Papal Encyclicals, 1740–1981.* 5 vols. Raleigh, NC: Pierian Press, 1981. Reprinted, Ann Arbor, MI: Pierian Press, 1990.

Papal Pronouncements: A Guide, 1740–1978, 2 vols. Ann Arbor, MI: Pierian Press, 1990.

Carrier, Hervé. *Gospel Message and Human Cultures: From Leo XIII to John Paul II.* Pittsburgh: Duquesne University Press, 1989.

Cervini, Fulvio, and Spantigati, Carla Enrica, eds. *Il tempo di Pio V, Pio V nel tempo: atti del Convegno Internazionale di Studi, Bosco Marengo, Alessandria, 11–13 marzo 2004.* Alessandria: Edizioni dell'Orso, 2006.

Chadwick, Owen. *Britain and the Vatican during the Second World War.* Cambridge and New York: Cambridge University Press, 1986.

Catholicism and History: The Opening of the Vatican Archives. New York: Cambridge University Press, 1978.

A History of the Popes 1830–1914. New York: Oxford University Press, 1998. Paperback, Oxford: Oxford University Press, 2003.

The Popes and European Revolution. New York: Oxford University Press, 1981.

Chastel, André. *The Sack of Rome, 1527.* Trans. Beth Archer. Princeton: Princeton University Press, 1983.

Chevallier, Pierre. *La séparation de l'église et de l'école: Jules Ferry et Léon XIII.* Paris: Fayard, 1981.

Chiron, Yves. *Pie XI (1857–1939).* Paris: Perrin, 2004.

Clancy, John. *Apostle for our Time: Pope Paul VI.* New York: P. J. Kennedy, 1963.

Collins, Jeffrey Laird. *Papacy and Politics in Eighteenth-Century Rome: Pius VI and the Arts.* Cambridge: Cambridge University Press, 2004.

Collins, Paul. *Upon this Rock: The Popes and their Changing Role.* Carlton, Vic.: Melbourne University Press, 2000.

Congar, Yves. *Église et papauté: regards historiques.* Paris: Cerf, 1994.

Cooke, Bernard, ed., *The Papacy and the Church in the United States.* New York: Paulist Press, 1989.

Cooney, John. *Scotland and the Papacy.* Edinburgh: P. Harris, 1982.

Coppa, Frank J. *The Modern Papacy since 1798.* New York: Longman, 1998.

The Papacy, the Jews, and the Holocaust. Washington, DC: Catholic University of America Press, 2006.

Politics and the Papacy in the Modern World. Westport, CT: Praeger, 2008.

Pope Pius IX: Crusader in a Secular Age. Boston: Twayne Publishers, 1979.

Coppa, Frank J., ed. *Controversial Concordats: The Vatican's Relations with Napoleon, Mussolini, and Hitler.* Washington, DC: Catholic University of America Press, 1999.

Corkery, James. *Joseph Ratzinger's Theological Ideas: Wise Cautions and Legitimate Hopes.* New York and Mahwah, NJ: Paulist Press, and Dublin: Dominican Publications, 2009.

Cornwell, John. *Breaking Faith: The Pope, the People, and the Fate of Catholicism.* London and New York: Viking, 2001.

Hitler's Pope: The Secret History of Pius XII. New York: Viking, 1999, and London: Penguin, 2000.

The Pontiff in Winter: Triumph and Conflict in the Reign of John Paul II. New York: Doubleday, 2004.

Craig, Mary. *Man from a Far Country: A Portrait of Pope John Paul II.* London: Hodder and Stoughton, 1979.

Curran, Charles E. *Dissent in and for the Church: Theologians and* Humanae vitae. New York: Sheed & Ward, 1969.

Loyal Dissent. Washington, DC: Georgetown University Press, 2006.

The Moral Theology of Pope John Paul II. Washington, DC: Georgetown University Press, 2005.

Deedy, John G., and Cort, John C. *The Catholic Church in the Twentieth Century: Renewing and Reimaging the City of God.* Collegeville, MN: Liturgical Press, 2000.

Del Noce, Augusto. *Pensiero della chiesa e filosofia contemporanea: Leone XIII, Paolo VI, Giovanni Paolo II.* Rome: Stadium, 2005.

Delzell, Charles F. *The Papacy and Totalitarianism between the Two World Wars.* New York: Wiley, 1974.

De Satgé, John. *Peter and the Single Church.* London: SPCK, 1981.

Dorr, Donal. *Option for the Poor: A Hundred Years of Vatican Social Teaching.* Maryknoll, NY: Orbis Books, 1992.

Dowd, Christopher. *Rome in Australia: The Papacy and Conflict in the Australian Catholic Missions, 1834–1884.* Leiden: Brill, 2008.

Duffy, Eamon. *Saints & Sinners: A History of the Popes.* New Haven: Yale University Press, 1997.

Dulles, Avery. *The Splendor of Faith: The Theological Vision of Pope John Paul II.* New York: Crossroad, 1999.

Duston, Allen, and Zagnoli, Roberto. *Saint Peter and the Vatican: The Legacy of the Popes.* Alexandria, VA: Art Services International, 2003.

Ellis, John Tracy. *Cardinal Consalvi and Anglo-Papal Relations, 1814–1824.* Washington, DC: Catholic University of America Press, 1942.

Eno, Robert B. *The Rise of the Papacy.* Wilmington, DE: M. Glazier, 1990.

Farmer, William Reuben, and Kereszty, Roch A. *Peter and Paul in the Church of Rome: The Ecumenical Potential of a Forgotten Perspective.* New York: Paulist Press, 1990.

Feldkamp, Michael F. *Pius XII und Deutschland.* Göttingen: Vandenhoeck & Ruprecht, 2000.

Fenwick, C. G. "The New City of the Vatican." *The American Journal of International Law* 23/2 (April 1929), 371–74.

Fiedler, Maureen, and Rabben, Linda, eds. *Rome has Spoken: A Guide to Forgotten Papal Statements and How they have Changed through the Centuries.* New York: Crossroad, 1998.

Fisher, Desmond. *Pope Pius XII and the Jews: An Answer to Hochhuth's Play* Der Stellvertreter. Glen Rock, NJ: Paulist Press, 1963.

Fogarty, Gerald. *The Vatican and the American Hierarchy from 1870 to 1965.* Stuttgart: Hiersemann, 1982.

Fosi, Irene. *All'ombra dei Barberini: fedeltà e servizio nella Roma barocca.* Rome: Bulzoni, 1997.

Gallagher, Charles R. *Vatican Secret Diplomacy: Joseph P. Hurley and Pope Pius XII.* New Haven: Yale University Press, 2008.

Gargan, Edward. *Leo XIII and the Modern World.* New York: Sheed and Ward, 1961.

Gattoni, Maurizio. *Clemente VII e la geo-politica dello Stato Pontificio.* Vatican City: Archivio Segreto Vaticano, 2002.

Gibson, David. *The Rule of Benedict: Pope Benedict XVI and his Battle with the Modern World.* San Francisco: HarperSanFrancisco, 2006.

Gilbert, Felix. *The Pope, his Banker, and Venice.* Cambridge, MA: Harvard University Press, 1980.

Godman, Peter. *Hitler and the Vatican: Inside the Secret Archives that Reveal the New Story of the Nazis and the Church.* New York: Free Press, 2004.

Gough, Austin. *Paris and Rome: The Gallican Church and the Ultramontane Campaign, 1848–1853.* Oxford: Oxford University Press, 1986.

Gouwens, Kenneth. *Remembering the Renaissance: Humanist Narratives of the Sack of Rome.* Leiden: Brill, 1999.

Gouwens, Kenneth, and Reiss, Sheryl E., eds. *The Pontificate of Clement VII: History, Politics, Culture.* Aldershot: Ashgate, 2005.

Granfield, Patrick. *The Limits of the Papacy: Authority and Autonomy in the Church.* New York: Crossroad, 1987.

The Papacy in Transition. Garden City, NY: Doubleday, 1980.

Grant, Frederick. *Rome and Reunion.* New York: Oxford University Press, 1965.

Greeley, Andrew M. *The Making of the Popes 1978: The Politics of Intrigue in the Vatican.* Kansas City: Andrews and McMeel, 1979.

Grès-Gayer, Jacques. *Théologie et pouvoir en Sorbonne: la faculté de théologie de Paris et la bulle* Unigenitus, *1714–1721.* Paris: Klincksieck, 1991.

Guasco, Maurilio, and Torre, Angelo., eds. *Pio V nella società e nella politica del suo tempo.* Bologna: Il Mulino, 2005.

Guitton, Jean. *The Pope Speaks: Dialogues of Paul VI with Jean Guitton.* New York: Meredith Press, 1968.

Hachey, Thomas E. *Anglo-Vatican Relations, 1914–1939: Confidential Annual Reports of the British Ministers to the Holy See.* Boston: G. K. Hall, 1972.

Haidacher, Anton. *Geschichte der Päpste in Bildern.* Heidelberg: F. H. Kerie, 1965.

Hales, E. E. Y. *The Emperor and the Pope: The Story of Napoleon and Pius VII.* Garden City, NY: Doubleday, 1961.

Pope John and his Revolution. Garden City, NY: Doubleday, 1965.

Revolution and Papacy, 1769–1846. Garden City, NY: Hanover House, 1960.

Hammond, Frederick. *Music and Spectacle in Baroque Rome: Barberini Patronage under Urban VIII.* New Haven: Yale University Press, 1994.

Halperin, Samuel. *Italy and the Vatican at War: A Study of their Relations from the Outbreak of the Franco-Prussian War to the Death of Pius IX.* Chicago: University of Chicago Press, 1939.

Hardt, Michael. *Papsttum und Ökumene: Ansätze eines Neuverständnisses für einen Papstprimat in der protestantischen Theologie des 20. Jahrhunderts.* Zürich: Schoningh, 1981.

Hasler, August. *How the Pope Became Infallible: Pius IX and the Politics of Persuasion.* Trans. Peter Heinegg. Garden City, NY: Doubleday, 1981.

Pius IX. Stuttgart: Hiersemann, 1977.

Hastings, Adrian. *Church and State: The English Experience.* Exeter: Exeter University Press, 1991.

Hebblethwaite, Peter. *In the Vatican.* Bethesda, MD: Alder & Alder, 1986.

Introducing John Paul II. London: Collins, 1982.

Paul VI: The First Modern Pope. London: HarperCollins, 1993.

Pope John XXIII: Shepherd of the Modern World. Garden City, NY: Doubleday, 1985.

The Year of Three Popes. New York: Collins, 1979.

Hehir, J. Bryan. "Papal Foreign Policy." *Foreign Policy* 78 (Spring 1990), 26–48.

Hendrix, Scott H. *Luther and the Papacy: Stages in a Reformation Conflict.* Philadelphia: Fortress Press, 1981.

Hibbert, Christopher. *Rome: The Biography of a City.* London: Penguin, 1985.

Hofmann, Paul. *The Vatican's Women: Female Influence at the Holy See.* New York: St. Martin's Press, 2002.

Holland, Joe. *Modern Catholic Social Teaching: The Popes Confront the Industrial Age, 1740–1958.* New York: Paulist Press, 2003.

Holmes, Derek. *The Papacy in the Modern World, 1914–1978*. New York: Crossroad, 1981.

The Triumph of the Holy See: A Short History of the Papacy in the Nineteenth Century. London: Burns & Oates, 1978.

Hook, Judith. *The Sack of Rome, 1527*. London: Macmillan, 1972. 2nd edn, 2004.

Horaist, Bruno. *La dévotion au pape et les catholiques français, sous le pontificat de Pie IX, 1846–1878*. Rome: École Française de Rome, 1995.

Irani, George Emile. *The Papacy and the Middle East: The Role of the Holy See in the Arab–Israeli Conflict, 1962–1984*. Notre Dame, IN: Notre Dame Press, 1986.

Jamme, Armand, and Poncet, Olivier. *Offices et papauté, XIV–XVIIe siècle: charges, hommes, destins*. Rome: École Française de Rome, 2005.

Joannes, Fernando. *The Bitter Pill: Worldwide Reaction to the Encyclical* Humanae vitae. Philadelphia: Pilgrim Press, 1970.

John Paul II. *Crossing the Threshold of Hope*. Ed. Vittorio Messori. Trans. Jenny McPhee and Martha McPhee. New York: Knopf, 1994.

Gift and Mystery: On the Fiftieth Anniversary of My Priestly Ordination. New York: Doubleday, 1997.

Sources of Renewal: The Implementation of the Second Vatican Council. Trans. P. S. Falla. San Francisco: Harper & Row, 1980.

Johns, Christopher M. S. *Papal Art and Cultural Politics: Rome in the Age of Clement XI*. Cambridge: Cambridge University Press, 1993.

Jones, Pamela M., and Worcester, Thomas, eds. *From Rome to Eternity: Catholicism and the Arts in Italy, ca. 1550–1650*. Leiden: Brill, 2002.

Kaiser, Robert Blair. *Pope, Council, and World: The Story of Vatican II*. New York: Macmillan, 1963.

Kane, Brian M. *Just War and the Common Good:* jus ad bellum *Principles in Twentieth Century Papal Thought*. San Francisco: Catholic Scholars Press, 1997.

Katz, Robert. *The Battle for Rome: The Germans, the Allies, the Partisans, and the Pope, September 1943–June 1944*. New York: Simon & Schuster, 2003.

Keely, Charles B. "Limits to Papal Power: Vatican Inaction after *Humanae vitae*." *Population and Development Review* 20 (1994), Supplement: *The New Politics of Population: Conflict and Consensus in Family Planning*, 220–40.

Kelly, J. N. D. *The Oxford Dictionary of Popes*. Oxford: Oxford University Press, 1986.

Kent, Peter C. *The Lonely Cold War of Pope Pius XII: The Roman Catholic Church and the Division of Europe, 1943–1950*. Montreal: McGill-Queen's University Press, 2002.

The Pope and the Duce: The International Impact of the Lateran Agreements. New York: St. Martin's Press, 1981.

Kent, Peter C., and Pollard, John F. *Papal Diplomacy in the Modern Age*. Westport, CT: Praeger, 1994.

Kertzer, David I. *The Popes against the Jews: The Vatican's Role in the Rise of Modern Anti-Semitism*. New York: Alfred A. Knopf, 2001.

Prisoner of the Vatican: The Popes' Secret Plot to Capture Rome from the New Italian State. Boston: Houghton Mifflin, 2004.

King, Ross. *Michelangelo and the Pope's Ceiling.* New York: Penguin, 2003.

Kirwin, William Chandler. *Powers Matchless: The Pontificate of Urban VIII, the Baldachin, and Gian Lorenzo Bernini.* New York: P. Lang, 1997.

Kittler, Glenn D. *The Papal Princes: A History of the Sacred College of Cardinals.* New York: Funk & Wagnalls, 1960.

Klaczko, Julian. *Rome and the Renaissance: The Pontificate of Julius II.* New York: G. P. Putnam's Sons, 1903.

Küng, Hans. *Infallible? An Inquiry.* Trans. Edward Quinn. Garden City, NY: Doubleday, 1971.

Kwitny, Jonathan. *Man of the Century: The Life and Times of Pope John Paul II.* New York: Henry Holt and Co., 1997.

La Due, William J. *The Chair of Saint Peter: A History of the Papacy.* Maryknoll, NY: Orbis Books, 1999.

Launay, Marcel. *La papauté à l'aube du XXe siècle: Léon XIII et Pie X (1878–1914).* Paris: Cerf, 1997.

Lawler, Justus George. *Popes and Politics: Reform, Resentment, and the Holocaust.* New York: Continuum, 2002.

Lemaître, Nicole. *Saint Pie V.* Paris: Fayard, 1994.

Le Roy, Albert. *La France et Rome de 1700 à 1715: histoire diplomatique de la bulle Unigenitus.* Geneva: Slatkine-Megariotis Reprints, 1976.

Levey, Michael. "Lawrence's Portrait of Pius VII." *Burlington Magazine* 117 (April 1975), 194–204.

Levillain, Philippe, ed., *The Papacy: An Encyclopedia.* 3 vols. Eng. trans. ed. John W. O'Malley. New York: Routledge, 2002.

Levillain, Philippe, and Ticchi, Jean-Marc, eds. *Le pontificat de Léon XIII: renaissances du Saint-Siège?* Rome: École Française de Rome, 2006.

Lohrmann, Klaus. *Die Päpste und die Juden: 2000 Jahre zwischen Verfolgung und Versöhnung.* Düsseldorf: Patmos, 2008.

Luxmoore, Jonathan. *The Vatican and the Red Flag: The Struggle for the Soul of Eastern Europe.* New York: G. Chapman, 1999.

MacEoin, Gary. *The Papacy and the People of God.* Maryknoll, NY: Orbis Books, 1998.

Mack Smith, Denis. *Modern Italy: A Political History.* Ann Arbor: University of Michigan Press, 1997.

Maffeo, Sabino. *The Vatican Observatory: In the Service of Nine Popes.* Vatican: Vatican Observatory Publications, 2001.

Mannion, Gerard, ed. *The Vision of John Paul II: Assessing his Thought and Influence.* Collegeville, MN: Liturgical Press, 2008.

Marchione, Margherita. *Pope Pius XII: Architect for Peace.* New York: Paulist Press, 2000.

Markus, R. A. *Pastors or Princes: A New Look at the Papacy and Hierarchy.* Washington, DC: Corpus Books, 1969.

Martina, Giacomo. *Pio IX.* 3 vols. Rome: Università Gregoriana Editrice, 1974–90.

Matelski, Marilyn. *Vatican Radio: Propaganda by the Airwaves*. Westport, CT: Praeger, 1995.

McBrien, Richard P. *Lives of the Popes: The Pontiffs from St. Peter to John Paul II*. San Francisco: Harper San Francisco, 1997.

McElrath, Damian. *The Syllabus of Pius IX: Some Reactions in England*. Louvain: Bibliothèque de l'Université, Bureau de la Revue, 1964.

McEnroy, Carmel. *Guests in their Own House: The Women of Vatican II*. New York: Crossroad, 1996.

McGinness, Frederick J. *Right Thinking and Sacred Oratory in Counter-Reformation Rome*. Princeton: Princeton University Press, 1995.

McInerny, Ralph. *The Defamation of Pius XII*. South Bend, IN: St. Augustine's Press, 2001.

McMullin, Ernan, ed. *The Church and Galileo*. Notre Dame, IN: University of Notre Dame Press, 2005.

McPhee, Sarah. *Bernini and the Bell Towers: Architecture and Politics at the Vatican*. New Haven: Yale University Press, 2002.

Melchior-Bonnet, Bernardine. *Napoléon et le pape*. Paris: Livre Contemporain, 1958.

Miller, J. Michael. *The Divine Right of the Papacy in Recent Ecumenical Theology*. Rome: Università Gregoriana Editrice, 1980.

Miller, J. Michael, ed. *The Encyclicals of John Paul II*. Huntington, IN: Our Sunday Visitor, 1996. Rev. edn. 2001.

Misner, Paul. *Papacy and Development: Newman and the Primacy of the Pope*. Leiden: Brill, 1976.

  Social Catholicism in Europe: From the Onset of Industrialization to the First World War. New York: Crossroad, 1991.

Moody, Joseph N. *Church and Society: Catholic Social and Political Thought and Movements, 1789–1950*. New York: Arts, Inc., 1953.

Murphy, Caroline. *The Pope's Daughter: The Extraordinary Life of Felice della Rovere*. Oxford: Oxford University Press, 2005.

Murphy, Francesca Aran, and Asprey, Christopher. *Ecumenism Today: The Universal Church in the 21st Century*. Burlington, VT: Ashgate: 2008.

Murphy, Paul I., with Arlington, R. René. *La popessa*. New York: Warner Books, 1983.

Murri, Romolo. *La* Rerum novarum *e Leone XIII*. Urbino: Quattro Venti, 1991.

Nell-Breuning, Oswald von. *Reorganization of Social Economy: The Social Encyclical Developed and Explained*. Trans. Bernard Dempsey. New York: Bruce Publishing Co., 1936.

Nocent, Adrien. *La célébration eucharistique avant et après Saint Pie V*. Paris: Éditions Beauchesne, 1977.

Noel, Gerard. *Pius XII: The Hound of Hitler*. New York: Continuum, 2008.

Noonan, James-Charles. *The Church Visible: The Ceremonial Life and Protocol of the Roman Catholic Church*. New York: Viking, 1996.

Noonan, John T. *A Church that Can and Cannot Change: The Development of Catholic Moral Teaching*. Notre Dame, IN: University of Notre Dame Press, 2005.

Noonan, Peggy. *John Paul the Great: Remembering a Spiritual Father*. New York: Viking, 2005.

Nussdorfer, Laurie. *Civic Politics in the Rome of Urban VIII*. Princeton: Princeton University Press, 1992.

Oakley, Francis. *The Conciliarist Tradition: Constitutionalism in the Catholic Church, 1300–1870*. Oxford : Oxford University Press, 2003.

O'Dwyer, Margaret. *The Papacy in the Age of Napoleon and the Restoration: Pius VII, 1800–1823*. Lanham, MD: University Press of America, 1985.

O'Grady, Desmond. *Rome Reshaped: Jubilees 1300–2000*. New York: Continuum, 1999.

O'Malley, John. "Giles of Viterbo: A Reformer's Thought on Renaissance Rome." *Renaissance Quarterly* 20:1 (Spring 1967), 1–11.

  A History of the Popes: From Peter to the Present. Lanham, MD: Sheed & Ward, 2010.

  Praise and Blame in Renaissance Rome: Rhetoric, Doctrine, and Reform in the Sacred Orators of the Papal Court, c. 1450–1521. Durham, NC: Duke University Press, 1979.

  What Happened at Vatican II. Cambridge, MA: Harvard University Press, 2008.

Onori, Lorenza Mocha, Schütze, Sebastian, and Solinas, Francesco, eds. *I Barberini e la cultura europea del Seicento*. Rome: De Luca Editori d'Arte, 2007.

Origins, vols. 1– (1971–).

Orsy, Ladislas. *Receiving the Council: Theological and Canonical Insights and Debates*. Collegeville, MN: Liturgical Press, 2009.

Ostrow, Steven F. *Art and Spirituality in Counter-Reformation Rome: The Sistine and Pauline Chapels in S. Maria Maggiore*. Cambridge: Cambridge University Press, 1996.

Padberg, John. "Ignatius, the Popes, and Realistic Reverence." *Studies in the Spirituality of Jesuits* 25:3 (May 1993), 1–28.

Padellaro, Nazareno. *Portrait of Pius XII*. Trans. Charles Full. New York: Knopf, 1966.

Panzer, Joel. *The Popes and Slavery*. New York: Alba House, 1996.

Paravicini Bagliani, Agostino. *Il corpo del papa*. Torino: Einaudi, 1994.

Partner, Peter. *Renaissance Rome, 1500–1559: A Portrait of a Society*. Berkeley: University of California Press, 1976.

Partridge, Loren, and Starn, Randolph. *A Renaissance Likeness: Art and Culture in Raphael's Julius*. Berkeley: University of California Press, 1980.

Passelecq, Georges, and Suchecky, Bernard. *The Hidden Encyclical of Pius XI: The Vatican's Lost Opportunity to Oppose Nazi Racial Policies that Led to the Holocaust*. Trans. Steven Rendall. New York: Harcourt, Brace and Company, 1997.

Pastor, Ludwig von. *The History of the Popes from the Close of the Middle Ages: Drawn from the Secret Archives of the Vatican and Other Original Sources*, ed. F. I. Antrobus et al., 40 vols., 3rd edn. (London: Kegan Paul, 1901–33). Also published as *The History of the Popes: From the Close of the Middle Ages*. Ed. F. I. Antrobus et al. 40 vols. St. Louis: Herder, 1923–69.

Pelletier, Gérard. *Rome et la Révolution française: la théologie et la politique du Saint-Siège devant la Révolution française (1789–1799)*. Rome: École Française de Rome, 2004.

Pesch, Rudolf. *Die biblischen Grundlagen des Primats*. Freiburg: Herder, 2001.

Pfister, Pierre. *Pius XII: The Life and Work of a Great Pope*. New York: Studio Publications, 1955.

Piolanti, Antonio. *Pius IX e la rinascità del Tomismo*. Vatican City: Libreria Editrice Vaticana, 1974.

Il Tomismo come filosofia cristiana nel pensiero di Leone XIII. Vatican City: Libreria Editrice Vaticana, 1983.

Pollard, John F. *Catholicism in Modern Italy: Religion, Society and Politics since 1861*. London: Routledge, 2008.

Money and the Rise of the Modern Papacy: Financing the Vatican, 1850–1950. Cambridge and New York: Cambridge University Press, 2005.

"The Papacy in Two World Wars: Benedict XV and Pius XII Compared." In Robert Mallet and Gert Sorenson, eds., *International Fascism, 1919–1945*. London: Routledge, 2002, 84–96.

The Unknown Pope: Benedict XV (1914–1922) and the Pursuit of Peace. New York: Geoffrey Chapman, 1999, Reprinted London: Continuum, 2005.

The Vatican and Italian Fascism, 1929–1932: A Study in Conflict. Cambridge and New York: Cambridge University Press, 1985.

Pollock, Robert C., ed. *The Mind of Pius XII*. New York: Crown Publishers, 1955.

Polverari, Alberto. *Vita di Pio IX*. 3 vols. Vatican City: Libreria Editrice Vaticana, 1986–88.

Prodi, Paolo. *The Papal Prince: One Body and Two Souls: The Papal Monarchy in Early Modern Europe*. Trans. Susan Haskins. Cambridge: Cambridge University Press, 1987.

Il sovrano pontefice: un corpo e due anime: la monarchia papale nella prima età moderna. Rev. edn. Bologna: Il Mulino, 2006.

Prodi, Paolo, and Reinhard, Wolfgang, eds. *Il concilio di Trento et il moderno*. Bologna: Il Mulino, 1996.

Quinn, John R. *The Reform of the Papacy: The Costly Call to Christian Unity*. New York: Crossroad, 1999.

Rafferty, Oliver. *The Catholic Church and the Protestant State: Nineteenth-Century Irish Realities*. Dublin: Four Courts Press, 2008.

Ranke, Leopold von. *The History of the Popes during the Last Four Centuries*. 3 vols. Trans. E. Foster. London: G. Bell and Sons, 1913.

Ratzinger, Joseph. *God and the World: A Conversation with Peter Seewald*. San Francisco: Ignatius Press, 2002.

The Ratzinger Report: An Exclusive Interview with Vittorio Messori on the State of the Church. San Francisco: Ignatius Press, 1985.

Salt of the Earth: The Church at the End of the Millennium: An Interview with Peter Seewald. San Francisco: Ignatius Press, 1997.

Ratzinger, Joseph, ed. *Dienst an der Einheit: Zum Wesen und Auftrag des Petrusamtes.* Düsseldorf: Patmos Verlag, 1978.

Rausch, Thomas P. *Pope Benedict XVI: An Introduction to his Theological Vision.* New York and Mahwah, NJ: Paulist Press, 2009.

Raybaud, Léon Pierre. *Papauté et pouvoir temporel sous les pontificats de Clément XII et Benoît XIV, 1730–1758.* Paris: Vrin, 1963.

Reese, Thomas J. *Inside the Vatican: The Politics and Organization of the Catholic Church.* Cambridge, MA: Harvard University Press, 1996.

Reinerman, Alan J. *Austria and the Papacy in the Age of Metternich.* Washington, DC: Catholic University of America Press, 1979.

Riccards, Michael P. *Vicars of Christ: Popes, Power, and Politics in the Modern World.* New York: Crossroad, 1998.

Rice, Louise. *The Altars and Altarpieces of New St. Peter's: Outfitting the Basilica, 1621–1666.* New York: Cambridge University Press, 1997.

Rietbergen, P. J. A. *Power and Religion in Baroque Rome: Barberini Cultural Policies.* Leiden: Brill, 2006.

Rittner, Carol, and Roth, John K. *Pope Pius XII and the Holocaust.* New York: Leicester University Press, 2002.

Rousseau, Richard W. *Human Dignity and the Common Good: The Great Papal Social Encyclicals from Leo XIII to John Paul II.* Westport, CT: Greenwood Press, 2002.

Royal, Robert. *The Pope's Army: 500 Years of the Papal Swiss Guard.* New York: Crossroad, 2006.

Russell, Robert J., Stoeger, William R., and Coyne, George V., eds. *John Paul II on Science and Religion: Reflections on the New View from Rome.* Vatican City: Vatican Observatory Publications, 1990.

Sanchez, José M. *Pius XII and the Holocaust: Understanding the Controversy.* Washington, DC: Catholic University of America Press, 2002.

Schall, James V. "*Fides et ratio:* Approaches to a Roman Catholic Political Philosophy." *The Review of Politics* 62:1 (Winter 2000), 49–75.

Schatz, Klaus. *Papal Primacy: From its Origins to the Present.* Trans. John A. Otto and Linda M. Maloney. Collegeville, MN: Liturgical Press, 1996.

Schimmelpfennig, Bernhard. *The Papacy.* Trans. James Sievert. New York: Columbia University Press, 1992.

Schuck, Michael J. *That They Be One: The Social Teaching of the Papal Encyclicals, 1740–1989.* Washington, DC: Georgetown University Press, 1991.

Schwaiger, Georg, and Seppelt, Franz. *Geschichte der Päpste, von Anfängen bis zur Gegenwart.* Munich: Kösel-Verlag, 1964.

Scotti, R. A., *Basilica: The Splendor and the Scandal: Building St. Peter's.* New York: Viking, 2006.

Shannon, William. *The Lively Debate: Response to Humanae vitae.* New York: Sheed & Ward, 1970.

Shaw, Christine. *Julius II: The Warrior Pope.* Oxford: Blackwell, 1993.

Shea, John Gilmary. *The Life of Pope Pius IX and the Great Events in the History of the Church during his Pontificate.* New York: T. Kelly, 1877.

Shea, William R., and Artigas, Mariano. *Galileo in Rome: The Rise and Fall of a Troublesome Genius*. New York and Oxford: Oxford University Press, 2003.

Signorotto, Gianvittorio, and Visceglia, Maria Antonietta, eds. *Court and Politics in Papal Rome, 1492–1700*. Cambridge: Cambridge University Press, 2002.

Silli, Antinono. *San Pio V: note agiografiche ed iconografiche*. Rome: Biblioteca B. Angelico, 1979.

Spinelli, Giovanni, ed. *Pio VII papa benedettino nel bicentenario della sua elezione*. Cesena: Badia di Santa Maria del Monte, 2003.

Stadtwald, Kurt. *Roman Popes and German Patriots: Antipapalism in the Politics of the German Humanist Movement from Gregor Heimburg to Martin Luther*. Geneva: Librairie Droz, 1996.

Stourton, Edward. *John Paul II: Man of History*. London: Hodder and Stoughton, 2006.

Szulc, Tad. *Pope John Paul II: The Biography*. New York: Scribner, 1995.

Tavard, George. *The Pilgrim Church*. New York: Herder and Herder, 1967.

Thierry, Jean-Jacques. *La vie quotidienne au Vatican: au temps de Léon XIII à la fin du XIXe siècle*. Paris: Hachette, 1963.

Thorvaldsen Museum. *Rome in Early Photographs, the Age of Pius IX: Photographs 1846–1878 from Roman and Danish Collections*. Copenhagen: Thorvaldsen Museum, 1977.

Tillard, J. M. R. *The Bishop of Rome*. Trans. John de Satgé. Wilmington, DE: Glazier, 1983.

Tittmann, Harold H. *Inside the Vatican of Pius XII: The Memoir of an American Diplomat during World War II*. New York: Doubleday, 2004.

Tobin, Greg. *Holy Father: Pope Benedict XVI: Pontiff for a New Era*. New York: Sterling Publishing, 2005.

Traeger, Jörg. *Der reitende Papst: ein Beitrag zur Ikonographie des Papsttums*. Munich: Schnell & Steiner, 1970.

Viaene, Vincent, ed. *The Papacy and the New World Order: Vatican Diplomacy, Catholic Opinion and International Politics at the Time of Leo XIII, 1878–1903*. Leuven: Katholieke Universiteit Leuven Press, 2005.

Von Arx, Jeffrey, ed. *Varieties of Ultramontanism*. Washington, DC: Catholic University of America Press, 1998.

Wallace, Lillian Parker. *Leo XIII and the Rise of Socialism*. Durham, NC: Duke University Press, 1966.

   The Papacy and European Diplomacy, 1869–1878. Chapel Hill: University of North Carolina Press, 1948.

Walsh, Michael J. *An Illustrated History of the Popes: Saint Peter to John Paul II*. New York: St. Martin's Press, 1980.

   John Paul II: A Biography. London: HarperCollins, 1994.

   Vatican City State. Santa Barbara, CA: Clio Press, 1983.

Weakland, Rembert G. *A Pilgrim in a Pilgrim Church: Memoirs of a Catholic Archbishop*. Grand Rapids, MI: Eerdmans, 2009.

Weigel, George. *Witness to Hope: The Biography of Pope John Paul II*. New York: Cliff Street Books, 1999.

Williams, George. *The Mind of John Paul II: Origins of his Thought and Action*. New York: Seabury Press, 1981.

Witte, John, ed. *The Teachings of Modern Roman Catholicism on Law, Politics, and Human Nature*. New York: Columbia University Press, 2007.

Wolffe, John. *God and Greater Britain: Religion and National Life in Britain and Ireland, 1843–1945*. London and New York: Routledge, 2005.

Wright, A. D. *The Early Modern Papacy: From the Council of Trent to the French Revolution, 1564–1789*. New York: Longman, 2000.

Wynn, Wilton. *Keepers of the Keys: John XXIII, Paul VI, and John Paul II, Three who Changed the Church*. New York: Random House, 1988.

Yzermans, Vincent A., ed. *The Major Addresses of Pope Pius XII*. St. Paul, MN: North Central Publishing Co., 1961.

Pope Pius XII and Catholic Education. St. Meinrad, IN: Grail Publications, 1957.

Zizola, Giancarlo, *The Utopia of Pope John XXIII*. Maryknoll, NY: Orbis Books, 1978.

Index